# PREVENTION OF DEVELOPMENTAL DISABILITIES

# PREVENTION OF DEVELOPMENTAL DISABILITIES

*Edited by*

## Siegfried M. Pueschel, M.D., Ph.D., M.P.H.
*Professor of Pediatrics*
*Brown University Program in Medicine*
*Director, Child Development Center*
*Department of Pediatrics*
*Rhode Island Hospital*
*Providence, RI*

*and*

## James A. Mulick, Ph.D.
*Associate Professor*
*of Pediatrics and Psychology*
*The Ohio State University*
*Department of Pediatrics*
*Children's Hospital*
*Columbus, OH*

·P A U L·H·
BROOKES
PUBLISHING Cº

Baltimore • London • Toronto • Sydney

**Paul H. Brookes Publishing Co.**
P.O. Box 10624
Baltimore, Maryland 21285–0624

Typeset by The Composing Room of Michigan, Inc., Grand Rapids, Michigan.
Manufactured in the United States of America by
The Maple Press Company, York, Pennsylvania.

**Library of Congress Cataloging-in-Publication Data**
Prevention of developmental disabilities / edited by Siegfried M.
  Pueschel and James A. Mulick.
      p.     cm.
  Includes bibliographical references.
  ISBN 1–55766–052–2
  1. Developmental disabilities—Prevention.   2. Maternal health
services.   3. Infant health services.   I. Pueschel, Siegfried M.
II. Mulick, James A. (James Anton).
  [DNLM:   1. Child Development Disorders—prevention &
control—United States.   2. Child Health Services—United
States.   3. Maternal Health Services—United States.   WA 310
  P944]
  RJ135.P739   1990
  613'.0432—dc20
  DNLM/DLC
  for Library of Congress                                    90–1622
                                                               CIP

# CONTENTS

v

# CONTRIBUTORS

**Dianne N. Abuelo, M.D.**
Director, Genetic Counseling Center
Department of Pediatrics
Rhode Island Hospital
593 Eddy Street
Providence, RI 02903

**Gail Barsel-Bowers, M.S.**
Genetic Counselor Coordinator
Child Development Center
Department of Pediatrics
Rhode Island Hospital
593 Eddy Street
Providence, RI 02903

**William J. Cashore, M.D.**
Professor of Pediatrics
Brown University
Neonatologist
Physician in Charge of the Normal
    Nurseries
Department of Pediatrics
Women & Infants Hospital of Rhode
    Island
101 Dudley Street
Providence, RI 02905

**Curtis L. Cetrulo, M.D.**
Professor of Obstetrics and Gynecology
Tufts University School of Medicine
Director of Maternal Fetal Medicine
St. Margaret's Hospital for Women
90 Cushing Avenue
Boston, MA 02125

**Donald R. Coustan, M.D.**
Professor of Obstetrics and Gynecology
Brown University Program in Medicine
Director of Obstetrics and Maternal-
    Fetal Medicine
Women & Infants Hospital of Rhode
    Island
101 Dudley Street
Providence, RI 02905–2401

**Allen C. Crocker, M.D.**
Associate Professor of Pediatrics
Harvard Medical School
Associate Professor of Maternal and
    Child Health
Harvard School of Public Health
Director, Developmental Evaluation
    Clinic
Children's Hospital
300 Longwood Avenue
Boston, MA 02115

**Mary E. D'Alton, M.D.**
Associate Professor of Obstetrics and
    Gynecology
Director, Maternal Fetal Medicine
Tufts University School of Medicine
90 Cushing Avenue
Boston, MA 02125

**Joan Edwards**
Executive Director
WNY Task Force on Prevention of
    MR/DD, Inc.
4242 Ridge Lea Drive
Suite #3
Amherst, NY 14226

**John R. Evrard, M.D., M.P.H.**
Professor Emeritus of Obstetrics and
  Gynecology
Brown University Program in Medicine
Director of Medical Education Emeritus
Women & Infants Hospital of Rhode
  Island
101 Dudley Street
Providence, RI 02905

**Robert Guthrie, Ph.D., M.D.**
Professor Emeritus of Pediatrics and
  Microbiology
State University of New York at Buf-
  falo and Buffalo Children's Hospital
Department of Pediatrics
Acheson Hall, Room 352
3435 Main Street
Buffalo, NY 14214

**Nancy B. Hansen, M.D.**
Assistant Professor of Pediatrics
The Ohio State University
Director of Neonatal Follow-Up Clinic
Division of Neonatology
Children's Hospital
700 Children's Drive
Columbus, OH 43205

**Alan R. Hinman, M.D., M.P.H.**
Director, Center for Prevention Services
Centers for Disease Control
Atlanta, GA 30333

**H. Eugene Hoyme, M.D.**
Associate Professor of Pediatrics and
  Obstetrics/Gynecology
Chief, Section of Genetics/
  Dysmorphology
Department of Pediatrics
University of Arizona, College of
  Medicine
Tucson, AZ 85724

**Nancy M. Johnson-Martin, Ph.D.**
Clinical Assistant Professor of Medical
  Psychology
Director, CHILD Project
Duke University Medical Center
Civitan Building
2213 Elba Street
Durham, NC 27705

**Edwin H. Kolodny, M.D.**
Professor of Neurology
Harvard Medical School
Director, Eunice Kennedy Shriver Cen-
  ter for Mental Retardation, Inc.
200 Trapelo Road
Waltham, MA 02254

**Harvey L. Levy, M.D.**
Associate Professor of Neurology
Harvard Medical School
Assistant Director
Newborn Screening Program
State Laboratory Institute
Massachusetts Department of
  Public Health
305 South Street
Boston, MA 02130

**Richard E. McClead, M.D.**
Associate Professor of Pediatrics
The Ohio State University
Division of Neonatology
Children's Hospital
700 Children's Drive
Columbus, OH 43205

**Kim S. McConnell, M.D.**
Developmental Pediatrician
Massachusetts Hospital School
3 Randolph Street
Canton, MA 02021

**Wayne A. Miller, M.D.**
Director, Prenatal Diagnostic
  Center, Inc.
80 Hayden Avenue
Lexington, MA 02173

**Brian L. G. Morgan, Ph.D.**
9 Island Avenue
Apartment 1404
Belle Isle
Venetian Causeway
Miami Beach, FL 33139

**James A. Mulick, Ph.D.**
Associate Professor of Pediatrics
  and Psychology
The Ohio State University
Department of Pediatrics
Children's Hospital
700 Children's Drive
Columbus, OH 43205-2696

**Edward R. Newton, M.D.**
Associate Professor
Director, Maternal-Fetal Fellowship
    Program
Department of Obstetrics
    and Gynecology
The University of Texas Health Science
    Center at San Antonio
7703 Floyd Curl Drive
San Antonio, TX 78284

**John S. O'Shea, M.D.**
Associate Professor of Pediatrics
Brown University
Director, Division of Ambulatory
    Pediatrics
Rhode Island Hospital
Providence, RI 02903

**Siegfried M. Pueschel, M.D., Ph.D.,
M.P.H.**
Professor of Pediatrics
Brown University Program in Medicine
Director, Child Development Center
Department of Pediatrics
Rhode Island Hospital
593 Eddy Street
Providence, RI 02903

**Patricia Sexton Scola, M.D., M.P.H.**
Department of Pediatrics
Rhode Island Hospital
593 Eddy Street
Providence, RI 02903

**Karen E. Senft, M.D.**
Director of Outpatient Pediatrics
Good Shepherd Rehabilitation Hospital
5th and St. John Streets
Allentown, PA 18103

**Paul T. von Oeyen, M.D.**
Assistant Professor of Obstetrics
    and Gynecology
Wayne State University School
    of Medicine
Assistant Director, Maternal-Fetal
    Medicine
Medical Director, Labor & Delivery
William Beaumont Hospital
3601 West 13 Mile Road
Royal Oak, MI 48072

**Betty R. Vohr, M.D.**
Associate Professor of Pediatrics
Brown University Program in Medicine
Director, Neonatal Follow-up Program
Women & Infants Hospital of Rhode
    Island
101 Dudley Street
Providence, RI 02905

**Joseph J. Volpe, M.D.**
Washington University School
    of Medicine
Department of Pediatrics
400 South Kings Highway
St. Louis, MO 63110

# PREFACE

This book is intended to provide a summary of developments of some of the major scientific and technological approaches in the prevention of developmental disabilities. There are many biomedical and environmental pathways along which, under certain circumstances, significant disability can result during the long period of human growth and development. The selection of topics to include in a book such as this one necessarily involves some difficult choices for editors and authors. Our decisions were based on criteria of practicality and demonstrated effectiveness. The topics included emphasize those approaches to prevention that have been widely used and that are still actively being refined to reduce the incidence or degree of disability among the population.

The current state of practice in the prevention of developmental disabilities is based, in large part, on the dramatic progress since the 1950s that has been made in understanding the etiology of specific handicapping conditions. Much of the evidence has been biomedical in nature. For example, it has been demonstrated repeatedly that many developmental disabilities are the result of chromosome disorders, mendelian genetic diseases, and multifactorial inherited conditions.

Genetic science has suggested a number of approaches in the prevention of disabilities through more accurate risk prediction, early detection, and various forms of medical intervention. Similarly, maternal infections, toxic exposure of the fetus to dangerous substances, and other physical conditions during pregnancy can adversely affect prenatal development and result in later disability. Unfavorable perinatal circumstances, metabolic derangements of the newborn, endocrine disturbances, central nervous system infections, as well as trauma, accidents, poisoning, and other environmental and physical problems also can result in developmental disability. Each of these demonstrated causes simultaneously provides an opportunity to discover, and then to implement, preventive measures. This book provides many examples of this process of discovery, problem solving, and implementation. Thus, it is an excellent guide to modern preventive science in the field of developmental disabilities for the student and the practitioner.

This book has been organized in a life-cycle approach that begins at conception and proceeds through pregnancy, infancy, and childhood, and ends with a discussion of the broad societal implications of state-of-the-art advances in prevention of handicapping conditions. It is our hope that this information will be applied to help ensure more successful pregnancies and improve the chances for infant survival.

Those interested in rising to the challenges of implementing preventive strategies will, we hope, find this book to be of value. The content would be appropriate for use in a course on prevention and public health and for courses on developmental issues in health planning. Such courses are often provided through specialized interdisciplinary programs focusing on developmental disabilities as well as through traditional educational programs in medicine, nursing, health administration, and allied health disciplines. The reference value of this book should be apparent to practicing physicians who need an up-to-date summary of prevention approaches, public health nurses, practitioners in other disciplines working with populations at risk for developmental disabilities, and public policy analysts and planners who work in areas related to maternal and child health. The responsibility for using this knowledge and urging further research and dissemination efforts rests with all adults in our society who want to provide a world full of hope and improved health to all children.

# ACKNOWLEDGMENTS

We would like to express our deep gratitude to Jill Rose for her expert secretarial skills. Because of her extraordinary efforts throughout the preparation of the manuscript we were able to complete this work on time. We also would like to thank Melissa A. Behm of Paul H. Brookes Publishing Company for her assistance, guidance, and support.

# PREVENTION OF DEVELOPMENTAL DISABILITIES

# I INTRODUCTION

# 1 | James A. Mulick

# IN THE CAUSE
# OF PREVENTION
## AN INTRODUCTION

There are few events that evoke more attention than the discovery of a child in need. A child's dependency and newness compel a special sort of commitment to help, to assure that the future will hold some measure of promise for growth, health, learning, and happiness. Assistance is likely to be given to such children, and action is seldom delayed when the approach to take is clearly understood and the tasks involved are well-defined.

Society has recognized that children with developmental disabilities are children in need. Massive efforts and large commitments of public and private resources have been expended to help treat their conditions and to improve their access to individualized education. Society's laws promote these actions and demand that professionals address the needs of children with disabilities with special vigor. The response to developmental disabilities has, on the whole, been generous and cooperative (Mulick & Pueschel, 1983), and society can be comforted by an appraisal of these facts.

The nature of developmental disabilities is part of the reason. Conditions that result in mental or physical limitations in a child's ability to follow a relatively normal developmental progression in multiple critical life activities, such as self-care, language, learning, capacity for independent living, and economic sufficiency, require extended and coordinated services. The government provides for these services as well as a means for their coordination at a state level in the Developmental Disabilities Assistance and Bill of Rights

The author was supported in part by U.S. Department of Health and Human Services MCH Special Project MCJ 443040-01-0 and MCH Special Project MCJ 009053-01-0. Preparation of the manuscript was supported in part through the generosity of Chris Rutkowski and *Rising Star Industries* of Torrance, California.

Act, as amended in 1978 (PL 95-602). Under this law and a variety of similar laws and regulatory measures, circumstances have improved for people with disabilities and their families. Children with mental retardation, cerebral palsy, autism, and other handicapping conditions receive an unprecedented measure of assistance through the resulting programs. Moreover, this increased attention to the problems represented by developmental disabilities has resulted in improved scientific understanding of many of the biological and behavioral processes involved in these conditions.

Another reason for wide recognition of the problems of developmental disabilities is the size of the affected population. In terms of mental retardation alone, using a statistical definition based only on the distribution of measured intelligence in the United States, there would be an estimated population of more than 5 million people in this category (Ingalls, 1978), and of these, perhaps 1–2 million would qualify under the Developmental Disabilities Act as needing lifelong coordinated services (Baroff, 1982). The total effect on society of this segment of the population with developmental disabilities can be appreciated if one considers the consequences of a need for lifelong care. Each stage in the life cycle may necessitate differing combinations of specialized services. The services may involve costly medical interventions, special education, respite care, social services, economic support, and residential options outside the family home. Each type of service involves varying amounts of professional and paraprofessional involvement, and these individuals must be educated and trained. Add to this the administrative and institutional structures needed to support service availability at all levels, and it is readily apparent that the social and economic costs of current standards for care are enormous. When the estimate is broadened to include possible effects on families of individuals with handicaps, the true extent of the direct effects of developmental disabilities on society can begin to be understood.

Concern about the families of children with handicaps is well-founded. Certainly many families make adequate adjustments to their child's needs (Weyhing, 1983), although not without cost and not without sacrifice. Many families are strengthened in ways that are difficult to quantify or analyze, and many can be helped to adjust through active intervention. However, families of children with handicaps must be considered to be at risk. There is some evidence that infants and children with handicaps are more likely to be exposed to neglect and physical violence at home than their peers without handicaps (Snyder, Hampton, & Newberger, 1983). Maternal reports of increased stress have been associated with the additional caregiving demands and some other characteristics of infants with handicaps (Beckman, 1983), and other research has suggested that the behavior and adjustment of adolescents with mental retardation can influence the social and emotional aspects of parenting behavior (Nihira, Meyers, & Mink, 1983). Other behavioral evidence of risk to the family is readily available (Wahler, 1980). The point to be made here is that the effects of a child with handicaps on the family are clearly bidirectional, and not merely a matter of parental or sibling attitude and responsibility.

The total impact of developmental disabilities on the economy, government, professionals, and family is enormous. The effects persist for extended periods of time, and, whether through genetic or sociocultural mechanisms, they can also affect future generations (Abuelo, 1983; Schilling, Schinke, Blythe, & Barth, 1982). There is great pressure from nearly all of those concerned with developmental disabilities to reduce their negative impact on and to enhance the prospects of children with handicaps and their families.

There is reason to believe that many disabilities or their detrimental effects can now be prevented. The commitment to serve the needs of children with handicaps and their families has yielded a rich harvest of new scientific knowledge. This book is concerned about new developments in biomedical and behavioral science that, if widely disseminated and acted upon, can prevent a significant number of developmental disabilities. The contents of this book are not exhaustive in terms of the entire field of prevention, but do present a practical survey of sound approaches. The reader is invited to consider ways to acknowledge the importance of this work and to contribute to the hope for society that it represents by using the most effective means available to advance the cause of prevention.

## CONCEPTUALIZING PREVENTION OPPORTUNITIES

The approach of this book is to consider the problem of preventing developmental disabilities from the perspective of normal development. What opportunities does an understanding of development give the professional interested in prevention? The answer to this question is represented in the organization of this book.

The life cycle provides a useful conceptual model. Human development begins at conception and follows a path that is at first closely tied to maternal factors during gestation, but becomes increasingly subject to wider and more complex environmental influences at birth. The search for preventive strategies must therefore begin with an examination of the period prior to conception, and inevitably with the preparation for parenthood.

Most young couples want to be emotionally, physically, and financially prepared for the birth of a child. Thus, it is important that prospective parents pursue family planning. This would include deciding when to begin a family, the desired number of children, and how the births should be spaced. Moreover, it is important that both parents, but especially the mother, be in good health, have a well-balanced diet, be free of infections, and develop a lifestyle that includes exercise and avoidance of harmful substances, such as drugs and alcohol. These issues are being brought sharply into focus now that the problems of acquired immunodeficiency syndrome (AIDS) and other blood borne and sexually transmitted diseases for sexually active people, and the children they conceive, are under public discussion (Kastner & Friedman, 1988). Furthermore, some young parents may have concerns about birth defects or genetic disorders, and this aspect is addressed through genetic counseling prior to pregnancy. These subjects and additional material on the importance of taking prevention seriously are covered in Part II, Prevention of Developmental Disabilities Prior to Conception, in this book.

The decisions made by parents prior to conception will pay off during the period of pregnancy. For example, the mother's life-style forms much of the basis for assuring an adequate fetal environment that provides needed nutrients and protection from toxic and teratogenic substances. Regular medical monitoring of the pregnancy not only allows ongoing counseling in these areas, but also provides an opportunity to utilize technological developments in prenatal diagnosis and to perform interventions needed to treat infections and avoid prematurity. Part III of this book, Prevention of Developmental Disabilities during Pregnancy, addresses the period of pregnancy and many of these issues concerning the gestational period.

Part IV, Prevention of Developmental Disabilities during the Perinatal and Neonatal Periods, is devoted to labor, delivery, and advances in neonatal care. This aspect of prevention concentrates on the management of maternal risk factors at the time of delivery and support for the premature or compromised neonate. Diagnosis of metabolic disorders is also included in this section, as well as early neurologic and developmental screening. Improved technology in the neonatal intensive care unit has revolutionized the care of infants who are at risk. However, such advances have given rise to some problems of their own. Follow-up of early problems and prompt referral for additional treatment is essential. This requires personnel who are trained in the techniques of developmental evaluation and who have adequate knowledge about the comprehensive array of long-term child and family services.

Early childhood is the final stage in this approach to prevention of developmental disabilities. It is a time when infants grow rapidly and acquire skills needed to control their own bodies enough to begin the lifelong task of exploration in the world of other people and interesting things. However, it is also a time when children are susceptible to health hazards and accidents. Both caregivers and professionals must be alert to such hazards as well as to the child's need for stimulation and opportunities to learn. The coverage of Prevention of Developmental Disabilities during Early Childhood, Part V, does not do justice to the many advances in relevant scientific knowledge. A single book devoted entirely to this period could hardly do so. For example, educational and technological advances developed to compensate for learning handicaps in young children (Bijou, 1983) or the influence of parenting style on child development (Wahler, 1980) are not included in this volume, despite their critical importance, due to limitations in space and their coverage elsewhere. Choices must be made. The editors' choice to stress early intervention and the areas of child safety, nutrition, immunoprophylaxis, and childhood lead exposure must be judged to reflect their view of the importance of these subjects rather than any evaluation of the truly immense list of competing topics.

## METHODS OF DISSEMINATION

The value of knowledge is in its use. Readers of this or any other volume on prevention represent a fraction of the potential audience capable of using the information. The young people who will someday bring children into the world, their families, teachers, medical and other health professionals, human services agency personnel, and policymakers all need access to some or all of the information contained in this volume. The underutilization of preventive strategies can be traced directly to lack of dissemination and lack of public demand. After all, new clinics for teenage parents, regionalized service activities for large rural geographic areas, bilingual community health projects for urban immigrant populations, and the like come into being only when there is sufficient recognition of the resultant benefits to both the target populations and the society that provides financial and political support. However, these authors and editors are well aware that the manner of dissemination used in this volume is far from the most effective with the majority of the target audience. Much more is needed and much more can be done.

Guthrie (1984) described a strategy for developing prevention efforts at the community level. Parents' groups, advocates, and primary care professionals can be a powerful force in both disseminating and generating the kind of political voice that results in concrete action and funding. Getting the knowledge to these groups is of major importance.

Health professionals who are aware of the possibilities for prevention can utilize many techniques. A gradual but effective dissemination tactic is that of individual counseling by health professionals of their patients during routine service contacts. This approach restricts the amount of information that can be conveyed, but capitalizes on the trust that is inherent in the professional-patient relationship.

Broader dissemination is possible through public lectures and presentations to parent organizations. Print media can be an important adjunct. For example, pamphlets can be developed on specific prevention topics and distributed to both consumers and professionals, depending on the content and purpose of the document. If left with groups following a presentation, a written summary can reinforce and preserve the impact of the program.

The commercial mass media has a powerful impact on the public. Preparation of brief media presentations, although costly in terms of professional time and funds, would serve to raise public awareness of specific aspects of prevention to a greater degree. The approach is limited rather severely, however, by the necessary brevity of any single spot in the mass media. Often reporters or feature writers can be interested in prevention issues, and may be persuaded to devote some additional space available to them to the topic. These points are relevant to both the print and broadcast mass media.

More specialized public service education outlets are increasingly available. One example is the national telephone TelMed information service. State health departments publish listings of prerecorded presentations on a large variety of topics that can be heard by people who dial a special telephone number. Prevention information will increasingly appear in this system. Similarly, cable television frequently provides health programming time to community or agency groups who have the capabilities of airing accurate information on prevention. Both of these systems allow a high degree of audience specificity, but are limited to users or subscribers who usually must be informed of the availability of the service by other means. Again, primary care providers can alert the people they serve to such programs, as can parent and advocacy groups.

Perhaps the best long-term dissemination resource available is the system of universal education in the United States. Young people at the middle school or high school level are exploring the possibilities of intimate relationships and actively seek information about their own bodies and their reproductive capacities. They need accurate information from trustworthy sources. Furthermore, they are socially and culturally prepared to learn, and they attend formal educational programs. Most schools provide classes in health, biology, general science, and home economics, and many include elective courses in human development and psychology. Information about the prevention of developmental disabilities and responsible parenthood can be incorporated within these and other aspects of the standard curriculum. Health professionals, parents, and educators must seek to assure the broad representation of prevention issues during these formative years of mandatory education. New York state has made a curriculum resource of this nature available to school districts (Litch, 1978, 1979), as have several other states. Even commercial textbook publishers may begin to include this kind of material in their products if the demand for it is made clear enough.

Obviously, teacher training will have to include similar curriculum material. In-service training programs for practicing teachers and courses for appropriate majors at the college level will have to be developed. Already a leader in disseminating service and treatment information, the American Association of University Affiliated Programs (AAUAP) for Persons with Developmental Disabilities has undertaken the challenge of prevention along with other professional and advocacy organizations (American Association of University Affiliated Programs [AAUAP] for Persons with Developmental Disabilities, 1983). AAUAP member programs are characterized by their many linkages to public and private agencies, colleges and universities, and school programs. They may be expected to be closely involved with new developments in preservice training at the college and graduate level, as well as serving as a reliable resource for in-service teacher training. Available in many states, these programs may also be consulted by organizations or individual professionals and interested citizens.

Specific approaches to dissemination will have to be tailored to meet local requirements. The effort will bring together individuals from many differing backgrounds who will have to work in concert to bring about the greatest possible awareness of the many practical steps that can be taken to advance the cause of preventing the kinds of disabling conditions discussed in this volume. There will be occasion for many who become involved in this process to confront profoundly disturbing questions of a moral and ethical nature; some such questions are introduced in this volume. The answers to such questions will emerge with time, deliberation, discussion, and, above all, involvement in the application of new scientific knowledge in an effort to help people with developmental disabilities and their families.

## CONCLUSION

Commitment to the prevention of developmental disabilities entails efforts by the scientific and professional community, government, and families. Advances in the biomedical and behavioral sciences must be put into practice by physicians and other professionals in response to growing demands in society to afford all children with the best opportunities available to achieve optimal growth and learning. Families should be encouraged to ask questions about how to ensure the health and happiness of children from the very start, and adequate medical advice and services should be made available to parents from the time they first decide to have children, through the critical periods of gestation and early childhood, and later as they seek to provide children with stability and sound guidance. Information about effective preventive strategies can and should be disseminated through cooperative efforts by individual practitioners, researchers and scholars, schools, the mass media, public agencies, and concerned groups of citizens. Prevention requires a great deal of effort and cooperation, not to mention revision of old habits that lead to action only after a problem occurs, but the results can be well worth such efforts as those described in this book—and even considerably more.

## REFERENCES

Abuelo, D. N. (1983). Genetic disorders. In J. L. Matson & J. A. Mulick (Eds.), *Handbook of mental retardation* (pp. 105–120). Elmsford, NY: Pergamon Press.
American Association of Universtiy Affiliated Programs (AAUAP) for Persons with

Developmental Disabilities. (1983). *Developmental handicaps: Prevention and treatment*. Washington, DC: AAUAP.

Baroff, G. S. (1982). Predicting the prevalence of mental retardation in individual catchment areas. *Mental Retardation, 20*, 133–135.

Beckman, P. J. (1983). Influence of selected child characteristics on stress in families of handicapped infants. *American Journal of Mental Deficiency, 88*, 150–156.

Bijou, S. W. (1983). The prevention of mild and moderate retarded development. In F. J. Menolascino, R. Neman, & J. A. Stark (Eds.), *Curative aspects of mental retardation* (pp. 223–241). Baltimore: Paul H. Brookes Publishing Co.

Guthrie, R. (1984). Prevention of developmental disabilities at the community level: A strategy for organization. In J. A. Mulick & B. L. Mallory (Eds.), *Transitions in mental retardation: Advocacy, technology and science* (pp. 261–272). Norwood, NJ: Ablex.

Ingalls, R. P. (1978). *Mental retardation: The changing outlook*. New York: John Wiley & Sons.

Kastner, T., & Friedman, D. (1988). Commentary: Pediatric acquired immune deficiency syndrome and the prevention of mental retardation. *Developmental and Behavioral Pediatrics, 9*, 47–48.

Litch, S. (1978). *Towards the prevention of mental retardation in the next generation: Vol. 1*. Albany: New York State Office of Mental Retardation and Developmental Disabilities.

Litch, S. (1979). *Towards the prevention of mental retardation in the next generation: Vol. 2*. Albany: New York State Office of Mental Retardation and Developmental Disabilities.

Mulick, J. A., & Pueschel, S. M. (1983). *Parent-professional partnerships in developmental disability services*. Cambridge, MA: Academic Guild Publishers.

Nihira, K., Meyers, C. E., & Mink, I. T. (1983). Reciprocal relationship between home environment and development of TMR adolescents. *American Journal of Mental Deficiency, 88*, 139–149.

PL 95-602, Developmental Disabilities Assistance and Bill of Rights Act, 1978.

Schilling, R. F., Schinke, S. P., Blythe, B. J., & Barth, R. P. (1982). Child maltreatment and mentally retarded parents: Is there a relationship? *Mental Retardation, 20*, 201–209.

Snyder, J. C., Hampton, R., & Newberger, E. H. (1983). Family dysfunction: Violence, neglect, and sexual misuse. In M. D. Levine, Q. B. Carey, A. C. Crocker, & R. T. Gross (Eds.), *Developmental-behavioral pediatrics* (pp. 259–275). Philadelphia: W. B. Saunders.

Wahler, R. G. (1980). Parent insularity as a determinant of generalization success in family treatment. In S. Salinger, J. Antrobus, & J. Glick (Eds.), *The ecosystem of the "sick" child: Implications for classification and intervention for disturbed and mentally retarded children* (pp. 187–199). New York: Academic Press.

Weyhing, M. C. (1983). Parental reactions to handicapped children and familial adjustments to routines of care. In J. A. Mulick & S. M. Pueschel (Eds.), *Parent-professional partnerships in developmental disability services* (pp. 125–138). Cambridge, MA: Academic Guild Publishers.

**2** | *Robert Guthrie*
*Joan Edwards*

# PREVENTION OF MENTAL RETARDATION AND DEVELOPMENTAL DISABILITIES
## AN OVERVIEW

Definitions are important in discussing a complex problem such as the prevention of mental retardation and developmental disabilities. All individuals may be mentally compromised to some degree, considering that it is extremely unlikely that any one individual has escaped completely all of the thousands of genetic influences and environmental agents that may adversely affect his or her mental development. Thus, a broader than usual definition of mental retardation is needed. If lead was eliminated from the environment of young children or alcohol from the environment of the fetus, then the prevention of some degree of mental retardation of human development would be rewarded. Whether a child has a potential IQ of 130 or of 90, he or she would benefit dramatically from preventive measures, no matter what reduction of IQ might otherwise have been present. Therefore, the goal of preventing lead poisoning or the effects of alcohol on the fetus is really aimed at improving the quality of life for a vast number of people in human society, far beyond the 2% or 3% who function in the "mentally retarded" range.

In considering specific causes of handicaps and their prevention, this chapter focuses primarily on some of the biomedical causes that are often associated with severe mental retardation. However, it is well-known that the vast majority of individuals usually described as mentally retarded by medical, legal, or educational standards have disabilities that are caused outside of the biomedical field. Prevention of these social, economic, and cultural causes is much more complex and difficult to organize and support, especially in a country like the United States.

Therefore, it is sensible to give a high priority to specific biomedical causes: 1) that are easily understood, 2) for which model prevention programs already exist, 3) that are of reasonable cost, 4) where there is little controversy over religious or political matters, 5) where there is a high prevalence of a preventable disorder, and 6) where significant cost-benefit can be demonstrated. Goals that are intellectually attractive and quite logical may be appealing to health professionals, but such goals must also be those of the community, for community cooperation is critical for success.

## DRAMATIC ADVANCES IN PREVENTION

### Cretinism

One of the first dramatic advances in the prevention of mental retardation in this century was the introduction of iodized salt in the 1930s to eliminate iodine deficiency, which is a cause of endemic cretinism. According to some authorities, this decreased severe mental retardation in mountainous countries, such as Switzerland, by 20%.

### Phenylketonuria

In the 1950s, specific prevention of phenylketonuria (PKU), an inherited form of mental retardation, by dietary control was introduced by Bickel, Gerrard, and Hicksman (1953). In 1961, a practical method for newborn screening was developed to detect this condition by use of a dried spot of blood on a filter paper (Guthrie, 1961). A blood specimen is taken prior to discharge of a baby from the hospital nursery and tested in a regional laboratory for a bacterial inhibition assay for phenylalanine. Thus, it is possible to detect PKU in an infant, provide early dietary treatment, and completely prevent the mental retardation ordinarily observed in phenylketonuria. However, the new problem of maternal PKU must be addressed.

### Amniocentesis

During the 1950s, a method for determining chromosomal abnormalities became available, and this led to the possibility of detecting these conditions prenatally in the 1960s. Amniocentesis is particularly valuable with older mothers where the increased risk of having a child with Down syndrome is greater than the risk of amniocentesis itself (see Miller, Chapter 8, this volume).

## Fetal Alcohol Syndrome

Possibly one of the most dramatic developments in the prevention of disabilities occurred in the 1970s with the recognition of fetal alcohol syndrome. It is now possible to prevent a form of mental retardation probably as frequent as Down syndrome by educating women to avoid taking alcohol during pregnancy (see Hoyme, Chapter 7, this volume).

## Rubella

In 1969, a vaccine for rubella, also known as German measles, was developed, and widespread immunization occurred. The vaccine is given to all children at the age of 1 or 2. Another development was the availability of a means of completely preventing Rh hemolytic disease in the newborn (see Pueschel, Scola, & McConnell, Chapter 6, this volume).

## Fragile-X Syndrome

During the 1970s, a specific X-linked, or sex-linked, form of mental retardation was discovered—the fragile-X syndrome. This discovery provided an explanation for the predominance of males over females in severely retarded populations (Sutherland, 1977; Turner & Turner, 1974). It has also been found that the fragile-X syndrome may be associated with autism (Brown et al., 1982). Fragile-X syndrome is preventable because of the development of a technique by which the fragile-X can be demonstrated in cells obtained by amniocentesis (Jenkins et al., 1981).

## Childhood Lead Poisoning

The 1980s has witnessed an interesting new phase of an old problem—childhood lead poisoning. The authors call this period the rediscovery of childhood lead poisoning. It is worth reviewing this problem because it is so immense and yet so poorly understood by the majority of the public as well as the professional community (see Senft & Pueschel, Chapter 20, this volume).

Some cities in the United States (e.g., Philadelphia, Chicago, New York) began to develop programs for detecting blood lead in children after the surgeon general made a statement about the danger of this problem in the 1960s. In the 1970s, federal money became available to combat lead poisoning. It is noteworthy that this occurred only after Senator Edward Kennedy and others exerted pressure that forced President Richard Nixon to release funds he had impounded for which Congress had already authorized and appropriated. The $6 million released was estimated to be only enough to deal with the problem of lead poisoning in one large city, such as Philadelphia. These funds were distributed throughout the country to programs that, to this day, are confined to large cities, where the risk is greatest. In some inner cities, as many as 20% of preschool children were determined to have undue lead exposure.

In 1982, these federal programs were still confined almost entirely to children in the central cities. Meanwhile, sources of lead other than old paint were discovered. In fact, there are so many sources of lead poisoning in children that it would be impossible to list them all here. A study by the United States Environmental Protection Agency (Webster, 1978) resulted in a statement appearing in the *New York Times* pointing out that a major source of lead resulting in childhood lead poisoning came from automobile exhaust. This lead was distributed in the environment wherever there was heavy motor traffic. It also became part of house dust and topsoil.

As more knowledge was gained about the extent of lead toxicity and its detrimental effect on children, the level of lead that was considered safe in a child's blood began to decrease. Now, at 25 ug/dl, it is less than half of the level that was considered safe in the 1970s (Centers for Disease Control, 1985). There are several types of evidence that led to this change. One is the studies carried out in experimental animals that demonstrated that very low, chronic exposure to lead causes damage to the central nervous system and results in changes of behavior (Needleman, 1980). Also, indirect evidence that clearly shows the detrimental effect of chronic lead exposure has begun to accumulate (Needleman et al., 1979) (see Table 2.1).

Another publication of a national survey involving 10,000 preschool children across the United States indicated that the threat of lead poisoning is even more widespread among children than heretofore believed (Annest, O'Connell, Roberts, & Murphy, 1981; Mahaffy, Annest, Roberts, & Murphy, 1982). Furthermore, data were presented demonstrating a close association between the blood lead level of preschool children and the use of lead in gasoline (Centers for Disease Control, 1982) (see Figure 2.1). The data showed that 4% of all children, age 6 months to 5 years, had levels of lead above 25 ug/dl, the cut-off point used by the Centers for Disease Control.

These figures are shocking and indicate that the present federally funded programs for detection and prevention of lead poisoning are only reaching a small fraction of the children who need to be screened. The maximum number of children screened in any one year in the United States, according to figures from the Centers for Disease Control, is less than .5 million. However, *all* children under age 6, approximately 15 million children, need to be screened.

Another important concern relating to low level lead exposure and infant development during the first year of life was discussed by Bellinger, Leviton, Neddleman, Waternaux, and Rabinowitz (1986). These investigators found that prenatal exposure to lead, which is relatively common among urban

**Table 2.1.** Percent of children ages 6 months to 5 years with lead poisoning levels of 30.0 ug/dl or more (United States, 1976–1980)

| Demographic variables | All[a] | White | Black |
|---|---|---|---|
| | | Race | |
| a. Both sexes | 4.0 | 2.0 | 12.2 |
|     Males | 4.4 | 2.1 | 13.4 |
|     Females | 3.5 | 1.8 | 10.9 |
| b. Annual family income | | | |
|     Under $6,000 | 10.9 | 5.9 | 18.5 |
|     $6,000–$14,999 | 4.2 | 2.2 | 12.1 |
|     $15,000 or more | 1.2 | 0.7 | 2.8 |
| c. Degree of urbanization | | | |
|     Urban, 1 million persons or more | 7.2 | 4.0 | 15.1 |
|     Central city | 11.6 | 4.0 | 15.1 |
|     Noncentral city | 3.7 | 4.5 | 18.6 |
|     Urban, less than 1 million persons | 3.5 | 3.8 | 3.3[b] |
|     Rural | 2.1 | 1.2 | 10.3[b] |

*Source*: Annest, J.L., O'Connell, D., Roberts, J., & Murphy, R.S. (1981). Blood lead levels from the second national health and nutrition examination survey, 1976–1980. In F.F. Cherry (Ed.), *Childhood lead poisoning prevention and control: A public health approach to an environmental disease* (pp. 93–102). New Orleans: Maternal and Child Health Section, Office of Health Services and Environmental Quality, Department of Health and Human Services; reprinted by permission.

[a]Includes data for races not shown separately.

[b]Number of sample persons in cell is less than 50.

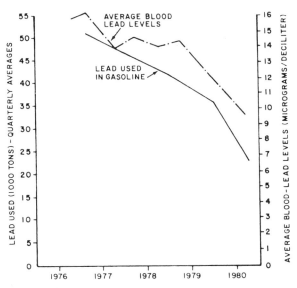

**Figure 2.1.** Lead used in gasoline production and average NHANES II blood-lead levels, February 1976–February 1980.

populations, was associated with a "less favorable" development of young infants.

Under the Reagan administration, the Environmental Protection Agency, the same agency that had taken a lead in pointing out the menace of lead in gasoline in 1978, made it clear that it wanted to relax the regulations and allow more lead in gasoline (Agency criticized for rule changes on lead in gas, 1982a, 1982b). This led to such an outcry from environmentalists and health authorities that, after public hearings and a great deal of publicity in the news media (Waldholz, 1982), the agency announced that it did not want to relax the regulations restricting the level of lead in gasoline, but would, in fact, tighten these regulations (Shabecoff, 1982).

The threat of lead to the development of young children has been established, facilities treat children with lead poisoning, and legal procedures have begun in an attempt to remove lead from the environment. It is clear that the next step required is that of screening *all* preschool children at least annually (Guthrie, 1982; Houk, 1981). In September, 1982, the United States Maternal and Child Health Service issued a public statement calling for this step (Bureau of Health Care Delivery and Assistance, 1982; Lin-Fu, 1979). Furthermore, steps have been taken in New York state to require all preschool children to be screened (Medical Tribune Report, 1982).

Large scale screening can be carried out easily utilizing Piomelli's method that tests the free erythrocytic protoporphyrin (FEP) in red blood cells. Blood specimens collected on filter paper can be used for this purpose (Orfanos, Murphey, & Guthrie, 1977; Piomelli, 1977; Piomelli, Davidown, Guinee, Young, & Gay, 1973). Piomelli has also pointed out that this is the most sensitive means of detecting iron deficiency (Piomelli, Brickman, & Carlos, 1976). Using the same type of blood specimen that was introduced in the 1960s for phenylketonuria screening, it is now possible to detect the two most common clinical conditions in preschool children, both of which are completely preventable: 1) nutritional anemia due to iron deficiency and 2) poisoning due to exposure to lead. It is hoped that in the near future, all preschool children will be screened for the presence of these two conditions at least annually, and more often in high-risk areas.

Once regional laboratories are established for receiving and testing dried blood specimens for FEP testing, these specimens will inevitably be used for detecting and preventing other causes of developmental disabilities and diseases in children in the same manner as the filter paper for phenylketonuria screening has been used for many other screening tests in newborn infants since the 1960s. With the rapid increase in awareness of the many man-made dangerous substances in the environment, tests for these substances will undoubtedly be applied to this same specimen to increase surveillance and further protect children's health.

## APPLICATIONS OF PREVENTIVE MEASURES

Now that some of the major preventable causes of mental retardation and developmental disabilities have been reviewed, the discussion is turned to what is being done to apply this knowledge. First, it should be mentioned that since 1970 it has been accepted that about 50% of mental retardation can be prevented by the end of this century. This statement was first made by President Nixon in 1971, based on information collected by the President's Committee on Mental Retardation. In 1977, at a national meeting on prevention organized by the President's Committee on Mental Retardation, Moser (1977) conservatively estimated that 29% of severe mental retardation could be prevented. With the knowledge gained about fetal alcohol syndrome and fragile-X syndrome, the total of preventable conditions associated with mental retardation is more than 40% (see Table 2.2).

## COST BENEFITS OF PREVENTION

One incentive, in addition to human reasons, for prevention of mental retardation is the tremendous cost benefit. At this time, when public health budgets are shrinking, it is important to point this out. In France, from 1970 to 1975, a perinatal prevention program was conducted that had been planned in such a way that one could estimate the amount of government funds that were saved as a result. It was estimated that 8 Francs were saved for each 1 Franc invested in the prevention program by the French government (*French Lessons on Handicap*, 1976).

In 1977, the General Accounting Office of the United States, in a report to Congress titled "Preventing Mental Retardation—More Can Be Done," estimated that a newborn screening program with seven tests for every infant born throughout the United States and treatment of the seven conditions detected would cost approximately $18 million per year for the 3 million children born annually. This would save more than $400 million in public funds for the care of individuals with disabilities if the conditions had not been prevented. The return on the investment is greater than 20 to 1 (Comptroller General of the United States, 1977). This could be doubled if one would

**Table 2.2.** Prevention of severe mental retardation (1982)

|  | Percent |
| --- | --- |
| Moser table (1977) | 29 |
| Fetal alcohol | 8 |
| Fragile-X | 5 |
| Total | 42 |

measure productivity and the addition to the gross national product by the individuals in whom the developmental disability had been prevented.

Another indication of the enormous cost benefits to be realized from prevention comes from the estimates of the total cost of care individuals with lead poisoning in the United States, which is on the order of $500 million to $1 billion per year (Provenzano, 1980). Of course, this is only for those who are *known* to have lead poisoning. Obviously, if everyone who is affected by lead poisoning is counted, the cost would be several times greater. The largest amount spent so far by the government is on the order of $10 million per year, which is only 1% of the estimated cost of treating those children who were not detected early, but were diagnosed as having lead poisoning later. If all preschoolers, approximately 15 million children, would be screened annually, this would cost about $30 million and treatment of children with lead poisoning would probably not add more than another $100 million. Thus, the cost benefits for a lead poisoning program would be greater than that for newborn screening for metabolic diseases.

For prevention of the effects of alcohol on the fetus, the New York state governor's task force estimated that a reduction of the incidence by one-third would save the state $40 million per year (Governor's Conference for the Prevention of Developmental Disabilities and Infant Mortality, 1981). This was based on an annual estimate of 386 cases of fetal alcohol syndrome and 3 to 4 times that of children with severe mental retardation (Russell, 1980).

Browder (1977) described the rubella vaccine program in Oregon during the 1970–1973 rubella epidemic. This epidemic, without the immunization program that cost $350,000, could have affected 150 children with congenital rubella (also known as German measles). The cost for the various types of medical, educational, and life-care services for these children would have been $11,953,000 or approximately 30 times the cost of the immunization program, which was $350,000. Browder estimated that the cost benefits for a national measles immunization program during a 10-year period are $130 million. Again, prevention proves to be extremely cost effective as well as ameliorating or eliminating a nonlethal, lifelong, severely handicapping condition.

## PREVENTION EFFORTS

Thus far this chapter has focused on the history of prevention in this century and the growing awareness of the cost benefits of prevention. This increased interest has resulted in many conferences on prevention in the United States at the national, state, and local levels. These conferences have led to a number of prevention efforts in various parts of this country that should be mentioned. First, however, keep in mind that some other countries have been ahead of the

United States in their prevention efforts. Scandinavia has had programs since the 1950s aimed at the prevention of birth defects and developmental disabilities. It was those programs that inspired the previously mentioned 5-year program in France, which took place from 1970–1975.

The Canadian Association for the Mentally Retarded (CAMR), the national parents' group, developed a prevention committee in the early 1970s that continues to be active. The combined efforts of professionals and parents' groups on prevention in Canada are impressive. In Saskatoon, for example, the Institute for Prevention of Mental Retardation at the University of Saskatchewan has been established, possibly the only one in the world.

Under the leadership of the CAMR's Prevention Committee, five regional symposia on prevention of mental retardation were held in Canada during 1981 by regional planning task forces. This led to a report in May 1982 to the Minister of National Health and Welfare with recommendations and priorities for action (National Prevention Committee, Canadian Association on Mental Retardation, 1982).

In the United States, the American Association on Mental Retardation (AAMR), representing Canada and the United States, formed a prevention committee in 1976, the same year that they celebrated their 100th year of existence. This committee has been active in setting up programs on prevention as part of the annual meeting of the AAMR. The American Association of University Affiliated Programs (AAUAP) also has a prevention committee and has been working closely with the committee of the AAMR.

Concerning the federal government, one has to point out the great interest of the President's Committee on Mental Retardation (PCMR) in prevention efforts. In fact, during the Carter and Reagan administrations, this has been one of the committee's main concerns. The 1980 report to the President was entirely on prevention (President's Committee on Mental Retardation [PCMR], 1980). In 1977, the PCMR organized an international summit conference on prevention involving the CAMR, AAMR, and the Association for Retarded Citizens of the United States (ARC) (Browder, 1977). In September, 1982, the PCMR cosponsored, along with the Atlanta Association for Retarded Citizens, a "National Showcase on Prevention" in Atlanta, attended by hundreds of participants from across the country.

Another conference on prevention, sponsored by the PCMR in cooperation with five other national organizations, focused on state-territorial planning for the prevention of mental retardation and related developmental disabilities (U.S. Department of Health and Human Services, 1983). The primary purpose of this conference was to stimulate a sincere commitment to a national effort to prevent mental retardation and to provide a forum that would facilitate the abilities of states to achieve success in conceptualizing, developing, implementing, and expanding state plans to prevent mental retardation and related developmental disabilities.

Other efforts for prevention have resulted in the passing of the Prevention of Disabilities Act (PL 100-202) designed to lessen the incidence of developmental disabilities throughout the United States. Funds were allocated to the Centers for Disease Control in Atlanta to award state efforts to prevent developmental disabilities. Requests for proposals were disseminated from among all 50 states. Twelve states applied and nine of them were awarded funds to establish prevention programs.

Still other efforts include a report by the National Advisory Child Health and Human Development Council (1989) on a prevention research program. Specific research programs focusing on low birth rate infants, intrauterine growth retardation, diabetes in pregnancy, maternal smoking, poor nutrition, and other conditions were described.

The interest of members of parents' organizations in prevention has increased. This has also been true for ARC, which formed a prevention committee in 1960 that was active for nearly 20 years and produced a useful book on guidelines for its members (National Association for Retarded Citizens, 1976).

The Atlanta Association for Retarded Citizens is only one of many that has been interested in prevention. The California Association for Retarded Citizens employed a full-time person to organize prevention activities over a 2-year period. This resulted in a report, "Agenda for Action," that is a blueprint of 64 action items that could be undertaken to prevent mental retardation (California Association for the Retarded, 1979). In 1983, the Office for Prevention of Developmental Disabilities, with a full-time staff, was established by the state of California.

Furthermore, state chapters, such as Illinois, Tennessee, Arkansas, New York, Rhode Island, Virginia, and others, have been active in encouraging prevention efforts. The Illinois Association for Retarded Citizens is unique in that it organized its own action program for the detection and prevention of lead poisoning. This program is independent of the Illinois State Health Department's program.

Although the federally funded lead poisoning programs have been primarily concentrated on large cities, the Illinois Association for Retarded Citizens demonstrated the extent of the problem in rural areas and in small towns long before the national survey mentioned previously (*Routine Screening of Children for Lead Poisoning*, 1976). A grant was obtained from the Knights of Columbus and the Illinois State Attorney General's Office to start a summer program in 1975, in which thousands of preschool children were screened in small towns and in rural areas around Illinois. Approximately 5,000 examinations of dried blood spot specimens were tested. Five percent of the children screened were confirmed to have lead poisoning, which is very close to the national figure of 4% found by the national survey. In addition, the Illinois Association for Retarded Citizens has been carrying out an intense educational program on prevention in the Chicago area with a large grant received from a private foundation (M. Young, personal communication, May 21, 1982).

## CONCLUSION

In this overview, the many areas of prevention in the biomedical field are discussed to justify the claim that 50% of mental retardation can be prevented. Some of the enormous cost benefits that result from prevention are summarized, and some of the efforts to direct attention to this problem at the national, regional, and state levels are outlined. Stressed in this chapter is the importance of the combined efforts of parents and professionals to persuade all levels of government that Benjamin Franklin was correct 200 years ago, in his statement that: "An ounce of prevention is worth a pound of cure." Transferred to the present era, this means that the current administration in the United States needs to be enlightened that one of the best investments that can be made with federal funds is in the prevention of lifelong, nonlethal handicapping conditions in children.

## REFERENCES

Agency criticized for rule changes on lead in gas. (1982a, April 1). *New York Times*.
Agency criticized for rule changes on lead in gas. (1982b, April 15). *New York Times*.
Annest, J. L., O'Connell, D., Roberts, J., & Murphy, R. S. (1981). Blood lead levels from the second national health and nutrition examination survey, 1976–1980. In F. F. Cherry, (Ed.), *Childhood lead poisoning prevention and control: A public health approach to an environmental disease* (pp. 93–102). New Orleans: Maternal and Child Health Section, Office of Health Services and Environmental Quality, Department of Health and Human Resources.
Bellinger, D., Leviton, A., Needleman, H. L., Waternaux, C., & Rabinowitz, M. (1986). Low level lead exposure and infant development in the first year. *Neurobehavioral Toxicology and Teratology*, *8*, 151–161.
Bickel, H., Gerrard, J., & Hicksman, E. M. (1953). Influence of phenylalanine intake on phenylketonuria. *Lancet*, *ii*, 313.
Browder, J. A. (1977, December 15–16). Immunizations and what can be done to improve their use. *Proceedings of an International Summit on Prevention of Mental Retardation from Biomedical Causes*, Racine, Wisconsin.
Brown, W. T., Jenkins, E. C., Friedman, E., Brooks, J., Wisniewski, K., Raguthu, S., & French, J. (1982). Autism is associated with the fragile-X syndrome. *Journal of Autism Developmental Disorders*, *12*, 303–308.
Bureau of Health Care Delivery and Assistance. (1982, September). *Division of maternal and child health report: Erythrocyte protoporphyrin screening of children for undue lead exposure and iron deficiency*. Health Resources and Services Administration, Public Health Service.
California Association for the Retarded. (1979). *Prevention: An agenda for action*. Sacramento: Author.

Centers for Disease Control. (1982). Blood levels in U.S. populations. *Morbidity and Mortality Weekly Report, 31*, 134.

Centers for Disease Control. (1985). *Preventing lead poisoning in young children.* Atlanta: Author.

Comptroller General of the United States. (1977). *Preventing mental retardation: More can be done* (Report No. HRD-77-37). Washington, DC: United States General Accounting Office.

French lessons on handicap. (1976). *Lancet, ii*, 941.

Governor's Conference for the Prevention of Developmental Disabilities and Infant Mortality. (1981). *Prevention action plan.* Albany: State of New York.

Governor's Task Force on Mental Retardation Prevention. (1981). *Tomorrow's children.* Nashville: Tennessee Children's Services Commission.

Guthrie, R. (1961). Blood screening for phenylketonuria. *Journal of American Medical Association, 178*, 863.

Guthrie, R. (1982, November 22). Speaking out: All preschoolers should be screened for lead toxicity. *Medical World News*, p. 94.

Houk, V. N. (1981). Lead poisoning prevention services. In F. F. Cherry (Ed.), *Childhood lead poisoning prevention and control: A public health approach to an environmental disease.* New Orleans: Maternal and Child Health Section, Office of Health Services and Environmental Quality, Department of Health and Human Resources.

Jenkins, E. C., Brown, W. T., Duncan, C., Brooks, J., Ben-Yishay, M., Giordano, F. M., & Nitowsky, H. M. (1981). Feasibility of fragile-X chromosome prenatal diagnosis demonstrated. *Lancet, ii*, 1292.

Lin-Fu, J. S. (1979). Lead exposure among children: A reassessment. *New England Journal of Medicine, 300*, 731–732.

Lin-Fu, J. S. (1980). Lead poisoning and undue lead exposure in children: History and current status. In H. L. Neddleman (Ed.), *Low level lead exposure: The clinical implications of current research.* New York: Raven Press.

Mahaffy, K. R., Annest, J. L., Roberts, J., & Murphy, R. S. (1982). National estimate of blood lead levels, United States, 1976–1980: Association with selected demographic and socioeconomic factors. *New England Journal of Medicine, 307*, 573–579.

Medical Tribune Report. (1982, November 10). Annual Pb screening for kids under 5 is sought in New York. *Medical Tribune.*

Moser, H. (1977, December 15–16). Prevention of mental retardation from biomedical causes. *Proceedings of an International Summit on Prevention of Mental Retardation from Biomedical Causes*, Racine, Wisconsin.

National Advisory Child Health and Human Development Council. (1989). *Prevention research program.* Bethesda, MD: National Institute of Health.

National Association for Retarded Citizens. (1976). *Prevention handbook: To our children's children* (2nd ed.). Arlington, TX: National Association for Retarded Citizens, Prevention and Public Health Subcommittee.

National Prevention Committee, Canadian Association on Mental Retardation. (1982). *Final report to the minister of National Health and Welfare on the prevention of mental retardation in Canada.* Toronto, Ontario: National Institute on Mental Retardation.

Needleman, H. L. (1980). *Low lead exposure: The clinical implications of current research.* New York: Raven Press.

Needleman, H. L., Gunnoe, C., Leviton, A., Reed, R., Peresie, H., Maher, C., & Barrett, P. (1979). Deficits in psychologic and classroom performance of children with elevated dentine lead levels. *New England Journal of Medicine, 300,* 689–696.

Orfanos, A. P., Murphey, W. H., & Guthrie, R. A. (1977). A simple fluorometric assay of free protoporphyrin in erythrocytes (FEP) as a screening test for lead poisoning. *Journal of Laboratory and Clinical Medicine, 89,* 659–665.

Piomelli, S. (1977). Free erythrocyte porphyrins in the detection of undue absorption of Pb and Fe deficiency. *Clinical Chemistry, 23,* 264–269.

Piomelli, S., Brickman, A., & Carlos, E. (1976). Rapid diagnosis of iron deficiency by measurement of free erythrocyte porphyrins and hemoglobin: The FEP/hemoglobin ratio. *Pediatrics, 57,* 136–141.

Piomelli, S., Davidown, B., Guinee, V. F., Young, P., & Gay, G. (1973). The FEP (free erythrocyte porphyrins test): A screening micromethod for lead poisoning. *Pediatrics, 51,* 254–259.

PL 100–202, Prevention of Disabilities Act, 1988; Public Health Act Section 301.

President's Committee on Mental Retardation (PCMR). (1980). *Mental retardation: Prevention strategies that work* (OHDS Publication No. 80–21029). Washington, DC: U.S. Department of Health and Human Services.

Provenzano, G. (1980). The social costs of excessive lead exposure during childhood. In H. L. Needleman (Ed.), *Low level lead exposure: The clinical implications of current research.* New York: Raven Press.

Routine screening of children for lead poisoning. (1976). *Pediatric News, 10.*

Russell, M. (1980). Impact of alcohol-related birth defects (ARBD) on New York State. *Neurobehavioral Toxicology, 2,* 277–283.

Shabecoff, P. (1982, August 1). Rules to reduce the lead in gas reported ready. *New York Times.*

Sutherland, G. P. (1977). Fragile sites on human chromosomes: Demonstration of their dependence on the type of tissue culture medium. *Science, 197,* 265–266.

Turner, G., & Turner, B. (1974). X-linked mental retardation. *Journal of Medical Genetics, 11,* 109–113.

U.S. Department of Health and Human Services, President's Committe on Mental Retardation. (1983, November). *Assessment of the national effort to combat mental retardation from biomedical causes* (conference proceedings).

Waldholz, M. (1982, May 27). Toxic tragedy: Lead poisoning takes a big, continuing toll as cures prove elusive. *The Wall Street Journal.*

Webster, B. (1978, May 2). Study cites hazards from airborne lead. *New York Times.*

# II

## PREVENTION OF DEVELOPMENTAL DISABILITIES PRIOR TO CONCEPTION

**3** | *John R. Evrard*
      | *Patricia Sexton Scola*

# PREPARATION
# FOR PARENTHOOD

Pregnancy is a test of fitness. Although a woman should be in an optimal state before conception, more often than not, pregnancy is a chance happening. The sexual drive in the human is such a potent force, subservient only to survival itself, that frequently reason does not prevail when the opportunity for sexual intercourse presents itself. Intercourse is a unique social interaction between two people that may result in a biologic event—pregnancy. Despite this reality, pregnancy, in an ideal situation, should be a planned event to ensure optimal outcome.

Developmental disabilities in the broad sense include a range of physical, mental, and emotional disorders that may vary from minimal to severe. Regardless of whether the aberration is due to an inherited disorder, a disease acquired in utero, improper nurturing of the child after birth, or others, the effects of the disability ultimately have the same result, a child with handicaps.

Errors in development that result from chromosome abnormalities or during early organogenesis are frequently associated with later disability. The risk of such major events producing a severe impact on physical or social functioning was determined to be 1.7% in a study of 10,000 consecutive births (Van Regemorter et al., 1984). Examples of these types of disorders include Down syndrome, a common chromosome disorder, and spina bifida, a major malformation. A program monitoring the incidence of birth defects in the United States found Down syndrome to occur at the rate of 7.63 per 10,000 births and spina bifida to occur at the rate of 5.1 per 10,000 births (Oakley, James, & Edmonds, 1984).

It is estimated that each year 250,000 infants are born with congenital defects. Of these, 200,000 are due to a structural defect or a metabolic disorder. Fifty thousand defects per year are due to problems associated with low birth weight infants (National Foundation, 1977). During 1986, 6.8% of all reported infant births were babies who weighed less than 2,500 g (Wegman, 1988).

Efforts to reduce the incidence of low birth weight infants would be useful since two-thirds of all perinatal deaths are associated with these babies. In addition, the metabolic and hypoxic insults observed in low birth weight infants are responsible for a number of developmental disabilities, such as retrolental fibroplasia, learning and speech difficulties, cerebral palsy, and poor motor coordination. Risk factors associated with low birth weight babies are:

1. *Late or no prenatal care for the mother:* Approximately 6% of white women beginning prenatal care in the first trimester produce a low birth weight infant. This increases to 16% without prenatal care. The comparable figures for the black population are 12% for those women beginning prenatal care in the first trimester and 25% for those receiving no care during pregnancy at all (National Foundation, 1977).
2. *Poverty:* The risk of producing a low birth weight baby for blacks is twice that of whites. This is a function of poverty and not ethnicity.
3. *Birth to young mothers:* The probability of producing a low birth weight baby increases with each decreasing year of age when the woman is 20 years or younger. For those under 16 years of age 10% of white women and almost 15% of black women have infants weighing less than 2,500 g (Wegman, 1988).

## ADOLESCENT PREGNANCY

Data clearly support the view that, with regard to developmental disabilities, one of the best preparations for parenthood is marriage. Nevertheless, the number of out of wedlock pregnancies is increasing, particularly among adolescents. Effective counseling, therefore, must be undertaken at an early age. With puberty occurring at younger ages each decade, the sexual urge perhaps reaches its peak in the teen years. Emotional and intellectual maturity lag behind this sexual awakening. Frequently, sexual activity begins without an appreciation of the end result. The biologic clock of pubescence cannot be ignored; therefore, society must educate children sexually in order to avoid untimely pregnancies.

There are approximately 11 million sexually active teenagers of which 4 million are females. At age 15, 20% of females are sexually active, and this rises to 71% by age 19. A decline in the total number of teenagers has resulted in their representing only 16% of women in the childbearing years in 1986 as compared to 1980 when they accounted for 20% of women in the childbearing population. Teenagers between 15 and 19 years gave birth to 12.6% of the total births in 1986. Of concern is the reported slight upward trend in births to those teens under 15 years of age (Wegman, 1988).

A frightening fact is that the younger the age at which sexual activity begins, the less likely it is that the individual is going to use contraception. Only 47% of women ages 15 through 19 years used a contraceptive method at the time of first sexual intercourse. Fifty percent of unwanted pregnancies are conceived within six months of initiation of sexual activity. Another fact is that two-thirds of sexually active teenagers do not use contraceptives regularly. In spite of a broader range of choices and accessibility to contraception, usage remains suboptimal and inconsistent by adolescents (Kulig, 1985).

What are the social consequences of adolescent pregnancy? Nine out of 10 adolescents who become pregnant now elect to keep the baby. Eight of 10 mothers age 17 and under are high school dropouts. Consequently, they have little education, few skills, and diminished prospects of a job. Six of 10 teenage marriages result in pregnancy and divorce within 5 years. Environmental risk factors that adversely effect pregnancy outcomes in teenagers include being black, living in rural areas, and receiving inadequate prenatal care. Such environmental concerns probably contribute more to poor outcomes than biological factors for older teenagers (Geronimus, 1986). The environment for an infant of a teenage parent is in many instances hardly conducive to nurturing and to development of full intellectual potential of the offspring. These authors submit that children who do not reach their full academic potential are just as handicapped as though they were born with a learning disability. It has also been demonstrated that the low birth weight infant and the infant born to an adolescent mother are more often the victim of child abuse, which is truly a handicapping factor. Thus, prevention of the adverse effects of many teenage pregnancies will also reduce the incidence of developmental disabilities.

## INCREASING ODDS
## FOR SUCCESSFUL PREGNANCIES

### Preconceptual Counseling

Any woman, irrespective of age, who is planning to become pregnant should undergo a physical examination, screening for high-risk conditions, and have certain tests performed. This is important for the detection and prevention of inherited diseases, for explaining the risks and testing procedures that can be used during pregnancy, and for nutritional counseling. In addition, environmental hazards, such as drugs, smoking, alcohol, the importance of prenatal care, as well as other risks during pregnancy, should be discussed.

The proportion of mothers having college degrees has risen dramatically since 1970. There has also been a parallel rise in the number of women entering the professions. Consequently, more women are postponing first births. Thus, it is not surprising to find that age specific birth rates for women 35 to 39 have increased from 3.9% in 1980 to 6.1% in 1986, but it is also reassuring that the rate of low birth weight deliveries to these women is comparable to the 20 to 24 year age group (Wegman, 1988). A long-term study of older women who had their first delivery after the age of 35 suggested that such women should not be considered to be high-risk obstetrical patients on the basis of age alone (Blickstein, Lancet, & Kessler, 1987). These women, however, must be advised about the increased risk of giving birth to a child with Down syndrome or other chromosome disorders. The risk of Down syndrome in infants of mothers age 30 to 34 is 1 in 669 births; between ages 35 and 39, it is 1 in 343; and it rises to 1 in 44 between ages 40 and 44 (Barsel, Abuelo, & Pueschel, 1982).

Preconceptual counseling and genetic screening should be recommended to those patients who have a pedigree suggestive of inherited disorders in family members, or whose ethnic background indicates an increased risk of a specific genetic disorder. For example, the counselor should assess the family history, establish the inheritance pattern if there is a genetic disease in the family, and give the estimated probability that a conceptus may have a certain disorder. The counselor also should advise the parents about preconceptual and prenatal testing. Prospective parents might also be interested in learning of the value of alpha-fetoprotein (AFP) testing in the maternal blood for screening for neural tube defects and chromosome disorders (see Kolodny, Abuelo, Barsel-Bowers, & Pueschel, Chapter 4; von Oeyen, Chapter 5; and Miller, Chapter 8, this volume).

## Rubella Testing

Another important aspect of prevention of birth defects is an adequate rubella testing and immunization program prior to pregnancy. Previous studies found immunity to rubella (also known as German Measles) to be lacking in 10% to 20% of the population. This has given rise to the suggestion that continued surveillance is necessary to evaluate current immunization programs (*Morbidity and Mortality Weekly Reports*, 1989). Since one-third of pregnancies occur before marriage, premarital testing for rubella immunity is not the most effective way to resolve the problem. High school girls, college women, and women attending family planning clinics should be tested, and those susceptible to rubella should be immunized. Some states have premarital rubella testing programs, but frequently, these programs are ineffective due to the fact that they do not require immunization of nonimmune females and because many women are pregnant at the time of marriage.

## Nutritional Status

Adequate nutritional status is also important for optimal pregnancy outcome. In teenagers the stresses of pregnancy are added to the nutritional needs for body maturation and are often superimposed on previously existing poor nutritional status. Reports from the literature indicate that both a low prepregnant weight and inadequate weight gain during pregnancy correlate with the birth of a low birth weight baby (Eastman & Jackson, 1968). When both factors are present, they become additive in their effects so that the infant born to an underweight woman who has gained less than 9 kg during pregnancy suffers double jeopardy. In a study by Bishop (1968), those women who were more than 5% underweight had a 22.8% incidence of low birth weight babies, whereas those underweight patients who had been treated with nutritional supplements had an incidence of 8.9% of low birth weight infants. Hemoglobin can also be used as a yardstick for nutritional status. The incidence of low birth weight babies of women with hemoglobin levels between 10 g/dl and 10.9 g/dl was found to be 12.8%, whereas the incidence was only 8.2% in those women having hemoglobin levels 11 g/dl (Bishop, 1968).

More important, Hagberg (1975) pointed out that fetal malnutrition plays an important role in the pathogenesis of cerebral palsy and mental retardation. In intrauterine life there is a time of rapid brain growth around the middle of gestation and during the third trimester (Brandt, 1981). At that time the number of adult cerebral neurons has already been achieved, and nutritional deprivation may result in poor motor coordination (see Morgan, Chapter 17, this volume).

## Eliminate Smoking, Alcohol, and Drugs

It is widely recognized that smoking during pregnancy results in infants with lower birth weights than those infants born to nonsmoking mothers. The effect of nicotine and end products of cigarette smoking has been of interest with considerable attention being paid to the role of increased cadmium levels from smoking as an adverse factor on fetal zinc metabolism (Kuhnert, Kuhnert, Debanne, & Williams, 1987). Premature placental calcifications occur statistically more frequently in pregnant women who smoke as compared to those who are nonsmokers and, thus, may be another factor in lowering birth weight (Brown, Miller, Khawli, & Gabert, 1988). In addition to the negative effect of smoking on fetal growth, there is also evidence that cigarette smoking during pregnancy is associated with an increased risk of late fetal and early neonatal death (Cnattingius, Haglund, & Meirik, 1988; Malloy, Kleinman, Land, & Schramm, 1988). An encouraging note is that those women who stop smoking before 16 weeks of gestation have infants whose birth weights are comparable to non-smokers (MacArthur & Knox, 1988).

Avoidance of alcohol during pregnancy is another topic to be emphasized prior to pregnancy. Numerous disorders in the infant have been ascribed to the intake of alcohol during pregnancy. These include prenatal and postnatal growth deficiency, developmental delay, microcephaly, and short palpebral fissures. Though these symptoms are clearly related to alcohol consumption during pregnancy, safe limits of alcohol consumption during pregnancy have not been established, and prospective parents should be so advised (see von Oeyen, Chapter 5; and Hoyme, Chapter 7, this volume).

Increasing attention has been directed toward pregnant women who use any illegal drugs during pregnancy. Complicating the management of such cases is the fact that frequently these patients may use several types of illicit drugs plus alcohol and cigarettes. Their life-style also may result in poor nutrition and inadequate prenatal care (Keith, Donald, Rosner, Mitchell, & Bianchi, 1986). Although the initial concern was that illegal use of drugs might result in a marked increase in congenital malformations, it now appears that the behavioral and neurologic development of infants who are born to addicted mothers are most affected (Chasnoff, 1986).

The effect of cocaine use during pregnancy has been of increasing concern. In one urban hospital cocaine has been detected in 17% of women receiving prenatal care (Frank et al., 1988). This has important implications in that intrauterine growth retardation and microcephaly have been significantly associated with cocaine use during pregnancy (Fulroth, Phillips, & Durand, 1989; Hadeed & Siegel, 1989). Intrauterine cocaine exposure has also been linked to cardiorespiratory complications in newborns (Chasnoff, Hunt, Kletter, & Kaplan, 1989). Furthermore, these infants have difficulty with sleep, wakefulness, and crying. Professionals working in the area of early intervention are now being made aware of techniques to help these infants and hopefully prevent later disability (Schneider, Griffith, & Chasnoff, 1989).

Public awareness of the need to discontinue smoking, alcohol, and drugs is reflected in a study in which more than half of the women reporting usage of smoking, alcohol, and drugs prior to pregnancy refrained from utilization during pregnancy. Cigarette smokers appeared to be most resistant to change with less than half of prior users able to quit smoking during pregnancy (Johnson, McCarter, & Ferenz, 1987).

Many prospective parents, both male and female, are the progeny of mothers who took diethylstilbestrol during their pregnancy. The parents may ask about the impact this may have on their childbearing. Data from the literature indicate that about 25% of males have epididymal cysts or small testicles, 26% have a low ejaculate of less than 1.5 ml, and in one study, 28 of 163 had severely pathologic sperm (Gill, Schumacker, & Bibbo, 1976). Concerning female progeny, in a study of 71 women whose mothers took diethylstilbestrol during pregnancy, the rate of premature delivery was 40% and the perinatal death rate was 25% (Cousins, Karp, Lacey, & Lucas, 1980) (see Hoyme, Chapter 7, this volume).

## Diabetes

Diabetes offers a unique opportunity to provide guidance to the affected woman. With the successful outcome of most pregnancies since insulin was introduced, the number of diabetics in this country has increased. It has been estimated that 1 in 1,000 births is to a diabetic woman, and 1 to 3 of 100 women develop gestational diabetes (Pederson, 1977). Gestational and insulin dependent diabetes, when not controlled, may result in macrosomic infants who may have multiple congenital anomalies. As Menutti (1985) pointed out, if metabolic control is to offset the incidence of malformation, women must be made aware of the risk before conception and be followed very closely during the early months of gestation. The delivery of macrosomic fetuses frequently is complicated, and shoulder dystocia, brachial plexus injury, hypoxia, and cervical spinal cord injury may occur.

Congenital malformations are more common in infants of diabetic mothers and are related to the length of time the mother has had diabetes. Priscilla White's classification demonstrates this (Table 3.1). In mothers with White's classification of A, B, and C, 4.9% of the infants have congenital anomalies, whereas in classes D and F, the frequency of congenital anomalies rises to 13.7%. Congenital cardiovascular disease in infants of diabetic mothers is 7.5 times more common than in the nondiabetic mother, and resultant fatalities are 28 times more frequently observed in those infants (Pederson, 1977). Central nervous system anomalies in babies of diabetic mothers are 8.5 times more common as are deaths due to central nervous system malformations. Although meticulous control of diabetes has lessened the probability of fetal and neonatal death, it has not lowered the incidence of congenital anomalies. Because embryogenesis and organogenesis occurs primarily in the first 2 months of fetal life, rigid preconceptual control of the diabetic mother may be the key to preventing congenital anomalies associated with maternal diabetes. It is reasonable to suggest that diabetic patients plan their pregnancies and

Table 3.1.  White's classification of diabetes

| Class | Description |
| --- | --- |
| A | Chemical diabetes |
| B | Onset after age 20 and < 10 years duration |
| C | Onset ages 10–19 years and 10–20 years duration |
| D | Duration > 20 years and onset before age 10 years; benign retinopathy |
| E | Calcification of leg vessels |
| F | Diabetic nephropathy |
| R | Proliferating retinopathy |

make certain that their disease is under adequate control from the time of conception to the termination of their pregnancy (see von Oeyen, Chapter 5; Hoyme, Chapter 7; and Hansen & McClead, Chapter 11, this volume).

## CONCLUSION

In conclusion, obtaining a preconceptual history, performing a physical examination, employing specific tests, and providing counseling to prospective parents about various risks and methods to increase the odds for successful outcome of pregnancy can be effective in the prevention of many developmental disabilities. The mutual cooperation of parents and professionals remains the best means of assuring the healthiest infant possible.

## REFERENCES

Barsel, G., Abuelo, D., & Pueschel, S. M. (1982). Incidence of Down syndrome in Rhode Island. *Journal of the American Medical Association, 248*, 645.

Bishop, E. (1968). Prevention of premature labor. *Proceedings of the National Conference for the Prevention of Mental Retardation through Improved Maternity Care*. Washington, DC: U.S. Department of Health, Education, and Welfare.

Blickstein, I., Lancet, M., & Kessler, I. (1987). Re-evaluation of the obstetrical risk for older primipara. *International Journal of Gynaecology and Obstetrics, 25*, 107–112.

Brandt, I. (1981). Brain growth, fetal malnutrition, and clinical consequences. *Journal of Perinatal Medicine, 1*, 3–26.

Brown, H. L., Miller, J. M., Khawli, O., & Gabert, H. A. (1988). Premature placental calcification in maternal cigarette smokers. *Obstetrics and Gynecology, 71*, 914–917.

Chasnoff, I. J. (1986). Perinatal addiction: Consequences of intrauterine exposure to opiate and nonopiate drugs. In I. J. Chasnoff (Ed.), *Drug use in pregnancy: Mother and child*. Boston: MTP Press.

Chasnoff, I. J., Hunt, C. E., Kletter, R., & Kaplan, D. (1989). Prenatal cocaine exposure is associated with respiratory pattern abnormalities. *American Journal of Diseases of Children, 143*, 583–587.

Cnattingius, S., Haglund, B., & Meirik, O. (1988). Cigarette smoking as risk factor for late fetal and early neonatal death. *British Medical Journal, 297*, 258–261.

Cousins, L., Karp, W., Lacey, C., & Lucas, W. (1980). Reproductive outcome of women exposed to diethylstilbestrol in utero. *Obstetrics and Gynecology, 56*, 70–76.

Eastman, N., & Jackson, E. (1968). Weight relationships in pregnancy. *Obstetrical and Gynecological Survey, 23*, 1003.

Frank, D. A., Zuckerman, B. S., Amaro, H., Aboagye, K., Bauchner, H., Cabral, H., Fried, L., Hingson, R., Kayne, H., Levenson, S. M., Parker, S., Reece, H., & Vinci, R. (1988). Cocaine use during pregnancy: Prevalence and correlates. *Pediatrics, 82*, 888–895.

Fulroth, R., Phillips, B., & Durand, D. J. (1989). Perinatal outcome of infants exposed to cocaine and/or heroin in utero. *American Journal of Diseases of Children, 143*, 905–910.

Geronimus, A. T. (1986). The effects of race, residence, and perinatal care on the relationship of maternal age to neonatal mortality. *American Journal of Public Health, 76*, 1416–1421.

Gill, W., Schumacker, G., & Bibbo, M. (1976). Structural and functional abnormalities in the sex organs of male offspring of mothers treated with diethylstilbestrol. *Journal of Reproductive Medicine, 16*, 147–153.

Hadeed, A. J., & Siegel, S. R. (1989). Maternal cocaine use during pregnancy: Effect on the newborn infant. *Pediatrics, 84*, 205–210.

Hagberg, B. (1975). Pre-, peri-, and post-natal prevention of neuropediatric handicaps. *Neuropaediatrie, 6*, 331–338.

Johnson, S. F., McCarter, R. J., & Ferenz, C. (1987). Changes in alcohol, cigarette, and recreational drug use during pregnancy: Implications for intervention. *American Journal of Epidemiology, 126*, 695–702.

Keith, L. F., Donald, W., Rosner, M., Mitchell, M., & Bianchi, J. (1986). Obstetric aspects of perinatal addiction. In I. J. Chasnoff (Ed.), *Drug use in pregnancy: Mother and child*. Boston: MTP Press.

Kuhnert, B. R., Kuhnert, P. M., Debanne, S., & Williams, T. G. (1987). The relationship between cadmium, zinc, and birth weight in pregnant women who smoke. *American Journal of Obstetrics and Gynecology, 157*, 1247–1251.

Kulig, J. W. (1985). Adolescent contraception: An update. *Pediatrics, 76*(Suppl.), 675–680.

MacArthur, C., & Knox, E. (1988). Smoking in pregnancy: Effects of stopping at different stages. *British Journal of Obstetrics & Gynaecology, 95*, 551–555.

Malloy, M. H., Kleinman, J. C., Land, G. H., & Schramm, W. F. (1988). The association of maternal smoking with age and cause of infant death. *American Journal of Epidemiology, 128*, 46–55.

Menutti, M. T. (1985). Teratology and genetic counseling of the diabetic mother. *Clinics in Obstetrics and Gynaecology, 28*, 486–495.

*Morbidity and Mortality Weekly Reports*. (1989). *38*, 11.

National Foundation. (1977). *Birth defects: Tragedy and hope*. White Plains, NY: The National Foundation, March of Dimes.

Oakley, G. P., James, L. M., & Edmonds, L. D. (1984). Temporal trends in reported malformation incidence for the United States: Birth defects monitoring program. *Clinical Pediatrics, 23*, 246–247.

Pederson, J. (1977). *The pregnant diabetic and her newborn*. Copenhagen, Denmark: Muns Gaard.

Schneider, J. W., Griffith, D. R., & Chasnoff, I. J. (1989). Infants exposed to cocaine in utero: Implications for developmental assessment and intervention. *Infants and Young Children, 2*, 25–36.

Van Regemorter, W., Dodion, J., Druart, C., Hayez, F., Vamos, E., Flament-Durand, J., Perlmutter-Cremer, N., & Rodesch, F. (1984). Congenital malformations in 10,000 consecutive births in a university hospital: Need for genetic counseling and prenatal diagnosis. *The Journal of Pediatrics, 104*, 386–390.

Wegman, E. (1988). Annual summary of vital statistics—1987. *Pediatrics, 82*, 817–827.

**4** | *Edwin H. Kolodny*
*Dianne N. Abuelo*
*Gail Barsel-Bowers*
*Siegfried M. Pueschel*

# PRECONCEPTUAL GENETIC SCREENING AND COUNSELING

Mendelian principles of inheritance have been known for more than a century, but the cytogenetic and biochemical tools to apply this knowledge directly to patients and their families were only developed in the 1950s and 1960s. An important concern with regard to this knowledge relates to the question of how it can be applied appropriately so that society may benefit from these advances.

Although information about genetics has been disseminated through newspapers, magazines, television, and biology courses in high schools and colleges, it may not reach a young couple in need of specific facts about genetics pertaining to their particular circumstances. Yet, many reproductive decisions can be made on the basis of genetic information derived from careful interviews with families and the results of relevant cytogenetic and biochemical tests. The actual carrier status or the risk of carrying a particular gene can be determined for an increasing number of genetic disorders. Predictability is replacing chance, and the prospects for the prevention and amelioration of many inherited disorders and birth defects have dramatically improved (Connor, 1989).

Genetic screening and counseling prior to conception is important preparation for parenthood. As part of this process, genetic defects within a family can often be clarified and the risk of recurrence can be estimated. It is hoped that this will reduce the risk that serious and life-threatening disease will recur in the same family and helps to assure proper early treatment for genetic disorders compatible with life. Although clinical geneticists and genetic counselors can provide such specific information, it is often the obstetrician, pediatrician, or family physician who is initially asked for genetic advice. Thus, obstetricians are increasingly recognizing the need to take a genetic history from each potential parent. Also, the pediatrician, who is primarily responsible for the care of the child with a developmental disability, is frequently involved in diagnosing birth defects and explaining their significance to families. At times, the neurologist provides genetic advice to the family. Such involvement is quite appropriate if one considers the fact that more than half of all childhood neurologic disorders have a genetic component (Bird & Hall, 1977). Other medical specialists are less often asked for genetic advice, yet, they also have a responsibility to either clarify for their patients the genetic aspects of the diseases they are treating or refer them for genetic counseling when appropriate.

## GENETIC COUNSELING

Genetic counseling can be defined as a communication process that deals with human problems associated with the occurrence or the risk of occurrence of a genetic disorder in a family. It is not counseling in the traditional sense of the word but primarily a process of educating an individual or couple about the nature and consequences of a genetic disorder, its mode of inheritance, whether it is preventable, and whether it can be diagnosed prenatally. Genetic counseling should provide information about the problems of a particular disorder and the options available for dealing with them. The majority of genetic counselors use a nondirective approach in that they attempt to provide patients with a thorough understanding of the problem, thereby enabling them to make their own reproductive decisions on the basis of what they have learned.

At one time genetic counseling was offered mainly to couples who had already had a child with a disability. Now more couples are seeking information about their genetic risks prior to conception. Table 4.1 lists the various groups of people for whom genetic counseling is considered appropriate.

### Mendelian Disorders

Mendelian or single-gene disorders are due to the presence of one or a pair of abnormal or mutant genes. These disorders are classified as autosomal dominant, autosomal recessive, X-linked dominant, and X-linked recessive.

#### Autosomal Dominant Disorders

In autosomal dominant disorders, the affected individual has a single abnormal gene that is paired with a normal gene. If the condition is not lethal and does not prevent reproduction, for each pregnancy there is a 50% chance that

**Table 4.1.** Indications for genetic counseling

Parents who have had a child with a birth defect or inherited disease

Persons with a birth defect or inherited disease themselves, or other family members with the defect or disease

Women over 35 who are pregnant or planning to become pregnant

Persons who are members of ethnic groups with a high incidence of a particular inherited disease (e.g., Tay-Sachs in Jewish people, sickle cell anemia in black people, thalassemia in people of Mediterranean origin)

Couples with a history of repeated miscarriage, stillbirth, or early infant death

Couples who have or are planning a consanguineous marriage (e.g., a marriage of first cousins)

Persons with a history of excessive exposure to drugs, chemicals, or radiation

it will be passed on to the next generation. Males and females are equally affected, thus autosomal dominant conditions can be passed from either parent to either sons or daughters. When normal parents have a child with an autosomal dominant disorder the condition is presumed to be the result of a new mutation. Again, if the condition is not lethal, the affected child will have a 50% chance of passing the condition on to his or her children.

Dominant genes are not always phenotypically expressed or, when they are expressed, the degree of expression may vary from individual to individual. Occasionally, a dominant gene is not expressed at all and is said to be nonpenetrant. In such a case, an individual who is phenotypically normal can pass on a dominant condition. Much more common than nonpenetrance is variability of expression of dominant disorders in which some individuals with a dominant gene are only mildly affected, whereas others are moderately or severely affected. For example, osteogenesis imperfecta tarda is a dominant disorder characterized by brittle bones, hearing loss, and blue sclerae when it is fully expressed. A parent who has a child with full expression of this condition may have only blue sclerae him- or herself and no other manifestations of the disorder. Nevertheless, there is still a 50% risk of passing the condition on to each offspring. Another example of variable expression is Marfan syndrome, which is an autosomal dominant connective tissue disorder characterized by tall stature, long extremities, cardiovascular abnormalities, and dislocation of the ocular lens. An affected individual may exhibit only tall stature and long extremities without any of the more serious manifestations of the disorder. Despite being mildly affected, however, such an individual again would be at a 50% risk of having a child with full expression of the disorder. Table 4.2 lists some dominant disorders and their major characteristics.

Most autosomal dominant disorders cannot yet be diagnosed prenatally. However, achondroplasia, a form of dwarfism, can be identified by ultrasonography during the second trimester of pregnancy.

**Table 4.2.** Common dominant disorders

| Disorder | Characteristics |
|---|---|
| Achondroplasia | Disproportionate short stature with large head |
| Huntington disease | Degenerative disease of the nervous system usually with adult onset |
| Myotonic dystrophy | Neuromuscular disorder with mask-like facial appearance and possible mental retardation |
| Marfan syndrome | Connective tissue disorder with tall stature, long fingers, cardiovascular abnormalities, and dislocated lens |
| Osteogenesis imperfecta tarda | Brittle bones, hearing loss, and blue sclerae |
| Polydactyly | Extra fingers and/or toes |

## Autosomal Recessive Disorders

Autosomal recessive disorders affect males and females with equal frequency. An affected individual has a pair or double dose of an abnormal or mutant gene. Both parents are usually phenotypically normal but are heterozygotes who carry the abnormal gene in single dose. If a couple has one child with an autosomal recessive disorder, the risk of recurrence is 25% for each subsequent pregnancy. There is a 50% chance that each future child will be a carrier and a 25% chance that a child will be unaffected and a noncarrier. Affected individuals and those of their siblings who are carriers are unlikely to have affected children unless they marry a carrier or another affected person with the same genetic disorder. Statistically, their children will be carriers.

For many of the autosomal recessive disorders a specific biochemical abnormality is known, making both carrier detection and prenatal diagnosis possible. This is true for Tay-Sachs disease as well as for many of the other inborn errors of metabolism and for the hemoglobinopathies, such as sickle cell disease and thalassemia. Phenylketonuria (PKU) is a condition for which the biochemical defect is known but for which prenatal diagnosis was not possible until the 1960s. However, new techniques using DNA analysis have made prenatal diagnosis of PKU available (Ledley et al., 1988). In the case of cystic fibrosis, the most common autosomal recessive disorder in Caucasians, discovery of the abnormal gene preceded recognition of the specific biochemical defect (Riordan et al., 1989). However, even before the gene was cloned, linkage analysis had mapped the gene sufficiently to permit carrier detection and prenatal diagnosis with the use of molecular genetic techniques (Dawson et al., 1989).

A consanguineous marriage considerably increases the chances of autosomal recessive disease in offspring because both individuals share the same genetic background, and thus both could be carriers. Similarly, individuals from small geographic isolates or the same ethnic or racial group will tend to share similar genes, again increasing the chances of autosomal recessive disease in offspring. For example, the increased incidence of Tay-Sachs disease among Ashkenazi Jews and French Canadians, of sickle cell disease in Blacks, and of thalassemia in Greeks and Italians has stimulated prevention efforts among these populations that are designed to identify those who are carriers of the genes for these diseases.

Occasionally, a couple who has had a child with a fatal or debilitating autosomal recessive disease may wish to utilize the option of artificial insemination for future pregnancies. Although this step reduces the risk of recurrence, there is a finite possibility that the sperm donor carries the same deleterious gene as the husband, particularly if the gene in question shows an ethnic predilection and if the donor has been selected because of ethnic and other resemblances to the husband. Therefore, if artificial insemination is employed, appropriate carrier detection, if technically possible, should be done on the donor.

### X-Linked Disorders

X-linked disorders affect the genes on the X chromosome and can be either X-linked recessive or X-linked dominant. However, there are extremely few X-linked dominant disorders; therefore, this discussion of X-linked inheritance focuses on X-linked recessive disorders that occur primarily in males with females usually being unaffected carriers.

Males have only a single X chromosome; thus, they are hemizygous for the genes on that chromosome, since these genes have no allele on the Y chromosome. As a result, males express X-linked recessive conditions. Females, however, are usually heterozygous for their deleterious X-linked genes and, thus, rarely express X-linked recessive disorders. However, if there is unfavorable lyonization with inactivation of a large percentage of the X chromosome with the normal allele, a heterozygous female may show mild, moderate, or occasionally severe manifestations of an X-linked recessive disorder.

For X-linked disorders that are not fatal or do not preclude reproduction, an affected male and noncarrier female will have only unaffected sons and carrier daughters. For example, this is the case for classical hemophilia. Carrier females are at 50% risk for having affected sons and 50% risk for having carrier daughters.

Careful study of family history will sometimes reveal an X-linked disorder. Typically, an affected child may have an affected brother, maternal uncle, or maternal male cousin. In such a case, the child's mother is considered an obligate carrier with a 50% risk for future affected sons. However, X-linked disorders sometimes occur in the absence of a positive family history as the result of a new mutation. In such situations, the mutation may have occurred in the mother who is thereby a carrier or it may have occurred in the affected child. In the latter case, the mother would not be a carrier and would be at negligible risk for recurrence in future offspring.

As a result of lyonization, carrier detection for most X-linked disorders is unreliable even when a specific biochemical abnormality is known. Since the carrier status is often difficult to determine, prenatal diagnosis should be offered to women who are probable or possible carriers of X-linked disorders, such as Hunter syndrome or Lesch Nyhan syndrome.

Duchenne muscular dystrophy is an X-linked recessive disorder in which carrier detection involves the measurement of an enzyme, creatine kinase (CK). This is a nonspecific test that allows detection of carriers only about 80% of the time. Women with significantly elevated CK levels are considered carriers, but women with normal CK levels cannot be considered noncarriers although the mathematical probability of being a carrier is reduced. Prenatal diagnosis of Duchenne muscular dystrophy is complex and often requires the availability of blood samples from multiple family members including a male affected with the disease (Bakker et al., 1989; Darras et al., 1988).

## Multifactorial Disorders

Many of the common congenital malformations, such as spina bifida, anencephaly, cleft lip and/or cleft palate, congenital heart defects, clubfoot, dislocation of the hip, pyloric stenosis, and hypospadias, are multifactorial disorders. They are the result of the interaction of multiple predisposing genes and, as yet, unknown environmental factors. There are several distinctive principles that govern recurrence risks for multifactorial conditions that differ from the rules that apply for Mendelian disorders:

1.  The risk of recurrence is usually between 2% to 5% provided there is only one affected first degree relative. If there are two affected offspring or one affected parent and one affected offspring, the risk of recurrence becomes 2 to 3 times greater and will further increase with each affected first degree relative.
2.  The risk of recurrence depends on the severity of the defect in the proband; the more severe the defect, the higher will be the risk. For example, parents who have a child with a bilateral cleft lip and palate have a higher risk (about 6%) than those who have a child with a unilateral cleft lip (2% to 3%).
3.  For those conditions in which the affected individual is more often of one sex, the recurrence risk is higher when the proband is of the sex that is less frequently affected. For example, cleft lip and/or cleft palate and pyloric stenosis both occur more frequently in males than in females. As a result, a couple with a daughter affected with either of these conditions has a higher risk of recurrence than a couple with an affected son. Likewise, an affected mother has a higher risk for having an affected child than does an affected father. This is explained on the basis of the sex that is least frequently affected having a greater genetic component or more predisposing genes than the sex that is most frequently affected.

Preconceptual genetic counseling is often requested by individuals who were born with multifactorial conditions (see Table 4.3) and by individuals who have affected siblings as well as other affected family members. Those who themselves have been affected can usually be reassured that the risk to their offspring is 5% or less. In those with affected siblings or other family members, the risk is greater than that of the general population but usually less than 1%. Prenatal diagnosis is possible for those inquiring about neural tube defects. For affected individuals and for those who have had affected children, sonography and amniocentesis for determination of alpha-fetoprotein (AFP) and acetylcholinesterase are recommended for each pregnancy. For those with relatives with neural tube defects, maternal serum AFP screening should be offered and amniocentesis made available when requested, particularly if the individual concerned is the sister or maternal aunt of an affected individual since data have indicated a risk approaching 1% for these individuals.

Screening for open neural tube defects, such as anencephaly and meningomyelocele, is suggested for all pregnancies in many areas of the United States and Europe. Measurements of maternal serum AFP during the 16th to 18th week of gestation will detect approximately 85% to 90% of open neural tube defects (U.K. collaborative study, 1977, 1979). However, the vast majority of abnormal maternal serum AFP tests are not due to neural tube defects, but often simply reflect discrepancies in gestational age or undiagnosed multiple pregnancy. Therefore, elevated maternal serum AFP tests should be followed up with ultrasound examination. After fetal age has been confirmed and multiple pregnancy has been ruled out, amniocentesis should be offered for amniotic fluid AFP and acetylcholinesterase determination (Collaborative acetylcholinesterase study, 1981; U.K. collaborative study, 1979). In addition to gestational age discrepancies, multiple pregnancy, and open neural tube defects, other reasons for elevated maternal serum and

Table 4.3. Approximate empiric recurrence risks for some common multifactorial disorders

| Abnormality | Recurrence risk for siblings and offspring |
| --- | --- |
| Cleft lip and/or cleft palate | 3%–5% |
| Spina bifida and anencephaly | 2%–3% |
| Cardiac defects | 2%–5% |
| Clubfoot | 2%–3% |
| Dislocation of hip | 4%–5% |
| Pyloric stenosis | 3%–5% |
| Hypospadias | 10% for brothers and sisters |

amniotic fluid alpha-fetoprotein include fetal demise and congenital abnormalities, such as duodenal atresia, omphalocele, and gastroschisis.

## Chromosome Disorders

Chromosome disorders can involve an abnormality in either the number or the structure of the chromosomes. Abnormalities in number can include either extra or missing chromosomes, such as trisomies (e.g., trisomy 21 due to the presence of an extra #21 chromosome) or monosomies (e.g., Turner syndrome due to a missing X chromosome). Abnormalities in structure include deletions, duplications, or inversions of chromosome material or translocations of material from one chromosome to another.

The incidence of major chromosome abnormalities in consecutive unselected live-born infants is approximately 0.7%. The occurrence of a chromosome abnormality in either an offspring or a close family member of a couple is one of the most common indications for genetic counseling (see Table 4.1).

It has been found that approximately 1 in 400 newborn males and 1 in 700 newborn females have abnormalities of the sex chromosomes; 1 in 800 newborns has an autosomal trisomy; and 1 in 500 has a balanced chromosome rearrangement. An unbalanced translocation occurs in approximately 1 in 2,000 newborns and is usually associated with congenital anomalies and mental retardation.

In general, in most cases of trisomy, the etiology is considered to be an accidental nondisjunctional event in the formation of either the egg or the sperm. Parental karyotypes generally do not need to be examined and the couple can be counseled that there is an empiric recurrence risk of approximately 1%. Parents of children with trisomy 21, trisomy 13, and trisomy 18 are routinely offered amniocentesis or chorionic villus biopsy (also called chorionic villus sampling [CVS]) for subsequent pregnancies (Fowler, Giles, Cooper, & Sardharwalla, 1989).

As opposed to amniocentesis, which is performed in the second trimester, chorionic villus biopsy can be performed in the first trimester. It allows prenatal diagnosis of chromosome disorders and biochemical defects, such as Tay-Sachs disease, as early as the 10th to 12th week of gestation (Hogge, Schonberg, & Golbus, 1985). However, chorionic villus biopsy carries a complication risk slightly higher than that of amniocentesis (Rhoads et al., 1989).

Genetic evaluation of the child with a structural chromosome abnormality involves karyotyping of both parents to determine whether one of them is a translocation carrier. Recurrence risks are low when neither parent is a carrier, but will be higher when one of the parents is found to have a balanced translocation. Risks of recurrence are also higher when the carrier parent is the mother. Amniocentesis or chorionic villus biopsy is indicated for subsequent pregnancies whether or not an abnormality is found in one of the parents. An example of a disorder resulting from a chromosome deletion is cri du chat syndrome. The affected individual has mental retardation and characteristic facial features, as well as a cat-like cry in early infancy. The syndrome is due to a deletion of part of the short arm of chromosome #5. In 10% to 15% of cases, a parent is found to be a balanced carrier. Down syndrome can also be due to translocation. The extra #21 chromosome, in whole or in part, can be translocated onto another chromosome. This can occur de novo or be inherited from a parent. Specific recurrence risk figures vary from 1% to 100% depending upon the karyotype findings and should be discussed with the parents along with their reproductive options during a formal genetic counseling session.

Another indication for karyotyping a couple is repeated pregnancy loss. Couples with multiple spontaneous abortions (three or more) are far more likely than the general population to be carriers of balanced translocations. This type of chromosome rearrangement may be of no clinical consequence to the carrier, but can result in a chromosomally unbalanced gamete. Detecting these at-risk couples by taking a careful history of pregnancy loss and screening them by karyotyping will allow for preconceptual genetic counseling aimed toward preventing the birth of a chromosomally unbalanced offspring.

Prenatal diagnosis should be offered to all pregnant women at increased risk for giving birth to an offspring with a disorder that is detectable during pregnancy. Unless there is a specific history suggesting an increased risk for a particular abnormality, such as neural tube defects or certain inherited biochemical disorders, this procedure will be primarily limited to testing women at risk for Down syndrome and other chromosome disorders. This includes women who are 35 years or older, since there exists known increased risks for trisomic live births associated with advanced maternal age, and younger women who have abnormal maternal serum AFP screening tests. Amniocentesis is usually performed at the 16th week of pregnancy, but it is occasionally done earlier for high-risk situations or for extreme parental anxiety (Benacerraf et al., 1988).

Merkatz, Nitowsky, Macri, and Johnson (1984) reported a link between low maternal serum AFP values and fetal trisomies. Cuckle, Wald, and Lindenbaum (1984) soon followed with the proposal to screen for Down syndrome using maternal serum AFP measurement. They indicated that certain combinations of low maternal serum AFP levels and maternal age could identify a population at higher risk for Down syndrome. As a result, many centers offer amniocentesis to women who are less than 35 years old if they have low AFP values. As compared to using advanced maternal age as the sole risk criterion for Down syndrome, this added use of low AFP values serves to raise the detection rate for Down syndrome from about 20% to 40%. Newer tests using other biochemical markers are reported to have even higher detection rates (Wald et al., 1988).

## GENETIC DISEASE IN THE MOTHER

Genetic conditions in the mother can have adverse affects on the fetus without direct transmission of the genetic defect to the fetus. Young women originally diagnosed by newborn screening programs as having phenylketonuria (PKU) have been successfully treated and are now approaching the reproductive age. If their low phenylalanine diet has not been continued and if pregnancy occurs, the mother's high blood phenylalanine level during pregnancy will expose the fetal brain to toxic levels of this amino acid. Therefore, these mothers must be managed with strict dietary control starting in the preconceptual period and their blood phenylalanine levels need to be monitored carefully throughout gestation (Levy, 1987; Pueschel, 1985; Pueschel, Hum, & Andrews, 1977).

For some disorders, a woman with a genetic disease may herself be harmed by pregnancy. For example, in Marfan syndrome, pregnancy significantly increases the risk of a dissecting aneurysm in mothers with pre-existing aortic dilatation. Therefore, in women with Marfan syndrome, the aortic root should be followed with serial echocardiograms for signs of enlargement and those patients whose pregnancies would present an extremely high risk should be counseled accordingly. Also, various hemoglobinopathies, such as sickle cell anemia and bleeding diatheses, may exacerbate during a pregnancy.

## FEASIBILITY OF GENETIC SCREENING

Couples frequently ask, "If so many diseases can now be detected prenatally, why not screen each potential parent to determine which of the many harmful mutant genes they may carry?" This question presupposes that a reliable screening procedure exists to detect these mutant genes or the gene products and that the resultant diseases can either be ameliorated by their early recognition or be preventable by pregnancy termination (Golbus, 1982). The feasibility of this approach depends upon numerous factors, including cost, test reliability, and availability of resources for testing and counseling. The cost to discover one carrier-carrier couple depends upon gene frequency and the technical requirements of the test. For example, to detect one Jewish couple at risk for offspring with type A Niemann-Pick disease (the heterozygote frequency is about 1 in 75 among Ashkenazi Jews), 8 times as many Ashkenazim would need to be screened to detect one Jewish couple at risk for Tay-Sachs disease (where the heterozygote frequency is about 1 in 25 among Ashkenazi Jews). Furthermore, the Tay-Sachs carrier test can be done using serum in an assay system that employs a highly sensitive synthetic substrate whereas the test for heterozygotes of Niemann-Pick disease requires leukocytes or cultured fibroblasts as well as the authentic lipid substrate sphingomyelin into which a radioactive label has been incorporated.

Various stringencies in testing requirements may make it difficult to collect and prepare the proper specimens needed for the actual heterozygote determination. Also, unless the test is highly specific and clearly differentiates between normal and carrier individuals, it will generate an intolerable number of false positive or false negative results. Moreover, there needs to be both a sufficient demand for the test to generate efficiencies of scale, and sufficient laboratory and counseling facilities available to handle the referrals generated by public expectations. Deliberations regarding cost effectiveness in genetic screening commonly compare the cost to prevent one new case of a serious early childhood disease with the actual costs for caring for the child until his or her death (Nelson, Swint, & Caskey, 1978). This sort of calculation ignores the emotional cost of the child's illness on his or her family. Thus, considerations of cost, technical feasibility, test reliability, predictive value, and availability of resources for testing and counseling act as major deterrents to the more widespread use of heterozygote screening for the prevention of genetic disease.

## TAY-SACHS CARRIER TESTING: PROTOTYPE FOR GENETIC SCREENING

### Suitability for Mass Screening

In the case of Tay-Sachs disease, selective genetic screening has had a significant effect. The number of new cases of Tay-Sachs disease has declined dramatically since the advent of widespread Tay-Sachs carrier testing. Beginning in Baltimore, Maryland, this program has spread to all major population centers in North America, Israel, and elsewhere. Three factors favor its success:

1. The existence of a defined subgroup of the population (Ashkenazi Jews and French Canadians) that is at increased risk for the Tay-Sachs disease trait
2. The existence of a relatively simple and inexpensive test for the carrier state
3. The availability of reliable prenatal diagnosis

### Operating Principles of Tay-Sachs Prevention Programs

Individuals submitting to Tay-Sachs carrier testing do so voluntarily. The results of their tests are kept confidential. Thorough pretesting education is stressed so that the client will understand the purpose of carrier testing and the significance of the test results that are generated. Pretest and posttest counseling are also provided to ensure that the information imparted is accurate and will help couples make informed decisions regarding their reproductive options. Each testing program also has access to a facility for prenatal diagnosis. These operating principles are applicable not only to Tay-Sachs carrier testing but to all programs of genetic disease screening. It would be unwise to legislate mandatory testing for carriers since the carrier state is harmless in the majority of instances and even in a carrier-carrier marriage does not inevitably cause disease in an offspring. Pretest and posttest education and counseling mitigate some of the psychosocial problems that genetic testing can create for the testee. These include anxiety concerning the result of testing, the loss of self-esteem that a carrier might experience, and concerns about choice of a mate and reproductive outcome (Clow & Scriver, 1977; Schneiderman, Lowder, & Rae-Grant, 1978; Stone, 1976).

## Impact of Tay-Sachs Carrier Testing Programs

At the end of 1978, 200,000 persons had been tested in the United States for Tay-Sachs carrier status (Greenberg & Kaback, 1982). From this experience it is clear that genetic screening affects not only the individuals who are tested but also their families, the families of children with the disease, physicians, clinics, hospitals, clinical laboratories, the clergy, school curricula, community agencies, public policy, and even the conduct of basic research. Questions are raised that only society can answer, such as, "Who pays for the cost of mass education campaigns, testing services, counseling, and care for an affected child?"

**Physician** The physician must now consider whom to test and when to test (Lowden, 1978). Should everyone be tested or only certain high-risk individuals? If married couples are tested, should it be only those who are planning to have children? Should both spouses be tested or will it be sufficient to test only one? Should the children of carriers and others below age 18 be tested? How should pregnant women be handled? And, what if they present themselves for testing after the time when amniocentesis for prenatal diagnosis is usually performed? Must physicians now take a complete genetic history, and must obstetricians now interview husbands as well? If physicians fail to recommend testing for this or other genetic diseases, are they liable for wrongful life and the emotional pain and suffering of the parents (Curran, 1977)?

**Testing Laboratories** Genetic screening involves life and death issues that place a heavy burden on testing laboratories. Stringent quality control must be maintained. This requires specimens from known heterozygote and homozygote affected individuals. The proper interpretation of test results may require the submission of medical information, a process that could prolong and complicate the testing process. Poor methodology, incomplete testing, or the wrong interpretation of the data could produce a false negative result that misinforms a couple concerning their risk for having children with a specific disease. Conversely, these factors could lead to a false positive result causing a couple needless anxiety and risks for each of their pregnancies because of the mistaken belief that prenatal diagnosis is required.

## MASS SCREENING FOR OTHER GENETIC CONDITIONS

Concomitant the increase in the number of recognized inherited diseases with a known molecular defect, there has been an increase in the number of conditions for which carrier testing is possible. Should testing be made available for all of these conditions or only for those causing severe and fatal disease of the nervous system in infancy or childhood? This question highlights an ethical dilemma from which geneticists cannot escape. If a fetus is diagnosed as having a genetic disorder compatible with a normal life expectancy, should that fetus be aborted? If not, does carrier screening for this disease serve any useful purpose? Screening might be warranted, for example, if early recognition of the disease would aid treatment of the affected child.

Genetic counselors giving nondirective counseling argue that individuals have a right to know their genetic constitution, and, if they elect to choose their offspring based upon tests for certain genetic traits, it is their prerogative to do so. Others would prefer to limit genetic screening to those traits that produce severe brain damage in the early years of life. What is clear in this debate is that the issue of whether or not to screen for a particular genetic trait is based upon the individual's own view of the severity of the disease in question. If a disease is regarded as serious, even if not life threatening, one is more apt to pursue carrier testing than if the disease is considered only a minor nuisance.

## CONCLUSION

Preconceptual genetic counseling educates prospective parents toward an understanding of their risks for having offspring with inherited disorders and with regard to their options either for prevention of the disorders or for planning optimal care for the affected child after birth. Parental options may include carrier testing in certain situations, refraining from reproduction, adoption, artificial insemination, prenatal diagnosis, or choosing to reproduce in spite of the genetic risks. The choice, of course, lies with the prospective parents. However, genetic disorders causing developmental disabilities can be prevented or ameliorated only with continued efforts aimed at education of the medical community, prospective parents, and society at large. (For further discussion see Miller, Chapter 8, this volume.)

## REFERENCES

Bakker, E., Bonten, E. J., Veenema, H., den Dunnen, J. T., Grootscholten, P. M., van Ommen, G. J. B., & Pearson, P. L. (1989). Prenatal diagnosis of Duchenne muscular dystrophy: A three-year experience in a rapidly evolving field. *Journal of Inherited Metabolic Disease, 12*(Suppl.1), 174–190.

Benacerraf, B. R., Greene, M. F., Saltzman, D. H., Barss, V. A., Penso, C. A., Nadel, A. S., Heffner, L. J., Stryker, J. M., Sandstrom, M. M., & Figoletto, F. D., Jr. (1988). Early amniocentesis for prenatal cytogenetic evaluation. *Radiology, 169*, 709–710.

Bird, T. D., & Hall, J. G. (1977). Clinical neurogenetics: A survey of the relationship of medical genetics to clinical neurology. *Neurology, 27*, 1057–1060.

Clow, C. L., & Scriver, C. R. (1977). Knowledge about and attitudes toward genetic screening among high school students: The Tay-Sachs experience. *Pediatrics, 59*, 86–91.

Collaborative acetylcholinesterase study. (1981). Amniotic fluid acetylcholinesterase electrophoresis as a secondary test in the diagnosis of anencephaly and open spina bifida in early pregnancy. *Lancet, ii*, 321–324.

Connor, J. M. (1989). Genetic aspects of prenatal diagnosis. *Journal of Inherited Metabolic Disease, 12*, 89–96.

Cuckle, H. S., Wald, N. J., & Lindenbaum, R. H. (1984). Maternal serum alpha-fetoprotein measurements: A screening test for Down syndrome. *Lancet, i*, 926.

Curran, W. J. (1977). Tay-Sachs disease, wrongful life and preventive malpractice. *American Journal of Public Health, 67*, 568–569.

Darras, B. T., Blattner, P., Harper, J. F., Spiro, A. J., Alter, S., & Francke, U. (1988). Intragenic deletions in 21 Duchenne muscular dystrophy (DMD)/Becker muscular dystrophy (BMD) families studied with the dystrophin cDNA: Location of breakpoints on *Hind*III and *Bg*/II exon-containing fragment maps, meiotic and mitotic origin of the mutations. *American Journal of Human Genetics, 43*, 620–629.

Dawson, D. B., Cummins, L. A., Schaid, D. J., Michels, V. V., Gordon, H., O'Connell, E. J., & Thibodeau, S. N. (1989). Carrier identification of cystic fibrosis by recombinant DNA techniques. *Mayo Clinic Proceedings, 64*, 325–334.

Fowler, B., Giles, L., Cooper, A., & Sardharwalla, I. B. (1989). Chorionic villus sampling: Diagnostic uses and limitations of enzyme assays. *Journal of Inherited Metabolic Disease, 12*, 105–117.

Golbus, M. S. (1982). The current scope of antenatal diagnosis. *Hospital Practice, 17*, 179–186.

Greenberg, D. A., & Kaback, M. M. (1982). Estimation of the frequency of hex-osaminidase A variant alleles in the American Jewish population. *American Journal of Human Genetics, 34*, 444–451.

Hogge, W. A., Schonberg, S. A., & Golbus, M. S. (1985). Prenatal diagnosis by chorionic villus sampling: Lessons of the first 600 cases. *Prenatal Diagnosis, 5*, 393–400.

Ledley, F. D., Koch, R., Jew, K., Beaudet, A., O'Brien, W. E., Bartos, D. P., & Woo, S. L. C. (1988). Phenylalanine hydroxylase expression in liver of a fetus with phenylketonuria. *The Journal of Pediatrics, 113*, 463–468.

Levy, H. L. (1987). Maternal phenylketonuria: Review with emphasis on pathogenesis. *Enzyme*, *38*, 312–320.

Lowden, J. A. (1978). Role of the physician in screening for carriers of Tay-Sachs disease. *Canadian Medical Association Journal*, *119*, 575–578.

Merkatz, I. R., Nitowsky, H. M., Macri, J. N., & Johnson, W. E. (1984). An association between low maternal serum alpha-fetoprotein and fetal chromosome abnormalities. *American Journal of Obstetrics and Gynecology*, *148*, 886–894.

Nelson, W. B., Swint, J. M., & Caskey, C. T. (1978). An economic evaluation of a genetic screening program for Tay-Sachs disease. *American Journal of Human Genetics*, *30*, 160–166, 663–665.

Pueschel, S. M. (1985). Maternal phenylketonuria. *Social Biology*, *32*, 31–44.

Pueschel, S. M., Hum, C., & Andrews, M. (1977). Nutritional management of the female with phenylketonuria during pregnancy. *American Journal of Clinical Nutrition*, *30*, 1153–1161.

Riordan, J. R., Rommens, J. M., Keran, B., Alon, N., Rozmahel, R., Grzelczak, Z., Zielenski, J., Lok, S., Plavsic, N., Chov, J. L., Drumm, M. L., Iannuzzi, M.C., Collins, F. S., & Tsui, L.C. (1989). Identification of the cystic fibrosis gene: Cloning and characterization of complementary DNA. *Science*, *245*, 1066–1073.

Rhoads, G. G., Jackson, L. G., Schlesselman, S. E., de la Cruz, F. F., Desnick, R. J., Golbus, M. S., Ledbetter, D. H., Lubs, H. A., Mahoney, M. J., Pergament, E., Simpson, J. L., Carpenter, R. J., Elias, S., Ginsberg, N. A., Goldberg, J. D., Hobbins, J. C., Lynch, L., Shiono, P. H. K., Wapner, R. J., & Zachary, J. M. (1989). The safety and efficacy of chorionic villus sampling for early prenatal diagnosis of cytogenetic abnormalities. *The New England Journal of Medicine*, *320* (10), 609–617.

Schneiderman, G., Lowder, J. A., & Rae-Grant, Q. (1978). Psychosocial aspects of a Tay-Sachs screening clinic. *American Journal of Psychiatry*, *135*, 1101–1102.

Stone, M. H. (1976). Possible hazards in screening of adolescents for Tay-Sachs disease. *New England Journal of Medicine*, *295*, 113.

U.K. collaborative study on alpha-fetoprotein in relation to neural-tube defects. (1977). Maternal serum alpha-fetoprotein measurement in antenatal screening for anencephaly and spina bifida in early pregnancy. *Lancet*, *i*, 1323–1332.

U.K. collaborative study on alpha-fetoprotein in relation to neural-tube defects. (1979). Amniotic fluid alpha-fetoprotein measurement in antenatal diagnosis of anencephaly and open spina bifida in early pregnancy. *Lancet*, *ii*, 652–662.

Wald, N. J., Cuckle, H. S., Densem, J. W., Nanchahal, K., Royston, P., Chard, T., Haddow, J. E., Knight, G. J., Palamaki, G. E., & Canick, J. A. (1988). Maternal serum screening for Down syndrome in early pregnancy. *British Medical Journal*, *297*, 883–887.

# III

## PREVENTION OF DEVELOPMENTAL DISABILITIES DURING PREGNANCY

# 5 | Paul T. von Oeyen

# OPTIMAL PRENATAL CARE

Optimal prenatal care should begin with family planning and prepregnancy counseling in an attempt to prevent significant problems that may occur early in gestation. Ideally, both prospective parents should be included in the initial counseling. Educational efforts, in addition to being aimed at prospective mothers, should include fathers in order to prepare them for the important role of providing encouragement and support during the course of pregnancy and parturition (see Evrard & Scola, Chapter 3, this volume).

Once pregnancy occurs, early prenatal care is essential to establish the estimated date of confinement, begin patient counseling, and develop a risk assessment. Establishing a risk assessment is an important purpose of the initial prenatal visit. The risk assessment is based on the medical history and physical examination, along with relatively few laboratory screening tests. It may, of course, be modified as pregnancy proceeds and if unforeseen problems develop. However, a major goal of prenatal care is to anticipate the possible development of both maternal and fetal problems so that they may be minimized or prevented entirely.

## RISK ASSESSMENT

Since the 1970s, many formalized systems of risk assessment have been promoted. These include point scoring systems defining high-risk pregnancies (Hobel, 1977; Nesbitt & Aubry, 1969), so that these pregnancies can be singled out for attention. Even without a formal scoring system, potential problems should be identified through the medical and obstetric histories, the physical examination, and appropriate laboratory tests. Although dividing pregnant women into specific "high-risk" and "low-risk" prenatal categories has merit in predicting pregnancy outcome, it must be remembered that intra-partum events still play a large role in determining final results.

## Medical History

Major medical problems can have a significant impact on both the maternal response to pregnancy and on fetal development. Chronic hypertension and renal disease are specifically associated with the risk of intrauterine growth retardation, as well as superimposed pregnancy induced hypertension. Diabetes mellitus is associated with increased risk of major congenital anomalies and stillbirth.

Maternal drug use through prescription medications, such as anticonvulsants for women with seizure disorders, or through over-the-counter or social drug use, such as alcohol, cocaine, and smoking, should be scrutinized. It should be determined if oral contraceptives were inadvertently continued before pregnancy was recognized. Maternal exposure in utero to diethyl-stilbestrol should be specifically ascertained due to the association with cervical and uterine pathology and subsequent adverse pregnancy outcome (Stillman, 1982). Recent viral or febrile illnesses should also be identified.

Past obstetric history is an excellent data source for determining problems in previous pregnancies (i.e., premature labor, difficult delivery) that may repeat themselves during the present pregnancy. For example, history of neonatal jaundice may be a clue to specific risk of blood incompatibility problems.

The menstrual history is most important for gestational dating. Abnormal bleeding episodes are often the first clues to early pregnancy problems, including threatened abortion or ectopic or molar pregnancy. Family history on both maternal and paternal sides for major medical problems and adverse pregnancy outcomes should be ascertained. Specific questions should concern congenital malformations, mental retardation, and possible genetic disorders (see Kolodny, Abuelo, Barsel-Bowers, & Pueschel, Chapter 4, this volume).

## Physical Examination

Initial blood pressure and weight are important as screening factors and are baselines for comparison of changes throughout pregnancy. A complete physical examination should be performed early in pregnancy and include cardiac and pulmonary auscultation, blood pressure reading, and thorough breast examination. Attention to a lump or other suspicious breast lesion should never be postponed due to pregnancy. Although cancer of the breast is relatively rare during pregnancy (less than 1% of all cases of breast cancer), delay in diagnosis will result in a poor treatment outcome (Ribiero, Jones, & Jones, 1986).

The pelvic examination provides both the initial confirmation and physical dating of the pregnancy by uterine size as well as an assessment of pelvic shape, size, and possibility of subsequent birth dystocia. Visual inspection of the vagina and cervix through speculum examination should be performed to check for abnormalities or infections and to facilitate the collection of specimens for culture and cytology.

## Initial Laboratory Tests

All pregnant women should undergo a basic battery of laboratory tests early in pregnancy. This should include identification of blood type, antibody screening, hemoglobin and/or hematocrit determination, serology testing for syphilis, hepatitis B surface antigen testing, and determination of rubella immunity. A urinalysis should be done, as well as a quantitative urine culture, to identify significant bacteriuria. All pregnant women should be made aware of the high risk and high perinatal transmission rate of acquired immunodeficiency syndrome (AIDS), and all women with high-risk factors should be offered voluntary human immunodeficiency virus (HIV) testing. A cervical culture for gonorrhea and cervical cytology should also be obtained. If definite positive signs of pregnancy have not already been established, a confirmatory pregnancy test should be performed. These tests should be carried out at the first prenatal visit.

With the data base obtained through medical history, physical examination, results of the initial laboratory tests, and assessment of social and psychologic factors, it will be possible to perform a risk assessment and develop a problem list for use as the pregnancy proceeds. The remainder of prenatal care consists primarily of timely screening for the development of various pregnancy complications that may threaten either the mother or the developing fetus. Optimal care should, of course, include education of the expectant mother in preparation for the physiologic effects of pregnancy and expectations for childbirth and parenthood.

## ESTABLISHMENT OF DATES

Establishing accurate dating early in pregnancy is essential for later assessment of such problems as intrauterine growth retardation, premature labor, or post dating. The time honored milestones of uterine size, fundal height growth, and time of first heard fetal heart tones are useful confirmatory facts but not accurate in themselves for dating. Time of quickening is notoriously variable and inaccurate for use of dating.

The traditional use of the last menstrual period as a starting point should always be qualified if there is a cycle irregularity or previous use of oral contraceptives. Some women persist in taking birth control pills after conception, and it is well known that ovulation time after ceasing oral contraceptives is highly variable. Early pelvic examination to compare uterine size with dates in the first trimester is useful, but errors of up to several weeks are common.

Ultrasound examination to establish or confirm dating is becoming so common as to prompt some practitioners to use this procedure in practically every pregnancy. Whether or not routine ultrasound examination should be done is quite controversial (Birnholz, 1980a; Campbell & Little, 1980; Grennert, Persson, & Gennser, 1978; Hegge, Franklin, Watson, & Calhoun, 1989), but to date, there is no verified evidence of ill effect from diagnostic ultrasound in human pregnancy (American Institute of Ultrasound in Medicine, 1988).

Like all other methods of dating pregnancy, ultrasound has its pitfalls and inherent inaccuracies. In the first trimester, crown-rump length is the best measurement for accurate dating, but errors may occur (Robinson & Fleming, 1975). However, most dating problems occur in patients who are first seen in the second or third trimester for prenatal care. Biparietal diameter (BPD), the standard fetal measurement for dating after the first trimester, becomes less precise as pregnancy advances toward term due to inherent biological variation between large and small babies and the observed slow down of biparietal growth in the third trimester. Thus, measurements made between approximately 16 and 26 weeks of gestation are more accurate for dating purposes than in early and late pregnancy, although measurements even during this time period are usually given an accuracy of about ±2 weeks (Sabbagha, Turner, Rockette, Mazer, & Orgill, 1974). Third trimester BPD (Birnholz, 1980b) or other measurements, such as femur length (O'Brien & Queenan, 1981) and interorbital distance (Mayden, Tortora, Berkowitz, Bracken, & Hobbins, 1982), may be of value but are less accurate for dating.

## NUTRITION AND WEIGHT GAIN

Proper nutrition in pregnancy has historically been a topic of much controversy. For example, in the past some obstetricians have advised restricting caloric intake in pregnant women, reasoning falsely that low weight gain would prevent the occurrence of pregnancy induced hypertension. This has been proven to be incorrect because the excessive weight gain often associated with pregnancy induced hypertension is due to edema rather than dietary habits (see Morgan, Chapter 17, this volume).

It is clear that birth weight can be significantly influenced by inadequate nutrition in pregnancy and that, in general, birth weight parallels maternal weight gain (Simpson, Lawless, & Mitchell, 1975). Adequate nutrition allowing for maternal weight gain of 9 kg to 14 kg (about 20 lbs. to 30 lbs.) is considered to be normal and is associated with the most favorable outcome in pregnancy (Naeye, 1979). The incidence of infants with low birth weight is greatest in pregnant women with low prepregnancy weights and low weight gains during pregnancy. Even obese women should gain at least 7 kg to 8 kg

(16 lbs. to 18 lbs.) during pregnancy, and weight reduction programs should never begin until postpartum.

All pregnant women should receive some form of nutrition counseling. Those at high risk for nutritional problems (e.g., the very young, the economically deprived, those underweight at the onset of pregnancy, or those already on special diets due to pre-existing medical disease or food fadism) should plan a more detailed nutritional intake with a professional dietician or nutritionist. In general, diets throughout pregnancy should be balanced with a variety of food groups and have an average daily increase of 300 kcal and 30 g protein above the normal nutritional intake (Food and Nutrition Board, 1979).

Some minerals may need to be supplemented during pregnancy. Among these is iron—to supply approximately 300 mg transferred to the placenta and fetus and 500 mg needed for maternal blood volume expansion (Pritchard & Scott, 1970). Also, approximately 30 g additional calcium is required during pregnancy (Pitkin, 1975). Unlike calcium, which can generally be mobilized from the maternal bones, iron stores are seldom adequate. Iron supplements using at least 30 mg daily of a simple ferrous salt are important throughout pregnancy in virtually all women in order to meet the demands of pregnancy and to prevent depletion of maternal iron stores (Scott, Pritchard, Saltin, & Humphryes, 1970). If dairy products cannot be ingested due to lactose intolerance, calcium supplements should be considered.

Prenatal vitamin supplementation is usually routinely given to pregnant women, even though evidence of specific benefits is lacking. For the most part, increased vitamin requirements during pregnancy can be supplied by an adequate, well-balanced diet. However, folic acid deficiency can lead to megaloblastic anemia. A dietary supplement of 1 mg folic acid daily during pregnancy provides an adequate prophylaxis for folate deficiency anemia and can be incorporated into prenatal vitamin preparation.

## PRENATAL SCREENING PROCEDURES

### Screening for Alloimmunization

In addition to blood typing, all pregnant women, regardless of their Rh status, should be screened initially for the presence of alloantibodies. If only Rh-negative women are screened for antibody formation, significant alloimmunization may go undetected from blood-group antigens other than Rho (D), such as Kell, Duffy, C, c, and others. These have assumed a higher percentage of total alloimmunization problems since the decrease in Rho (D) sensitization due to postpartum Rh immune globulin administration to Rh-negative women. Many blood group antigens that induce IgG antibodies can produce hemolytic disease of the fetus and newborn that may be just as hazardous as

Rho (D) sensitization. Because initial sensitization can occur during the course of pregnancy, it is recommended that all patients undergo a repeat general antibody screening during the third trimester, even if the initial screen is negative.

Rh immune globulin prophylaxis of the nonsensitized Rh-negative mother can be expanded from postpartum use to routine antepartum administration to prevent the approximately 2% chance of Rh sensitization that may occur during the third trimester (Bowman, Chown, Lewis, & Pollock, 1978). Screening for antibodies should be done just prior to the standard 300 ug injection of Rh immune globulin at 28 weeks of gestation. Such programs have been initiated in many areas throughout the United States and Canada and give hope for virtually wiping out the occurrence of Rh-induced erythroblastosis fetalis.

Potentially preventable sources of Rh sensitization include inappropriate administration of Rh immune globulin after spontaneous or induced abortion, ectopic pregnancy, amniocentesis, or an episode of bleeding or suspected placental abruptio where the potential for fetal-maternal hemorrhage exists. All of these problems together, however, are a relatively minor source of new Rh alloimmunization compared to the failure to administer Rh immune globulin properly postpartum (estimated to be about 4,896 cases each year) and those that will occur because of antepartum sensitization during the third trimester (estimated to be about 5,670 cases each year) (Frigoletto, 1982). These alloimmunizations, which are a threat to future pregnancies, can only be prevented by a combination of routine antepartum Rh immune globulin prophylaxis at 28 weeks gestation of all Rho (D) negative pregnant women at risk, as well as diligence in administering postpartum Rh immune globulin to all unsensitized Rh-negative women delivering Rho (D) positive infants.

## Screening for Anemia

The definition of anemia during pregnancy is complicated by the average 45% increase in maternal blood volume that occurs during pregnancy (Ueland & Metcalfe, 1975). The plasma volume initially rises and is followed by an increase in the volume of circulating red cells, which usually never matches the plasma volume increase. This results in a relative dilution of erythrocytes, a normal physiologic effect of the hypervolemia of pregnancy. Thus, a hemoglobin value of less than 10 g/dl as a definition of anemia in pregnancy compared to a value of less than 12 g/dl for nonpregnant women has been suggested (Pritchard & Scott, 1970).

All black women should undergo hemoglobin electrophoresis to rule out sickle cell trait as well as other hemoglobinopathies. Women with the sickle cell trait should be made aware of the genetic implications, and it should be recommended that the father also have a hemoglobin electrophoresis done. Hemoglobin electrophoresis to screen for beta thalassemia should also be performed on the blood of all anemic women with a Mediterranean origin. All women with significant hemoglobinopathies, such as sickle cell disease, SC disease, and homozygous beta thalassemia, should be maintained at a hematocrit of at least 25% or higher to ensure adequate oxygen carrying capacity to the fetus. Patients with sickle cell trait and heterozygous beta thalassemia on the allelic gene (sickle cell beta thalassemia disease) may be asymptomatic during most of the course of pregnancy, and these conditions are sometimes overlooked. Often these women do not have complications until labor and delivery, when they are also at high risk for sickle crises and fetal distress.

All anemic pregnant women should be evaluated initially with a reticulocyte count, a peripheral smear, and red cell indices. Iron deficiency is still the most common cause of anemia in pregnancy, and even nonanemic patients benefit from iron therapy during pregnancy to provide for the demands of blood volume expansion and fetal red cell production, while still maintaining adequate bone marrow stores. Megaloblastic anemias are most often due to folate deficiency, which can be prevented by routine folate supplementation (Pritchard, Scott, & Whalley, 1969). Vitamin $B_{12}$ deficiencies are rare.

Women with an acquired hemolytic anemia and a positive direct Coombs test should also be screened for associated thrombocytopenia. Black women are at higher risk for a drug induced hemolytic anemia due to deficiency of glucose 6-phosphate dehydrogenase. Women with chronic renal failure, rheumatoid arthritis, or other inflammatory processes may have an associated anemia of chronic disease.

## Screening for Diabetes Mellitus

The hormonal and metabolic changes of pregnancy result in "glucose intolerance," that is, gestational diabetes, in 1%–3% of pregnant women. Many now believe that all pregnant women should be screened for gestational diabetes at 26 to 28 weeks of gestation, when the anti-insulin hormonal effects of pregnancy are becoming most pronounced. Risk factors for developing gestational diabetes include: 1) maternal age over 30, 2) overweight, 3) a family history of diabetes (e.g., parents, siblings, aunts, uncles), 4) a history of a prior unexplained stillbirth, 5) gestational diabetes in a previous pregnancy, 6) a history of a previous macrosomic infant ($\geq$4,100 g), and 7) glycosuria. Although routine urine dipstick for glucose should be done at every prenatal visit, glycosuria should by no means be relied upon for diabetic screening.

The diagnosis of gestational diabetes is based on specific criteria concerning the blood glucose response to a 100 g oral glucose tolerance test (OGTT) (see Table 5.1). The original study used the Somogyi-Nelson whole blood glucose analysis, which gives values approximately 12% lower than the plasma or serum glucose determination used more commonly in clinical labo-

Table 5.1. Oral glucose tolerance test (OGTT) in pregnancy

| Plasma glucose after 100 g oral glucose load (mg/100 ml) | | | |
|---|---|---|---|
| Fasting | 1 hour | 2 hours | 3 hours |
| 105 | 185 | 165 | 145 |

Exceeding any two values warrants the diagnosis of gestational diabetes.

ratories. Coustan and Lewis (1978) proposed slightly lower values for plasma or serum glucose limits for the OGTT based on reducing the original whole blood glucose values by 5 mg/dl to account for nonglucose reducing substances. To avoid having to perform a full 3 hour OGTT in large numbers of patients, an oral 50 g glucose loading test (GLT) can be performed first as a screening test (O'Sullivan, Mahan, & Dandrow, 1973). Then, only those women with an abnormal 1 hour glucose level after the GLT need to be screened further with the 3 hour OGTT. Obviously, raising the criteria for the 1 hour glucose loading test will result in fewer oral glucose tolerance tests being necessary, but it will also risk lowering the sensitivity of the screening procedures. However, a lower cutoff point on the 1 hour GLT (e.g., 130 mg/dl) will increase the sensitivity of screening but result in more normal 3 hour OGTTs being performed. It is most important, however, to make the screening test sensitive enough to identify the greatest rate of gestational diabetics so that this important complication of pregnancy is not missed. It is therefore reasonable to screen all women with a 50 g, 1 hour GLT at 26 to 28 weeks of gestation. A formal 100 g, 3 hour OGTT would then be performed on those women with a 1 hour plasma glucose value of 130 mg/dl or greater. It is also wise to screen patients with the risk factors mentioned above at 18 to 20 weeks to detect the more overt gestational diabetics earlier in pregnancy.

The presence of type 1, insulin-dependent diabetes mellitus (IDM) presents a perinatal risk factor not usually found in gestational diabetic pregnancies: the excess occurrence of congenital malformations. Infants of type 1 diabetic mothers have an incidence of major congenital anomalies ranging from 5% to 9% or at least three times the expected rate of anomalies in nondiabetic pregnancy (Gabbe, 1977; Kitzmiller et al., 1978; Pedersen, 1977). As other causes of perinatal mortality and morbidity in diabetes have been reduced, congenital malformations have taken the lead as the most important single cause of death in IDM (see Hoyme, Chapter 7, this volume).

The types of anomalies most commonly seen, expressed as the ratio of incidence in IDM when compared with those in controls, are shown in Table 5.2 (Kitzmiller, Cloherty, & Graham, 1982; Kucera, 1971; Mills, Baker, & Goldman, 1979). Cardiac anomalies are about four times more frequent in infants of diabetic mothers. Anencephaly and other central nervous system

Table 5.2.  Major congenital malformations in infants of diabetic mothers

| Malformation | Ratio of incidence IDM/non-IDM | Gestational age (weeks) |
|---|---|---|
| Caudal regression | 252 | 5 |
| Spina bifida, hydrocephalus, or other central nervous system | 2 | 6 |
| Anencephalus | 3 | 6 |
| Cardiac anomalies | 4 | |
| Transposition of great vessels | | 7 |
| Ventricular septal defect | | 8 |
| Atrial septal defect | | 8 |
| Anal/rectal atresia | 3 | 8 |
| Renal anomalies | 5 | |
| Agenesis | 6 | 7 |
| Cystic kidney | 4 | 7 |
| Ureter duplex | 23 | 7 |
| Situs inversus | 84 | 6 |

Adapted from Kitzmiller, Cloherty, and Graham (1982); Kucera (1971); and Mills, Baker, and Goldman (1979).

defects are respectively three and two times more common in IDM. These defects have special significance in that open neural tube defects are potentially detectable in early pregnancy. For this reason, screening in early pregnancy with maternal serum alpha-fetoprotein and ultrasound, with amniocentesis as a back up, should be offered to pregnant type 1 diabetic women in the second trimester. Other congenital anomalies found more commonly in IDM include anal-rectal atresia, renal anomalies, and situs inversus.

The other important information shown in Table 5.2 is the latest gestational age at which these malformations are known to occur. All of these malformations must occur very early in pregnancy, between approximately the 5th and 10th week of gestation. It is apparent that any intervention that might reduce the incidence of congenital anomalies has to be applied early in pregnancy.

Evidence has been accumulating that the metabolic derangement of poor diabetic control in early pregnancy is related to the risk of major congenital anomalies in IDM. A correlation has been made between the initial hemoglobin A1c (HbA1c) value, a retrospective measure of diabetic control, and the incidence of congenital anomalies in the offspring of insulin dependent diabetic mothers (see Table 5.3) (Miller et al., 1981). Women with first trimester HbA1c values greater than 8.5%, as measured in this particular laboratory, had a much higher incidence of infants with major malformations than those with HbA1c values below 8.5%. Thus, HbA1c, or other glycosy-

Table 5.3. Initial HbA1c and major congenital anomalies

| Initial HbA1c < 14 weeks | No anomalies | Major congenital Anomalies | | Total |
|---|---|---|---|---|
| ≤6.9% | 19 | 0 | 3.4% | 19 |
| 7.0%–8.5% | 37 | 2 | | |
| 8.6%–9.9% | 27 | 8 | 22.4% | 35 |
| ≥10.0% | 18 | 5 | | 23 |
| | 101 | 14 | 12.9% | 116 |

Adapted from Miller et al. (1981).
Note: Chi-square = 8.9 and P < 0.01 for HbA1c ≤ 8.5% versus HbA1c > 8.5%

lated hemoglobin measurements, may have some predictive value of risk for malformation in diabetic pregnancy.

An even better use for HbA1c screening of diabetic women would be to assess the state of diabetic control before these women attempt conception. If insulin-dependent women could be counseled before pregnancy, they might be able to lower the risk for congenital malformations in their offspring by improving their diabetic control before or at the time of conception and during early pregnancy. All too often diabetic women do not seek medical attention until they are already pregnant, after completion of embryogenesis (see Evrard & Scola, Chapter 3, this volume).

## Screening for Congenital Infections

Congenital infections are a significant cause of developmental problems. Therefore, screening for these infections and emphasizing their prevention are important goals of prenatal care. Agents associated with toxoplasmosis, rubella, cytomegalic inclusion disease, herpes simplex infection, and others may result in serious perinatal mortality and morbidity (see Pueschel, Scola, & McConnell, Chapter 6, this volume).

There has been a varying degree of success in screening for these diseases. Screening for rubella immunity early in pregnancy, preferably prior to pregnancy, is a useful tool for identifying pregnancies potentially at risk for congenital infection if subsequent exposure is suspected or anticipated. Women who are seronegative should be vaccinated postpartum with attenuated rubella virus.

The usefulness of screening every pregnant woman for infection with the protozoan *Toxoplasma gondii*, in contrast, is problematic. Women found with an absence of IgG toxoplasma antibody when screening in early pregnancy are at risk for acquiring infection during pregnancy and should be counseled to avoid potential sources of infection, such as exposure to cat litter or ingestion of uncooked beef. However, there is difficulty in interpreting the status of women with a low or high initial toxoplasma antibody titer. Repeat titers to determine a rise in IgG or the presence of a high IgM antibody titer will be necessary to attempt a differentiation of a recent versus a chronic infection. In the face of maternal infection, treatment with spiramycin can be given and a more definitive diagnosis of fetal infection can be attempted with amniocentesis and fetal blood sampling (Daffos et al., 1988). In the United States, spiramycin is available only by special request from the Food and Drug Administration. If fetal infection is proven early enough in gestation, a choice can be made between pregnancy termination and continuing treatment with pyremethamine and sulfadiazine. A negative toxoplasma antibody test in early pregnancy should probably be followed up with retesting in the third trimester and at delivery to detect possible acquired infections, but ideally screening should be performed prior to pregnancy.

Cytomegalovirus antibody is found in a majority of American women, indicating a widespread prevalence of this virus. Although the virus easily crosses the placenta, only a small percentage of newborns are seriously affected. The value of screening for maternal cytomegalovirus is questionable (Stagno, Pass, Dworsky, & Alford, 1982) because no satisfactory treatment exists for the small percentage (but overall large number) of neonates that have significant infection. Pregnant women should be advised to avoid contact with individuals known to be shedding cytomegalovirus. Blood transfusions, another potential source of infection, should be limited to strict indications. Screening should ideally be performed prior to pregnancy.

The herpes simplex virus has little likelihood of transplacental transmission, but it is a great hazard to the neonate contaminated from the birth canal at time of delivery. Because the predictability of antepartum viral cultures for viral shedding at the time of delivery is poor, and systemic neonatal disease from recurrent herpes is uncommon (Arvin et al., 1986), specific cultures during pregnancy are not necessary except to confirm the diagnosis from a questionable lesion. If herpes simplex lesions are present, or the most recent culture has been positive, delivery should be performed by cesarean section.

The concept of the TORCH (Toxoplasmosis, Other, Rubella, Cytomegalovirus, Herpes simplex) infections has been expanded to several other agents. All pregnant women (Arevalo & Washington, 1988) should be screened for hepatitis B. Infants born to mothers who are hepatitis B surface antigen HBSAg positive should be considered for passive immunization with hyperimmune globulin as well as given the hepatitis B vaccine.

Pregnant women should also be screened for tuberculosis, especially in urban low socioeconomic groups where the prevalence of tuberculosis is greatest. This can be done with the subcutaneous PPD, with follow-up chest X-rays (with the abdomen shielded) of women with positive reactions.

Routine cervical cultures of all pregnant women for group B streptococcal colonization appears to be of questionable value (Ledger, 1980). However, patients at high risk with positive cultures should probably be treated prophylactically at the time of labor and delivery to prevent neonatal colonization.

*Mycoplasma hominis*, *Ureaplasma urealyticum*, and *Listeria monocytogenes* are other infectious agents suspected as causes of perinatal infection and subsequent early pregnancy loss, premature labor, and neonatal infection. Screening all pregnant women does not appear to be warranted, although culturing selected high-risk patients may be worthwhile.

## Screening for Sexually Transmitted Diseases

Syphilis should be screened for in all pregnancies. The nonspecific serologic tests for syphilis (VDRL, RPR, or Hinton test), if positive, should be followed by a specific antitreponemal antibody test (FTA-ABS). Populations considered to be at risk should be rescreened in the third trimester to avoid the tragic occurrence of congenital syphilis caused by maternal exposure subsequent to a negative serologic test in early pregnancy.

Cervical screening cultures for gonorrhea should also be repeated in the third trimester to detect infections acquired subsequent to an early pregnancy screening. Rectal and throat cultures should be obtained in patients with a history suggesting any risk.

Human immunodeficiency virus (HIV) testing should be offered to all pregnant mothers in high-risk groups, including intravenous drug users and sexual partners of men who are bisexual or intravenous drug users, due to the high risk of perinatal transmission of AIDS (Minkoff, 1987). Care should be taken to provide confidentiality in reporting results, and adequate counseling should be available for both informed consent and follow-up of abnormal results.

Genital herpes, discussed previously in this chapter, is also a sexually transmitted disease that is seen with increased frequency. To avoid infecting the infant during delivery, a caesarean section is recommended when an active genital lesion is present.

## Screening for Urinary Tract Infections

All pregnant women should be screened for significant bacteriuria whether or not they have symptoms of urinary tract infection. In at least 25% of cases, pregnant women with untreated asymptomatic bacteriuria subsequently develop symptomatic urinary tract infection (Cunningham, MacDonald, & Gant, 1989). Besides concern for maternal renal damage from pyelonephritis, urinary tract infection may be a cause of premature labor (Kass, 1965). A number of simplified screening tests for bacteriuria are commercially available, but when urinary tract infection is suspected, a quantitative urine culture with colony count and antibiotic sensitivities from a midstream clean catch specimen must be performed. Bladder catheterization is associated with a 9% risk of initiation of infection and should be avoided if possible (Brumfitt, Davies, & Rosser, 1961). Women with a history of frequent urinary tract infections should be screened with cultures each trimester and those with recurrent infections should be considered for continuous antibiotic therapy.

## Screening for Cervical Cancer

Cervical cytology (Pap smear) should be performed at the initial visit of all prenatal patients. Not only is this often the best opportunity for cervical cancer screening, but also any abnormalities can be detected early in pregnancy so that appropriate therapy can be planned. Abnormal smears should be confirmed and colposcopy performed to identify the site and extent of lesions. Cervical biopsies should be done with caution during pregnancy since bleeding may be a problem. It is imperative, however, to investigate any suspicion of cancer, because treatment must not be delayed. Treatment for dysplasia or carcinoma in situ, however, may be postponed until after delivery. If a cone biopsy is necessary for diagnostic purposes, it is best carried out in early pregnancy because of the risk of hemorrhage, as mentioned above, and the subsequent risk of either cervical incompetence or stenosis, with resultant perinatal complications.

## Screening for Genetic Abnormalities

Prenatal diagnosis should be offered to all pregnant women at increased risk for giving birth to children with disorders that can be detected during pregnancy. Although traditionally this has primarily involved testing women age 35 or older for fetal Down syndrome or other chromosomal aneuploidies, there has been an explosion in the number of genetic and other congenital disorders that can be detected prenatally as well as an expansion of techniques allowing faster and earlier prenatal diagnosis (see Hoyme, Chapter 7, this volume).

All pregnant women should have a genetic and family history taken as part of their routine prenatal risk assessments, including such risk factors as maternal age, race and ethnic background, family history of neural tube defects or other congenital anomalies, any prior history of reproductive loss, and possible exposure to environmental teratogens (e.g., drugs) or agents capable of causing congenital infection. All women should also be offered maternal serum alpha-fetoprotein (AFP) screening at 16 weeks of gestation after proper counseling. Besides detection of approximately 85%–90% of open neural tube defects (U.K. collaborative study, 1977), elevated maternal serum AFP may indicate the possible presence of a variety of disorders, such as multiple pregnancy, fetal demise, and congenital abnormalities (i.e., duodenal atresia, omphalocele, and gastroschisis). Low values, however, have been found to be associated with increased risk for fetal autosomal trisomies (Merkatz, Nitowsky, Macri, & Johnson, 1984). A woman's age and maternal serum AFP level may be combined to give a more precise risk for the most common trisomy, Down syndrome (Cuckle, Wald, & Thompson, 1987). This calculated risk can be put into perspective by comparison to that of an unscreened pregnant 35-year-old woman at 16 weeks (approximately 1 in 270). Further refinements of prenatal risk for trisomies may become possible by combining various parameters, such as serum estriol and human chorionic gonadotropin measurements along with maternal serum AFP and maternal age (Wald et al., 1988).

As a screening test, a maternal serum AFP value outside of the normal range necessitates follow-up evaluation and should never be acted upon alone. An ultrasound examination should be performed to confirm dates, rule out twins, or missed abortion. If these do not adequately explain the maternal serum AFP value, amniocentesis is indicated to measure amniotic fluid AFP and acetylcholinesterase, and to perform karyotyping. The majority of structural abnormalities can be detected by an experienced ultrasound examiner, but amniocentesis should be offered even in the absence of abnormal findings on ultrasound.

Although amniocentesis for abnormal maternal serum AFP values cannot be done earlier than the screening test itself (15–17 weeks gestation), earlier karyotyping for other indications, such as advanced maternal age or a previous history of a chromosomal abnormality, can be performed by either early amniocentesis (12–15 weeks gestation) or chorionic villus biopsy. One multicenter study of the safety and efficacy of chorionic villus biopsy concluded that the excess pregnancy loss rate from the former compared to amniocentesis was only 0.8% after statistical adjustment for differences between the study groups (Rhoads et al., 1989).

## Screening for Multifetal Pregnancy

Pregnancies with multiple fetuses are clearly at increased risk for perinatal mortality and morbidity. Complications include premature labor and delivery, intrauterine growth retardation, placental or cord accidents, malpresentation, congenital malformations, and fetal-fetal hemorrhage. Unfortunately, too many multifetal pregnancies, especially twins, are not suspected until late in pregnancy or during labor (Powers, 1973).

The most important factor in the early diagnosis of multifetal pregnancy is a high index of suspicion. A family history of dizygotic twins on the maternal side and the use of infertility drugs (i.e., clomiphene, pituitary gonadotropin) greatly increase the odds for multiple ovulation and multifetal pregnancy. A significant discrepancy in uterine size and gestational dates (size greater than dates) always raises the suspicion of multifetal pregnancy. Palpation of extra fetal parts and simultaneous auscultation of fetal heart tones at different rates are proof of multifetal pregnancy. By far the best confirmation of multifetal pregnancy, however, is with ultrasound imaging.

The importance of early and accurate diagnosis of twins could be used as one justification for recommending second trimester ultrasound examinations in all pregnancies. When multifetal pregnancy is confirmed by ultrasound, serial examinations are necessary to evaluate fetal growth and to screen for discordance in size, which can be a sign of fetal-fetal transfusion secondary to intravascular anastomosis. Conjoined twins are rare, occurring in approximately 1 of 70,000 births (Tan, Goon, Salmon, & Wee, 1971).

Although it may be difficult to perform or interpret other means of evaluating fetal well-being in multifetal pregnancy (e.g., nonstress tests and contraction stress tests), the ultrasound components of the biophysical profile may be useful for evaluating the status of multiple fetuses in utero (Manning, Platt, & Sipes, 1980).

## Screening for Intrauterine Growth Retardation

Intrauterine growth retardation may be associated with multiple obstetric or medical complications, including multifetal pregnancy, chronic renal disease, and pregnancy induced hypertension. However, in the majority of cases, intrauterine fetal growth problems occur without any obvious predictive association. All pregnancies, therefore, should be screened for fetal growth retardation, with the most basic tool being serial measurement of the fundal height (McDonald measurement). Even in experienced hands, however, up to 50% of small-for-gestational-age infants are not detected until birth. Again, the obstetrician must have a high index of suspicion. To aid in making fundal growth problems more obvious, a simple growth curve can be used to detect deviation from the norm. Careful serial measurements are important during follow-up examinations.

Once the suspicion is raised on clinical grounds, further evaluation of the fetus with ultrasound should be done, including both abdominal and head measurements so that asymmetric (high head-to-body circumference ratio) and symmetric growth retardation problems can be distinguished (Campbell, 1977). Symmetric growth retardation is more likely to be due to intrinsic fetal problems, such as congenital infection or chromosome abnormalities. Thorough ultrasound examination for signs of malformations should also be done simultaneously. Oligohydramnios always raises the suspicion of intrauterine growth retardation.

In general, fetal growth problems can best be evaluated with serial ultrasound examinations and calculation of estimated fetal weight gain. This weight gain should average approximately 200 g per week at the time of greatest fetal growth during the late second and early third trimesters (Birnholz, 1980b).

## Screening for Late Pregnancy Complications

All pregnant women should have more frequent antepartum visits during the third trimester, with repeated blood pressure and urine protein measurements.

This should detect, among other problems, signs of pregnancy induced hypertension. It is also important to check for signs of premature cervical dilatation and labor. Finally, several of the initial laboratory screening tests (hemoglobin or hematocrit, blood antibody formation, syphilis serology, and gonorrhea cultures) should be repeated.

## CONCLUSION

Prenatal care in modern obstetrics comprises more than care of the pregnant woman. Pregnant women must be educated on the many aspects of pregnancy that may affect the well-being of the fetus. They must be prepared physically and emotionally for the events of labor and delivery. Optimal prenatal care involves the simultaneous care and evaluation of two individuals, the mother and her fetus. The explosion of knowledge and novel technology has made it possible to survey the fetus as an individual in his or her own right. For continued advances in the prevention of developmental disabilities, an emphasis on prenatal care of the fetus, as well as optimal care of the mother, must be made.

## REFERENCES

American Institute of Ultrasound in Medicine. (1988). *Bioeffects considerations for the safety of diagnostic ultrasound.* Bethesda, MD: Author.

Arevalo, J. A., & Washington, A. E. (1988). Cost-effectiveness of prenatal screening and immunization for hepatitis B virus. *Journal of the American Medical Association, 259,* 365–369.

Arvin, A. M., Hensleigh, P. A., Prober, C. G., Au, D. S., Yasu Kawa, L. L., Wittek, A. E., Palumbo, P. E., Paryani, S. G., & Yeager, A. S. (1986). Failure of antepartum maternal cultures to predict the infant's risk of exposure to herpes simplex virus at delivery. *New England Journal of Medicine, 315,* 796–800.

Birnholz, J. C. (1980a). The case for routine use of ultrasound in pregnancy. *Seminars in Ultrasound, 1,* 235.

Birnholz, J. C. (1980b). Ultrasound characterization of fetal growth. *Ultrasonic Imaging, 1,* 135–149.

Bowman, J. M., Chown, B., Lewis, M., & Pollock, J. M. (1978). Rh-isoimmunization during pregnancy: Antenatal prophylaxis. *Canadian Medical Association Journal, 118,* 623–627.

Brumfitt, W., Davies, B. I., & Rosser, E. (1961). Urethral catheter as a cause of urinary tract infection in pregnancy and puerpetium. *Lancet, ii,* 1059.

Campbell, S. (1977). Ultrasound measurement of fetal head to abdomen circumference ratio is assessment of growth retardation. *British Journal of Obstetrics and Gynaecology, 84,* 165–174.

Campbell, S., & Little, D. J. (1980). Clinical potential of real-time ultrasound. In M. J. Bennett & S. Campbell (Eds.), *Real-time ultrasound in obstetrics* (pp. 27–38). Oxford: Blackwell Scientific Publications.

Coustan, D. R., & Lewis, S. B. (1978). Insulin therapy for gestational diabetes. *Obstetrics and Gynecology*, *51*, 306.

Cuckle, H. S., Wald, N. J., & Thompson, S. G. (1987). Estimating a woman's risk of having a pregnancy associated with Down's syndrome using her age and serum alpha-fetoprotein level. *British Journal of Obstetrics and Gynaecology*, *94*, 387–402.

Cunningham, F. G., MacDonald, P. C., & Gant, N. F. (1989). *Williams Obstetrics* (18th ed.). Norwalk, CT: Appleton & Lange.

Daffos, F., Forestier, F., Capella-Pavlovsky, M., Thulliez, P., Aufrant, C., Valenti, D., & Cox, W.L. (1988). Prenatal management of 746 pregnancies at risk for congenital toxoplasmosis. *New England Journal of Medicine*, *318*, 271–275.

Food and Nutrition Board. (1979). *Recommended dietary allowances* (9th ed.). Washington, DC: National Research Council, National Academy of Sciences.

Frigoletto, F. D. (1982). Risk perspectives of Rh sensitization. In F. D. Frigoletto, J. F. Jewett, & A. A. Konugres (Eds.), *Rh hemolytic disease: New strategy for eradication* (pp. 136–152). Boston: G. K. Hall.

Gabbe, S. G. (1977). Congenital malformations in infants of diabetic mothers. *Obstetrical and Gynecological Survey*, *32*, 125–132.

Grennert, L., Persson, P. H., & Gennser, G. (1978). Benefits of ultrasonic screening of a pregnant population. *Acta Obstetricia et Gynaecologica Scandinavica*, *78* (Suppl.), 5.

Hegge, F. N., Franklin, R. W., Watson, P. T., & Calhoun, B. C. (1989). An evaluation of the time of discovery of fetal malformations by an indications-based system for ordering obstetric ultrasound. *Obstetrics and Gynecology*, *74*, 21–24.

Hobel, C. J. (1977). Identification of the patient at risk. In R. J. Bolognese & R. H. Schwarz (Eds.), *Perinatal medicine: Clinical management of the high-risk fetus and neonate*. Baltimore: Williams & Wilkins.

Kass, E. H. (1965). *Progress in pyelonephritis*. Philadelphia: Davis.

Kitzmiller, J. L., Cloherty, J. P., & Graham, C. A. (1982). Management of diabetes and pregnancy. In G. P. Kozak (Ed.), *Clinical diabetes mellitus* (pp. 203–214). Philadelphia: W. B. Saunders.

Kitzmiller, J. L., Cloherty, J. P., Younger, M. D., Tabatabaii, A., Rothchild, S. B., Sosenko, I., Epstein, M. F., Singh, S., & Neff, R. K. (1978). Diabetic pregnancy and perinatal morbidity. *American Journal of Obstetrics and Gynecology*, *131*, 560.

Kucera, J. (1971). Rate and type of congenital anomalies among offspring of diabetic women. *Journal of Reproductive Medicine*, *7*, 61.

Ledger, W. J. (1980). Bacterial infections during pregnancy. In E. J. Quilligan & N. Kretchmer (Eds.), *Fetal and maternal medicine* (pp. 345–364). New York: John Wiley & Sons.

Manning, F. A., Platt, L. D., & Sipes, L. (1980). Antepartum fetal-evaluation: Development of a fetal biophysical profile. *American Journal of Obstetrics and Gynecology*, *136*, 787–795.

Mayden, K., Tortora, M., Berkowitz, R., Bracken, H., & Hobbins, J. (1982). Orbital diameters: A new parameter for prenatal diagnosis and dating. *American Journal of Obstetrics and Gynecology*, *144*, 289–297.

Merkatz, I. R., Nitowsky, H. M., Macri, J. N., & Johnson, W. E. (1984). An association between low maternal serum alpha-fetoprotein and fetal chromosome abnormalities. *American Journal of Obstetrics and Gynecology*, *148*, 886–894.

Miller, E., Hare, J. W., Cloherty, J. P., Dunn, P. J., Gleason, R. E., Soeldner, J. S., & Kitzmiller, J. L. (1981). Elevated maternal hemoglobin A1c in early pregnancy and major congenital anomalies in infants of diabetic mothers. *New England Journal of Medicine*, *304*, 1331–1334.

Mills, J. L., Baker, L., & Goldman, A. S. (1979). Malformations in infants of diabetic mothers occur before the seventh gestational week: Implications for treatment. *Diabetes*, *28*, 292–293.

Minkoff, H. (1987). Care of pregnant women infected with human immunodeficiency virus. *Journal of the American Medical Association*, *258*, 2714–2717.

Naeye, R. (1979). Weight gain and the outcome of pregnancy. *American Journal of Obstetrics and Gynecology*, *135*, 3.

Nesbitt, R. E. L., Jr., & Aubry, R. H. (1969). High risk obstetrics: II. Value of semi-objective grading system in identifying the vulnerable group. *American Journal of Obstetrics and Gynecology*, *103*, 972.

O'Brien, G. D., & Queenan, J. T. (1981). Growth of the ultrasound fetal femur length during normal pregnancy: Part 1. *American Journal of Obstetrics and Gynecology*, *141*, 833–837.

O'Sullivan, J. B., Mahan, C. M., & Dandrow, R. V. (1973). Screening criteria for high-risk gestational diabetic patients. *American Journal of Medicine*, *116*, 895.

Pedersen, J. (1977). *The pregnant diabetic and her newborn*. Baltimore: Williams & Wilkins.

Pitkin, R. M. (1975). Calcium metabolism in pregnancy: A review. *American Journal of Obstetrics and Gynecology*, *121*, 724.

Powers, W. F. (1973). Twin pregnancy: Complications and treatment. *Obstetrics and Gynecology*, *42*, 795.

Pritchard, J. A., & Scott, D. E. (1970). Iron demands during pregnancy. In L. Hallberg, H. G. Harwerth, & A. Vannotti (Eds.), *Iron deficiency: Pathogenesis, clinical aspects, therapy*. New York: Academic Press.

Pritchard, J. A., Scott, D. E., & Whalley, P. J. (1969). Folic acid requirements in pregnancy induced megaloblastic anemia. *Journal of the American Medical Association*, *208*, 1163.

Rhoads, G. G., Jackson, L. G., Schlesselman, S. E., de la Cruz, F. F., Desnick, R. J., Golbus, M. S., Ledbetter, D. H., Lubs, H. A., Mahoney, M. J., Pergament, E., Simpson, J. L., Carpenter, R. J., Elias, S., Ginsberg, N. A., Goldberg, J. D., Hubbins, J. C., Lynch, L., Shiono, P. H., Wapner, R. J., & Zachery, J. M. (1989). The safety and efficacy of chorionic villus sampling for early prenatal diagnosis of cytogenetic abnormalities. *New England Journal of Medicine*, *320*, 609–617.

Ribiero, G., Jones, D. A., & Jones, M. (1986). Carcinoma of the breast associated with pregnancy. *British Journal of Surgery*, *73*, 607.

Robinson, H. P., & Fleming, J. E. (1975). A critical evaluation of sonar "crown-rump length" measurements. *British Journal of Obstetrics and Gynaecology*, *82*, 702–710.

Sabbagha, R. E., Turner, H. J., Rockette, H., Mazer, J., & Orgill, J. (1974). Sonar BPD and fetal age: Definition of the relationship. *Obstetrics and Gynecology*, *43*, 7.

Scott, D. E., Pritchard, J. A., Saltin, A. S., & Humphryes, S. M. (1970). Iron deficiency during pregnancy. In L. Hallberg, H. G. Harwerth, & A. Vannotti (Eds.), *Iron deficiency: Pathogenesis, clinical aspects*. New York: Academic Press.

Simpson, J. W., Lawless, R. W., & Mitchell, A. C. (1975). Responsibility of the obstetrician to the fetus: II. Influence of prepregnancy weight and pregnancy weight gain on birthweight. *Obstetrics and Gynecology*, *45*, 481–487.

Stagno, S., Pass, R. F., Dworsky, M. E., & Alford, C. (1982). Maternal cytomegalovirus infection and perinatal transmission. *Clinical Obstetrics and Gynecology*, *25*, 563.

Stillman, R. J. (1982). In utero exposure to diethylstilbestrol: Adverse effects in the reproductive tract and reproductive performance in male and female offspring. *American Journal of Obstetrics and Gynecology, 142*, 905–921.

Tan, K. L., Goon, S. M., Salmon, Y., & Wee, J. H. (1971). Conjoined twins. *Acta Obstetricia et Gynecologica Scandinavica, 50*, 379.

Ueland, K., & Metcalfe, J. (1975). Circulatory changes in pregnancy. *Clinical Obstetrics and Gynecology, 18*, 41.

U.K. collaborative study on alpha-fetoprotein in relation to neural tube defects. (1977). Maternal serum alpha-fetoprotein measurement in antenatal screening for anencephaly and spina bifida in early pregnancy. *Lancet, i*, 1323–1332.

Wald, N. J., Cuckle, H. S., Densem, J. W., Nanchahal, K., Royston, P., Chard, T., Haddow, J. E., Knight, G. J., Palomak, G. E., & Carrick, J.A. (1988). Maternal serum screening for Down's syndrome in early pregnancy. *British Medical Journal, 297*, 883–887.

**6** | Siegfried M. Pueschel
Patricia Sexton Scola
Kim S. McConnell

# INFECTIONS
# DURING
# PREGNANCY

Since the early 1960s, much has been learned about the natural history of infectious processes during pregnancy and their effect on the embryo and fetus. Similarly, significant progress has been made in the prevention of some of the infectious diseases that interfere with normal embryonic and fetal development. In spite of these advances, however, there are still many unknown areas in this field that will require further study.

This chapter focuses primarily on such diseases as rubella, cytomegalic inclusion disease, herpes simplex, toxoplasmosis, and human immunodeficiency virus infections occuring during pregnancy. Other viral diseases that are discussed are those that affect the embryo/fetus if the mother is infected during pregnancy, although in some instances definite evidence of an increased risk to the fetus is lacking.

## RUBELLA

### Historical Considerations

De Bergen and Orlow first described rubella as a specific disease entity in 1758 (Wesselhoeft, 1947). Subsequently, German physicians displayed great interest in rubella and the term German measles came into use. Veale (1866) gave this infectious disease its present name, rubella.

It was not until 1941 that the Australian ophthalmologist Gregg and McAlistair (1941) reported a relationship between maternal rubella infection during early pregnancy and specific congenital anomalies in the offspring. In particular, he observed an increased prevalence of congenital cataracts following maternal rubella infection. In subsequent years, other investigators confirmed Gregg's observations. The propagation and isolation of the rubella virus in the 1960s paved the way for the development of a vaccine against rubella infections.

## Epidemiology

In studying the epidemiology of rubella, it was observed that major rubella epidemics occur in 6–9 year cycles. The incidence of rubella varies with the epidemic cycle, the number of susceptible persons within a given population, and the interpersonal contacts within groups. During the 1964 rubella epidemic, the highest attack rate was noted in the 5- to 9-year-old age group, whereas in the time period from 1975 to 1977, the highest attack rate occurred in the 15- to 19-year-old age group.

## Congenital Rubella

In order for a pregnant woman to contract rubella, she must be susceptible to the rubella virus, and she must be exposed to a person with rubella during the time period of active viral shedding. The pregnant woman's viremia produces placental infection, and viruses are readily transferred to the embryo/fetus. The risk of infection of the embryo/fetus is also determined by the gestational age when exposure occurs. The incidence of infection is highest during the first 4–5 months of pregnancy, with the greatest risk in the first 8 weeks of gestation. The risk of fetal damage declines with advancing pregnancy, although little is known about events in second and third trimester rubella infection (Dudgeon, 1975). The incidence of congenital rubella is 22% when the infection occurs during the first month, 20% in the second, 9% in the third, and 3% in the fourth month of pregnancy (Dudgeon, 1975). Placental and fetal infection usually persists throughout the remainder of the pregracy.

Rubella virus can be recovered from numerous organs, including liver, spleen, lungs, kidneys, and brain, from aborted embryos and fetuses. Infants born with congenital rubella usually harbor live virus that can be obtained from the throat, rectum, and urine of the neonate (Cooper & Krugman, 1967). Infants with congenital rubella will often shed rubella virus during the first year of life; by the first birthday, this only occurs in 10%–20% of these children, and by 1.5 years, investigators are unable to demonstrate viral persistence in the nasopharynx (Rawls, Phillips, Melnick, & Desmond, 1967). The virus, however, may be found in cataracts and other tissues for many years.

Fetal infection may result in abortion, stillbirth, or multiple congenital anomalies in a live-born infant. The most common manifestation of congenital rubella at the time of birth is growth retardation with the majority of infected infants weighing less than 2,500 g. About one-third of infants with congenital rubella will have cataracts that may be either bilateral or unilateral.

Most often cataracts are present at birth, but they may also develop later in infancy. Retinopathy, pigmentary defects, microphthalmia, and congenital glaucoma occur less often. Sensorineural hearing loss, which is usually bilateral, is a frequently observed congenital anomaly (Cooper, 1968). Some degree of hearing impairment is noted in nearly all children with congenital rubella. On occasion, their only manifestation is deafness. Approximately 10%–20% of all neonates with congenital rubella will have meningoencephalitis at the time of birth, which presents a full anterior fontanelle, irritability, hypotonia, seizures, and/or lethargy. Active central nervous system infection has been demonstrated to persist for more than a year in some children with congenital rubella. Children with congenital rubella may also have persistent infections other than those mentioned above, such as interstitial pneumonitis, hepatitis, nephritis, and myositis. Approximately 40%–50% of these infants will have mental retardation. Furthermore, behavior disorders and autistic features, including difficulties relating to people, have been observed. Among cardiovascular abnormalities, patent ductus arteriosus is most often diagnosed. In two-thirds of the patients, other cardiac lesions may be present, such as pulmonary artery stenosis and ventricular septal defect. In severe cases of congenital rubella, myocarditis may lead to death. Other malformations, including tracheoesophageal fistulas and jejunal atresia, are rare (Cooper, 1968; Cooper et al., 1969). Other associated disorders involving the immune, hematologic, and skeletal systems have also been reported.

## Prevention of Congenital Rubella

Of utmost importance is the prevention of congenital rubella. Although large-scale trials of passive immunization with immunoglobulin have been carried out in the past, there is no evidence that this will provide a significant protective effect; therefore, the use of passive immunization is not recommended (Dudgeon, 1969). However, active immunization can provide effective and durable immunity. Parkman, Meyer, Kirschstein, and Hopps (1966) developed an attenuated rubella strain that had lost its virulence after a series of subcultures in monkey kidneys. Shortly thereafter, improved rubella vaccine, produced in different culture media, showed that these vaccines were highly immunogenic and free of side effects. They did not appear to lead to transmissible infections despite virus excretion having been noted following immunization. Most important, these new vaccines conferred protection against natural infection.

During the 1970s, millions of doses of rubella vaccine were administered in many countries throughout the world. Active immunization with live attenuated rubella virus vaccine using an RA-27-3 strain grown in WI38 human embryonic lung-tissue culture is now available in the United States. Immunization with this vaccine produces antibodies in 90% or more of those immunized.

Rubella vaccine is recommended for children 1 year of age and older. It should not be given to infants less than 1 year of age because of persisting maternal antibodies that may interfere with seroconversion. Vaccination for rubella is routinely administered to young children (usually as a triple vaccine containing rubella, mumps, and rubeola viruses) when they are about 15 months of age. Hence, the vast majority of children today are vaccinated against rubella. Many states have laws that allow young children to enter the school system only if they have received the rubella vaccine. Also, colleges, universities, other educational and training facilities, as well as military bases often seek proof of rubella immunity from all individual employees who are in their childbearing years.

Yet, there are still many adolescents and young adults who, having been neither vaccinated nor exposed to wild rubella virus, have no immunity against it. The U.S. Public Health Service recommends that adolescent girls and adult women be given rubella vaccine only if they are shown to be susceptible to rubella by serologic testing. Some states have initiated a premarital serology test for rubella immunity. If a woman has been found to be seronegative, rubella vaccine can be administered if the woman is not pregnant and is willing to postpone pregnancy for at least 3 months. If, during antenatal screening for rubella susceptibility a seronegative woman is identified, she should be instructed to avoid exposure to a rubella-infectious person and be vaccinated in the postpartum period. Also, employees working in hospitals and clinics should have serologically demonstrated immunity to rubella, and if seronegative, should receive the rubella vaccine since they may contact rubella from infected patients and, if infected, might transmit rubella to pregnant patients.

Moreover, it is recommended that patients with rubella infection should not have contact with susceptible pregnant women. Rubella containment is an important part of prevention. Also, rubella reporting is paramount as it permits public health authorities to organize vaccination programs so that small outbreaks of rubella can be prevented from developing into major epidemics.

There are some situations when rubella vaccine should not be given. As mentioned above, live rubella vaccine is contraindicated in pregnancy and during a 3 month period prior to conception. In altered immune states, such as immune deficiency syndromes, leukemia, lymphoma, or during therapy with steroids and antimetabolites, rubella vaccine should not be administered. In addition, rubella vaccination should not be carried out during intercurrent illnesses when interference from another viral agent might preclude effective rubella immunization.

The policy for administrating rubella vaccine is by no means uniform. For example, in Great Britain, the rubella vaccine is offered primarily to all girls during adolescence. In the United States, however, mass vaccination of both sexes is implemented for all young children. The vaccination strategy is based on the observation that the highest attack rate of acquired rubella occurs in school-age children and that these children are the major source of infection for pregnant women.

The antibody response following rubella immunization is generally 4–6 times lower than after natural infection. Yet, the antibody levels are sustained over many years following vaccination. There have been concerns about the possible risk of reinfection in the vaccinated individual. Levine, Berkowitz, and St. Geme (1982) described congenital rubella subsequent to maternal gestational reinfection where the mother had been exposed to wild strains of rubella twice, but it is not known whether reinfection of the immunized woman could be harmful to the developing fetus. The risk of a reinfection is believed to be very small.

De la Mata and DeWals (1988) reported that a policy for the prevention of congenital rubella is present in 16 of 17 European countries surveyed. Three countries are maintaining their selective strategy of vaccinating teenage girls, but in eight countries this strategy has changed to mass vaccination of infants. In five other countries an approach combining both mass immunization and selective vaccination has been adopted. The authors conclude that mass vaccination of all young children combined with systematic revaccination either of all children or of teenage girls is probably the most effective approach for eliminating congenital rubella in Europe.

In the Netherlands, the Health Council has advocated the introduction of an elimination strategy of rubella by vaccinating 1- and 9-year-old children (de Boo, van Druten, & Plantinga, 1987). In Sweden, a two dose vaccination program has been aimed at eliminating rubella. Children are vaccinated at 18 months and 12 years with a combined vaccine against measles, mumps, and rubella (Böttiger, Christenson, Romanus, Taranger, & Strandell, 1988). An immunization program to eliminate rubella in Finland has also used a combined live vaccine given twice at the ages of 14 to 18 months and 6 years (Peltola et al., 1986). All countries who studied their immunization program have reported relatively good serum conversion of the children immunized.

In the United States, a combination of measles, mumps, rubella, and varicella vaccines has been used in a comparative clinical trial with 15–17 months old healthy children. The vaccines stimulated virtually 100% seroconversion for all component viruses. Antibodies to rubella viruses as well as the others were persistent at one year follow-up studies (Arbeter et al., 1986).

In a summary statement regarding congenital rubella syndrome in the United States, the Centers for Disease Control reported a significant reduction of congenital rubella syndrome since the 1970s. Declines of the congenital rubella syndrome rates parallel the decline in the overall rubella incidence. Thus, it is apparent that the vaccination strategy practiced in the United States, immunizing all young children, brought about a significant reduction of rubella and particularly of the congenital rubella syndrome.

## Vaccination during Pregnancy

When a pregnant woman who is susceptible to rubella is vaccinated with attenuated rubella virus, the virus can cross the placenta and infect the embryo/fetus. Attenuated rubella virus has been found in aborted embryos from rubella-susceptible women who were vaccinated before or during the early weeks of pregnancy. Ebbin, Wilson, Chandor, and Wehrle (1973) studied inadvertent immunization of rubella during pregnancy. They found that 9 out of 60 patients were susceptible to rubella prior to immunization; 6 of the 9 women had normal deliveries, 2 had spontaneous abortions, and 1 preferred a therapeutic abortion. In the latter case, attenuated rubella virus was isolated from the fetus.

In another study of inadvertent administration of rubella vaccine during pregnancy, Modlin, Herrmann, Brandling-Bennett, Eddins, and Hayden (1976) reported on 145 women who had their pregnancies terminated. They recovered rubella vaccine from products of the conceptuses in 9 instances, but no clinical or serologic evidence of rubella infection was found in infants when the pregnancy was allowed to go to term. The investigators concluded that the maximal risk of infection of a fetus after vaccination of the mother during pregnancy was somewhere between 5% and 10%.

The Centers for Disease Control (1984–1985) indicated that more than 350 women are known to have received rubella vaccine inadvertently during pregnancy. No recognizable anomalies commonly associated with the congenital rubella syndrome were observed in the offspring of 173 women who carried the pregnancy to term. Although there is no apparent risk to the fetus, it is generally recommended that rubella vaccine not be given during pregnancy and not during a 3-month period prior to pregnancy, as mentioned above.

## Change in Epidemiology

Undoubtedly, immunization of persons susceptible to rubella with an effective vaccine has brought about a change in the epidemiology of rubella. The last large scale epidemic in the United States occured in 1963–1964. From past experience of cyclic recurrences of rubella epidemics, one would have expected a major epidemic to occur in 1970–1971. Yet, such an epidemic did not take place because of a large scale immunization program that was initiated about that time.

In 1985, a total of 604 cases of rubella were reported in the United States, which represents a 20% decrease from the 1984 total of 752 cases and a 99% decline from 1969 when the rubella vaccine was licensed. The decline in overall rubella incidence is paralleled by the significant drop of congenital rubella syndrome cases. Whereas 57 confirmed congenital rubella cases occured in 1979, only 2 such cases were reported in 1985, which is a 96% decline (Centers for Disease Control, 1987). A provisional total of 221 cases of rubella was reported in the United States in 1988. This is the lowest annual total since rubella became a nationally notifiable disease in 1966 (Rubella and congenital rubella syndrome, 1989). In 1987, 6 infants with congenital rubella syndrome were reported to the National Congenital Rubella Syndrome Registry of which 3 were considered to be indigenous, and in 1988, only one infant with congenital rubella syndrome was reported (Rubella and congenital rubella syndrome, 1989). These data provide convincing evidence that the large-scale immunization programs implemented since 1974 have been most effective in preventing congenital rubella syndrome.

## CYTOMEGALIC INCLUSION DISEASE

### Historical Considerations

The term cytomegalia was used by Goodpasture and Talbot (1921) to describe cells with large inclusions found in skin lesions of sick infants. The possibility of a viral etiology was strengthened by Cole and Kuttner's (1926) report of a filterable virus from guinea pig submaxillary glands transmitting cytomegalia. Later, the observation of cells with inclusions in the urine of infants with cytomegalic inclusion disease offered an important diagnostic tool to identify children with this infectious disease. Isolation of the virus from the salivary gland, adenoid tissue, and liver in the mid 1950s provided confirmation of cytomegalovirus as the causative agent in cytomegalic inclusion disease.

### Epidemiology

Cytomegalovirus is ubiquitous with no seasonal variation. Cytomegalovirus infection has been found in 0.5%–2.4% of all births (Pass, Stagno, Myers, & Alford, 1980). An accurate appreciation of the incidence and prevalence in other than the newborn period is hampered by the fact that a positive viral culture may result from primary infection, chronic infection, or reactivation.

### Congenital Cytomegalovirus Infection

The most likely route for fetal infection is transplacental at the time of maternal viremia or by an ascending infection via the birth canal. The effect of maternal infection on the fetus may differ at various gestational ages. A fetal infection can cause generalized encephalitis, chromosome damage, mitotic inhibition, and altered embryogenesis. Of those women with a primary cytomegalovirus infection, approximately 50% of their offspring have positive viral studies (Stagno et al., 1982). The investigation by Pass et al. (1980) of 34 symptomatic patients found the most common manifestations to be petechiae, hepatosplenomegaly, and jaundice. Microcephaly occurred in 50% of the patients. Ten of the 34 patients died and 1 was lost to follow-up. Mental retardation or significant psychomotor delay was present in 14 of the remaining 23 patients. In addition, 7 patients had hearing loss, 5 had seizures, and 7 had other neurologic manifestations. The only 2 asymptomatic patients were under 2 years of age at last assessment.

Suggestive of more subtle problems in gestationally infected infants was the longitudinal study by Williamson et al. (1982). Three of the four children with normal IQs and hearing loss had defects of sequencing, short-term memory, word retrieval, and temporal or spatial concepts not attributable to the hearing loss.

A bimodal distribution of intelligence and general development with one group demonstrating severe delays and the other less severe intellectual deficits was identified in a prospective study of 32 children with symptomatic cytomegalovirus infection evaluated by Conboy et al. (1987). The presence of microcephaly, neurologic abnormality, and chorioretinitis were significantly associated with lower intelligence that suggested that infants with such findings would need close follow-up. Even school-age children with less severe disabilities frequently required special education services because of learning problems, speech difficulties, or hyperactivity. This further confirms the necessity for continued developmental assessment of infants born with symptomatic cytomegalovirus infection who appear to have a relatively benign outcome.

Asymptomatic congenital cytomegalovirus infection is also not without risk because from 5% to 20% of patients will later have abnormalities, such as sensorineural hearing loss and school difficulties (Hanshaw, 1982). Saigal, Lunyk, Larke, and Chevnesky (1982) identified 64 of 15,212 newborns who had cytomegalovirus-positive urine cultures. Of this group only 4 were symptomatic at birth. Prospectively, 47 children were available for long-term audiologic assessment and comparison with 44 matched controls. Sensorineural hearing loss was detected in 17% of the children with cytomegalovirus-positive cultures and in none of the matched controls. All but one of the seven children with impaired hearing had asymptomatic cytomegalovirus infection in the neonatal period. Hanshaw (1982) estimated that cytomegalovirus-induced sensorineural hearing loss may occur in approximately 2,000 newborns yearly and is probably the leading cause of nonhereditary congenital sensorineural hearing loss.

The implication to the fetus of a primary maternal cytomegalovirus infection as differentiated from a reactivated infection requires further clarification. Stagno et al. (1982) performed serologic examinations on 3,712 pregnant women of which 2,698 were from a middle to upper income group and 1,014 from a low income group. In the middle and upper income group, 45% were serosusceptible to cytomegalovirus, but only 18% of the low income group were serosusceptible. The incidence of primary cytomegalovirus infection in susceptible women was not significantly different between the two income groups, although there was an increased risk of primary cytomegalovirus infection in the higher income group due to the greater percentage of serosusceptible women in that group. According to the authors, primary cytomegalovirus infection was more likely to cause clinically apparent disease in the newborn than maternal recurrent infection. The risk of recurrent infection as the cause of congenital cytomegalovirus infection in seropositive women was determined to be 0.5% in the higher income group and 1.5% in the lower income group. At least one case of reactivated maternal infection resulting in symptomatic cytomegalovirus infection has been documented (Ahlfors, Harris, Ivarrson, & Svanberg, 1981). In addition, the possibility of cytomegalovirus infection being acquired at the time of birth or during the neonatal period must also be considered.

## Prevention of Congenital Cytomegalovirus Infection

Cytomegalovirus is ubiquitous, and asymptomatic infections occur frequently. The cytomegalovirus may be shed over an extended period and it is difficult to protect a susceptible pregnant patient. If the immune status of the pregnant patient is unknown, direct exposure to a clinically recognized cytomegalovirus infected person and their secretions should be avoided. Pass, August, Dworsky, and Reynolds (1982) discussed the risk to day-care center employees who are of childbearing age and are exposed to children who are excreting cytomegalovirus. Young women working in educational programs with infants and preschoolers need to be aware of the risk of cytomegalovirus infection during pregnancy and may want to determine their antibody status (Bale, Blackman, Murph, & Andersen, 1986). Good hygiene remains an important preventive measure in such settings.

Blood transfusion is also seen as a potential source of cytomegalovirus infection in infants. There is a special risk to premature infants in terms of mortality and morbidity. A study of blood transfusion practices and the incidence of cytomegalovirus infection in a neonatal intensive care unit showed an overall incidence of congenital cytomegalovirus of 0.7% (Griffin et al., 1988). During the study period, none of the seronegative infants had cytomegalovirus detected in the urine, but five (2%) of the seropositive group acquired infection. The infants with acquired infection all weighed 1,200 g or less. They were hospitalized for more than 1 month and received multiple blood transfusions. The possibility of perinatally acquired infection rather than transfusion acquired infection could not be entirely ruled out since all the newborns excreting cytomegalovirus after 1 week of age were initially seropositive.

Since the rubella vaccine has been of great value in the prevention of congenital rubella, the development of a cytomegalovirus vaccine to prevent mental retardation has been suggested. Elek and Stern (1974) tested a live vaccine from the Ad 169 strain and considered its development as important in the prevention of mental retardation. Of 26 volunteers, 25 became seropositive after subcutaneous injection. Fourteen volunteers were asymptomatic and 12 developed mild local reactions. The Towne 125 vaccine developed from live human cytomegolovirus was evaluated by Glazer et al. (1979). It caused seroconversion in all 12 seronegative renal transplant candidates with only mild local reaction at the inoculation site. In a preliminary study by Fleisher, Starr, Friedman, and Plotkin (1982), 10 seronegative pediatric nurses of childbearing age were vaccinated and serial specimens obtained. Serologic response began at 2–4 weeks and peaked at 4–8 weeks. All volunteers had a cell-mediated immune response with only local reactions to the inoculation. The oncogenic potential, antigenic variability, and duration of antibody response are all areas that need further investigation. Clinical trials involving large numbers of immunized women with long-term follow-up of their offspring are still necessary before immunization is accepted as the major means to prevent the devastating effects of cytomegolovirus infection.

## HERPES SIMPLEX VIRUS

### Historical Considerations

The term herpes, from the Greek "to creep," is attributed by Nahmias and Dowdle (1968) to Greek physicians who described lesions that spread by "creeping." Around 100 A.D., Herodatus noted oral lesions associated with fever. Separation of smallpox from herpes lesions, and further subdivision of herpetic lesions into herpes zoster and oral and genital herpes simplex lesions, continued into the 20th century. By the 1960s, it was possible to differentiate herpes simplex virus (HSV) strains by antigenic differences. Nahmias and Dowdle (1968) clarified the relationship of HSV type 1 as the causative factor in most nongenital infections and HSV type 2 in most genital or neonatal infections. Subsequently, restriction endonuclease analysis of DNA and poly peptide analysis became available for determination of various strains of HSV.

### Epidemiology

HSV has a worldwide distribution without significant seasonal variation or epidemic cycle. The incidence and prevalence vary with age, socioeconomic level, and geographic distribution. The attack rate of HSV type 2 is a reflection of sexual activity and promiscuity.

### Congenital HSV Infection

Primary HSV infection during pregnancy has been considered as a possible cause of spontaneous abortion and congenital anomalies, although this has not been well documented. Evidence for intrauterine HSV infection was reported by Hutto et al. (1987) after reviewing 13 infants with clinical evidence of HSV infection. Viral isolation in each instance was HSV-2 positive. Two of the infants died during the first week of life, and of the remaining, 10 were severely neurologically impaired and 1 was blind. Primary genital infection was reported by 4 of the mothers, recurrent infection by 1 mother, and a negative history of lesions by the remaining women.

Passage through an infected birth canal is the primary cause of neonatal HSV infection. A progressive increase in the rate of neonatal infection was reported in a study from King County, Washington, by Sullivan-Bolyai, Hull, Wilson, and Corey (1983) with a rate of 11.9/100,000 live births in the years from 1978 to 1981 compared to the years 1966 to 1969 when the rate was 2.6/100,000 live births. Clinically symptomatic genital herpes was observed in the mother or father of 65% of the HSV-2 positive infants. In the remainder, serologic or cultural evidence of infection was detected in the mothers. A nongenital source accounted for the six newborns who were HSV-1 positive.

The newborn infant may present localized skin lesions, central nervous system disease, or disseminated systemic infection with multisystem involvement. Central nervous system disease usually becomes evident at an average age of 11 days and disseminated disease at 16 days, although symptoms may be apparent at any time from birth to 1 month of age. HSV infection is difficult to diagnose in those infants with systemic manifestations who do not have typical skin, mucocutaneous, or eye lesions.

Neonatal HSV infection has been recognized as a serious problem by the Committee on Fetus and Newborn and Committee on Infectious Diseases, American Academy of Pediatrics (1980). These committees noted that there was a 60% case fatality rate and major neurologic and ocular sequelae in half of the survivors. In a study of 56 HSV infected newborns, Whitley, Nahmias, Visintine, Fleming, and Alford (1980) observed that of the 26 considered premature, complications associated with prematurity such as respiratory distress, bacterial infections, and hypoglycemia occurred in 18 infants. Of the 30 normal term infants, 20 had an uncomplicated neonatal course and were discharged prior to the detection of HSV infection. Ten full-term infants had an abnormal course and a prolonged nursery stay with bacterial infections as the main reason for the extended hospitalization.

## Prevention of Congenital HSV Infection

Prevention of HSV infection in the neonate at this time lies primarily in the management of the infected mother. Recommendations by the American Academy of Pediatrics for pregnancies at risk include careful weekly monitoring during the last 8 weeks of pregnancy of those women who develop genital HSV during pregnancy, have a past history of genital lesions, or a sexual partner with herpetic lesions. Obstetricians should be aware of the risk to the offspring if the mother is infected. Both primary and recurrent HSV infections may occur without clinical symptoms. Positive viral cultures or clinically

observed lesions are considered indications for cesarean section prior to the
onset of labor. If there has been rupture of the membranes for less than 4–6
hours, cesarean section may still be considered. Brunell (1980) pointed out
that a rapid, inexpensive, and accurate screening mechanism for HSV would
greatly enhance the rate of detection of HSV-infected women without clinical
symptoms.

An infant born vaginally to a mother with acute genital HSV requires
isolation from other infants and appropriate isolation techniques by caregivers. Observation in the hospital for up to 2 weeks is indicated and viral
cultures should be obtained. Although at low risk of developing HSV infection, the infant born to a HSV infected mother after cesarean section and
before rupture of the membranes should also be segregated and followed
closely as an outpatient for a month.

Kleiman, Schreiner, Eitzen, Lemons, and Jansen (1982) surveyed 161
neonatal referral centers and determined that 83% excluded hospital personnel
with overt HSV lesions from direct patient care and 27% from all hospital
work. The argument was brought forth that such an isolation policy may not
be warranted because it is based on specific case reports of HSV transmission
from nursery personnel to newborns and on studies that found a higher percentage of HSV type 1 infected newborns than could be accounted for by the
incidence for HSV type 1 genital infections in women. However, support of
an isolation policy may be strengthened by data from one study that detected
this virus in oropharyngeal secretions of 78% and on the hands of 67% of 11
adult volunteers during 15 episodes of active labial herpes (Turner, Shehab,
Osborne, & Hendley, 1982). Furthermore, in the same study, the virus survived up to 2 hours on skin, 3 hours on cloth, and 4 hours on plastic materials.
It was concluded that clothing should be changed and contaminated surfaces
cleaned with alcohol or benzalkonium chloride.

Breastfeeding by a mother with HSV infection is permissible if there are
no active lesions on the breast and other lesions are well covered. Handwash-
ing precautions are necessary, however.

Vidarabine has been evaluated in the treatment of neonatal HSV infection with a significant reduction in mortality after such treatment (Whitley,
Nahmias, Soong, et al., 1980). In localized central nervous system disease,
mortality was reduced from 50% to 10% and morbidity from 83% to 50%
with vidarabine therapy. Although the mortality in disseminated disease with
vidarabine therapy decreased from 85% to 57%, the morbidity remained high.
Vidarabine decreased mortality and morbidity was further confirmed by a
follow-up study performed by Whitley et al. (1983). Disseminated HSV-2 in
a pregnant woman was successfully treated at 32 weeks of gestation with
parenteral acyclovir as reported by Cox, Phillips, DePaolo, and Faro (1986).
The infant survived with no abnormalities. Continued evaluation of antiviral

drugs, such as vidarabine and acyclovir, will provide needed information on the prevention of death or disability from neonatal HSV infection.

## TOXOPLASMOSIS

### Historical Considerations

The protozoan *Toxoplasmosis gondii* was first described by Nicolle and Manceaux (1908) and Splendore (1908). In 1939, Wolf, Cowen, and Paige observed that this protozoan could produce human disease. A few years later, proven cases of acquired infections were reported by Pinkerton and Henderson (1941).

### Gestational Toxoplasmosis

In the United States, approximately 20% to 30% of women in the childbearing age exhibit serologic evidence of previous *Toxoplasma gondii* infection. In France and certain tropical countries, the prevalence figure is significantly higher. In this country the frequency of primary toxoplasmosis infection during the gestational period is estimated to be approximately 2 per 1,000, whereas in Europe 20–80 per 1,000 pregnant women have acute toxoplasmosis. About one-third of pregnant females infected with toxoplasmosis transmit this organism to their offspring (Monif, 1974).

In a prospective study, Kimball, Kean, and Fuchs (1971) performed serologic tests in 4,048 women at their first prenatal visits and later at delivery. They found that of 2,765 women who initially were seronegative, 6 showed seroconversion at the time of delivery; and of 1,283 patients who had a positive antibody titer during the first examination, 17 displayed a substantial rise of the titer at the end of the gestational period. In another study, Ruoss and Bourne (1972) examined 3,187 pregnant women for antibodies to toxoplasmosis and observed that 22% of the patients had antibodies when first seen at the prenatal clinic. Two patients had antibodies at a high dilution at the initial examination and 7 patients developed antibodies during the second half of the pregnancy. None of these 9 women, however, experienced any significant illness.

A diagnosis of primary maternal infection may be established by the demonstration of rising antibody titers in serum samples obtained at 2–4 week intervals. Yet, a definite diagnosis cannot always be made, because a high antibody titer may be present at the initial serologic determination and may persist for several years.

### Congenital Toxoplasmosis

Clinical manifestations of acute intrauterine toxoplasmosis infection depend on a number of factors, including the time during pregnancy when the infection occurred, the virulence of the organism, the number of protozoa transferred across the placenta, and the immunologic status of the mother. The congenital infection differs markedly from the acquired form of toxoplasmosis one may see in later life. The primary site of pathologic infestation of in utero acquired toxoplasmosis is the central nervous system. Infection of the cerebral cortex and basal ganglia may cause significant neuropathology at the time of birth and during later life. Such central nervous system insult may result in hydrocephalus, mental retardation, intracerebral calcifications, seizures, and cerebral palsy. Chorioretinitis is also often observed in these infants.

Remington and Desmonts (1973) reported that nearly 45% of women who acquire toxoplasmosis during the gestational period gave birth to congenitally infected infants. According to these investigators, the rate of transmission is related to the gestational age when the infection occurs. Desmonts and Couvreur (1974) noted similar observations of the incidence of fetal infections that increased from 17% when maternal toxoplasmosis was acquired during the first trimester, to 25% in the second trimester, and to 65% during the third trimester of gestation.

Desmonts and Couvreur (1974) followed 183 pregnancies in which toxoplasmosis was acquired during pregnancy. Of 59 infants with documented infection, a subclinical illness was observed in 39 children, 11 had a very mild form of the disease, 7 exhibited severe ocular or cerebral involvement, and 2 died. In another study of 24 children who did not have any signs of toxoplasmosis in the newborn period, significant symptoms became apparent later (Wilson, Remington, Stagno, & Reynolds, 1980). A total of 13 of the 24 children (group I) either had positive umbilical cord serum IgM antibodies for toxoplasmosis or were detected as the result of testing for IgA and IgM toxoplasma antibodies. In the remaining 11 children (group II), the diagnosis was made only after the children presented later with ophthalmologic or neurologic symptoms suggestive of congenital toxoplasmosis infection. The vast majority of children (85%) in group I and all children in group II had chorioretinitis. Three children in group I and 8 children in group II developed unilateral and/or bilateral blindness. Various neurologic, intellectual, and audiologic deficits were observed in children in both groups. According to this study, it is not justifiable that professionals should be unconcerned with toxoplasmosis infections, because approximately 75% of congenitally infected newborns had pathologic findings on detailed ophthalmologic and neurologic investigations.

Congenital toxoplasmosis usually occurs as a complication of a first infection, accidentally acquired by a susceptible pregnant woman. Antibodies against toxoplasmosis found in the woman prior to the pregnancy are usually protective. Although the risk of a second infected infant is very small, congenital infestation with *Toxoplasma gondii* in successive offspring may occur (Garcia, 1968; Langer, 1963).

Sever et al. (1988) analyzed antibody titers to toxoplasmosis in 22,845 pregnant women who had been followed in the Collaborative Prenatal Project. The investigators found a predicted doubling in the frequency of deafness among children born to women with antibodies to toxoplasmosis, a 60% increase in microcephaly, and a 30% increase of mental retardation in association with the presence of high maternal antibody titers to *Toxoplasma gondii*.

Carter and Frank (1986) reported that there are between 140 to 1,400 cases of congenital toxoplasmosis per year in Canada; of these, 70 to 280 infants are severely affected at birth, and many of the others suffer sequelae later in life.

Foulon, Naessens, Volckaert, Lauwers, and Amy (1984) investigated the incidence of congenital toxoplasmosis in Belgium. They assessed the susceptible population of 1,403 women every 6 weeks and found 20 of these women (1.4%) seroconverted. Ten of the seroconverters had a therapeutic abortion and of the remaining 10, two gave birth to congenitally infected infants.

**Diagnostic Tests**

The most important diagnostic criteria are the serologic tests together with high index of clinical suspicion. Serologic tests include the Sabin-Feldman dye test, complement fixation test, indirect hemagglutination test, indirect fluorescent antibody test, IgM fluorescent antibody test, and the ELISA technique. The dye test, the oldest of the serologic tests, is described as a sensitive and specific measure of toxoplasma antibodies. The indirect fluorescent antibody test is most often used in state health department laboratories. The IgM fluorescent antibody test was probably the most specific test available until it was replaced by the more effective ELISA test.

Antibodies against *Toxoplasma gondii* can be found in humans within the first few weeks of an infection. They rise to a peak during the following 2 months and then usually persist at a slightly lower level throughout the life of the individual. Serologic confirmation of a recent infection with *Toxoplasma gondii* can be inferred when the titer of the Sabin-Feldman dye test has increased more than eightfold or when the indirect immuno fluorescent antibody titer increases at least fourfold. Diagnostic confirmation can also be sought by the isolation of live parasites. This requires preparation of lymph node, muscle, or placental tissue. After grinding and mincing, the tissues are inoculated intraperitoneally into laboratory mice. Specific histologic changes in lymph nodes obtained from infected mice have been described by Dorfman and Remington (1983).

In congenital infections, antibodies must be demonstrated in both maternal and infant serum. The diagnosis of congenital toxoplasmosis after birth is usually made by demonstration of persistent or rising levels of specific IgG antibodies, by the presence of IgM antibodies in cord blood or infant serum, or by the recovery of the protozoa from placenta or cord blood (Stagno, 1980). A negative IgM determination at birth will need to be followed by a repeat test 2 or 3 weeks later.

A method of diagnosing and treating congenital toxoplasmosis in utero is based on the identification of maternal acute infection, followed by culture of fetal blood and amniotic fluid, testing of fetal blood for toxoplasma specific IgM, nonspecific measures of infection, and ultrasound examination of the fetal brain (Daffos et al., 1988). Of 746 documented cases of maternal toxoplasma infection, the diagnosis was made antenatally in 39 of 42 fetuses.

## Treatment of Toxoplasmosis

A primary infection with *Toxoplasma gondii* during pregnancy is an indication for therapy (Desmonts & Couvreur, 1974). For first and second trimester toxoplasma infections, Desmonts and Couvreur (1974) found that treatment with spiramycin reduced the overall frequency of fetal infection. Also, Daffos et al. (1988) treated all mothers who had been diagnosed to have toxoplasma infection with spiramycin throughout pregnancy. If fetal infection was documented, pyrimethamine and a sulfonamide were added to the therapeutic regime. The investigators found that of the 15 infected fetuses with congenital toxoplasmosis who were carried to term, all but 2, who had chorioretinitis, remained clinically well during follow-up examinations. Thus, these authors conclude that prenatal diagnosis of congenital toxoplasmosis is practical and that prenatal therapy for women who wish to continue their pregnancies reduces the severity of the manifestations of the disease. Spiramycin is not available in the United States; however, with special permission from the Food and Drug Administration, spiramycin can be purchased from Canada and used as an "investigational drug" with an IND number in the United States.

The most frequently administered antitoxoplasma chemotherapeutic agents are pyrimethamine and the sulfonamides. These drugs are often used in combination. Frenkel (1971) showed that the synergistic effect of these drugs interferes with biosynthesis of folic acid in the parasite. However, these drugs also result in folic acid depletion in humans and may cause bone marrow depression. In addition, pyrimethamine has been found to have teratogenic effects and may cause severe leukopenia and thrombocytopenia. Frenkel (1971) suggested that because of the hematologic complications caused by pyrimethamine it should not be administered during the first trimester of pregnancy. Araujo and Remington (1974) provided evidence that clindamycin is effective in the treatment of toxoplasmosis. Yet, since clindamycin has not been tested in humans it is not recommended as therapy for toxoplasmosis. Although trimethoprim-sulfamethoxazole has been used successfully for toxoplasmosis infection in nonpregnant adults, it should not be administered during pregnancy since trimethoprim is also teratogenic. Some investigators have raised the question whether pyrimethamine and sulfonamides should be used for the protection of the fetus when the maternal infection occurs after the first trimester. Although Desmonts' (1974) data suggested that the transfer of the toxoplasma parasites via the placenta to the fetus may be delayed by using such therapy, there are no definite data available to suggest that once the maternal infection has occurred these drugs can protect the fetus.

Charles (1980) indicated that in the majority of toxoplasmosis infections during pregnancy, no specific antitoxoplasmosis therapy is required. As noted above, there are conflicting reports on effective treatment of toxoplasmosis. More investigations are needed to provide information on effective long-term treatment outcome.

**Prevention of Toxoplasmois**

In order to prevent infection from *Toxoplasma gondii*, it has been recommended that seronegative females stay away from cats shortly before and during pregnancy. The litter of house cats, which may contain feces of infected cats, also should be avoided by pregnant women and should be disposed of by some other member in the household if the cat is to remain in the house of the pregnant woman.

It has also been suggested that young girls be exposed to cats before they reach the childbearing age. This practice must be questioned, however, because the acquired disease can produce chorioretinitis in the affected person at any age. Moreover, it has been shown that a woman does not necessarily have to acquire a primary infection with toxoplasmosis during gestation in order to transmit the organism to the fetus. It has been reported that persistent parasitemia may exist in spite of high toxoplasma antibody levels. In addition, congenital infection in successive pregnancies, although a rare event, may occur. Langer (1963) found *Toxoplasma gondii* organisms in the brain of two successive stillborn infants. Also, Garcia (1968) observed *Toxoplasma gondii* infection in offspring in successive pregnancies. Thus, unlike most viral diseases, toxoplasma immunity does not necessarily confer protection to subsequent pregnancies.

There are other preventive measures that can diminish the possibility of acquiring toxoplasmosis infection. Women who are about to become pregnant or who are pregnant should avoid eating raw meat or meat that has not been thoroughly cooked. It is also advised that pregnant women wash their hands with soap after handling raw meat. Because freezing will kill both trophozoites and encysted organisms, it is safe for pregnant women to handle and eat meat that has been frozen.

Since many infected infants will be asymptomatic and will not be clinically identified until perhaps years later when neurologic, ophthalmologic, or other symptoms become apparent, a reliable newborn screening program for toxoplasmosis would be desirable. Unfortunately, IgM quantification and toxoplasma IgM antibody determination in cord sera, which had been proposed as neonatal screening for toxoplasmosis infections, have a low sensitivity and limited specificity and thus are inadequate for screening purposes. Another assay to identify neonatal toxoplasmosis measures the blastogenic response of lymphocytes incubated with toxoplasma antigens (Pass, Reynolds, August, & Stagno, 1979; Wilson, Desmonts, Couvreur, & Remington, 1979). This method would be valuable in particular during the first 6 months of life when maternally derived IgG antibodies may interfere with the serologic diagnosis. However, studies indicate that during the first few months of life, the lymphocyte transformation assay is not superior to the serial detection of IgG antibodies by direct immunofluorescence or the Sabin-Feldman dye tests (Stagno, 1980).

Although the incidence of congenital toxoplasmosis in the United States is relatively low (0.1%–0.2%), it is significantly higher than other disease entities where effective screening programs are in place, such as phenylketonuria and congenital hypothyroidism. Thus, a reliable screening procedure at reasonable cost carried out during pregnancy to identify primary toxoplasmosis and/or the development of a sensitive screening method for newborn children would provide important information that could lead to effective therapeutic intervention.

## HUMAN IMMUNODEFICIENCY VIRUS

### Historical Considerations

Infection with human immunodeficiency virus (HIV), the etiologic agent responsible for acquired immunodeficiency syndrome (AIDS), has been reported worldwide with the number of cases increasing in epidemic proportions. Following initial reports in 1981 of a new immunodeficiency disease affecting homosexual men and later heterosexual adults, including intravenous drug users and persons of Haitian descent (Centers for Disease Control, 1981, 1982), it became apparent that children were also affected. The first reported pediatric cases involved children who had received blood transfusions and later developed symptoms of immunodeficiency (Oleske et al., 1983; Rubinstein et al., 1983).

An infectious etiology was confirmed in 1983 when the virus was isolated from affected persons (Barre-Sinoussi et al., 1983). Initially named the human T-cell lymphotropic virus-III (HTLV-III) and AIDS-related virus (ARV) by separate groups of researchers (Gallo et al., 1984), the virus was renamed in 1985 by the International Committee on Taxonomy of Viruses, and is now officially known as human immunodeficiency virus. Since then, the spectrum of disease caused by HIV infection in children and adults has become increasingly better understood as more infected persons, symptomatic and asymptomatic, are identified.

## Epidemiology

Like adults, children may be infected with HIV through sexual contact or by exposure to blood products contaminated with the virus. However, the majority of cases of pediatric HIV infection have resulted from vertical transmission from an infected mother to her fetus or newborn (Rogers et al., 1987). Most of the women who transmit HIV infection to their children are intravenous drug users; others have acquired the virus via heterosexual relationships with infected partners and some are of Haitian descent (Centers for Disease Control, 1988b). Many of the women are asymptomatic for HIV infection at the time of their pregnancy and may unknowingly transmit the virus to their unborn children (Oleske, Connor, & Boland, 1988).

Most cases of pediatric HIV infection in the United States have been from urban areas with the majority reported in the states of Florida, New York, and New Jersey (Friedland & Klein, 1987; Rogers et al., 1987). Anonymous testing of cord blood from infants born to mothers in Massachusetts showed an overall prevalence of maternal seropositivity of 0.21% with the highest rate of 0.8% in women delivering in inner city hospitals (Hoff et al., 1988). In New York inner-city hospitals, the prevalence of HIV seropositivity among childbearing women is as high as 3% (Centers for Disease Control, 1988a). Among children with AIDS, approximately 52% are black, 24% are white, and 23% are Hispanic (Centers for Disease Control, 1989).

By the end of 1988, 1,346 cases of AIDS in children under age 13 years had been reported to the Centers for Disease Control (CDC). The 1987 revision of the CDC case definition for AIDS broadened the scope of clinical manifestations of pediatric AIDS and eliminated some of the previous underreporting that had resulted from the use of the earlier case definition (Centers for Disease Control, 1987). However, it is important to understand that infection with HIV produces a spectrum of effects from asymptomatic to critically ill. About half of the children with HIV infection do not meet case criteria for AIDS. It has been estimated that by 1991 there will be 10,000–20,000 children in the United States with HIV infection (Oleske et al., 1988).

## Clinical Manifestations of HIV Infection in Children

The incubation period for AIDS is variable. Most children with congenital HIV infection become symptomatic within the first 2 years of life, but others have been asymptomatic for more than 7 years (Rogers et al., 1987). In general, there is a shorter incubation period for AIDS in children than in adults. The median age of diagnosis of AIDS for congenitally acquired infection is 10 months (Onorato, Markowitz, & Oxtoby, 1988).

Common manifestations include lymphadenopathy, failure to thrive, hepatosplenomegaly, and fevers. As in adults, the associated immunologic abnormalities lead to recurrent infections, including opportunistic infections, such as *Pneumocystis carinii* pneumonia. HIV infected children are more likely than infected adults to have recurrent bacterial infections and are at risk for sepsis and meningitis. Fungal infections are common, particularly chronic oral candidiasis and Candida esophagitis. Lymphocytic interstitial pneumonitis, common among children but rarely seen in adults, is of unknown etiology. Conversely, lymphomas that are more common in HIV infected adults are rarely seen in children.

HIV causes primary infection of the central nervous system (Epstein et al., 1986), and most children with symptomatic HIV infection show some degree of encephalopathy, static or progressive. Belman and colleagues (1988) found evidence of central nervous system dysfunction in 61 of 68 children with symptomatic HIV infection. Developmental delays, mental retardation, microcephaly, and cerebral atrophy are frequent manifestations. Pseudobulbar palsy and spasticity may also occur. Seizures are relatively infrequent.

A constellation of dysmorphic facial features associated with congenitally acquired HIV infection has been described (Marion, Wiznia, Hutcheon, & Rubinstein, 1986). These features include a prominent boxlike forehead, hypertelorism, patulous lips, and a well-formed triangular philtrum. However, they are not universally present in children with congenitally acquired HIV infection, and there is existing controversy as to whether such features represent an AIDS embryopathy (Cordero, 1988).

**Diagnostic Tests**

Diagnostic tests available for children are the same that are used for adults. The most often used tests are antibody tests, including the enzyme linked immunosorbant assay (ELISA), Western Blot, and the indirect fluorescent antibody test (IFA). Antigen tests are becoming more widely available but may not be positive unless the virus is actively replicating. Culture tests are very specific but not readily available. A new technique for detection of the virus is the polymerase chain reaction test, by which the presence of viral DNA is amplified for more accurate detection.

There are limitations to all of these tests including the fact that routinely available antibody tests that measure IgG do not distinguish between passively acquired maternal antibody and antibody produced by the child. This makes the presence of infection in a child under age 15 months difficult without other accompanying symptoms or evidence of immune dysfunction. Also, it is not possible to know if an infant who has converted from a positive to negative antibody test due to loss of maternal antibodies is truly uninfected or has failed to produce antibodies to the virus. The development of HIV specific IgM assays would address these problems. It has been recommended that children born to seropositive mothers who subsequently become seronegative continue to be followed for months or years even if they remain asymptomatic (Lepage, Batungwanayo, & van de Perre, 1989).

## Treatment of HIV Infection

There is no cure for HIV infection at the present time and treatment has been essentially supportive. Controlled trials are now underway to evaluate new drugs, some of which are already used to treat HIV infected adults. These drugs include zidovudine (AZT) and dideoxycytidine (Pizzo et al., 1988). Intravenous immunoglobulin has been reported to decrease the number of infections, but to date this has not been confirmed by controlled studies (Ochs, 1987). Other therapies include specific antifungal and antibiotic medications as well as nutritional support, sometimes with parenteral hyperalimentation.

In addition to specific medical therapeutic needs, these children have extensive social-emotional and developmental needs. Families of HIV infected children are usually of low socioeconomic background, they have limited resources, and they have problems that may include other relatives infected with HIV, drug abuse, and inability to care for the infected child. A multidisciplinary team consisting of physicians, nurses, social workers, psychologists, and therapists is needed to address these complex medical and psychosocial issues.

The prognosis for children with asymptomatic infection is uncertain; for children with AIDS, the prognosis remains grim. Median survival after diagnosis of AIDS is less than 1 year (Rogers et al., 1987).

## Prevention of HIV Infection

At present, the only means of prevention of congenital HIV infection is prevention of pregnancy in an HIV infected woman. Since many infected women are asymptomatic and unaware of their status at the time of pregnancy, intensive efforts must be directed toward identification and education of women at risk so that they can make informed choices regarding pregnancy.

## OTHER INFECTIONS

There are numerous other infectious agents that potentially can be teratogenic to the embryo or fetus.

## Influenza

The first prospective study of influenza in early pregnancy was carried out by Campbell (1953). Some investigators who studied influenza infection during pregnancy and its effect upon the fetus did not find evidence that the influenza virus caused significant fetal anomalies (Walker & McKee, 1959; Wilson, Heins, Imagawa, & Adams, 1959), whereas others found a teratogenic effect in conceptuses (Coffey & Jessop, 1963; Hakosolo & Saxen, 1971; Hardy, Azarowicz, Mannini, Medearis, & Cooke, 1961). Coffey and Jessop (1963) reported an increased incidence of central nervous system abnormalities in infants born to women who had been infected with influenza during the epidemic of 1957–1958 in Ireland. They found that out of 60 females studied, 24 had infants with congenital anomalies, 18 of whom had central nervous system defects. During the same time period, Hardy and colleagues (1961) studied the effects of maternal influenza infection on fetal outcome in the United States. They noted that 10% of the infants born to mothers, who had influenza infections during the first trimester, had a significantly increased risk of congenital anomalies. Similarly, Leck (1963) reported that maternal influenza infections during the first trimester increased the risk of congenital anomalies, particularly those of the central nervous system. It also has been suggested that drug therapy during influenza infections might be teratogenic and thus increase the risk of congenital anomalies in the offspring (Charles, 1980). Although some reports show a significant increase of congenital anomalies in infants born to mothers who have been infected with influenza virus during early pregnancy, it is not possible to draw definite conclusions about the effect of influenza virus on intrauterine embryonic/fetal development.

**Mumps**

As in the case of influenza, the role of mumps virus in congenital disease also remains controversial. Manson, Logan, and Loy (1960) observed no significant difference of fetal complication between 101 cases of maternal mumps infection and the control group. Connelly, Reynolds, and Crawford (1964), however, found congenital anomalies in infants whose mothers had been infected with mumps in early pregnancy. In addition, other retrospective studies indicate that mumps may have an adverse effect on the embryo/fetus during the first trimester. Experimental studies showed that after maternal infection, the virus could be isolated from the fetus 1 week later (St. Geme, Paralta, & van Pelt, 1972).

Intrauterine infection with this virus has been implicated in the pathogenesis of primary endocardial fibroelastosis (Shone, Armas, Manning, & Keith, 1966; St. Geme, Noren, & Adams, 1966). Yet, Gersony, Katz, and Nadas (1966) and Chen, Thompson, and Rose (1971) failed to prove a relationship between mumps infection during pregnancy and primary endocardial fibroelastosis in the offspring.

**Measles**

Although measles, or rubeola infection, during pregnancy is a rare event, abortion, stillbirths, and congenital abnormalities have been reported after gestational infection (Stevenson, 1973). Of 99 live births to mothers who had measles during pregnancy, Manson et al. (1960) found 7 infants with congenital anomalies. Siegel (1973), however, did not detect any congenital anomalies in the offspring of 44 mothers who had been infected with measles during the first trimester. Most reports that imply an association of maternal measle infection and congenital anomalies in the offspring are retrospective in nature and the abnormalities observed are vague in type, questioning the likelihood of the measles virus as a significant intrauterine teratogen.

## Coxsackie Virus

Kibrick and Benirschke (1956) reported the first case of intrauterine infection with coxsackie B-III virus. Coxsackie virus was cultured from the spinal cord of a female infant who died 7 days after birth from serious respiratory difficulties, myocarditis, and meningoencephalitis. In a prospective study, Brown and Evans (1967) observed a significantly increased number of offspring with congenital heart disease whose mothers had experienced infections with coxsackie B-III and B-IV virus in the first trimester of pregnancy when compared with a control group. In another study involving 22,935 women, Brown and Karunas (1972) found that infections with B-III and B-IV strains of coxsackie virus in early pregnancy were associated with cardiovascular defects in the offspring. Other investigators also reported an increased incidence of urogenital anomalies, such as hypospadias, epispadias, and cryptorchidism in infants of mothers who had gestational coxsackie B-IV infections. In addition, intrauterine coxsackie infection can cause central nervous system, hepatic, and myocardial disease in the offspring.

## Varicella

Brunell (1966) reported that varicella infection during the last trimester of pregnancy may result in premature labor and delivery of an immature infant. Similarly, Manson et al. (1960) observed a high incidence of prematurity in infants born to varicella infected mothers. Siegel and Fuerst (1966), however, did not find prematurity associated with maternal varicella.

Manson et al. (1960) observed major congenital anomalies in 7 of 293 infants born to mothers who had varicella during pregnancy. Muscle atrophy, lymph node hypoplasia, and skin defects were described by some researchers (Rinvik, 1969; Savage, Mossa, & Gordon 1973). Srabstein et al. (1974) noted ophthalmologic anomalies and neurologic disorders in infants whose mothers were exposed to varicella virus during the first trimester of pregnancy. Blattner (1974) also reported frequent ocular anomalies in infants whose mothers had varicella in early pregnancy. Feldman (1952) suggested that latent infection may be present in the absence of any abnormalities following gestational varicella infection. Also, Dudgeon, Marshall, and Soothill (1969) indicated that the varicella virus can survive in the fetus throughout fetal life. Although varicella infection during pregnancy can result in congenital anomalies, the latter are observed infrequently.

## Syphilis

Syphilis is caused by the organism *Treponema pallidum*. It was the most devastating sexually transmitted disease for many centuries. Congenital infections due to transplacental transmission are associated with multisystem disease. Early manifestations include enlarged liver, spleen, and lymph nodes, bone involvement, and skin lesions that lead to failure to thrive and sometimes death if untreated. Other manifestations are those of disfigurement and central nervous system involvement. Fortunately, premarital and prenatal blood testing are now widely practiced. These programs in combination with the availability of penicillin to treat infected mothers and infants has markedly decreased the impact of syphilis as a contributor to developmental disabilities since the 1960s.

## CONCLUSION

This chapter focuses on specified infectious processes during pregnancy that may cause significant fetal insults. Also, various preventive measures are discussed that are available at the present time. Further research is needed to bring about more effective prevention of gestational infections, such as cytomegalic inclusion disease, toxoplasmosis, and others.

## REFERENCES

Ahlfors, K., Harris, S., Ivarrson, S., & Sranberg, L. (1981). Secondary cytomegalovirus infection causing symptomatic congenital infection. *New England Journal of Medicine, 305*, 284.

Araujo, F. G., & Remington, J. S. (1974). Effect of clindamycin on acute and chronic toxoplasmosis in mice. *Antimicrobial Agents and Chemotherapy, 5*, 647–651.

Arbeter, A. M., Baker, L., Starr, S. E, Levine, B. L., Books, E., & Plotkin, S. A. (1986). Combination measles, mumps, rubella and varicella vaccine. *Pediatrics, 78*, 742–747.

Bale, J. F., Blackman, J. A., Murph, J., & Andersen, R. D. (1986). Congenital cytomegalovirus infection: Information for educational personnel. *American Journal of Diseases of Children, 140*, 128–131.

Barre-Sinoussi, F., Chermann, J. C., Rey, F., Nugeyre, M. T., Chamaret, S., Gruest, J., Daughet, C., & Axler-Bier, C. (1983). Isolation of a T-lymphocytic retrovirus from a patient at risk for acquired immunodeficiency syndrome (AIDS). *Science, 220*, 868–871.

Belman, A. L., Diamond, G., Dickson, D., Horoupian, D., Llena, J., Lantos, G., & Rubinstein, A. (1988). Pediatric acquired immunodeficiency syndrome: Neurologic syndromes. *American Journal of Diseases of Children, 142*, 29–35.

Blattner, R. J. (1974). The role of viruses in congenital defects. *American Journal of Diseases of Children, 128*, 781–786.

Böttiger, M., Christenson, B., Romanus, V., Taranger, J., & Strandell, A. (1988). Swedish experience of two dose vaccination programme aiming at eliminating measles, mumps, and rubella. *British Medical Journal, 295*, 1264–1267.

Brown, G. C., & Evans, T. N. (1967). Serologic evidence of coxsackie virus etiology of congenital heart disease. *Journal of the American Medical Association, 199*, 151–155.

Brown, G. C., & Karunas, R. S. (1972). Relationship of congenital anomalies and maternal infection with selected enteroviruses. *American Journal of Epidemiology, 95*, 207–217.

Brunell, P. A. (1966). Placental transfer of varicella-zoster antibody. *Pediatrics, 38*, 1034–1038.

Brunell, P. A. (1980). Prevention and treatment of neonatal herpes. *Pediatrics, 65*, 1150–1153.

Campbell, W. A. B. (1953). Influenza in early pregnancy and effects on the fetus. *Lancet, i*, 173–174.

Carter, A. O., & Frank, J. W. (1986). Congenital toxoplasmosis: Epidemiologic features and control. *Canadian Medical Association Journal, 135*, 618–623.

Centers for Disease Control. (1981). Kaposi's sarcoma and *Pneumocystis* pneumonia among homosexual men—New York City and California. *Morbidity and Mortality Weekly Report, 30*, 305–308.

Centers for Disease Control. (1982). Task Force on Kaposi's sarcoma and opportunistic infections: Epidemiologic aspects of the current outbreak of Kaposi's sarcoma and opportunistic infections. *New England Journal of Medicine, 306*, 248–252.

Centers for Disease Control. (1984–1985). Rubella and congenital rubella syndrome— United States. *Morbidity and Mortality Weekly Report, 35*, 129–135.

Centers for Disease Control. (1987). Revision of the CDC surveillance case definition for acquired immunodeficiency syndrome. *Morbidity and Mortality Weekly Report, 36*(Suppl.), 1–15.

Centers for Disease Control. (1988a). Quarterly report to the domestic policy council on the prevalence and rate of spread of HIV and AIDS in the United States. *Morbidity and Mortality Weekly Report, 37*, 223–226.

Centers for Disease Control. (1988b). Update: Acquired immunodeficiency syndrome (AIDS)—Worldwide. *Morbidity and Mortality Weekly Report, 37*, 286–288, 293–295.

Centers for Disease Control. (1989). Update: Acquired immunodeficiency syndrome— United States, 1981–1988. *Morbidity and Mortality Weekly Report, 38*, 229–236.

Charles, D. (1980). *Infections in obstetrics and gynecology*. Philadelphia: W. B. Saunders.

Chen, S. C., Thompson, M. W., & Rose, V. (1971). Endocardial fibroelastosis: Family studies with special reference to counseling. *Journal of Pediatrics, 79*, 385–392.

Coffey, V. P., & Jessop, W. J. E. (1963). Maternal influenza and congenital deformities: A follow-up study. *Lancet, i*, 748–751.

Cole, R., & Kuttner, A. G. (1926). A filterable virus present in the submaxillary glands of guinea pigs. *Journal of Experimental Medicine, 44*, 855–873.

Committee on Fetus and Newborn, Committee on Infectious Diseases, American Academy of Pediatrics. (1980). Perinatal herpes simplex virus infections. *Pediatrics, 66*, 147–148.

Conboy, T. J., Pass, R. F., Stagno, S., Alford, C. A., Myers, G. J., Britt, W. J., McCollister, F. P., Summers, M. N., McFarland, C. E., & Boll, T. J. (1987). Early clinical manifestations and intellectual outcome in children with symptomatic congenital cytomegalovirus infection. *Journal of Pediatrics, 111*, 343–348.

Connelly, J. P., Reynolds, S., & Crawford, J. D. (1964). Viral and drug hazards in pregnancy. *Clinical Pediatrics*, *3*, 587–597.

Cooper, L. Z. (1968). Rubella: A preventable cause of birth defects. In D. Bergsma, S. Krugman, & C. Jackson (Eds.), Intrauterine infections. *Birth Defects Original Article Series*, *4*, 23–35.

Cooper, L. Z., & Krugman, S. (1967). Clinical manifestations of postnatal and congenital rubella. *Archives of Ophthalmology*, *77*, 434–439.

Cooper, L. Z., Ziring, P. R., Ockerse, A. B., Fedun, B. A., Kiely, B., & Krugman, S. (1969). Clinical manifestations and management. *American Journal of Diseases of Children*, *118*, 18–29.

Cordero, J. F. (1988). Issues concerning AIDS embryopathy (The Pediatric Forum). *American Journal of Diseases of Children*, *142*, 9.

Cox, S. M., Phillips, L., DePaolo, H. D., & Faro, S. (1986). Treatment of disseminated herpes simplex virus in pregnancy with parenteral acyclovir. *Journal of Reproductive Medicine*, *31*, 1005–1007.

Daffos, F., Forestier, F., Capells-Pavlovsky, M., Thulliez, P., Aufront, C., Valenti, D., & Cox, W. L. (1988). Prenatal management of 746 pregnancies at risk for congenital toxoplasmosis. *New England Journal of Medicine*, *318*, 271–275.

de Boo, T. M., van Druten, J. A., & Plantinga, A. D. (1987). Predicting the dynamic effects of rubella vaccination programmes. *Statistics in Medicine*, *6*, 843–851.

De la Mata, I., & DeWals, P. (1988). Policies for immunization against rubella in European countries. *European Journal of Epidemiology*, *4*, 175–180.

Desmonts, G. (1974). Congenital toxoplasmosis. *New England Journal of Medicine*, *291*, 366–367.

Desmonts, G., & Couvreur, J. (1974). Congenital toxoplasmosis: A prospective study of 378 pregnancies. *New England Journal of Medicine*, *290*, 1110–1116.

Dorfman, R. F., & Remington, J. S. (1983). Value of lymph node biopsy in the diagnosis of acute acquired toxoplasmosis. *New England Journal of Medicine*, *289*, 878–881.

Dudgeon, J. A. (1969). Congenital rubella: Pathogenesis and immunology. *American Journal of Diseases of Children*, *118*, 35–44.

Dudgeon, J. A. (1975). Congenital rubella. *Journal of Pediatrics*, *87*, 1078–1086.

Dudgeon, J. A., Marshall, W. C., & Soothill, J. F. (1969). Immunological responses to early and late intrauterine virus infections. *Journal of Pediatrics*, *75*, 1149–1166.

Ebbin, A. J., Wilson, M. G., Chandor, S. B., & Wehrle, P. F. (1973). Inadvertent rubella immunization in pregnancy. *American Journal of Obstetrics and Gynecology*, *117*, 505–512.

Elek, S. D., & Stern, H. (1974). Development of a vaccine against mental retardation caused by cytomegalovirus in utero. *Lancet*, *i*, 1–5.

Epstein, L. G., Sharer, L. R., Oleske, J. M., Connor, E. M., Goudsmit, J., Bagdon, L., Robert-Guroff, M., & Koenigsberger, M. R. (1986). Neurologic manifestations of human immunodeficiency virus infection in children. *Pediatrics*, *78*, 678–687.

Feldman, G. V. (1952). Herpes zoster neonatorum. *Archives of Disease in Childhood*, *27*, 126–127.

Fleisher, G. R., Starr, S. E., Friedman, H. M., & Plotkin, S. A. (1982). Vaccination of pediatric nurses with live attenuated cytomegalovirus. *American Journal of Diseases of Children*, *136*, 294–296.

Fouleon, W., Naessens, A., Volckaert, T. M., Lauwers, S., & Amy, J. J. (1984). Congenital toxoplasmosis: A prospective survey in Brussels. *Obstetrics and Gynaecology*, *91*, 419–423.

Frenkel, J. K. (1971). Toxoplasmosis: Mechanisms of infection, laboratory diagnosis and management. *Current Topics in Pathology*, *54*, 28–75.

Friedland, G. H., & Klein, R. S. (1987). Transmission of the human immunodeficiency virus. *New England Journal of Medicine*, *317*, 1125–1135.

Gallo, R. C., Salahuddin, S. Z., Popovic, M., Shearer, G. M., Kaplan, M., Haynes, B. F., Palker, T. J., Redfield, R., Oleske, J., Safai, B., White, G., Foster, P., & Markham, P.D. (1984). Frequent detection and isolation of cytopathic retroviruses (HTLV-III) from patients with AIDS and at risk for AIDS. *Science*, *224*, 500–503.

Garcia, A. G. P. (1968). Congenital toxoplasmosis in two successive sibs. *Archives of Disease in Childhood*, *43*, 705–710.

Gersony, W. M., Katz, S. L., & Nadas, A. S. (1966). Endocardial fibroelastosis and the mumps virus. *Pediatrics*, *37*, 430–434.

Glazer, J. P., Friedman, H. M., Grossman, R. A., Starr, S. E., Barker, C. F., Perloff, L. J., Huang, E., & Plotkin, S. A. (1979). Live cytomegalovirus vaccination of renal transplant candidates. *Annals of Internal Medicine*, *91*, 676–683.

Goodpasture, E. W., & Talbot, F. B. (1921). Concerning the nature of "protozoan-like" cells in certain lesions of infancy. *American Journal of Diseases of Children*, *21*, 415–421.

Gregg, N. Mc. (1941). Congenital cataract following German measles in the mother. *Transactions of the Ophthalmological Society of Australia*, *3*, 35–46.

Griffin, P. M., O'Shea, M., Brazy, J. E., Koepke, J., Klein, D., Malloy, C., & Wilfert, C. M. (1988). Cytomegalovirus infection in a neonatal intensive care unit. *American Journal of Diseases of Children*, *142*, 1188–1193.

Hakosolo, J., & Saxen, L. (1971). Influenza epidemic and congenital defects. *Lancet*, *ii*, 1346–1347.

Hanshaw, J. B. (1982). On deafness, cytomegalovirus and neonatal screening. *American Journal of Diseases of Children*, *136*, 886–887.

Hardy, J. M., Azarowicz, E. N., Mannini, A., Medearis, D. N., Jr., & Cooke, R. E. (1961). The effect of Asian influenza on the outcome of pregnancy. *American Journal of Public Health*, *51*, 1182–1188.

Hoff, R., Berardi, V. P., Weiblen, B. J., Mahoney-Trout, L., Mitchell, M. L., & Grady, G. F. (1988). Seroprevalence of human immunodeficiency virus among childbearing women. *New England Journal of Medicine*, *318*, 525–530.

Hutto, C., Arvin, A., Jacobs, R., Steele, R., Stagno, S., Lyrene, R., Willett, L., Powell, D., Andersen, R., Werthammer, J., Ratcliff, G., Nahmias, A., Christy, C., & Whitley, R. (1987). Intrauterine herpes simplex infection. *Journal of Pediatrics*, *110*, 97–101.

Kibrick, S., & Benirschke, K. (1956). Acute aseptic myocarditis and meningoencephalitis in newborn children infected with coxsackie virus group B, type 3. *New England Journal of Medicine*, *255*, 883–889.

Kimball, A. C., Kean, B. H., & Fuchs, F. (1971). Congenital toxoplasmosis: A prospective study of 4,048 obstetric patients. *American Journal of Obstetrics and Gynecology*, *111*, 211–218.

Kleiman, M. B., Schreiner, R. L., Eitzen, H., Lemons, J. A., & Jansen, R. D. (1982). Oral Herpes virus infection in nursery personnel: Infection control policy. *Pediatrics*, *70*, 609–612.

Langer, H. (1963). Repeated infections of *Toxoplasma gondii*. *Obstetrics and Gynecology*, *21*, 318–329.

Leck, I. (1963). The incidence of malformations following influenza epidemics. *British Journal of Preventive Social Medicine*, *17*, 70–80.

Lepage, P., Batungwanayo, J., & van de Perre, P. (1989). Seronegativity and HIV infection. *Archives of Disease in Childhood, 64*, 135–137.

Levine, J. B., Berkowitz, C. D., & St. Geme, J. W., Jr. (1982). Rubella virus reinfection during pregnancy leading to late-onset congenital rubella syndrome. *Journal of Pediatrics, 100*, 589–591.

Manson, M. M., Logan, W. P. D., & Loy, R. M. (1960). Rubella and other virus infections during pregnancy. *The report on public health and medical subjects* (Rep. No. 101). London: Ministry of Health.

Marion, R. W., Wiznia, A. A., Hutcheon, R. G., & Rubinstein, A. (1986). Human T-cell lymphotropic virus type III (HTLV-III) embryopathy. *American Journal of Diseases of Children, 140*, 638–640.

Modlin, J. F., Herrmann, K. L., Brandling-Bennett, A. D., Eddins, D. L., & Hayden, G. F. (1976). Risk of congenital abnormality after inadvertent rubella vaccination of pregnant women. *New England Journal of Medicine, 294*, 972–974.

Monif, G. R. G. (1974). *Infectious diseases in obstetrics and gynecology.* New York: Harper & Row.

Nahmias, A. J., & Dowdle, W. R. (1968). Antigenic and biologic differences in herpes hominis. *Progress in Medical Virology, 10*, 110–159.

Nicolle, C., & Manceaux, L. (1908). Sur une infection à Corps de leishman du gondi [About an infection of leishmania (on neighboring organisms) of gondi]. *C. R. Academy of Science, 147*, 763–766.

Ochs, H. D. (1987). Intravenous immunoglobulin in the treatment and prevention of acute infections in pediatric acquired immunodeficiency syndrome patients. *Pediatric Infectious Disease, 6*, 509–511.

Oleske, J. M., Connor, E. M., & Boland, M. G. (1988). A perspective on pediatric AIDS. *Pediatric Annals, 17*, 319–321.

Oleske, J. M., Minefor, A., Cooper, R., Thomas, K., de la Cruz, A., Ahdieh, H., Guerrero, I., Joshi, V., & Desposito, F. (1983). Immune deficiency syndrome in children. *Journal of the American Medical Association, 249*, 2345–2349.

Onorato, I. M., Markowitz, L. E., & Oxtoby, M. J. (1988). Childhood immunization, vaccine-preventable diseases and infection with human immunodeficiency virus. *Pediatric Infectious Disease, 6*, 588–595.

Parkman, P. D., Meyer, H. M., Jr., Kirschstein, R. L., & Hopps, H. E. (1966). Attenuated rubella virus: Vol. I. Development and laboratory characterization. *New England Journal of Medicine, 275*, 569.

Pass, R. F., August, A. M., Dworsky, M., & Reynolds, D. W. (1982). Cytomegalovirus infection in a day care center. *New England Journal of Medicine, 307*, 477–479.

Pass, R. F., Reynolds, D. W., August, A., & Stagno, S. (1979). Cellular immune response to toxoplasma in children with congenital toxoplasmosis (CT). *Clinical Research, 27*, 810A.

Pass, R. F., Stagno, S., Myers, G. J., & Alford, C. A. (1980). Outcome of symptomatic congenital cytomegalovirus infection: Results of long-term longitudinal follow up. *Pediatric, 66*, 758–762.

Peltola, H., Karanko, V., Kurki, T., Hukkanen, V., Virtanen, M., Pentinen, K., Nissinen, M., & Heinonen, O. P. (1986). Rapid effect on endemic measles, mumps, and rubella of nationwide vaccination programme in Finland. *Lancet, i*, 137–139.

Pinkerton, H., & Henderson, R. G. (1941). Adult toxoplasmosis: A previously unrecognized disease entity simulating the typhus-spotted fever group. *Journal of the American Medical Association, 116*, 807–814.

Pizzo, P. A., Eddy, J., Falloon, J., Balis, F. M., Murphy, R. F., Moss, H., Wolters,

P., Brouwers, P., Jaronski, P., Rubin, M., Broder, S., Yarchoan, R., Brunetti, A., Maha, M., Nusinoff-Lehrman, S., & Poplack, D. G. (1988). Effect of continuous intravenous infusion of zidovudine (AZT) in children with symptomatic HIV infection. New England Journal of Medicine, 319, 889–896.

Rawls, W. E., Phillips, C. A., Melnick, J. L., & Desmond, M. M. (1967). Persistent virus infection in congenital rubella. Archives of Ophthalmology, 77, 430–433.

Remington, J. S., & Desmonts, G. (1973). Congenital toxoplasmosis variability in the IgM-fluorescent antibody response and some pitfalls in diagnosis. Journal of Pediatrics, 83, 27–30.

Rinvik, R. (1969). Congenital varicella encephalomyelitis in surviving newborns. American Journal of Diseases of Children, 117, 231–235.

Rogers, M. F., Thomas, P. A., Starcher, E. T., Noa, M. C., Bush, T. J., & Jaffee, H. W. (1987). Acquired immunodeficiency syndrome in children: Report of the Centers for Disease Control National Surveillance. Pediatrics, 79, 1008–1014.

Rubella and congenital rubella syndrome: United States, 1985–1988. (1989). American Journal of Diseases of Children, 143, 893–894.

Rubinstein, A., Sicklick, M., Gupta, A., Bernstein, L., Klein, N., Rubinstein, E., Spigland, I., Fruchter, L., Litman, N., Lee, H., & Hollander, M. (1983). Immunodeficiency with reversed T4/T8 ratios in infants born to promiscuous and drug-addicted mothers. Journal of the American Medical Association, 249, 2350–2356.

Ruoss, C. F., & Bourne, G. L. (1972). Toxoplasmosis in pregnancy. British Journal of Obstetrics and Gynaecology, 79, 1115–1118.

Saigal, S., Lunyk, O., Larke, R. P. B., & Chevnesky, M. A. (1982). The outcome in children with congenital cytomegalovirus infection. American Journal of Diseases of Children, 136, 896–901.

Savage, M. O., Mossa, A., & Gordon, R. R. (1973). Maternal varicella infections as a cause of fetal malformations. Lancet, i, 352–354.

Sever, J. L., Ellenberg, J. H., Ley, A. C., Madden, D. L., Fucciello, D. A., Tzan, N. R., & Edmonds, D. M. (1988). Toxoplasmosis: Maternal and pediatric findings in 23,000 pregnancies. Pediatrics, 82, 181–192.

Shone, J. D., Armas, S. M., Manning, J. A., & Keith, J. D. (1966). Mumps antigen skin test in endocardial fibroelastosis. Pediatrics, 37, 423–429.

Siegel, M. (1973). Congenital malformations following chickenpox, measles, mumps, and hepatitis: Results of a cohort study. Journal of the American Medical Association, 226, 1521–1524.

Siegel, M., & Fuerst, H. T. (1966). Low birth weight and maternal virus disease: A prospective study of rubella, measles, mumps, chickenpox, and hepatitis. Journal of the American Medical Association, 197, 680–684.

Splendore, A. (1908). Un nuovo protozoa parassita dei conigli: Incontrato nelle lesioni anatomiche d'una malattia che recorda in multi punti II kola-azer dell'uomo. [A new protozoah parasite deicomigli: Found in anatomical lesions in multiple areas in a disease Kola-azer]. Rev. Soc. Sci. Sao Paolo, 3, 109–112.

Srabstein, J. C., Morris, N., Larke, R. P. B., de Sa, D. J., Castelino, B. B., & Sum, E. (1974). Is there a congenital varicella syndrome? Journal of Pediatrics, 84, 239–243.

Stagno, S. (1980). Congenital toxoplasmosis. American Journal of Diseases of Children, 134, 635–637.

Stagno, S., Pass, R. F., Dworsky, M. E., Henderson, R. E., Moore, E. G., Walton, P. D., & Alford, C. A. (1982). Congenital cytomegalovirus infection: The relative importance of primary and recurrent infection. New England Journal of Medicine, 306, 945–949.

Stevenson, R. E. (1973). The fetus and the newly born infant: Influences of the prenatal environment. St. Louis: C. V. Mosby.

St. Geme, J. W., Jr., Noren, G. R., & Adams, P. (1966). Proposed embryopathic relation between mumps virus and primary endocardial fibroelastosis. *New England Journal of Medicine*, 275, 339–347.

St. Geme, J. W., Jr., Paralta, H., & van Pelt, L. F. (1972). Intrauterine mumps virus infection of the Rhesus monkey: Abbreviated viral replication in the fetus as an explanation for postnatal split immunologic recognition. *Journal of Infectious Diseases*, 126, 249–255.

Sullivan-Bolyai, J., Hull, H. F., Wilson, C., & Corey, L. (1983). Neonatal herpes simplex virus infection in King County, Washington: Increasing incidence and epidemiologic correlates. *Journal of the American Medical Association*, 250, 3059–3062.

Turner, R., Shehab, Z., Osborne, K., & Hendley, J. O. (1982). Shedding and survival of herpes simplex virus from fever blisters. *Pediatrics*, 70, 547–549.

Veale, H. (1866). History of an epidemic of Rötheln, with observations on its pathology. *Edinburgh Medical Journal*, 12, 404–414.

Walker, W. M., & McKee, A. P. (1959). Asian influenza in pregnancy: Relationship to fetal anomalies. *Obstetrics and Gynecology*, 13, 394–398.

Wesselhoeft, C. (1947). Rubella (German measles). *New England Journal of Medicine*, 236, 943–950, 978–988.

Whitley, R. J., Nahmias, A. J., Soong, S., Galasso, G. G., Fleming, C. L., & Alford, C. A. (1980). Vidarabine therapy of neonatal herpes simplex virus infection. *Pediatrics*, 66, 495–501.

Whitley, R. J., Nahmias, A. J., Visintine, A. M., Fleming, C. L., & Alford, C. A. (1980). The natural history of herpes simplex virus infection of mother and newborn. *Pediatrics*, 66, 489–494.

Whitley, R. J., Yeager, A., Kartus, P., Bryson, Y., Connor, J. D., Alford, C. A., Nahmias, A., & Soong, S. (1983). Neonatal herpes simplex infection: A follow-up evaluation of vidarabine therapy. *Pediatrics*, 72, 778–785.

Williamson, W. D., Desmond, M. M., LaFevers, N., Taber, L. H., Catlin, F. I., & Weaver, T. G. (1982). Symptomatic congenital cytomegalovirus. *American Journal of Diseases of Children*, 136, 902–905.

Wilson, C. B., Desmonts, G., Couvreur, J., & Remington, J. S. (1979). Lymphocyte transformation in the diagnosis of congenital toxoplasma infection. *Program and Abstracts 19th Interscience Conference on Antimicrobial Agents and Chemotherapy* (Abstract No. 449).

Wilson, C. B., Remington, J. S., Stagno, S., & Reynolds, D. W. (1980). Development of adverse sequelae in children born with subclinical congenital toxoplasma infection. *Pediatrics*, 66, 767–774.

Wilson, M. G., Heins, H. L., Imagawa, D. T., & Adams, J. M. (1959). Teratogenic effects of Asian influenza. *Journal of the American Medical Association*, 171, 638–641.

Wolf, A., Cowen, D., & Paige, B. (1939). Human toxoplasmosis: Occurrence in infants of encephalomyelitis, verification by transmission to animals. *Science*, 89, 226–227.

# 7 | H. Eugene Hoyme

# TERATOGENIC CAUSES OF DEVELOPMENTAL DISABILITIES

A teratogen is defined as "a drug, chemical, infectious, or environmental agent which by acting during the embryonic or fetal period alters morphology or subsequent function in the postnatal period" (Shepard, 1979, p. 2). The concept that environmental agents are significant causative factors in the etiology of developmental disabilities is a relatively new one. It was not until the recognition in 1961 when prenatal exposure to thalidomide caused serious human fetal malformations that the medical community, and the public in general, became acutely aware of environmental insults causing serious birth defects in human fetuses (Lenz, 1961; McBride, 1961).

This chapter discusses mechanisms of teratogenesis, methods of teratogen identification, and known human teratogens and nonteratogens. It is important to recognize the role teratogens play in the etiology of developmental disabilities, because these disabilities are potentially totally preventable through public education and awareness.

## MECHANISMS OF TERATOGENESIS

Teratogens exert their most significant adverse effects during the metabolically active periods of embryonic growth and development (Wilson, 1973). A teratogenic insult before implantation (prior to 14 days postconception in the human) has little effect on morphogenesis because of an "all or none" phenomenon—the embryo either dies or regenerates completely. Insults during the period of organogenesis (days 14 to 60) are most apt to produce major morphologic alterations, because this is the period of the most rapid cellular proliferation and differentiation. During the remainder of gestation, the fetus is less susceptible to major morphologic changes; however, subtle and minor changes in structure and function can occur. The developing human nervous system is particularly susceptible to teratogenic insults throughout gestation, a point that is illustrated by discussion of the teratogenic effects of alcohol later in this chapter.

Animal studies have been particularly useful in defining how teratogens work. Mechanisms of teratogenesis can be more completely delineated in animals, because teratogenic insults can be carefully controlled and the results scrupulously monitored in a laboratory setting. Animal studies have shown that teratogens exhibit time specificity of action within a species. Animal studies have also found marked species-to-species variation in response to various teratogens. For example, aspirin, corticosteroids, and several vitamin deficiencies are teratogenic in mice and rats but appear to be safe in humans (Shepard, 1979). This species-to-species variation implies that there exist genetic differences that help determine susceptibility to teratogens. Fraser and his colleagues have illustrated this genetic difference in susceptibility by studying the incidence of cleft lip in certain inbred strains of mice (Fraser, 1969; Fraser & Pashayan, 1970). The A/J mouse inhibits a higher natural incidence of cleft lip and cleft palate than do other strains. In addition, most environmental agents, such as aspirin and corticosteroids known to produce clefts, are more effective in the A/J mouse. As with mice, it follows that certain human genotypes are more likely susceptible than others to the adverse effects of specific teratogens. Animal studies have also shown that there exists in most cases a linear relationship between maternal teratogen dosage and the degree of adverse fetal effects. For example, both sucrose and sodium chloride given in large doses can alter fetal morphogenesis (Shepard, 1979). Finally, animal studies have shown that there is a high degree of correlation, approximately 70%, between mutagenicity and teratogenicity of various agents (Shepard, 1979).

## METHODS FOR
## IDENTIFICATION OF HUMAN TERATOGENS

With the advent of environmental exposures to potentially toxic materials, such as those at Love Canal and the exposure of both servicemen and civilians to Agent Orange in Vietnam, the subject of teratogenesis has become a controversial topic at the forefront of public attention. Unfortunately, rumors, anecdotal reports, and marginal scientific studies all too often receive undue attention by the popular press causing unnecessary anxiety in pregnant women exposed to suspected teratogens. A survey of 15 popular magazines revealed that 55% of the articles regarding teratology are inaccurate (Gunderson, Martinez, Carey, Kochenour, & Emery, 1986). The constant barrage of the public by such reports may lead to generalized apathy toward all educational efforts aimed at decreasing or preventing exposures to known human teratogens. One of the tasks for professionals dealing with developmental disabilities is to aid the public in interpreting scientific reports and to discern those agents for which clear evidence of teratogenicity in humans exists.

Much of the public confusion about teratogens lies in the methods previously used for screening agents for teratogenicity. Animal studies have been widely used; however, no human teratogen has ever been identified by animal studies. Thalidomide is the prime example of a human teratogen that was not identified by premarketing animal studies. There are at least 14 publications indicating a lack of teratogenicity of thalidomide in mice and rats (Cahen, 1966). It was later found to be a potent teratogen in rabbits, monkeys, and humans. This wide interspecies variation in susceptibility led Fraser (1964) to conclude that "the final proof of whether a drug is likely to be teratogenic in man must be sought in man" (p. 169).

In terms of studies in humans, retrospective epidemiologic investigations have been most frequently used to attempt to identify teratogens. However, no human teratogen has been identified through a retrospective epidemiologic study. These attempts have failed because of flaws inherent in the methods employed (Jones, 1981; Shepard, 1982). In many of these studies, pregnancy records of women who have given birth to children with major malformations are examined. These studies rely heavily on an accurate maternal history, often taken months after exposure. Over-the-counter drugs and agents in the workplace are often not accurately considered in such investigations. In other studies, birth records of children with intrauterine exposure to a particular agent are examined for major malformations. Such studies do not detect patterns of malformation and would most likely have failed to detect the fetal alcohol syndrome or the fetal hydantoin syndrome. In addition, intrauterine growth deficiency, the most sensitive indicator of teratogenic insult, is generally not reported on birth or death certificates. Another drawback to epidemiologic studies is the large number of cases needed to prove the teratogenicity of a particular agent at a certain probability level. It is possible that there exist small subpopulations of individuals with genetically heightened teratogenic susceptibility to a relatively safe drug or agent. Epidemiologic studies might overlook the existence of such at-risk individuals.

However, those human teratogens previously identified have been discerned because of the observations of astute clinicians, thalidomide (Lenz, 1961; McBride, 1961) and alcohol (Jones, Smith, Ulleland, & Streissguth, 1973) being good examples. Prospective clinical studies in populations of humans have heretofore not been possible because of the obvious moral and ethical problems inherent in them.

An alternative method for determining teratogenicity in humans is the utilization of a teratogen registry (Jones, 1981). Although—as mentioned above—ethical considerations preclude administering potential teratogens to human populations to study their effects, pregnant women are carrying out their own "experiments of nature" all the time. The pregnant American woman takes an average of 11 different drugs during her pregnancy (Doering & Stewart, 1978). A teratogen registry takes advantage of this experiment of nature. A woman with a potential teratogenic exposure (or her physician) usually contacts the registry by telephone. At the time of the first telephone contact, data regarding the nature, time, and dosage of the exposure are recorded and a summary of available information about the potential teratogen is given to the caller. The woman is then invited to participate in the registry follow-up. One month following the expected date of confinement, women who expressed interest in follow-up are contacted for an appointment. At the follow-up visit, the child is examined by a dysmorphologist and the results are discussed with the family. A letter is then sent to the obstetrician and pediatrician, and the case is entered into the registry data bank. In this way, prospective data regarding teratogenic exposure can be obtained.

More accurate reporting of the nature of exposure is possible because the exposed woman is ascertained shortly after her exposure. Additionally, in the follow-up visit, the child is examined carefully to detect any apparent malformation. The California Teratogen Registry, the first such registry, was established in 1979 (Jones, 1981). Many such services have now been established throughout the United States and Canada. This pooling of data collected could prove to be a very useful tool for identification of new human teratogens.

## KNOWN HUMAN TERATOGENS

Those agents for which sufficient data exist to indicate definitive teratogenicity in humans are set forth in the following three subsections: infectious agents; drugs, chemicals, and environmental agents; and maternal disease or altered metabolic state.

### Infectious Agents

A number of infectious agents (toxoplasmosis, rubella, Herpes virus hominis I and II, syphilis, cytomegalovirus, HIV, and others) have been associated with adverse fetal development when contracted by pregnant women during early gestation (Shepard, 1980). The nature and scope of these prenatal infections are discussed by Pueschel, Scola, and McConnell, in Chapter 6, this volume.

## Drugs, Chemicals, and Environmental Agents

*Alcohol*

Although fetal alcohol syndrome was not described in the medical literature until 1973 (Jones et al., 1973), in retrospect, civilization has been at least subliminally aware of the adverse effects of alcohol on pregnancy outcome for centuries. For example, there are biblical references warning against alcohol abuse in early pregnancy: "Behold, thou shalt conceive, and bear a son; and now drink no wine nor strong drink . . . " (Judges 13:7). And Vulcan, the blacksmith of the gods in Roman mythology, was purportedly the handicapped son of a chronic alcoholic woman. Despite this underlying awareness, alcoholism and the adverse effects of alcohol on the fetus continue to be massive public health problems. Depending on the population studied, the incidence of full-blown fetal alcohol syndrome varies from 1 in 300 to 1 in 2,000 live births. Fetal alcohol syndrome occurs in 30%–40% of all infants born to chronic alcoholic women (Streissguth, Landesman-Dwyer, Martin, & Smith, 1980).

The primary features of the disorder are prenatal onset growth deficiency, delayed development, and a variety of structural defects (Streissguth et al., 1980). Children with fetal alcohol syndrome are usually below the third percentile in height, weight, and head circumference, with head circumference being the most severely affected. The most significant adverse effects of alcohol on fetal development are those on the central nervous system, including mental retardation (average IQ of 60), poor motor development, tremulousness, hyperactivity, and decreased attention span (Streissguth et al., 1980). A variety of gross and ultrastructural abnormalities in brain development have been noted (Clarren, Alvord, Sumi, Streissguth, & Smith, 1978; Majewski, Fischbach, Pfeiffer, & Bierich, 1978). The facial characteristics of fetal alcohol syndrome include short palpebral fissures, flat nasal bridge, epicanthal folds, short nose, indistinct philtrum, thin upper lip, and hypoplastic midface. Other anomalies include joint contractures, altered palm crease patterns, nail hypoplasia, and congenital heart defects (present in about 30% of cases) (Streissguth et al., 1980).

Since the initial description of this disorder, it has become apparent that there exists a spectrum of effects of alcohol on fetal development, with fetal alcohol syndrome representing the most severe manifestation of these effects. Although 33% of infants of chronic alcoholic women manifested full-blown fetal alcohol syndrome, 43% had a partial effect, and only 24% of infants were found to be normal (Olegard et al., 1979). With respect to moderate amounts of alcohol intake during pregnancy, Hanson, Streissguth, and Smith (1978) found that 11% of offspring born to women who drank between one and two ounces of absolute ethanol daily during the first trimester of pregnancy have features consistent with the prenatal effects of alcohol. No definitive data are available concerning either lesser amounts of alcohol or "binge drinking" during gestation. Thus, until further studies are complete, as the American Medical Association's Council on Scientific Affairs (1983) stated, "the safest course is abstinence" (see Evrard & Scola, Chapter 3, and von Oeyen, Chapter 5, this volume).

## Cigarette Smoking

Studies indicate that maternal cigarette smoking during pregnancy leads to a decrease in birth weight of 170 g to 250 g (Youmoszai, Kacie, & Haworth, 1968). The minimum number of cigarettes necessary to cause growth deficiency has not been established; however, Russell, Raylor, and Madison, (1966) showed intrauterine growth deficiency in infants whose mothers smoked 5 or more cigarettes daily. The degree of growth deficiency seems to be directly proportional to the number of cigarettes smoked daily, with the most markedly growth deficient babies seen in the heaviest smokers (Simpson, 1957). Birth length has been studied less completely; however, Hardy and Mellitis (1972) reported birth length to be 1.3 cm less in offspring of smokers as compared to nonsmokers. There has been no difference noted in head circumference.

Effects of maternal smoking on long-term behavior and developmental performance of offspring are controversial. Positive studies have shown effects on reading ability and social adjustment (Davie, Butler, & Goldstein, 1972), mathematical skills (Dunn, McBurney, Ingram, & Hunter, 1977), and overall cognitive abilities (Nichols, 1977). However, Hardy and Mellitis (1972) found no effects on developmental performance at 4 or 7 years of age in offspring of smoking versus nonsmoking mothers (see Evrard & Scola, Chapter 3, and von Oeyen, Chapter 5, this volume).

## Aminopterin

Aminopterin and its methyl derivative, methotrexate, are folic acid antagonists. Aminopterin is a potent abortifacient when administered prior to 40 days gestation (Shepard, 1980). When taken later in the first trimester, a variety of serious structural defects and intrauterine growth deficiency have been noted. Milunsky, Graef, and Gaynor (1968) reviewed eight such cases: four ended in abortion, two died in the perinatal period, and two survived. All manifested intrauterine growth deficiency, defects in calvarial ossification, prominent eyes, hypoplastic supraorbital ridges, ocular hypertelorism, small low-set ears, micrognathia, and limb anomalies. Follow-up of the affected children who survived revealed growth deficiency and mild developmental delay (Howard & Rudd, 1976; Milunsky et al., 1968).

## Diethylstilbesterol

In 1971, it was first reported that the incidence of clear cell adenocarcinoma of the vagina was greater in women whose mothers had been treated with diethylstilbesterol during the first trimester of their pregnancies (Herbst, Ulfelder, & Poskanzer, 1971). Subsequently, over 2 million women who were prenatally exposed to diethylstilbesterol have been ascertained, and only 350 cases of adenocarcinoma have been found. Thus, the associated risk of adenocarcinoma in this group is quite small. Other problems associated with maternal diethylstilbesterol exposure have been delineated. Structural defects of the genital tract have been found in prenatally exposed females, leading to reproductive problems (Kaufman, Binder, Gray, & Adam, 1977), and genitourinary anomalies have been diagnosed in prenatally exposed males (Gill, Schumacher, & Bibbo, 1976). The exact incidence and impact of these defects have not been determined.

## Diphenylhydantoin

Prenatal exposure to diphenylhydantoin (Dilantin) has been associated with a pattern of malformation termed the "fetal hydantoin syndrome." The possible teratogenic effects of anticonvulsants were first suggested by Meadow in 1968. Hanson and Smith (1975) looked specifically at Dilantin and subsequently described the characteristics of fetal hydantoin syndrome. It is now felt that Dilantin exerts a spectrum of effects on fetal development, with the fetal hydantoin syndrome representing the most severe manifestation of those effects. Features of the fetal hydantoin syndrome include prenatal onset growth deficiency, mild to moderate mental deficiency, wide anterior fontanel, ocular hypertelorism, metopic ridge, depressed nasal bridge, short nose, bowed upper lip, cleft lip and cleft palate, hypoplasia of distal phalanges, nail hypoplasia, and low arch dermal ridge patterns (Smith, 1987).

There is some evidence that barbiturates taken in conjunction with diphenylhydantoin may increase the risk to the fetus (Speidel & Meadow, 1972). No safe minimum level of hydantoin intake, below which there is no increased teratogenic risk, has been determined. Hanson, Myrianthopolous, Harvey, and Smith (1976) found the risk for the hydantoin exposed fetus having the fetal hydantoin syndrome to be 10%, and the risk for having some manifestations of the disorder to be 33%. Of most significance, they found a 38% prevalence of developmental delay in exposed children.

## Heroin and Methadone

Structural defects have not been associated with prenatal exposure to either heroin or methadone. However, both intrauterine growth deficiency and prematurity have been prominent features of such exposure in utero (Stone, Salerno, Green, & Zelson, 1971; Zelson, Lee, & Casalino, 1973). The degree and incidence of intrauterine growth deficiency are more marked following exposure to heroin than following exposure to methadone. Zelson et al. (1973) found a 35% incidence of growth deficiency in heroin exposed pregnancies versus a 22% incidence in the methadone exposed group.

In a study of 3- and 6-year-old children born to heroin addicted mothers, Wilson, McCreary, Kean, and Baxter (1979) noted both growth deficiency and a 14% prevalence of microcephaly. They also found these children to have poor social adjustment and poor perceptual and organizational abilities. IQs were not affected. Perception and learning have been less well studied in children who were exposed to methadone in utero.

## Isotretinoin and Etretinate

Vitamin A and its congeners have been found to be teratogenic in a variety of laboratory animals (Kamm, 1982). Isotretinoin, 13-cis retinoic acid (Accutane), has been marketed as a mode of treatment for severe cystic acne. Because of its teratogenicity in animals, it has been advised that women who are pregnant or who plan to become pregnant not be treated with isotretinoin.

Reports have delineated a recognizable pattern of malformations in infants of women taking Accutane during the first trimester of pregnancy (De La Cruz, Sun, Vangvanichyakorn, & Desposito, 1984; Fernhoff & Lammer, 1984; Lammer, 1985; Lott, Bocian, Pribam, & Leitner, 1984). Lammer (1985) reported characteristic craniofacial, cardiac, and central nervous system malformations in 19 prenatally exposed infants. The craniofacial malformations included microtia or anotia in 15 of the 19 children, micrognathia in 5, and cleft palate in 3. Cardiac anomalies reflected abnormalities in aortic-pulmonary septation in 7 children, 4 of whom also had thymic anomalies. Central nervous system malformations were noted in 17 of the infants which included hydrocephalus in 9 and microcephaly in 4. Lammer speculated that abnormal differentiation and migration of cephalic neural crest cells in early embryogenesis might be the underlying mechanism of isotretinoin teratogenesis. Of 18 women ascertained during pregnancy to be taking isotretinoin, 13 (72%) had spontaneous abortions, 4 (22%) had normal children, and 1 (6%) had a malformed child (Fernhoff & Lammer, 1984).

The risk of poor fetal outcome, therefore, appears to be great in pregnancies with first trimester isotretinoin exposure. These data indicate that isotretinoin should not be prescribed to sexually active women unless effective contraceptive methods are used. Women taking isotretinoin should be counseled about the potential risks to the fetus should they become pregnant while taking this medication.

Another vitamin A derivative, etretinate (Tegison), has caused additional concern. This medication for severe psoriasis has been proven to be teratogenic in both animals and humans. It is stored in fat and has been documented in the serum in small amounts up to 1 year after the medication has been discontinued. The pattern of malformation observed closely resembles that associated with isotretinoin (Lammer, 1988).

## Lithium

Nora, Nora, and Toews (1974) first observed an increase in Ebstein anomaly, a rare malformation of the tricuspid valve, among infants prenatally exposed to lithium. Results from a registry of lithium treated pregnancies confirm this association with congenital heart defects. Weinstein and Goldfield (1975) found 11 cases of congenital heart defects among 143 offspring with intrauterine lithium exposure. Four of these 11 children had Ebstein anomaly. These data suggest that lithium is teratogenic in humans during early gestation. Lithium may be safely resumed by a pregnant woman once morphogenesis of the heart is essentially complete (about 45 days post conception).

## Methyl Mercury

The tragic story of the methyl mercury poisoning of Minimata Bay in Japan drew attention to the fact that industrial pollutants can cause serious human fetal maldevelopment. Between 1952 and 1965, offspring born to women who had ingested fish contaminated with mercury manifested severe neurologic dysfunction with mental retardation, microcephaly, and spasticity. Murakami (1972) reviewed 25 cases of fetal Minimata disease and reported that cerebral palsy was the main feature. Other structural defects were rare.

Organic mercury has no affinity to the developing central nervous system post partum. It appears that central nervous system damage can only occur following exposure in either the embryonic or the fetal periods of development (Shepard, 1979).

## Radiation

Some studies indicate that although high doses of radiation are damaging to the fetus, diagnostic X-rays are not believed to be teratogenic (Brent & Gorson, 1972; Jones, 1981; Swartz & Reichling, 1978). From a practical standpoint, risk to the fetus does not become significant until after a dose of greater than 10 rads has been absorbed. Most diagnostic X-ray studies involve doses of 500 millirads or less (Jones, 1981). Large doses of radiation following the atomic blasts in Hiroshima and Nagasaki were associated with increased fetal loss and an increased rate of microcephaly and mental retardation in surviving exposed fetuses (Blot & Miller, 1973; Plummer, 1952). Similar results might be expected following large therapeutic doses of radiation in the treatment of malignancies.

## Tetracycline

Tetracycline taken after the 4th month of pregnancy may lead to brownish staining of the deciduous teeth in the exposed child (Baden, 1970). The teeth are also more susceptible to caries and manifest hypoplastic enamel. Although the permanent teeth are usually not affected, administration close to term may lead to staining of the crowns of the permanent teeth.

## Thalidomide

Thalidomide is the prototype of the human teratogen. As mentioned earlier, thalidomide illustrates many of the general principles of teratogens, marked interspecies variability in susceptibility and time specificity of action. Thalidomide, a sedative-hypnotic agent, is a potent teratogen in man with as little as 0.9 ug/ml in the circulation sufficient to harm the developing fetus (Beckmann & Kampf, 1961). One study showed that ingestion by the mother of 100 mg or more on days 21–36 following conception resulted in fetal malformations (Nowack, 1965). Best estimates of the number of affected children born who were prenatally exposed to thalidomide are between 7,000 and 8,000 (Lenz, 1966). Most affected babies were born in West Germany, England, Wales, Canada, and Japan. Only 17 affected children were born in the United States, where the drug was not approved for general usage.

The pattern of malformation seen in affected infants includes phocomelia, polydactyly, syndactyly, facial capillary hemangiomata, hydrocephaly, renal anomalies, cardiovascular anomalies, ear and eye defects, and intestinal anomalies (Mellin & Katzenstein, 1962); intelligence is normal. Despite the wealth of studies concerning thalidomide, its exact mechanism of action in terms of teratogenesis remains unknown.

## Trimethadione

German, Kowal, and Ethlers (1970) first suggested that prenatal exposure to the anticonvulsant trimethadione (Tridione) caused malformations in the fetus. Subsequently, Zackai, Mellman, Neiderer, and Hanson (1975) described the fetal Tridione syndrome. Features include prenatal onset growth deficiency, mental deficiency, midfacial hypoplasia, short nose with anteverted nares, flat nasal bridge, mild synophrys with an unusual upslant to the eyebrows, strabismus, ptosis, cleft lip and cleft palate, unusual cupped or rectangular pinnae with overlapping helices, and cardiovascular and genital defects. The incidence of this disorder in the offspring of women taking Tridione is unknown.

## Valproic Acid

A teratogenic effect of valproic acid intake during pregnancy was suggested by Robert (1982) from the birth defects surveillance system of the Institut Europeen des Genomutations in Lyon, France. There, during 1976 and between 1978 and 1982, 146 cases of meningomyelocele were ascertained. Among these, 9 (6.2%) of the mothers had epilepsy and had taken valproic acid during the first trimester. Statistical analysis of the data shows a significant increase in meningomyelocele in those women who took valproic acid during early gestation. The frequency of spina bifida in pregnancies exposed to valproate is unknown. However, some studies indicate that the risk is 1%–1.5% (Bjerkedal et al., 1982; Lindhout & Schmidt, 1986).

Additional malformations have been reported in exposed infants, including a variety of facial alterations comprising the fetal valproate syndrome. Facial characteristics include prominent forehead, flat nasal bridge, short nose with anteverted nares, ocular hypertelorism, small down-turned mouth, and a long thin upper lip (Ardinger et al., 1988; DiLiberti, Harndon, Dennis, & Curry, 1984).

## Warfarin

Ingestion of the anticoagulant warfarin (Coumadin) during pregnancy has led to a pattern of fetal malformation termed the fetal warfarin syndrome. Principal features include prenatal onset growth deficiency, seizures, marked nasal hypoplasia, and chondrodysplasia punctata (Shaul & Hall, 1977). It now appears that the central nervous system anomalies encountered are secondary to exposure in the second and third trimesters, whereas the facial abnormalities and stippled ephiphyses are associated with Coumadin exposure during weeks 6–9 post conception. The incidence of the fetal warfarin syndrome in offspring at risk due to maternal Coumadin exposure is unknown. However, in one review, Hall, Panti, and Wilson (1980) found an adverse pregnancy outcome in one-third of 418 offspring reported in the literature with prenatal Coumadin exposure.

## Maternal Disease or Altered Metabolic State

### Hyperthermia

There exists a large body of animal data that implicated hyperthermia as a potent teratogen in guinea pigs (Edwards, 1969), rabbits (Brinsmade & Rubsaamen, 1957), rats (Skreb & Frank, 1963), hamsters (Kilham & Ferm, 1976), and others. Retrospective studies have reported maternal hyperthermia as being teratogenic in humans (Miller, Smith, & Shephard, 1978; Smith, Clarren, & Harvey, 1978). Pleet, Graham, Harvey, and Smith (1980) reported a series of 23 retrospectively ascertained children prenatally exposed to temperatures of 38.9°C or above between 4 and 14 weeks of gestation. They noted a pattern of malformation, including prenatal onset growth deficiency, central nervous system defects (mental retardation, microcephaly, hypotonia, and microphthalmia), variable first and second branchial arch defects, as well as midface hypoplasia, micrognathia, cleft lip with or without cleft palate, and malformed ears. Although these retrospective studies are not conclusive, they suggest teratogenic effects of hyperthermia on the human fetus.

## Maternal Diabetes Mellitus

The overall incidence of congenital anomalies in infants of diabetic mothers is two to four times greater than in infants born to women without diabetes (Breidahl, 1966; Soler, Walsh, & Malins, 1976). The anomalies involve the cardiovascular, skeletal, spinal, genitourinary, gastrointestinal, and central nervous systems. Two particular patterns of malformation have been seen with increased frequency in infants of diabetic mothers: the caudal regression sequence (Gabe, 1977) and the femoral hypoplasia—unusual facies syndrome (Johnson, Carey, Gooch, Peterson, & Beattie, 1983). Both may result from an early gestational teratogenic insult to the caudal mesoderm of the developing embryo. Milunsky, Alpert, Kitzmiller, Younger, and Neff (1982) reported a tenfold increase in neural tube defects in infants of diabetic mothers (19.5/1,000). They now recommend routine maternal serum alpha-fetoprotein screening as part of regular prenatal care for diabetic women in light of these data.

Studies indicate that tight control of diabetes prior to and during early gestation in diabetic women decreases the risk for congenital anomalies as compared to the offspring of diabetic women who are poorly controlled (Miller et al., 1981) (see Evrard & Scola, Chapter 3, and Coustan, Chapter 10, this volume).

## Maternal Phenylketonuria

Since newborn screening on a widespread basis for phenylketonuria (PKU) was begun in the 1960s, there are now thousands of normal children and adolescents with PKU. These children were ascertained early in life, maintained on a low phenylalanine diet, and many of them are now coming of reproductive age. Because half of these individuals are female, their offspring are potentially subject to the adverse effects of high maternal phenylalanine levels during pregnancy. Lenke and Levy (1980) reviewed 524 pregnancies in 155 mothers with phenylketonuria or hyperphenylalaninemia. The clinical features of those offspring who were subjected to high maternal phenylalanine levels include mental retardation, microcephaly, congenital heart disease, and prenatal onset growth deficiency. Later neurologic sequelae include seizures and spasticity. Additionally, women with PKU may have an increased frequency of spontaneous abortion (Mabry, 1978).

The goal of managing pregnancies in women with PKU is to provide a low phenylalanine diet throughout the gestational period in order to minimize risks to the embryo/fetus. The earlier the diet is instituted (preferably prior to conception), the better the outcome. Ideally, phenylalanine blood levels between 4 and 6 mg/dl should be maintained to decrease fetal risks (Lenke & Levy, 1980) (see Cashore, Chapter 12, this volume).

## KNOWN NONTERATOGENS IN HUMANS

Drugs, chemicals, and environmental agents for which there exist sufficient data to indicate nonteratogenicity in humans include amphetamines, Clomid, corticosteroids, diagnostic X-rays, LSD, and Tofranil. Multiple studies have failed to demonstrate significant adverse fetal effects of these agents during human pregnancy (Jones, 1981).

## TERATOGEN COUNSELING

In counseling the pregnant woman following a potentially teratogenic exposure, it is most important to first obtain the clinical facts with respect to the exact nature of the exposure and timing of gestation. Second, all available data must be collected before advising the patient. More often than not, the data will be inconclusive as to the teratogenicity of a particular insult. Although no easy answers may be forthcoming, there are several principles that are quite helpful when counseling the pregnant patient at risk (Jones, 1981). Pregnant women deserve to know all the facts regarding an exposure that they may have had, whether the facts are conclusive or not. The opportunity to discuss the data with a knowledgeable, sympathetic counselor may be therapeutic in and of itself. Careful examination of a prenatally exposed child, focusing on particular parental concerns, may be the only way to alleviate parental anxiety.

## CONCLUSION

This chapter summarizes the most important agents that have been found to be teratogenic, including infectious agents, certain drugs, chemicals, and environmental compounds, as well as maternal disease and altered metabolic states in the pregnant woman. Moreover, mechanisms of teratogenesis and methods of teratogen identification are described. Particular emphasis is placed on the role teratogens play in the etiology of handicapping conditions and how public education and awareness of these concerns can prevent developmental disabilities from occuring.

## REFERENCES

American Medical Association's Council on Scientific Affairs. (1983). Fetal effects of maternal alcohol use. *Journal of the American Medical Association, 249,* 2517–2521.

Ardinger, H. H., Atkins, J. F., Blackston, D., Elsas, L. J., Clarren, S. K., Livingstone, S., Hannery, D. B., Pellock, J. M., Herod, M. J., Lammer, E. J., Majewski, H., Schinzel, A., Toriello, H. V., & Hanson, J. W. (1988). Verification of the fetal valproate syndrome phenotype. *American Journal of Medical Genetics*, 29, 171–185.

Baden, E. (1970). Environmental pathology of the teeth. In R. J. Gorlin & H. M. Goldman (Eds.), *Thoma's oral pathology* (6th ed., Vol. I, pp. 184–238). St. Louis: C. V. Mosby.

Beckmann, R., & Kampf, H. H. (1961). Zur quantitativen Bestimmung und zum qualitativen Nachweis von Thalidomid [The quantitative diagnosis and qualitative proof of Thalidomide]. *Arzneimittel Forschung, 11*, 45–48.

Bjerkedal, T., Cziezel, A., Goujard, J., Kallen, B., Mastroiacova, P., Nevin, N., Oakley, G., & Robert, E. (1982). Valproic acid and spina bifida. *Lancet, ii*, 1096.

Blot, W. J., & Miller, R. W. (1973). Mental retardation following in utero exposure to the atomic bombs of Hiroshima and Nagasaki. *Radiology, 106*, 617–619.

Breidahl, H. D. (1966). The growth and development of children born to mothers with diabetes. *Medical Journal of Australia, 1*, 268–270.

Brent, R., & Gorson, R. O. (1972). Radiation exposure in pregnancy. *Current Problems in Radiology, 2*, 3–12.

Brinsmade, A. B., & Rubsaamen, H. (1957). Zur teratogenetischen Wirkung von unspezifischem Fieber auf den sich entwickelnden Kaninchenembryo [Evaluation of teratogenic effects of non-specific fever on rabbit embryoes]. *Beiträge zur Pathologie und Anatomie, 117*, 154–155.

Cahen, R. L. (1966). Experimental and clinical chemoteratogenesis. *Advances in Pharmacology and Chemotherapy, 4*, 263–349.

Clarren, S. K., Alvord, E. C., Sumi, M., Streissguth, A. P., & Smith, D. W. (1978). Brain malformation related to prenatal exposure to ethanol. *Journal of Pediatrics, 92*, 64–67.

Davie, R., Butler, N., & Goldstein, H. (1972). *From birth to seven: The second report of the national child development study (1958 cohort)*. London: Longman, in association with the National Children's Bureau.

De La Cruz, E., Sun, S., Vangvanichyakorn, K., & Desposito, F. (1984). Multiple congenital malformations associated with maternal isotretinoin therapy. *Pediatrics, 74*, 428–430.

DiLiberti, J. H., Harndon, P. A., Dennis, N. R., & Curry, C. J. R. (1984). The fetal valproate syndrome. *American Journal of Medical Genetics, 19*, 473–481.

Doering, P. L., & Stewart, R. B. (1978). The extent and character of drug consumption during pregnancy. *Journal of the American Medical Association, 239*, 843–846.

Dunn, H. G., McBurney, A. K., Ingram, S., & Hunter, C. M. (1977). Maternal cigarette smoking during pregnancy and the child's subsequent development: Vol. II. Neurological and intellectual maturation to the age of 6½ years. *Canadian Journal of Public Health, 68*, 43–50.

Edwards, M. J. (1969). Congenital defects in guinea pigs: Fetal resorptions, abortions, and malformations following induced hyperthermia during early gestation. *Teratology, 2*, 213–328.

Fernhoff, P. M., & Lammer, E. J. (1984). Craniofacial features of isotretinoin embryopathy. *Journal of Pediatrics, 105*, 595–597.

Fraser, F. C. (1964). Experimental teratogenesis in relation to congenital malformations in man. In M. Fishbein (Ed.), *Proceedings of the Second International Conference on Congenital Malformations*. New York: International Medical Congress Ltd.

Fraser, F. C. (1969). Gene-environment interactions in the production of cleft palate. In H. Nishimura, J. R. Miller, & M. Yasuda (Eds.), *Methods for teratologic studies in experimental animals and man* (pp. 34–49). Tokyo: Igaku Shoiu Ltd.

Fraser, F. C., & Pashayan, H. (1970). Relation of face shape to susceptibility to congenital cleft lip. *Journal of Medical Genetics, 7,* 112–117.

Gabe, S. G. (1977). Congenital malformations in infants of diabetic mothers. *Obstetrical and Gynecological Survey, 32,* 125–132.

German, J., Kowal, A., & Ethlers, K. H. (1970). Trimethadione and human teratogenesis. *Teratology, 3,* 349–361.

Gill, W. B., Schumacher, G. F. B., & Bibbo, M. (1976). Structural and functional abnormalities in the sex organs of male offspring of mothers treated with DES. *Journal of Reproductive Medicine, 16,* 147–153.

Gunderson, S. A., Martinez, L. P., Carey, J. C., Kochenour, N. K., & Emery, M. G. (1986). Critical review of articles regarding pregnancy exposures in popular magazines. *Teratology, 33,* 82C.

Hall, J. G., Panti, R. M., & Wilson, K. M. (1980). Maternal and fetal sequelae of anticoagulation during pregnancy. *American Journal of Medicine, 68,* 122–140.

Hanson, J. W., Myrianthopolous, N. C., Harvey, M. A. S., & Smith, D. W. (1976). Risks to the offspring of women treated with hydantoin anticonvulsant, with emphasis on the fetal hydantoin syndrome. *Journal of Pediatrics, 89,* 662–668.

Hanson, J. W., & Smith, D. W. (1975). The fetal hydantoin syndrome. *Journal of Pediatrics, 87,* 285–290.

Hanson, J. W., Streissguth, A. P., & Smith, D. W. (1978). The effects of moderate alcohol consumption during pregnancy on fetal growth and morphogenesis. *Journal of Pediatrics, 92,* 457–460.

Hardy, J. B., & Mellitis, D. D. (1972). Does maternal smoking during pregnancy have a long-term effect on the child? *Lancet, ii,* 1332–1336.

Herbst, A. L., Ulfelder, H., & Poskanzer, D. C. (1971). Adenocarcinoma of the vagina: Association of maternal stilbesterol therapy with tumor appearance in young women. *New England Journal of Medicine, 284,* 878–881.

Howard, N. J., & Rudd, N. L. (1976). *The natural history of amniopterin-induced embryopathy.* Paper presented at the Birth Defects Conference, University of British Columbia, Vancouver.

Johnson, J. P., Carey, J. C., Gooch, W. M., Peterson, J., & Beattie, J. F. (1983). Femoral hypoplasia-unusual facies syndrome in infants of diabetic mothers. *Journal of Pediatrics, 102,* 866–872.

Jones, K. L. (1981). Teratogens: What we know and don't know about them. In M. M. Kaback (Ed.), *Genetic issues in pediatric and obstetric practice* (pp. 109–130). Chicago: Yearbook Medical Publishers, Inc.

Jones, K. L., Smith, D. W., Ulleland, C. N., & Streissguth, A. P. (1973). Pattern of malformation in offspring of chronic alcoholic mothers. *Lancet, i,* 1267–1271.

Kamm, J. J. (1982). Toxicology, carcinogenicity, and teratogenicity of some orally administered retinoids. *Journal of the American Academy of Dermatology, 6,* 652–659.

Kaufman, R. H., Binder, G. L., Gray, P. M., & Adam, E. (1977). Upper genital tract changes associated with exposure in utero to diethylstilbesterol. *American Journal of Obstetrics and Gynecology, 128,* 52–59.

Kilham, L., & Ferm, V. H. (1976). Exencephaly in fetal hamsters exposed to hyperthermia. *Teratology, 14,* 323–326.

Lammer, E. J. (1985). Retinoic acid embryopathy. *Proceedings of the Greenwood Genetics Center, 4,* 81.

Lammer, E. J. (1988). A phenocopy of the retinoic acid embryopathy following maternal use of etretinate that ended one year before conception. *Teratology*, *37*, 472.

Lenke, R. R., & Levy, H. L. (1980). Maternal phenylketonuria and hyper-phenylalaninemia. *New England Journal of Medicine*, *303*, 1202–1208.

Lenz, W. (1961). Kindliche Missbildungen nach Medikamenten Einnahme während der Gravität? [Malformations in children prenatally exposed to drugs]. *Deutsche Medizinische Wochenschrift*, *86*, 255–257.

Lenz, W. (1966). Malformation caused by drugs in pregnancy. *American Journal of Diseases of Children*, *112*, 99–106.

Lindhout, D., & Schmidt, D. (1986). In-utero exposure to valproate and neural tube defects. *Lancet*, *ii*, 1392–1393.

Lott, J. T., Bocian, M., Pribam, H. W., & Leitner, M. (1984). Fetal hydrocephalus and ear anomalies associated with maternal use of isotretinoin. *Journal of Pediatrics*, *105*, 597–600.

Mabry, C. C. (1978). *Maternal phenylketonuria*. Paper presented at the 13th Conference of Collaborative Study of Children Treated for PKU, Tahoe, NV.

Majewski, F., Fischbach, H., Pfeiffer, J., & Bierich, J. R. (1978). Zur Frage der Interruptio bei alkoholkranken Frauen [The question of induced abortion in alcoholic women]. *Deutsche Medizinische Wochenschrift*, *103*, 895–898.

McBride, W. G. (1961). Thalidomide and congenital abnormalities. *Lancet*, *ii*, 1358.

Meadow, S. R. (1968). Anticonvulsant drugs and congenital abnormalities. *Lancet*, *ii*, 1296.

Mellin, G. W., & Katzenstein, M. (1962). The saga of thalidomide. *New England Journal of Medicine*, *267*, 1184–1193.

Miller, E., Hare, J. W., Cloherty, J. P., Dunn, J. P., Gleason, R. E., Soeldner, S., & Kitzmiller, J. L. (1981). Elevated maternal hemoglobin A1C in early pregnancy and major congenital anomalies in infants of diabetic mothers. *New England Journal of Medicine*, *304*, 1331–1334.

Miller, P., Smith, D. W., & Shepard, T. (1978). Maternal hyperthermia as a possible cause of anencephaly. *Lancet*, *ii*, 519.

Milunsky, A., Alpert, E., Kitzmiller, J. L., Younger, M. D., & Neff, R. K. (1982). Prenatal diagnosis of neural tube defects: Vol. VIII. The importance of serum alpha-fetoprotein screening in diabetic pregnant women. *American Journal of Obstetrics and Gynecology*, *142*, 1030–1032.

Milunsky, A., Graef, J. W., & Gaynor, M. F. (1968). Methotrexate-induced congenital malformations with a review of the literature. *Journal of Pediatrics*, *72*, 790–795.

Murakami, U. (1972). The effect of organic mercury on intrauterine life. In M. A. Klingberg (Ed.), *Proceedings of the First International Symposium on the Effect of Prolonged Drug Usage on Fetal Development: Advances in Experimental Medicine and Biology* (Vol. 27, pp. 301–336). New York: Plenum.

Nichols, P. L. (1977). *Minimal brain dysfunction: Association with perinatal complications*. Paper presented at the Society for Research in Child Development, New Orleans.

Nora, J. J., Nora, A. H., & Toews, W. H. (1974). Lithium, Ebstein's anomaly and other congenital heart defects. *Lancet*, *ii*, 594–595.

Nowack, E. (1965). The sensitive period in thalidomide embryopathy. *Humangenetik*, *1*, 516–536.

Olegard, R., Sabel, K. G., Aronssen, M., Sandin, B., Johansson, P. R., Carlsson, C., Kyllerman, M., Iverson, K., & Hrbek, A. (1979). Effects on the child of alcohol abuse during pregnancy: Retrospective and prospective studies. *Acta Paediatrica Scandinavica*, *275*(Suppl.), 112–121.

Pleet, H. B., Graham, J. M., Harvey, M. A., & Smith, D. W. (1980). Patterns of malformation resulting from the teratogenic effects of first trimester hyperthermia. *Pediatric Research, 14,* 587–590.

Plummer, G. (1952). Anomalies occurring in children exposed in utero to the atomic bomb in Hiroshima. *Pediatrics, 10,* 687–693.

Robert, E. (1982). Valproic acid and spina bifida: A preliminary report—France. *Morbidity and Mortality Weekly Report, 31,* 565–566.

Russell, C. S., Raylor, R., & Madison, R. N. (1966). Some effects of smoking in pregnancy. *British Journal of Obstetrics and Gynaecology, 73,* 742–746.

Shaul, W. L., & Hall, J. G. (1977). Multiple congenital anomalies associated with oral anticoagulants. *American Journal of Obstetrics and Gynecology, 127,* 191–198.

Shepard, T. H. (1979). Teratogenicity of therapeutic agents. *Current Problems in Pediatrics, 10,* 5–42.

Shepard, T. H. (1980). *Catalogue of teratogenic agents* (3rd ed.). Baltimore: The Johns Hopkins University Press.

Shepard, T. H. (1982). Detection of human teratogenic agents. *Journal of Pediatrics, 101,* 810–815.

Simpson, W. J. (1957). A preliminary report on cigarette smoking and the incidence of prematurity. *American Journal of Obstetrics and Gynecology, 73,* 808–815.

Skreb, N., & Frank, Z. (1963). Developmental abnormalities in the rat induced by heat. *Journal of Embryology and Experimental Morphology, 11,* 445–448.

Smith, D. W. (1987). *Recognizable patterns of human malformation* (4th ed.). Philadelphia: W. B. Saunders.

Smith, D. W., Clarren, S. K., & Harvey, M. A. (1978). Hyperthermia as a possible teratogenic agent. *Journal of Pediatrics, 92,* 878–883.

Soler, N. G., Walsh, C. H., & Malins, J. M. (1976). Congenital malformations in infants of diabetic mothers. *Quarterly Journal of Medicine, 45,* 303–313.

Speidel, B. D., & Meadow, S. R. (1972). Maternal epilepsy and abnormalities of the fetus and newborn. *Lancet, ii,* 839–843.

Stone, M. L., Salerno, L. G., Green, M., & Zelson, C. (1971). Narcotic addition in pregnancy. *American Journal of Obstetrics and Gynecology, 109,* 716–723.

Streissguth, A. P., Landesman-Dwyer, J. C., Martin, J. C., & Smith, D. W. (1980). Teratogenic effects of alcohol in human and laboratory animals. *Science, 209,* 353–361.

Swartz, H. M., & Reichling, B. A. (1978). Hazards of radiation exposure for pregnant women. *Journal of the American Medical Association, 239,* 1907–1908.

Weinstein, M. R., & Goldfield, M. (1975). Cardiovascular malformations with lithium used during pregnancy. *American Journal of Psychiatry, 132,* 529–531.

Wilson, G. S., McCreary, R., Kean, J., & Baxter, C. (1979). The development of preschool children of heroin-addicted mothers: A controlled study. *Pediatrics, 63,* 135–141.

Wilson, J. G. (1973). *Environment and birth defects.* New York: Academic Press.

Youmoszai, M. K., Kacie, A., & Haworth, J. C. (1968). Cigarette smoking during pregnancy: The effect upon hematocrit and acid-base balance of the newborn. *Canadian Medical Association Journal, 99,* 197–200.

Zackai, E. H., Mellman, W. J., Neiderer, B., & Hanson, J. W. (1975). The fetal trimethadione syndrome. *Journal of Pediatrics, 87,* 280–284.

Zelson, C., Lee, S. J., & Casalino, M. (1973). Neonatal narcotic addiction. *New England Journal of Medicine, 289,* 1216–1218.

**8** | *Wayne A. Miller*

# PRENATAL
# GENETIC
# DIAGNOSIS

A proper frame of reference to best present prenatal genetic diagnosis is to provide a review of the scope of genetic disorders. Approximately 20% of recognized pregnancies terminate spontaneously in the first trimester (Fabricant, Boue, & Boue, 1980). Fully 40% to 60% of these are found to have chromosome abnormalities (Alberman & Creasy, 1977; Creasy, Crolla, & Alberman, 1976; Geisler & Kleinebrecht, 1978). Of the remainder, approximately 70% have some other developmental abnormality. In addition, approximately 2% to 4% of all live-born infants are found to have some type of birth defect. These birth defects account for 50% of all perinatal deaths, 15% of all infant deaths, and 20% to 30% of all pediatric hospital admissions. Viewed from another perspective, genetic disorders lead to a loss in life-years four times greater than all types of heart disease and eight times greater than all types of cancer (Erbe, 1977).

Few of the more serious disorders are treatable, and it is doubtful that the majority of these disorders will ever be amenable to treatment. Therefore, since the early 1970s, emphasis has been placed on developing techniques to identify some of the more serious malformations and genetic disorders in utero. The main object is to allow the parents the option of terminating an affected pregnancy. However, it is this author's opinion that if termination is not a consideration for the couple, prenatal diagnostic techniques should still be offered to the couple at risk. The main reasons include: 1) giving the parents time to accustom themselves to the fact of having a child with disabilities, therefore, partially eliminating the period of anger, disappointment, and despair that often occurs immediately after the birth of a child with a birth defect; 2) identifying those situations that call for alterations in obstetrical

management; and 3) arranging for specialized pediatric services in the immediate postnatal period. An example would be the identification of a child with
spina bifida. In this case, obstetrical management should be altered to include
delivery by cesarean section rather than by vaginal delivery. A pediatric
neurosurgical team should be readily available so that correction of the defect
can be accomplished as soon as possible after the delivery, with subsequent
appropriate follow-up care by an interdisciplinary team that has expertise in
the field.

## TECHNIQUES FOR
## PRENATAL GENETIC DIAGNOSIS

There are seven techniques available for prenatal genetic diagnosis. These are
amniocentesis, early amniocentesis, ultrasonography, amniography, fetoscopy, percutaneous umbilical blood sampling (PUBS), and chorionic villus
biopsy.

### Amniocentesis

Amniocentesis is probably the best known technique for prenatal genetic
diagnosis. It involves removing 15 ml to 25 ml of amniotic fluid at about the
16th week of gestation. There are some centers that perform amniocentesis
between the 12th and 14th week of gestation. Fetal cells present in the amniotic fluid can be grown in culture and used for cytogenetic, DNA, and/or
biochemical analyses. Through cytogenetic analysis, both numerical and
structural abnormalities of the chromosomes can be readily identified. Moreover, there are approximately 70 inborn errors of metabolism that can be
diagnosed using amniotic fluid cells. These are presented in Table 8.1.

A new and exciting application for amniotic fluid cell analysis is based
on recombinant DNA technology. Using techniques that can identify structural changes in the gene or those DNA polymorphisms closely linked to the
gene in question, genetic diseases can be diagnosed. More than 50 genetic
disorders have been linked to DNA polymorphisms, and the actual DNA
mutation has been identified in about 45 disorders.

The supernatant fluid can be used for a number of viral or biochemical
studies. The most common application is the test for alpha-fetoprotein (AFP).
In the early 1970s, it was recognized that AFP is present in amniotic fluid
from all pregnancies and that the amount is inversely proportional to the stage
of gestation. It was also observed at that time that the levels of AFP were
markedly elevated in pregnancies affected by various fetal malformations
(Brock, 1976; Macri, Weiss, Tillitt, Balsam, & Elligers, 1976; Milunksy &
Alpert, 1976). Although AFP determinations are a relatively precise test,
there are a number of situations that can lead to false positive elevations. The
likelihood that an elevated AFP value indicates a fetal malformation is directly proportional to the degree of abnormality. A new assay for a specific

**Table 8.1.** Inborn errors of metabolism diagnosable prenatally by biochemical assay

Lipidoses
  Adrenoleukodystrophy
  Ceroid-lipofuscinosis
  Cholesterol ester storage disease
  Fabry disease
  Farber disease
  Gaucher disease, several forms
  $G_{m1}$ gangliosidosis, Types 1 and 2
  $G_{m2}$ gangliosidosis
    Tay-Sachs disease
    Sandhoff disease
    AB variant
  Krabb disease
  Metachromatic leukodystrophy, several forms
  Multiple sulfatase deficiency
  Niemann-Pick disease, several forms
  Refsum disease
  Wolman disease

Mucopolysaccaridoses
  β-Glucuronidase deficiency
  Hurler/Scheie syndromes
  Hunter syndrome
  I-cell disease
  Morquio syndrome, A and B
  Maroteaux-Lamy syndrome, several forms
  Sanfilippo syndrome, A, B, C, and D

Carbohydrate and glycoprotein metabolism disorders
  Aspartylglucosaminuria
  Fucosidosis
  Galactosemia
  Glucose-6-phosphate dehydrogenase deficiency
  Glucose phosphate isomerase deficiency
  Glycogen storage disease, Type II, III, IV, and VIII
  Mannosidosis
  Pyruvate decarboxylase deficiency
  Pyruvate dehydrogenase complex deficiency, several forms

Amino acid metabolism disorders
  Dihydropteridine reductase deficiency
  Hereditary tyrosinemia, Type I
  Hyperprolinemia, Type II
  Lysine disorders
    Hyperlysinemia
    Saccharopinuria
  Sulfur pathway disorders
    Cystathionine synthase deficiency (homocystinuria)
    Sulfite oxidase deficiency
  Urea cycle disorders
    Argininosuccinicaciduria
    Citrullinemia
    Ornithine carbamyltransferase deficiency

Miscellaneous disorders
  Acatalasia, several forms
  Adenosine deaminase deficiency
  Agammaglobulinemia
  Chronic granulomatous disease
  Combined immunodeficiency due to adenosine deaminase or nucleoside phosphorylase deficiency
  Congenital adrenal hyperplasia, 21-hydroxylase deficiency
  Cytochrome oxidase C deficiency
  Cystinosis
  Hypercholesterolemia, several forms
  Lesch-Nyhan syndrome
  Lysosomal acid phosphatase deficiency
  Menkes disease
  Mucolipidosis, Types II, III, and IV
  Orotic aciduria, Types 1 and II
  Porphyria
    Acute intermittent porphyria
    Congenital erythropoietic porphyria
    Protoporphyria
  Prolidase deficiency
  Triosephosphate isomerase deficiency
  Wiskott-Aldrich syndrome
  X-linked ichthyosis
  Zellweger syndrome

*(continued)*

Table 8.1. (continued)

| Organic acid disorders | Vitamin metabolism disorders |
|---|---|
| Glutaric aciduria | 5,10-Methylenetetrahydrofolate |
| 3-Hydroxy-3-methylglutaryl-CoA lyase | reductase deficiency |
| deficiency | Methylmalonic acidemia |
| Isovaleric acidemia | Collagen disorders |
| Maple syrup urine disease, several | Ehlers-Danlos syndrome, Types IV, V, |
| forms | and VIII |
| Methylmalonic acidemia, several | Hydroxylysine deficient collagen |
| forms | disease |
| Mevalonic aciduria | |
| Propionic acidemia | |

isozyme of acetylcholinesterase was developed in the early 1980s (Haddow, Morin, Holman, & Miller, 1980). As opposed to the quantitative AFP assay, the acetylcholinesterase is a qualitative assay (Schedit, Stanley, & Bryla, 1978). For any measured level of alpha-fetoprotein, a positive acetylcholinesterase scan will increase the likelihood of the presence of a fetal defect by sixteenfold.

### Early Amniocentesis

Since 1987, a number of groups have reported the ability to perform amniocentesis at 11 to 14 weeks of gestation. Although the data are preliminary, improvements in ultrasound, operative technique, and laboratory procedures appear to allow performance of amniocentesis at these earlier gestational ages with success, accuracy, and safety approaching that of amniocentesis performed at 16 to 18 weeks of gestation (Benacerraf et al., 1988; Hanson, Zorn, Tennant, Marianos, & Samuels, 1987; Miller, Davies, & Thayer, 1987). Initial information on pregnancy outcome does not indicate a higher rate of prematurity, low birth weight, or fetal injury (Miller, Davies, & Thayer, 1988). The smaller volume of amniotic fluid removed during this procedure makes it difficult to obtain sufficient cells for most biochemical assays and some DNA studies; therefore, this author does not recommend its use in these situations.

### Ultrasonography

Ultrasonography, which is the use of low-energy, high-frequency sound waves to visualize intrauterine structures, is strongly recommended as an adjunct procedure to amniocentesis. However, with technologic refinements since 1983, ultrasound has come into its own as a diagnostic procedure for determining fetal malformations. To date, no short-term risks from use of ultrasound have been identified (Kim et al., 1975); however, long-term follow-up of children with exposure in utero has yet to be performed. For this reason, this author feels that ultrasound should be used only if there is a definite indication and should not be used routinely in pregnancies.

## Amniography

Amniography involves removal of a small amount of amniotic fluid and replacement of this fluid with an equal amount of radio-opaque dye. Fluorograms are then taken to observe the external shape of the fetus. With the refinements in ultrasound, amniography has been replaced. However, an X-ray taken 24 hours after installation of the dye may be useful in identifying fetal gastrointestinal malformations.

## Fetoscopy

Fetoscopy is the use of a small fiberoptiscope to visualize the intrauterine contents. It was originally developed for direct visualization of the fetus. Because of the small field of vision with the 21 gauge instrument, the rigidity of the instrument, the failure of the fetus to cooperate in terms of exposing specific parts of its anatomy, and its increased risk, the application of fetoscopy is somewhat limited. It has proven to be useful, however, in obtaining samples of fetal blood and for fetal skin biopsies.

## Percutaneous Umbilical Blood Sampling

Ultrasound can also be used to guide a needle into an umbilical blood vessel to obtain a sample of fetal blood, a procedure known as percutaneous umbilical blood sampling (PUBS). Because of the reported lower fetal loss rate, this procedure is rapidly replacing fetoscopy as the method of choice for obtaining fetal blood.

## Chorionic Villus Biopsy

Chorionic villus biopsy, a new technique for first-trimester prenatal genetic diagnosis, is being developed and evaluated. This procedure involves transcervical or transabdominal sampling of placental tissue at 9–11 weeks gestation. The cells obtained can then be used for cytogenetic, biochemical, or DNA studies. One study indicated that the fetal loss rate due to chorionic villus biopsy is only slightly higher than that of amniocentesis.

## INDICATIONS FOR APPLICATION

Each of these techniques has a cost either in terms of risk to the mother and fetus or in financial terms and, therefore, should only be applied in specific situations where the couple has been identified as being at risk for a diagnosable fetal malformation or birth defect. There are seven categories for identifying couples with risks. These are:

1. *Maternal age 35 years or greater*   The incidence of chromosome abnormalities increases with advanced maternal age. Graphically, the slope increases rather slowly from 20 to 34 years, at which time it starts to increase markedly. The risk of chromosome abnormalities doubles every 2.5 years after the maternal age of 35 years. A paternal age effect has been identified; however, this is much smaller than the maternal age effect. It is estimated that at any given maternal age, each year difference in paternal age indicates a 1% increase or decrease in the maternal age-related risk. At a maternal age of 35 years, the risk for some type of significant chromosome abnormality is approximately 1 in 200 to 1 in 300 live births. Because the commonly quoted risk for problems after an amniocentesis is approximately 1 in 250, it is recommended that at a maternal age of 35 years the parents consider having an amniocentesis performed. There is nothing magical about the maternal age of 35 years. Maternal ages 34, 35, or 36 constitute a gray zone where the risk of having an affected fetus approximately equals the risk of the procedure. At a maternal age of 37 years or greater, the risk of having an affected fetus is clearly higher than the risk of an amniocentesis. At age 33 years or lower, the risk of an affected fetus is clearly less than that of the procedure.

2. *Either parent being a carrier of a balanced chromosome translocation* When either parent is a carrier of a balanced chromosome translocation, there is no net gain or loss of choromosome material, and the individual is clinically normal. The same individual, however, has an increased risk of passing on an abnormal amount of genetic information to his or her offspring. The risk is dependent on the type of translocation that is involved, the chromosomes that are affected, and the sex of the carrier. In general, empirical studies have shown the risk to range between 2% and 100% for producing a genetically abnormal offspring. Certain Robertsonian translocations, which involve the joining of both chromosomes of a pair, lead to a situation in which only chromosomally abnormal offspring can be produced (e.g., 21/21 translocation). A point of information in regard to identification of such carriers is that an obstetrical history of recurrent fetal loss or the birth of malformed infants indicates a need to perform chromosome studies on the parents. In couples with the obstetrical history of recurrent fetal loss, the risk that one parent is a carrier of a balanced translocation is approximately 1 in 20 (Portnoi, Joye, van den Akker, Morlier, & Taillemite, 1988; Sachs, Johoda, Van Hemel, Hoogeboom, & Sandkuyl, 1985; Schmidt, Nitowsky, & Dar, 1976).

3. *Previous birth of a chromosomally abnormal infant* Empirical studies have shown that the risk of recurrence of a chromosomally abnormal infant is between 1% and 2%.

4. *Known risk for a Mendelian disorder that can be diagnosed in utero* Most of the Mendelian disorders are autosomal recessives, indicating a risk of 25% for recurrence or occurrence for the couple (see Kolodny, Abuelo, Barsel-Bowers, & Pueschel, Chapter 4, this volume). A list of the disorders diagnosable in utero is presented in Table 8.1.

5. *Previous child born with a neural tube defect* Empirical studies have shown that couples who have had a child with a neural tube defect have a recurrence risk of between 1% and 3%.

6. *Mother is a carrier of an X-linked disorder not diagnosable in utero* When the mother is a carrier of an X-linked disorder not diagnosable in utero, couples may choose fetal sex identification and elect to continue only female pregnancies. Male fetuses have a 50% risk of being affected, while female fetuses will be carriers and only rarely affected. Depending on the severity of the disorder, the couple may choose to terminate all male pregnancies. The difference between this category and those mentioned previously is that the diagnosis does not identify the affected fetus but rather a fetus at high risk of being affected.

7. *Birth of a previous child with multiple malformations* If the couple has had a child with multiple malformations, then they should undergo a more complete evaluation to identify whether the disorder is genetic in origin, whether there is a recurrence risk, and whether the malformation is expressed sufficiently early in gestation for diagnosis by one of the previously mentioned techniques.

The first five categories are definite indications for performing prenatal diagnostic studies. If couples are identified as belonging to one of these categories, they are at a definite risk of having a child with a birth defect that can be diagnosed. The other two categories are not as precise and involve different considerations or further investigations.

## APPLICATIONS OF DIAGNOSTIC TECHNIQUES

### Amniocentesis and Early Amniocentesis

An absolutely necessary adjunct to amniocentesis is the performance of ultrasound prior to insertion of the needle. The complete ultrasound examination should be performed with a full bladder, the woman should then be allowed to void, and then additional scans of the uterus should be taken to identify the point of needle insertion. Needle insertion should be done with direct ultrasound guidance. In review of records since the mid-1980s, it has become clear that sample quality has significantly improved by the use of ultrasound. Sample quality directly relates to the success and accuracy of the chromosome analysis (Miller & Kacoyanis, 1982). Ultrasound is also critical for the determination of gestational age. By use of biparietal diameter, abdominal circumference, and femur length measurements, a person well-trained in obstetrical ultrasound can identify the day of conception within ±5 days. Such a determination is necessary for proper interpretation of the measured values of AFP, since they vary with gestational age. Ultrasound is also useful for identifying multiple fetuses. If separate amniotic sacs are identified, samples must be taken from each sac to obtain a complete appraisal of the pregnancy.

Localization of the placenta is necessary to identify the point of needle insertion. Unlike the fetus, who can move out of harm's way, the placenta is immobile. It contains the major blood vessels that supply the fetus and can be the site of traumatic injury that can lead to fetal demise. If there is an anterior placenta and the woman is at less than 17 weeks of gestation, delaying the procedure for 1 to 2 weeks is recommended. At this later time, there should be a window through which to place the needle. If it is necessary to go through an anterior placenta, then the point of insertion of the umbilical cord into the placenta should be identified and a point that is approximately two-thirds of the way from the site of insertion to the placental margin should be selected. The reasons for avoiding the point of insertion of the umbilical cord are obvious. Through post amniocentesis-ultrasound examinations, it has been found that there was a higher rate of partial separation of the placenta if the chosen point was near the placental margin for insertion of the needle. An additional reason for ultrasound examination prior to amniocentesis is for identification of major malformations, such as anencephaly.

The procedure of amniocentesis itself is straightforward. After the point for the needle insertion is identified, a sterile prep and drape of the abdomen are carried out and the amniocentesis needle is introduced to the amniotic cavity. The use of a local anesthetic is a personal choice of the physician. However, using a 22-gauge long needle for amniocentesis negates the need for a local anesthetic. The needle that is used has a stylet to avoid obtaining maternal cells during passage through the abdominal wall. The first few milliliters of amniotic fluid are kept in a separate syringe and either discarded or used for an AFP assay. This flushing action will decrease the incidence of maternal cell contamination in the amniotic fluid cultures. Between 15 ml and 25 ml of amniotic fluid are obtained and sent to the laboratory for initiation of cultures and an AFP assay.

The technique for early amniocentesis, performed at 11–14 weeks gestation, is identical. However, because of the smaller amount of amniotic fluid present at this stage, the author recommends that the amount of fluid obtained be limited to 1 cc per gestational week. This earlier application of amniocentesis is still considered experimental because the relative safety compared to a 16 to 18 week amniocentesis is not well-defined.

The question of the safety of amniocentesis is still unresolved. The National Institutes of Health study performed in the early 1970s indicated that there was no statistically significant increase in the rate of fetal loss after amniocentesis, whereas the British Research Council study indicated that the risk may be as high as about 1 in 80 (Medical Research Council Working Party on Amniocentesis, 1978; Miskin et al., 1974). The reality probably lies somewhere in between. In the author's study of over 10,000 women who underwent amniocentesis, the incidence of fetal loss was less than would be expected if amniocentesis were not performed. Indeed, the rate of fetal loss is so low that no matter what statistical test is used, amniocentesis is statistically significant protection against fetal loss. This is obviously a quirk of the sample, as there are at least seven cases of fetal loss in the author's study that can be directly attributable to the amniocentesis procedure. Although in each of these seven cases there was a predisposing cause for the fetal loss, it is most likely that the immediate cause of the miscarriage was the amniocentesis procedure. The National Institute of Child Health and Human Development (NICHD) (1976) study also showed that in about 6% of primary attempts to obtain fluid, the obstetrician is unsuccessful. Using the technique outlined above, the author believes that the rate of failure to obtain amniotic fluid with one needle insertion should be less than 1% and with two needle insertions should be less than 0.1%. The same study also showed a cell culture failure rate of approximately 9%. Again, the author's experience indicates that this is unacceptable. If adequate samples are provided, the success rate should be greater than 99%. An adequate sample is defined as one that is not grossly bloody and contains more than 15 ml of amniotic fluid. The major cause of erroneous diagnoses in the NICHD study was maternal cell contamination. By taking the precaution of discarding the first milliter of amniotic fluid that is obtained and by counting at least 15 cells from two separate cultures, this problem should be overcome.

**Ultrasonography**

Ultrasound techniques can identify most fetal neural tube defects. Hydrocephalus can be recognized by serial determinations of the size of the lateral ventricles of the brain. Ventral wall defects, such as omphalocele and gastroschisis, can be visualized. Kidney size and structure can be evaluated, and kidney function can be determined by measuring the rate of urine production. The size, presence, and the length of the long bones of the arms and legs can be measured by ultrasound and used to diagnose various forms of short-limb dwarfism. Cardiac silhouette imaging, to identify the presence of all chambers and, in a few institutions, to measure blood flow through the various chambers, can be performed. Another use for ultrasound is to direct the placement of the fetoscope and to direct it to specific positions on the fetus during visualization (Haney, 1978; Harrison, Campbell, & Craft, 1975; Higginbottom, Bagnell, Harris, Slater, & Porter, 1976; Kaffe, Gedunlow, Walker, & Hirschhorn, 1977; Kleinman, Hobbins, Lynch, Talner, & Jaffe, 1980; Rodeck, 1978; Rodeck & Campbell, 1978).

## Amniography

In most cases, diagnosis of neural tube defects by amniography has been replaced by ultrasound. This is because the risks of miscarriage from amniography are approximately the same as those from amniocentesis, whereas ultrasonography is noninvasive. Radiation exposure in utero should be avoided and ultrasound seems to be more accurate in its diagnostic capabilities. However, amniography is useful in evaluating certain ventral wall defects that may not be apparent by ultrasound, and it is useful in providing an evaluation of the fetal gastrointestinal tract by use of a 24-hour delay film.

## Fetoscopy and
## Percutaneous Umbilical Blood Sampling

Fetoscopy is used for direct visualization of the fetus and for obtaining samples of specific fetal tissues. The amniotic fluid cells that are obtained by amniocentesis are relatively undifferentiated and, therefore, express only some of the enzyme systems of the intact individual. By taking fetal blood through the sampling of umbilical or placental vessels and by carrying out a fetal skin biopsy from the buttocks or the thighs, more highly specialized tissues can be obtained. The disorders to be diagnosed by this method are different from those that are feasible through amniotic fluid cell cultures (Alter et al., 1976; Kan, Golbus, Trecartin, & Filly, 1977; Mahoney & Hobbins, 1977; U.K. collaborative study, 1977). Examples of disorders that have been diagnosed by fetoscopy include neural tube defects, sickle cell anemia, thalassemia, hemophilia, and congenital ichthyosis. In situations where chromosome analysis from amniotic fluid cell cultures yields confusing or inconclusive results, fetal blood sampling with lymphocyte stimulation and chromosome examination of metaphase spreads can be used to clarify the situation. In any applications of fetoscopy, the risk of fetal loss is about 5% and the risk of premature delivery is about 10%. As noted previously, ultrasound guided blood sampling is replacing fetoscopy as the preferred technique. Fetal loss rates associated with ultrasound guided blood sampling have been reported as 1% to 2% with a similar decrease in the rate of prematurity. The technique appears to be applicable at any stage of gestation after 18 weeks.

## Chorionic Villus Biopsy

Chorionic villus biopsy requires a trained ultrasonographer and obstetrician. The ultrasonographer scans the uterus to determine the viability of the pregnancy by observing fetal heart motion, measuring gestational age by the crown-rump length, and the location of the placenta. The obstetrician introduces the sampling instrument into the placental tissue under direct ultrasound guidance and obtains the chorionic villi tissue.

Although a number of different methods and instruments are used, they fall into two major categories: transvaginal and transabdominal sampling. Only 10 mg to 20 mg of chorionic villi are usually sampled, yet this is far more viable tissue than is obtained by amniocentesis and is sufficient for most biochemical assays and DNA analysis. Therefore, studies can be performed immediately rather than being delayed for 2–5 weeks until sufficient cells are generated by culture as is necessary with amniotic fluid specimens. In addition, trophoblast tissue has a relatively rapid mitotic rate, and techniques have been developed to allow for direct preparation of the fresh sample for cytogenetic analyses. This again precludes the need for cell culture and allows for diagnosis in a matter of hours rather than weeks. Because of technical problems and limitations, however, most laboratories have chosen to use both the direct technique and cultured chorionic tissue for chromosome analysis in order to overcome the frequent problems of maternal cell contamination and unexplained mosaicism (Callen et al., 1988; Canadian Collaborative CVS-Amniocentesis Clinical Trial Group, 1989; Hunter, 1988). This combined approach requires 5 to 14 days for complete studies. Even with these precautions, about 1% to 2% of women undergoing chorionic villus biopsy will need amniocentesis to clarify confusing or conflicting cytogenetic results from the chorionic villus sample.

The fetal loss rate after chorionic villus biopsy is reported to be 2% to 4%. Since there is limited information available on the rate of spontaneous fetal loss after evidence of fetal viability at 8–11 weeks gestation, it is somewhat difficult to assess the true procedure-related loss rate. However, it is estimated that in experienced hands, there is approximately a 0.7% excess fetal loss over that reported with amniocentesis (Rhoads et al., 1989). Since most experienced amniocentesis operators report a procedure related loss of less than 0.2%, the chorionic villus biopsy associated loss rate is about 0.9% or four to five times the loss rate associated with amniocentesis. Similarly, the rates of maternal complications, such as vaginal bleeding and uterine cramping, are reportedly higher (Crane, Beaver, & Cheung, 1988). Serious maternal complications that are rare include uterine infections leading to septic shock, and, in some cases, the uterus has been removed (Barela et al., 1986; Black & Schulman, 1988). In addition to the above considerations, it is of note that there is a higher rate of unsuccessful procedures and a higher laboratory failure rate associated with chorionic villus biopsy. Also, chorionic villus biopsy does not allow testing for neural tube defects.

The obvious advantage of chorionic villus biopsy is that is is performed at an earlier stage of gestation than amniocentesis. The potential benefits from this earlier diagnosis are sufficiently great to warrant the use of chorionic villus biopsy in high-risk situations, such as couples at risk for Mendelian defects, X-linked disorders, and unbalanced chromosome rearrangements. This procedure can also be considered by couples at lesser risk, if they are appraised of the risks and limitations of chorionic villus biopsy in comparison to amniocentesis.

## MATERNAL SERUM ALPHA-FETOPROTEIN SCREENING

With the exception of testing that is performed for advanced maternal age and for those few biochemical disorders in which heterozygote carriers can be identified, most of the couples who are identified as being candidates for prenatal diagnosis come to attention after the birth of an affected child. This is an inadequate form of prevention of these defects. For example, even if all subsequent pregnancies with an affected offspring were screened by amniocentesis, only 5% of affected fetuses would be identified. Therefore, it is obvious that screening techniques that allow us to identify couples that are at risk are a necessary area of development.

At about the same time that elevated amniotic fluid AFP was identified as being associated with neural tube defects, alpha-fetoprotein was also observed in maternal serum. It was found that in the majority of pregnancies with neural tube defects, the levels of maternal serum AFP were also elevated (Ferguson-Smith, 1978). Standard protocol requires a first serum sample to be taken between 16 and 18 weeks of gestation. The range of normal is set so that 5% of the population will be identified as having an elevated value. Protocols will vary from one center to another. It is suggested that women with mild elevations of maternal serum AFP have a second sample drawn and analyzed within 1–2 weeks of the first, while those women with more marked elevations of AFP proceed immediately to the next stage of the protocol.

For those women with one elevated serum AFP determination, a second sample should be obtained about 2 weeks after the first. Approximately 20% of the women who have an increased AFP value in the first blood sample will have a normal value on the second sample and will need no further testing. Those women with one significantly elevated or two slightly elevated serum samples should be offered an ultrasound examination that may show a neural tube defect, but it will also be useful for determination of the gestational age and for identification of a multiple pregnancy. Approximately 20% of the women who have ultrasound examinations will be found to have a multiple pregnancy, which is the cause of their elevated maternal serum AFP values. An additional 30% will be 2 weeks or more further along in gestation than expected. Because serum AFP values increase with advancing gestational age, reinterpretation of the measured value on the basis of the correct gestational age usually indicates that the measured values are within the range of normal.

Within the screened population approximately 1% will have two abnormal serum samples and normal ultrasound. Because the risk of a fetal defect is approximately 10%, these women should be offered amniocentesis so that AFP assays and acetylcholinesterase scans can be performed on the fluid. A decision on whether to perform chromosome analysis should be based on the parents' ages and personal concerns. If these biochemical parameters are abnormal, a fetal defect is most likely the cause. The women with abnormal maternal serum AFP and normal amniotic fluid AFP are at increased risk of having a premature baby, a small-for-gestational-age baby, or a fetal demise. The extent of this risk can be defined, given the increase of the serum AFP level. Utilizing standard protocols, it is clear that with such a screening program, between 80% and 90% of all open neural tube defects could be identified.

Low serum AFP values have been reported to be associated with a higher risk for Down syndrome (Cuckle, Wald, & Lindenbaum, 1984; Merkatz, Nitowsky, Macri, & Johnson, 1984). An individual risk can be determined for any pregnant woman based on her age-related risk and the level of measured AFP (Palomaki & Haddow, 1987). Standard protocols recommend follow-up testing, such as ultrasound and amniocentesis, if this combined risk is equal to or greater than the risk that a 35 year old has for Down syndrome. Unlike maternal serum AFP screening for neural tube defects, a second sample is contraindicated in Down syndrome screening because both the Down syndrome median and the normal median are usually both above the value of maternal serum AFP being evaluated, and repeat testing would be expected to move upward, regardless of fetal status. Ultrasound examination is important because gestational age is crucial to interpretation of the measured value. In this author's experience, about 20% of the patients interpreted as having low maternal serum AFP values are at an earlier gestation than expected and reinterpretation of the measured value based on accurate gestational age yields a normal value. Yet, maternal serum AFP is not a good screening test since only 20% to 25% of the Down syndrome fetuses would be identified through the standard protocols. A screening test with this low level of sensitivity would not usually be applied. However, since maternal serum AFP is already being used for neural tube defect screening, low values should be interpreted and acted upon. A prospective collaborative study indicated that a chromosomally abnormal fetus is found in 1 out of ever 86 women who are identified as being at high risk by this protocol (New England Regional Genetics Group, 1989).

Numerous other hormones and proteins have been evaluated as maternal serum markers for Down syndrome (Wald et al., 1988). At this time, two additional markers show promise as screening adjuncts: 1) unconjugated estriol in maternal serum is lower in Down syndrome pregnancies (Canick et al., 1988) and 2) chorionic gonadotrophin is elevated in association with Down syndrome pregnancies (Bogart, Pandian, & Jones, 1987). Table 8.2 shows the sensitivity of these different parameters, singly and in different

Table 8.2. Sensitivity of specified maternal serum markers

| | Percent of all pregnant women undergoing amniocentesis | Percent of all Down syndrome fetuses identified |
|---|---|---|
| Age alone | 5 | 20 |
| MSAFP | 3 | 25 |
| Age and MSAFP | 8 | 40 |
| Age and HCG | 5 | 49 |
| Age, HCG, AFP | 5 | 56 |
| Age, HCG, uE3 | 5 | 57 |
| Age, HCG, AFP, uE3 | 5 | 61 |

MSAFP, maternal serum alpha-fetoprotein; HCG, maternal serum chorionic gonadotrophin; uE3, maternal serum unconjugated estriol.

combinations, while maintaining a uniform specificity. A number of different protocols are under investigation.

## RECOMBINANT DNA TECHNOLOGY

A new and exciting application for amniotic fluid cells is based on the use of recombinant DNA technology. Using techniques that can identify structural changes in the gene or DNA polymorphisms closely linked to the gene in question, genetic diseases can be diagnosed using any cell type, since all cells—regardless of their state or stage of differentiation—contain the entire genome, even if they do not express the specific gene product. If techniques were available that allowed geneticists to look directly at the gene or at some closely associated part of the genome, diagnosis of any genetic disorder could be done from any cell type whether or not the gene product is expressed in that cell type (Antonarakis, 1989).

The cornerstone of this technology is the ability to extract DNA from cells and cleave it into fragments of different size by use of a restriction endonuclease. Restriction endonucleases are enzymes that recognize a specific sequence in a DNA molecule and cut the DNA molecule at that point. Under proper conditions a restriction endonuclease will cut a strand each and every time it "sees" a specific sequence of bases, yielding a unique and reproducible pattern of fragment sizes for every individual. These fragments can then be separated by size using agarose gel electrophoresis.

Another crucial aspect of this technology is the generation of a DNA probe to identify the DNA fragment of interest. These probes are mirror image fragments of nucleic acid molecules that have base sequences complementary to that of the DNA one wishes to study. Under proper conditions the probe will only recombine with DNA fragments that contain sequences complementary to itself. Probes can be prepared from radioactively labeled, enzymatically labeled, or fluorophore labeled precursors. After hybridization, the gene of interest can be identified by autoradiography, colorimetry, or fluorescent excitation.

Because individuals have variations in their DNA base sequence, digestion by restriction endonuclease can yield different size fragments containing the DNA sequence to be studied. Since restriction endonucleases differ in their recognition sites, the patterns produced in an individual by different enzymes can differ markedly in the DNA fragments. These variations, or DNA fingerprints, are called restriction fragment length polymorphisms (RFLP).

As stated earlier, either direct analysis of the gene and its integrity or analysis of a physically near site that expresses a polymorphism can be performed. In the first case where direct analysis of the gene is involved, direct detection of an abnormal gene through a number of various techniques, including inability to hybridize with a DNA probe or a different response to cleavage by restriction endonucleases, can be used to differentiate between a normal and an abnormal gene. In the second situation where analysis of a physically near site is involved, variations in size of the DNA fragments, RFLP, produced by specific endonucleases, are used to identify the presence of an abnormal gene. If such a polymorphism is closely linked to the gene in question, this linkage may allow one to trace the abnormal gene through a family and thereby identify its presence or absence in the fetus by the presence or absence of specific polymorphisms. DNA amplification by polymerase chain reaction (PCR) is a new development in recombinant DNA technology that can be applied to either RFLP or direct gene analysis. Using oligonucleotide primers to direct synthesis of new complementary DNA strands, a desired segment of DNA can be amplified 10 million times within a few hours. With this large number of copies of the specific DNA sequence, analyses can be accomplished on smaller amounts of DNA in a short period of time using nonradioactive probes (Erlich, Gelfand, & Saiki, 1988; Kogan, Doherty, & Gitschier, 1987).

Both of these techniques have been applied successfully in the prenatal diagnosis of sickle cell anemia. The first test developed was a difference in RFLP obtained through use of a specific endonuclease between individuals with hemoglobin A and certain individuals with hemoglobin S. Individuals with hemoglobin S mutation frequently lose a restriction endonuclease Hpa1 recognition site, and therefore, their DNA yields a DNA fragment containing the globin gene that is 13 kilobases long instead of 7.6 kilobases or 7.0 kilobases when digested with this enzyme. This difference is reflected by differential migration due to size difference during electrophoresis of DNA fragments containing the globin gene. The point mutation that causes this difference in RFLP is not within the globin gene itself, but it is sufficiently close that such a polymorphism can be used to identify the abnormal gene because it travels with the gene as a marker during meiosis. The sickle gene is not always on the 13 kilobase fragment; in some individuals it is found in the 7.6 kilobase fragment. In addition, some individuals with Hgb A are found to have 13 kilobase fragments. In order for the test to be meaningful, family studies have to be done to determine which chromosome carries the mutant gene in a particular family.

Another technique identifies a specific endonuclease that cleaves within the globin A gene whereas the globin S gene is left intact, resulting in DNA fragments of different sizes. This test actually identifies a variation within the structural gene itself.

More than 50 genetic diseases have been linked to RFLPs, including cystic fibrosis, Huntington disease, neurofibromatosis, thalassemia, hemophilia A and B, phenylketonuria, Duchenne and Becker muscular dystrophies, and myotonic dystrophy (Watkins, 1988). Direct DNA analysis is possible in more than 45 genetic disorders in which the specific mutation is known (Landegren, Kaiser, Caskey, & Hood, 1988). With the expansion of this field, it is likely that the number of genetic disorders diagnosable in utero by recombinant techniques will expand rapidly in the coming years. Indeed, it is theoretically possible that any genetic disorder of Mendelian inheritance can be diagnosed using these techniques, whether the biochemical basis is understood or not.

## CONCLUSION

New developments in prenatal genetic diagnosis make it possible for many chromosomal and genetic disorders to be identified prior to birth. These new techniques include amniocentesis, ultrasonography, amniography, festoscopy, percutaneous umbilical blood sampling, and chorionic villus biopsy. In addition, maternal serum alpha-fetoprotein screening is routinely available for neural tube defect and chromosomal defect identification. Finally, recombinant DNA technology can be used to identify structural changes in the gene and DNA polymorphisms closely linked to the gene, thus, diagnosing genetic disease.

## REFERENCES

Alberman, E., & Creasy, M. R. (1977). Frequency of chromosomal abnormalities in miscarriages and perinatal deaths. *Journal of Medical Genetics, 14*, 313–315.
Alter, B. P., Modell, C. B., Fairweather, D., Hobbins, J. C., Mahoney, M. J., Frigoletto, F. S., Sherman, A. S., & Nathan, D. G. (1976). Prenatal diagnosis of hemoglobinopathies: A review of 15 cases. *New England Journal of Medicine, 295*, 1437–1443.

Antonarakis, S. (1989). Diagnosis of genetic disorders at the DNA level. *New England Journal of Medicine*, *320*, 153.

Barela, A. I., Kleinman, E. G., Golditch, I. M., Menke, D. J., Hogge, W. A., & Golbus, M. S. (1986). Septic shock with renal failure after chorionic villus sampling. *American Journal of Obstetrics and Gynecology*, *154*, 1100–1102.

Benacerraf, B. R., Greene, M. F., Saltzman, D. H., Barss, V. A., Penso, C. A., Nadel, A. S., Heffner, L. J., Stryker, J. M., Sandstrom, M. M., & Frigoletto, F. D. (1988). Early amniocentesis for prenatal cytogenetic evaluation. *Radiology*, *169*, 709–714.

Black, S. H., & Schulman, J. D. (1988). Prenatal sampling and bicornuate uterus. *Prenatal Diagnosis*, *8*, 476–477.

Bogart, M. H., Pandian, M. R., & Jones, O. W. (1987). Abnormal maternal serum chorionic gonadotrophin levels in pregnancies with fetal chromosome abnormalities. *Prenatal Diagnosis*, *7*, 623–630.

Brock, D. J. H. (1976). Mechanisms by which amniotic fluid alpha-fetoprotein may be increased in fetal abnormalities. *Lancet*, *ii*, 345–346.

Callen, D. F., Korban, G., Dawson, G., Gugasyan, L., Krumins, E. J. M., Eichenbaum, S., Petrass, J., Purvis-Smith, S., Smith, A., Den Dulk, G., & Martin, N. (1988). Extra embryonic/fetal karyotypic discordance during diagnostic chorionic villus sampling. *Prenatal Diagnosis*, *8*, 453–460.

Canadian Collaborative CVS-Amniocentesis Clinical Trial Group. (1989). Multicenter randomised clinical trial of chorionic villus sampling and amniocentesis. *Lancet*, *i*, 1–6.

Canick, J. A., Knight, G. J., Palomaki, G. E., Haddow, J. E., Cuckle, H. S., & Wald, N. J. (1988). Low second trimester maternal serum unconjugated estriol in pregnancies with Down's syndrome. *British Journal of Obstetrics and Gynaecology*, *95*, 330–333.

Crane, J. P., Beaver, H. A., & Cheung, S. W. (1988). First trimester chorionic villus sampling versus mid-trimester genetic amniocentesis: Preliminary results of a controlled prospective trial. *Prenatal Diagnosis*, *8*, 355–366.

Creasy, M. R., Crolla, J. A., & Alberman, E. D. (1976). A cytogenetic study of human spontaneous abortion using banding techniques. *Human Genetics*, *31*, 177–196.

Cuckle, H. S., Wald, N. J., & Lindenbaum, R. H. (1984). Maternal serum AFP measurement: A screening test for Down syndrome. *Lancet*, *i*, 926–929.

Erbe, R. W. (1977). Prenatal diagnosis of inherited disease. In P. L. Altman & D. D. Katz (Eds.), *Human health and disease* (pp. 91–96). Bethesda, MD: Federation of American Societies for Experimental Biology.

Erlich, H. A., Gelfand, D. H., & Saiki, R. K. (1988). Specific DNA amplification. *Nature*, *331*, 461–463.

Fabricant, J. D., Boue, J., & Boue, A. (1980). Cytogenetic abnormalities in spontaneous abortions. In J. T. Queenan (Ed.), *Management of high risk pregnancy* (pp. 71–82). Oradell, NJ: Medical Economics.

Ferguson-Smith, M. A. (1978). Maternal age and Down syndrome. *Lancet*, *ii*, 213.

Geisler, M., & Kleinebrecht, J. (1978). Cytogenetic and histologic analyses of spontaneous abortions. *Human Genetics*, *45*, 239–251.

Haddow, J. E., Morin, M. E., Holman, M. S., & Miller, W. A. (1980). Acetylcholinesterase and fetal malformations: A modified qualitative technique for diagnosis of neural tube defects. *Clinica Chimica Acta*, *27*, 61–63.

Haney, A. F. (1978). Fetal measurements. *Perinatal Care*, *2*, 22–28.

Hanson, F. W., Zorn, E. M., Tennant, F. R., Marianos, S., & Samuels, S. (1987). Amniocentesis before 15 weeks gestation: Outcome, risks and technical problems. *American Journal of Obstetrics and Gynecology, 156,* 1524–1531.

Harrison, R., Campbell, S., & Craft, I. (1975). Risks of fetomaternal hemorrhage resulting from amniocentesis with and without placental localization. *Obstetrics and Gynecology, 46,* 389–391.

Higginbottom, J., Bagnell, K. M., Harris, P. F., Slater, J. H., & Porter, G. A. (1976). Ultrasound monitoring of fetal movements. *Lancet, i,* 719–721.

Hunter, A. (1988). False-positive and false-negative findings on chorionic villus sampling. *Prenatal Diagnosis, 8,* 475.

Kaffe, S., Gedunlow, L., Walker, B. A., & Hirschhorn, K. (1977). Prenatal diagnosis of bilateral renal agenesis. *Obstetrics and Gynecology, 49,* 478–480.

Kan, Y. W., Golbus, M. S., Trecartin, R. F., & Filly, R. A. (1977). Prenatal diagnosis of beta-thalassemia and sickle cell anemia. *Lancet, i,* 269–271.

Kim, H. J., Hsu, L. Y. F., Paciuc, S., Cristian, S., Quintana, A., & Hirschhorn, K. (1975). Cytogenetics and fetal wastage. *New England Journal of Medicine, 293,* 844–847.

Kleinman, C. S., Hobbins, J. C., Lynch, D. C., Talner, N. S., & Jaffe, C. C. (1980, December). Prenatal echocardiography. *Hospital Practice, 15,* 81–88.

Kogan, S. C., Doherty, A. B. M., & Gitschier, J. (1987). An improved method for prenatal diagnosis of genetic diseases by analysis of amplified DNA sequences. *New England Journal of Medicine, 317,* 985.

Landegren, U., Kaiser, R., Caskey, C. T., & Hood, L. (1988). DNA diagnostics: Molecular techniques and automation. *Science, 242,* 229–237.

Macri, J. N., Weiss, R. R., Tillitt, R., Balsam, D., & Elligers, K. W. (1976). Prenatal diagnosis of neural tube defects. *Journal of the American Medical Association, 236,* 1251–1254.

Mahoney, M. J., & Hobbins, J. C. (1977). Prenatal diagnosis of chondroectodermal dysplasia (Ellis van Creveld syndrome) using fetoscopy and ultrasound. *New England Journal of Medicine, 297,* 258–260.

Medical Research Council Working Party on Amniocentesis. (1978). An assessment of the hazards of amniocentesis. *British Journal of Obstetrics and Gynaecology, 85,* 1–41.

Merkatz, I. R., Nitowsky, H. M., Macri, J. N., & Johnson, W. E. (1984). An association between low maternal serum alpha-fetoprotein and fetal chromosome abnormalities. *American Journal of Obstetrics and Gynecology, 148,* 886–891.

Miller, W. A., Davies, R. M., & Thayer, B. A. (1987). Success, safety and accuracy of early amniocentesis (abstract). *American Journal of Human Genetics, 41,* A281.

Miller, W. A., Davies, R. M., & Thayer, B. A. (1988). First trimester amniocentesis (abstract). *American Journal of Human Genetics, 43,* A240.

Miller, W. A., & Kacoyanis, S. T. (1982). Factors influencing the success and safety of amniocentesis. *American Journal of Human Genetics, 34,* 102a.

Milunksy, A., & Alpert, F. (1976). Prenatal diagnosis of neural tube defects: I. Problems and pitfalls: Analysis of 2,495 cases using the alpha-fetoprotein results. *Obstetrics and Gynecology, 48,* 6–12.

Miskin, M., Doran, T. A., Rudd, N., Gardner, H. A., Liedgren, S., & Benzie, R. (1974). Use of ultrasound for placental localization in genetic amniocentesis. *Obstetrics and Gynecology, 43,* 872–877.

National Institute of Child Health and Human Development (NICHD). (1976). National registry for amniocentesis study group mid-trimester amniocentesis for prenatal diagnoses: Safety and accuracy. *Journal of the American Medical Association*, *236*, 1471–1476.

New England Regional Genetics Group. (1989). Prenatal collaborative study of Down syndrome in pregnant women under age 35. *American Journal of Obstetrics and Gynecology*, *160*, 575–581.

Palomaki, G. E., & Haddow, J. E. (1987). Maternal serum alpha-fetoprotein, age and Down syndrome risk. *American Journal of Obstetrics and Gynecology*, *156*, 852–862.

Portnoi, M. F., Joye, N., van den Akker, J., Morlier, G., & Taillemite, J. L. (1988). Karyotypes of 1142 couples with recurrent abortion. *Obstetrics and Gynecology*, *72*, 31–34.

Rhoads, G. G., Jackson, L. G., Schesselman, S. E., de la Cruz, F. F., Desnick, R. J., Golbus, M. S., Ledbetter, D. H., Lubs, H. A., Mahoney, M. J., & Pergament, E. (1989). The safety and efficacy of chorionic villus sampling for early prenatal diagnosis of cytogenetic abnormalities. *New England Journal of Medicine*, *320*, 609–617.

Rodeck, C. H. (1978). Value of fetoscopy in prenatal diagnosis. *Journal of the Royal Society of Medicine*, *73*, 29–33.

Rodeck, C. H., & Campbell, S. (1978). Early prenatal diagnosis of neural tube defects by ultrasound-guided fetoscopy. *Lancet*, *i*, 1128–1129.

Sachs, E. S., Johoda, M. G. J., Van Hemel, J. O., Hoogeboom, A. J. M., & Sandkuyl, L. A. (1985). Chromosome studies of 500 couples with two or more abortions. *Obstetrics and Gynecology*, *65*, 375–378.

Schedit, P. C., Stanley, F., & Bryla, D. A. (1978). One year follow-up of infants exposed to ultrasound in utero. *American Journal of Obstetrics and Gynecology*, *131*, 743–748.

Schmidt, R., Nitowsky, H. M., & Dar, H. (1976). Cytogenetic studies in reproductive loss. *Journal of the American Medical Association*, *236*, 369–373.

U.K. collaborative study on alpha-fetoprotein in relation to neural tube defects. (1977). Maternal serum alpha-fetoprotein measurement in antenatal screening for anencephaly and spina bifida. *Lancet*, *i*, 1323–1332.

Wald, N. J., Cuckle, H. S., Densem, J. W., Nanchahel, K., Royston, P., Chard, T., Haddow, J. E., Knight, G. J., Palomaki, G. E., & Canick, J. A. (1988). Maternal serum screening for Down's syndrome in early pregnancy. *British Medical Journal*, *297*, 883–887.

Watkins, P. C. (1988). Restriction fragment length polymorphism (RFLP): Applications in human chromosome mapping and genetic disease research. *BioTechniques*, *6*, 310–312.

# 9

*Curtis L. Cetrulo*
*Mary E. D'Alton*
*Edward R. Newton*

# ETIOLOGY
# OF PRETERM
# LABOR

Little (1862) is credited with the first description of cerebral palsy associated with perinatal events. In the title of his original article he talked about "abnormal parturition, difficult labor, premature birth, and asphyxia neonatorum" (p. i). One-third of all children with neurologic handicaps are born prematurely, and deliveries at less than 30 weeks carry a high risk of developmental disability.

In 1980 the Food and Drug Administration approved for the first time a tocolytic agent (ritodrine HCl) specifically for the management of premature labor. Most obstetricians felt that with an effective tocolytic agent, most cases of preterm labor could be stopped. However, by 1982 it was obvious that there had been no documented change in the prevalence of preterm deliveries. Eight to ten percent of all births in this country occur before 37 weeks of gestation. Despite other advances and new technology, preterm births still account for more than 85% of all neonatal deaths. It is clear that time has shifted the focus of attention from curative, crisis-oriented methods to epidemiologic prenatal research of pathophysiologic mechanisms to prevent preterm delivery. To predict the risk of preterm birth prior to the onset of labor, new tools of assessment must be developed.

The new pharmacologic approach has failed in part because preterm labor has not been recognized early enough for its effective inhibition. In one study by Herron, Katz, and Creasy (1982), only 20% of patients in premature labor came to the hospital early enough for treatment with tocolytic drugs. An additional reason why the prevalence of preterm delivery has not decreased is the need for intentional preterm delivery, sometimes due to placental insufficiency or bleeding, prenatal developmental problems including certain congenital anomalies, and other fetal or maternal indications.

## ETIOLOGY

There are many causes of preterm labor and delivery. As Table 9.1 indicates, at least 40% of preterm deliveries occur for no apparent reason. However, many factors have been recognized as being predictive of preterm delivery. For example, a multiple pregnancy is at risk for preterm delivery, and a woman who has delivered one premature baby carries a risk of 35% that her next delivery will also be preterm. If a woman has had two or more previous preterm deliveries, the risk that future deliveries will be preterm increases to 70%.

Papiernik and Berkhouer (1969) were the first to report criteria for identifying a population at risk for preterm deliveries. Their system, which was published 5 years later (Papiernik & Kaminski, 1974), included 30 predictive characteristics that are grouped under four headings:

*General and social factors*
Unwed mother: pregnancy of a woman unmarried at the time of the examination
Low weight: mother's weight before pregnancy lower than 45 kg
Diminutive size: mother's height less than 1.5 m
More than two children without domestic help
Unfavorable age: less than 20 years or more than 40 years of age
Low social class: nonskilled workers or precarious financial situation

*Unfavorable obstetrical or gynecological antecedents*
Dilation and curettage (D&C): previous D & C for spontaneous or induced abortion
Uterine malformation: malformation either diagnosed by hysterography or evident during the pregnancy (uterus arcuatus, uterus septus, uterus didelphys, hemiuterus)
Cylindrical uterus: minor malformation of the uterus; for example, parallelism of the walls of the uterus diagnosed during the pregnancy
Previous late abortion: previous abortion from the third to the sixth month of pregnancy

**Table 9.1.** Causes of preterm labor and delivery

| | |
|---|---|
| Spontaneous labor | |
| No known cause | 40% |
| Maternal/fetal complications | 25% |
| Multiple pregnancy | 10% |
| Intentional | 25% |
| —placental insufficiency, bleeding, congenital anomalies, premature rupture of membranes that leads to chorioamnionitis | |

Previous premature birth: previous delivery of a child weighing less than 2,500 g
Short interval since last pregnancy: less than 1 year between the last delivery and fecundation of the present pregnancy
Contractibility of the uterus: painful contractions are also induced by examination and are of regular rhythm and of longer duration than the usual spontaneous contractions
Presenting part: lower than 1 or +1, as far as the level of the sciatic spines
Thinned lower uterine segment: very thin and in shape of a cupola
Shortened cervix: cervix shorter than 2 cm
Patency of the internal os: palpable at the internal cervical os

*Danger signals at examination*
Metrorrhagia during pregnancy: bleeding during the second or third trimester of pregnancy
Suspicion of placenta previa: association between metrorrhagia and irregular presentation
Multiple pregnancy: confirmed by radiography and/or ultrasonography
Polyhydramnios
Proteinuria
Hypertension: systolic 130 and/or diastolic 90
Excessive weight gain: more than 9 kg at 32 weeks
Loss of weight during the previous month: loss of at least 1 kg during the previous month
Less than 5 kg weight gain at 32 weeks of pregnancy

*Factors of fatigue*
Work outside the home
Strenuous work: for work involving strenuous physical effort, standing, or continuous nervous tension (at-risk occupations include nurses, telephone operators, punchcard operators, cleaning staff, sales staff, hairdressers, and dentists)
Apartment above third floor in building without elevator
Long daily commuting time: more than 1 to 5 hours daily

Papiernik and Berkhouer (1969) were the first to recognize the central role of stress and fatigue and the importance of cervical changes in the etiology of preterm labor. Others (Creasy, Gummer, & Liggins, 1980; Hobel, 1982) expanded on Papiernik and Berkhouer's list of risk factors and stressed the importance of four historical factors that identify the patient at risk for preterm delivery. These four factors are: 1) age, 2) weight, 3) history of genitourinary infection, and 4) smoking.

Hobel (1982) also noted the importance of low progesterone levels as a predictor of preterm labor. Both Hobel (1982) and Creasy et al. (1980) agreed with Papiernik and Berkhouer (1969) that frequent pelvic examinations should be performed in the period from 20 to 32 weeks in order to identify cervical effacement and dilatation, especially in a high-risk group of patients. Shown in Table 9.2 is a risk prediction system developed by Creasy et al. (1980) that is similar to that of Papiernik and Berkhouer. This system also has four subgroups; however, a quantification of risk is attempted, with point totals of 0–5 representing low risk and those greater than or equal to 10 indicating high risk for preterm delivery.

**Table 9.2.** System for predicting spontaneous preterm birth

| Points | Socioeconomic status | Past history | Daily habits | Current pregnancy |
|---|---|---|---|---|
| 1 | Two children at home<br>Low socioeconomic status | One abortion<br>Less than 1 year since last birth | Work outside home | Unusual fatigue |
| 2 | Mother younger than 20 or older than 40<br>Single parent | Two or three abortions | More than 10 cigarettes per day<br>Heavy work<br>Long tiring trip | Less than 13 kg weight gain by 32 weeks<br>Albuminuria<br>Hypertension<br>Bacteriuria |
| 3 | Very low socioeconomic status<br>Shorter than 150 cm<br>Lighter than 45 kg | | | Breech at 32 weeks<br>Weight loss of 2 kg<br>Head engaged<br>Febrile illness |
| 4 | Younger than 18 | Pyelonephritis | | Metrorrhagia after 12 weeks<br>Effacement<br>Dilation<br>Uterine irritability |
| 5 | | Uterine anomaly<br>Second trimester abortion<br>DES exposure | Hydramnios | Placenta previa |
| 10 | | Premature delivery<br>Repeated second trimester abortions | Twins | Abdominal surgery |

From Creasy, R. K., Gummer, B. A., & Liggins, G. C. (1980). System for predicting spontaneous preterm birth. Obstetrics and Gynecology, 55 (6), 692–695; reprinted by permission.

Point totals of 1–5 represent low risk; 6–9 indicates medium risk; point totals $\geq$ 10 indicate high risk for preterm delivery.

Since the diagnosis of premature labor is a patient diagnosis, education of the patient at risk for preterm labor is most important. Patients identified at high risk should be followed weekly, and the importance of early preterm labor detection should be stressed (Creasy et al., 1980). Instructions about the subtle and insidious symptoms of preterm labor are emphasized, including palpation of painless contractions; regular uterine contractions with or without pain for 1 hour or longer; dull back, lower abdominal, and thigh pain or pressure; intestinal "cramping" with or without diarrhea or indigestion; and change in vaginal discharge.

Women at high risk for preterm labor should avoid orgasm or breast stimulation and report any signs of urinary tract infection. If participating in intercourse, condoms should be used to avoid the influence that seminal prostaglandins have on uterine contractibility.

Education of medical personnel is also important and includes in-service training for attending and resident physicians, as well as primary care nurses in the expanded role (Creasy et al., 1980). The program stresses:

Prompt response to patient complaints with frequent pelvic examinations and fetal monitoring
Liberal admission for observation
Aggressive tocolytic treatment
Recognition of contraindications to tocolysis, including premature rupture of membranes, 4 cm or more of cervical dilatation, severe bleeding, active cardiovascular disease, and fetal demise or congenital anomalies incompatible with sustained life

Applying this approach of risk identification, weekly prenatal visits, and parent education, Herron et al. (1982) were able to reduce significantly the incidence of preterm delivery in a high-risk group. They are quick to point out, however, the need for an "improved discriminating tool," especially for the primigravida woman. They note that there has been little improvement in the incidence of indicated preterm delivery for bleeding problems and other causes of placental insufficiency, including hypertension syndromes of pregnancy and diabetes.

Guyer, Wallach, and Rosen (1982), in discussing prevention strategies for reducing the incidence of low birth weight infants, listed infection as one of four critical influences; the others were smoking, nutrition, and adequacy of prenatal care. Furthermore, they pointed out the association between urinary tract infection and low birth weight infants.

Included in any list of causes of preterm birth is premature rupture of membranes, a leading cause of preterm delivery and perinatal deaths. Some evidence suggests that infection of the amniotic fluid may preceed frank rupture of the membranes, and bacteria in the amniotic fluid of unruptured membranes may cause labor. Bobbitt and Ledger (1977, 1978) were the first to suggest that unrecognized amnionitis in an afebrile asymptomatic mother with intact membranes could be the cause of premature labor. In support of this suggestion, Naeye and Peters (1980) have shown that chorioamnionitis with intact membranes was a significant contributor to low birth weight infants and perinatal mortality. They found that chorioamnionitis was twice as frequent when membranes ruptured just after preterm labor began. This suggests that chorioamnionitis preceded and was the cause of the premature rupture of the fetal membranes. Miller, Pupkin, and Hill (1980) have demonstrated a wider spectrum of bacteria capable of colonizing amniotic fluid in the presence of intact membranes.

Cedarquist, Zervoudaks, Ewool, and Litwin (1979) reported the relationship between prematurely ruptured membranes and fetal immunoglobulin production. They demonstrated that 63% of umbilical cord blood samples in patients with premature rupture of membranes had increased levels of IgM or IgA, which is usually evidence of long standing fetal infection. Creatsas, Pavlatos, Lolis, Aravantinos, and Kaskarelis (1981) found that women with premature rupture of membranes prior to term are more likely to have anaerobes in endocervical cultures than women without premature rupture of membranes at term.

Curbelo, Bejar, Benirschke, and Gluck (1981) examined bacteria commonly associated with perinatal infections. They found that bacteroides fragilis, peptostreptococcus, fusobacterium, and streptococcus viridans had very high phospholipase $A_2$ activity and suggested that this enzyme could participate in triggering premature labor.

An interpretation of all these studies is that subclinical anaerobic infection can occur with intact membranes and can lead to premature rupture of membranes and preterm delivery. Furthermore, it can be postulated that this infection may cause premature labor, followed by premature rupture of membranes and preterm delivery or premature labor and preterm delivery without premature rupture of membranes (see Table 9.3). It should be stressed that the endocrine sequence that starts preterm labor may not be the same as that which starts labor at term.

Illingsworth (1958) reported 21 genetic causes of cerebral palsy. Ellenberg and Nelson (1979) and Bennett, Chandler, and Robinson (1981) also reported genetic problems in preterm delivery. They found that cerebral palsy developed in preterm births at an increased rate if, in addition to being preterm, children were small for gestational age when compared to preterm children appropriate for gestational age. This implies that intrauterine or genetic factors may contribute to preterm birth.

Holm (1982) described a group of children with birth weights less than 2,268 g who had prenatal causes of cerebral palsy, including brain malforma-

**Table 9.3.** Possible scenarios

1. Premature rupture of membranes ⟶ Infection ⟶ Premature labor ⟶ Preterm delivery
2. Premature labor ⟶ Premature rupture of membranes ⟶ Infection ⟶ Preterm delivery
3. Infection ⟶ Premature labor ⟶ Premature rupture of membranes ⟶ Preterm delivery
4. Infection ⟶ Premature labor ⟶ Preterm delivery

tions, congenital anomalies, recognizable syndromes, and neurologic abnormalities. Two lethal congenital anomalies associated with an increased incidence of preterm delivery are anencephaly with polyhydramnios and bilateral renal agenesis (Potter syndrome) with lack of amniotic fluid.

## PRETERM DELIVERY DUE TO DELIBERATE OBSTETRIC INTERVENTION

Pregnancies at risk for placental insufficiency occasionally have an indication for preterm delivery. In studying the causes of births that occur early, pregnancies complicated by hypertensive disease, including preeclampsia and chronic hypertension, Rh incompatibility, and infection, are often on the list of etiologic factors that indicate deliberate obstetric intervention (see Table 9.4).

When preterm delivery threatens, maternal and fetal care should include a careful admission history, physical examination, and an assessment of gestational age (see Figure 9.1 and Table 9.5). The physical examination should include an initial cervical examination, followed by sequential cervical examinations to assess progression, dilatation, and effacement of the cervix or descent of the presenting part.

**Table 9.4.** Preterm delivery due to deliberate obstetric intervention

Pregnancies at risk for placental insufficiency occasionally have an indication for preterm delivery.

Factors that indicate preterm delivery:
1. Preeclampsia and other hypertensive syndromes of pregnancy
2. Diabetes
3. Bleeding—both placenta previa and placental abruption
4. Severe intrauterine fetal growth retardation
5. Heart disease
6. Rh incompatability
7. Infection—as a result of premature rupture of membranes

1. MENSTRUAL HISTORY

   LNMP_____

   LMP_____

   PMP_____

   Menarche_____Interval_____Duration_____

   Hx Menstrual Irregularity_____

2. HISTORY OF ORAL CONTRACEPTIVES (When Stopped)

   Date_____

3. QUICKENING

   Date_____

4. CLINICAL EVALUATION

   a. First uterine size estimate

      Date_____Size_____

      By Whom_____

   b. Fetal heart tones

      Date First Heard_____By Whom_____

   c. Pregnancy Test: Type_____Date_____Result_____

   d. Ultrasound: Date_____Gestation_____

   e. Reliability of Dates_____

   f. EDC_____Estimate Based on_____

   _____

5. COMMENTS:_____

   _____

   _____

   _____        _____
        Signature                          Date

**Figure 9.1.** Gestational age estimation sheet.

Monitoring of fetal heart rate and uterine contractions should be a part of any surveillance of preterm labor. Accelerations of the fetal heart rate with fetal movements and the lack of deceleration with contractions rule out fetal jeopardy. An ultrasound examination to confirm gestational age and identify the presenting part is helpful. A biophysical profile is also appropriate, with notations made of fetal breathing movements, fetal tone, and an assessment of amniotic fluid volume.

The neonatology department of the hospital should be notified after initial assessment of the patient. For most women bed rest is prescribed, which is often therapeutic. Glucocorticoids are given if the gestational age is

**Table 9.5.** Treatment of threatened premature labor

Maternal/fetal care

A. Admission history and physical examination

B. Cervical assessment—Premature labor = as a result of progressive dilatation and effacement of cervix or descent of the presenting part prior to 37 weeks

C. Careful assessment of gestational age

D. Ultrasound examination and antepartum monitoring
   1) Confirm presenting part
   2) Fetal well-being—biophysical profile
   3) Gestational age assessment

E. Notify neonatology department (Intensive care nursery)

F. Bed rest

G. Tocolytic agents

H. Steroids if gestational age is less than 34 weeks or if amniotic fluid evaluation indicates fetal pulmonary immaturity

I. Delivery at a perinatal center

J. Aggressive perinatal care if estiamted fetal weight is greater than 600 gm. or gestational age 26 weeks or greater (i.e., cesarean section for fetal distress, breech)

less than 34 weeks and if amniotic fluid studies indicate fetal pulmonary immaturity. If contractions continue and/or if cervical changes are noted, tocolysis is usually begun.

## TOCOLYSIS

As ritodrine HC1 is the only drug approved for use in premature labor, the discussion on tocolysis is limited to this agent. Other agents, such as magnesium sulfate or terbutaline, are probably equally effective, and their indications and contraindications are similar.

Ritodrine HCl is a potent beta sympathomimetic agent with predominantly beta-2 effects on the uterus. Ritodrine HCl decreases the intensity and frequency of uterine contraction through a calcium-dependent mechanism in the myometrial cell. The cardiovascular effects of maternal tachycardia and hypotension are usually not significant, and there are only mild and transient effects on the newborn. In the United States, one collaborative study (Merkatz, Peter, & Barden, 1980) showed the statistical advantages of using ritodrine HCl over the other agents. These included decreased neonatal mortality, reduced incidence of respiratory distress syndrome, increased number of pregnancies attaining 36 weeks, increased mean gestational age, more days gained, and a larger number of infants weighing 2,500 g or more.

Women who are experiencing contractions between 20 and 36 weeks of pregnancy are candidates for use of this potent beta sympathomimetic agent. Whether or not one should wait for a cervical change before starting therapy is something that is left up to the individual practitioner. Occasionally, it is reasonable to wait for a cervical change. For example, if the woman's cervix is closed and uneffaced and if contractions are occurring, it might be reasonable to wait for a change in cervical effacement and dilatation. However, if the cervix is from 2 cm to 3 cm dilated and 50% effaced, it may not be reasonable to wait because the cervix may rapidly become dilated to 5 cm or 6 cm and, at this point, tocolysis will not be very effective.

Contraindications to the use of this agent include: 1) active vaginal bleeding, 2) eclampsia or preeclampsia, 3) maternal cardiac disease, 4) intrauterine infection, and 5) fetus malformations incompatible with sustained life. Maternal hyperthyroidism is also a contraindication, as is any maternal or fetal condition that is incompatible with prolongation of the pregnancy.

The administration of this agent has limited success when an incompetent cervix exists, when ruptured membranes are present, or when the cervix is dilated more than 4 cm and is 80% to 90% effaced. Similarly, ritodrine HCl is often not effective in an untreated urinary tract infection. Maternal side effects include tachycardia, hypotension, arrhythmias, hypokalemia, and pulmonary edema. Metabolic changes include changes in glucose tolerance with increased glycogenolysis and changes in blood lipids. In addition, many women become very agitated when this drug is used. The fetal side effects include fetal tachycardia and occasionally the fetal heart rate decreases if maternal hypotension is severe. Newborn hypotension has not been reported, but neonatal hypoglycemia and hypocalcemia have been observed with neonatal irritability following ritodrine administration.

Ritodrine HCl is administered intravenously, using a Harvard or other calibrated infusion pump. The initial dose is 50 ug/minute with increases of 50 ug/minute every 10 minutes. The dose is reduced if unacceptable side effects develop. The maximum dose that could be used is 350 ug/minute, and the drug is discontinued if labor progresses at the maximum dose. Ritodrine HCl infusion is usually continued for 12 hours after the arrest of labor, at which time oral therapy is provided during the last half hour of the intravenous dose. The initial oral dose is 10 mg/30 minutes before discontinuing the intravenous therapy, and then 10 mg every 2 hours or 20 mg every 4 hours for 24 hours. The maximum oral dose is 120 mg in 24 hours.

During use of ritodrine HCl it is necessary to monitor the maternal heart rate, electrocardiogram, blood pressure, and uterine activity. The fetal heart rate should also be monitored, and an accurate estimate of maternal intake and output should be kept. The patient should be at bed rest in the lateral recumbent position during the infusion. Blood for complete blood count, electrolytes, glucose, and lactate levels should be obtained. It is especially important to monitor the potassium level, as hypokalemia has been a frequent complication of intravenous infusion of ritodrine HCl. Similarly, when any tocolytic agent is given in conjunction with steroids, there is a risk of developing pulmonary edema. The lungs should be frequently auscultated during the intravenous infusion of ritodrine.

It is mandatory that preterm delivery occur at a perinatal center with an intramural intensive care nursery. The outcome for the premature baby is significantly improved when the delivery occurs in such a tertiary care center (Paneth et al., 1982).

The final treatment of threatened preterm delivery should include aggressive perinatal care that seeks to ensure intact survival if the gestational age has reached 26 weeks, or if the estimated fetal weight is 600 g or greater. This includes obstetrical intervention by cesarean section and the availability of an experienced resuscitation team at delivery. Herschel, Kennedy, Kayne, Henry, and Cetrulo (1982) have demonstrated good outcomes in the low birth weight infant with this approach.

A new approach is the use of home uterine contraction monitoring to identify patients with increased uterine activity who are at increased risk of preterm delivery (Katz, Newman, & Gill, 1986; Morrison, Martin, Martin, Gookin, & Wiser, 1987). This new technology is being evaluated in many institutions in the United States and Europe.

## CONCLUSION

Preventing preterm delivery involves the early identification of patients at risk for delivery prior to 37 weeks. Once these women have been identified, education of the at-risk population and staff care for these patients is emphasized. Treatment is aimed at continuing the pregnancy until fetal pulmonary maturity is assured. Preterm delivery should occur at a perinatal center to ensure optimal survival.

## REFERENCES

Bennett, F. C., Chandler, L. S., & Robinson, N. M. (1981). Spastic diplegia in premature infants: Etiologic and diagnostic considerations. *American Journal of Diseases of Children, 135,* 732–737.
Bobbitt, J. R., & Ledger, W. J. (1977). Unrecognized amnionitis and prematurity: A preliminary report. *Journal of Reproductive Medicine, 19,* 8–12.
Bobbitt, J. R., & Ledger, W. J. (1978). Amniotic fluid analysis. *Obstetrics and Gynecology, 51,* 56–62.
Cedarquist, L. L., Zervoudaks, I. A., Ewool, L. C., & Litwin, S. D. (1979). The relationship between prematurely ruptured membranes and fetal immunoglobulin production. *American Journal of Obstetrics and Gynecology, 134,* 784–788.
Creasy, R. K., Gummer, B. A., & Liggins, G. C. (1980). System for predicting spontaneous preterm birth. *Obstetrics and Gynecology, 55* (6), 692–695.

Creatsas, G., Pavlatos, M., Lolis, D., Aravantinos, D., & Kaskarelis, D. (1981). Bacterial contamination of the cervix and prematurre rupture oof membranes. *American Journal of Obstetrics and Gynecology*, *139*, 522–525.

Curbelo, V., Bejar, R., Benirschke, K., & Gluck, L. (1981). Premature labor: Vol. I. Prostaglandin precursors in human placental membranes. *Obstetrics and Gynecology*, *57* (4), 473–478.

Ellenberg, J. H., & Nelson, K. B. (1979). Birthweight and gestational age in children with cerebral palsy or seizure disorder. *American Journal of Diseases of Children*, *133*, 1044–1048.

Guyer, B., Wallach, L. A., & Rosen, S. L. (1982). Birth weight standardized neonatal mortality rates and the prevention of low birth weight: How does Massachusetts compare with Sweden? *New England Journal of Medicine*, *306*, 1230–1233.

Herron, M. A., Katz, M., & Creasy, R. K. (1982). Evaluation of a preterm birth prevention program: Preliminary report. *Obstetrics and Gynecology*, *59*, 452–456.

Herschel, M., Kennedy, J. L., Kayne, H. L., Henry, M., & Cetrulo, C. L. (1982). Survival of infants born at 24 to 28 weeks gestation. *Obstetrics and Gynecology*, *60*, 154–158.

Hobel, C. J. (1982). Premature birth: Spotting the risks. *Contemporary Obstetrics and Gynecology*, *19*, 209–232.

Holm, V. A. (1982). The causes of cerebral palsy. *Journal of the American Medical Association*, *247*, 1473–1477.

Illingsworth, R. S. (1958). *Recent advances in cerebral palsy*. Boston: Little, Brown.

Katz, M., Newman, R., & Gill, P. (1986). Assessment of uterine activity in ambulatory patients at high risk of preterm labor and delivery. *American Journal of Obstetrics and Gynecology*, *154*, 44–47.

Little, W. J. (1862). On the influence of abnormal parturition, difficult labour, premature birth and asphyxia neonatorum on the mental and physical conditions of the child, especially in relation to deformities. *Transactions of the London Obstetrical Society*, *3*, 293–344.

Merkatz, I. R., Peter, J. B., & Barden, T. P. (1980). Ritodrine hydrochloride: A betamimetic agent for use in preterm labor. II. Evidence of efficacy. *Obstetrics and Gynecology*, *56*, 7–12.

Miller, J. M., Pupkin, M. J., & Hill, G. B. (1980). Bacterial colonization of amniotic fluid from intact fetal membranes. *American Journal of Obstetrics and Gynecology*, *136*, 796–804.

Morrison, J., Martin, J. N., Jr., Martin, R. W., Gookin, K. S., & Wiser, W. L. (1987). Prevention of preterm birth by ambulatory assessment of uterine activity: A randomized study. *American Journal of Obstetrics and Gynecology*, *158*, 536–543.

Naeye, R. L., & Peters, E. C. (1980). Causes and consequences of premature rupture of fetal membranes. *Lancet*, *1*, 192–194.

Paneth, N., Siely, J. L., Wallenstein, S., Marcus, M., Pakter, J., & Susser, M. (1982). Newborn intensive care and neonatal mortality in low birth weight infants. *New England Journal of Medicine*, *307*, 149–155.

Papiernik, E., & Berkhouer, E. (1969). Coeffecient de risque d'accouchement prématuré (C.R.A.P.) [Risk factors of premature labor]. *Presse Medicale*, *77*, 793–794.

Papiernik, E., & Kaminski, M. (1974). Multifactorial study of risk of prematurity at 32 weeks of gestation: Vol. I. A study of the frequency of 30 predictive characteristics. *Journal of Perinatal Medicine*, *2*, 30–36.

# IV

## PREVENTION OF DEVELOPMENTAL DISABILITIES DURING THE PERINATAL AND NEONATAL PERIODS

# 10 | Donald R. Coustan

# PREVENTION OF COMPLICATIONS DURING LABOR AND DELIVERY

As Cetrulo, D'Alton, and Newton point out in Chapter 9, "abnormal parturition, difficult labor, premature birth, and asphyxia neonatorum" is associated with cerebral palsy (Little, 1862). However, nearly 100 years passed before this association became the subject of obstetric investigation. The concept that preventable events at delivery cause neurologic damage leading to most cases of cerebral palsy has been assumed to be true, without regard to the evidence available in the scientific literature.

Other chapters in this volume discuss the problems of prematurity, infections, environmental teratogens, and genetic disorders that may lead to developmental disabilities in the offspring. All of these problems precede the process of being born, although many cannot be detected prior to birth.

## EPIDEMIOLOGIC STUDIES

In one study from the greater Seattle area, Holm (1982) evaluated 142 children with confirmed cerebral palsy born after January 1, 1970, and examined before December 30, 1979. Half of these babies had one or more prenatal risk factors, another 25% had low birth weight, and 10% were term babies. Of the latter, only 8 (5.6%) had some identifiable problem leading to birth asphyxia; whereas the other 6 had unexplained low Apgar scores. Thus, in this retrospective study, complications recognizable as labor-delivery problems were present in only a small proportion (less than 6%) of children with cerebral palsy.

Table 10.1 summarizes seven retrospective studies of children with cerebral palsy. As shown, 23%–100% of the babies were born prematurely

157

Table 10.1. Retrospective case control studies of cerebral palsy and circumstances

| Year of publication | Author(s) | Normal | Premature delivery | | Breech delivery | | Forceps delivery | | Cesarean section | |
|---|---|---|---|---|---|---|---|---|---|---|
| | | | Cerebral palsy | Control group | Cerebral palsy | Control group | Cerebral palsy | Control group | Cerebral palsy | Control group |
| 1955 | Eastman and DeLeon | 96 | 35.4% | 9.2% | 8.3% | 3.2% | 6.3%* | 2.0% | 4.2% | 4.6% |
| 1958 | Skatvedt | 391 | 28.2% | 4.1% | 8.1% | | 6.8% | | 1.9% | |
| 1962 | Steer and Bonney | 317 | 28.6% | 9.5% | 9.0% | 3.3% | 24.0% | 32.0% | 5.0% | 7.5% |
| 1962 | Eastman et al. | 753 | 31.2% | 8.2% | 9.0% | 3.5% | 7.7%* 37.8%** | 4.7% 35.6% | 6.4% | 4.5% |
| 1978 | Mayer and Wingate | 158 | 28.5% | | 12.6% | | 28.3% | | | |
| 1981 | Bennett et al. | 18 | 100% | | 16.2% | 14.3% | | | | |
| 1982 | Holm | 142 | 23.2% | | | | | | | |

*Midforceps deliveries
**All forceps deliveries

and 8%–16% were breech deliveries. However, those studies that distinguished midforceps deliveries from others found that cerebral palsy victims were two to three times more likely to have been delivered by midforceps than the average population. Delivery by cesarean section did not seem to be associated with an increased risk of cerebral palsy.

Unfortunately, it is impossible to draw conclusions about causality from such retrospective studies. In the first place, many of these studies are based on recollection of birth events by the mother years later. Recall bias, a phenomenon in which people with a bad outcome are more likely to remember events surrounding that outcome, could explain some of the differences. In addition, all of the variables investigated are not independent of each other.

For example, breech delivery is almost uniformly associated with an increased likelihood of cerebral palsy (see Table 10.2). However, certain antecedent conditions of the mother or fetus are associated with a greater likelihood of breech presentation. Prematurity, low birth weight, oligohydramnios (diminished volume of amniotic fluid), and structural or functional abnormalities of the fetus are all factors associated with both cerebral palsy and breech presentation.

If the focus is on genetic disorders and correct for birth weight, then abnormal babies are 2–13 times more likely to assume breech position than normal infants (see Table 10.3). When these abnormal babies end up with mental retardation, they contribute to the statistics linking breech delivery to mental retardation. Yet, no one would seriously suggest that the mental retardation was solely due to breech delivery. This underscores the importance of controlling for confounding variables in such studies.

**Table 10.2.** Known factors associated with breech presentation and potential reasons for failure in assuming the vertex presentation

| Factors | Potential reasons |
| --- | --- |
| Uterine and placental | |
| Bicornuate to double uterus | Aberrant shape of pregnant uterine cavity |
| Placenta previa or placenta in cornus of uterus | Aberrant shape of pregnant uterine cavity |
| Fetal | |
| Twins | Aberrant crowding |
| Prematurity | Less uterine constraint to fetal positioning |
| Low birth weight | Less uterine constraint to fetal positioning |
| Polyhydramnios | Less uterine constraint to fetal positioning |
| Oligohydramnios | Undue uterine constraint to fetal movement |
| Abnormalities in form or function of the fetus | Limitation in the capacity of the fetus to assume the vertex position |

From Braun, F. H. T., Jones, K. L., & Smith, D. W. (1975). Breech presentation as an indicator of fetal abnormality. *Journal of Pediatrics, 86,* 419–421; reprinted by permission.

Table 10.3. Frequency of breech presentation in various disorders

| Disorder | Number of cases | Percentage of breech presentation | Expected percentage for birth weight | Relative difference |
|---|---|---|---|---|
| Prader-Willi syndrome | 22 | 50 | 3.9 | 12.8 |
| 18 trisomy syndrome | 14 | 43 | 7.1 | 6.1 |
| Smith-Lemli-Opitz syndrome | 20 | 40 | 3.2 | 12.5 |
| Fetal alcohol syndrome | 10 | 40 | 8.2 | 4.9 |
| Potter anomaly | 87 | 36 | 7.7 | 4.7 |
| Zellweger syndrome | 15 | 27 | 3.7 | 7.2 |
| Myotonic dystrophy | 14 | 21 | 3.7 | 5.7 |
| 13 trisomy syndrome | 8 | 12 | 6.0 | 2.0 |
| Werdnig-Hoffman syndrome | 10 | 10 | 2.6 | 3.8 |
| de Lange syndrome | 52 | 10 | 5.6 | 1.7 |
| 21 trisomy syndrome | 39 | 5 | 2.7 | 2.0 |

From Braun, F. H. T., Jones, K. L., & Smith, D. W. (1975). Breech presentation as an indicator of fetal abnormality. *Journal of Pediatrics, 86,* 419–421; reprinted by permission.

## ANIMAL STUDIES

Experimental data concerning brain damage has been provided by animal studies. It is well-known that anoxia or severe hypoxia can cause death of the fetus or neonate. The assumption has been that sublethal amounts of hypoxia are responsible for brain damage. The extensive investigations by Myers' (1972, 1975) group at the National Institutes of Health (NIH) have shown that, at least in the primate fetus, total anoxia induced by clamping the umbilical cord and preventing lung breathing can be applied for up to 35 minutes, yet the fetus can still be resuscitated. However, if the anoxia lasts approximately 20 minutes or more before resuscitation, the fetus or newborn will eventually die of cardiogenic shock after a few hours or days. Anesthetized nonhuman primate fetuses subjected to total anoxia lasting up to 13 minutes do not sustain any brain injury. Only those fetuses anoxic for more than 13, but less than 20 minutes, sustain brain injury, and then injury is generally noted in brainstem structures. This type of brainstem injury is not found in human offspring suspected of having sustained perinatal injury, with the possible exception of cord prolapse; rather, cerebral injury is the rule.

Myers' group (Adamsons & Myers, 1977) also produced partial fetal hypoxia by compressing the maternal aorta, by the administration of excessive oxytocin to the mother, and in a number of other ways. If the asphyxia was severe enough to bring the fetal arterial pH to levels below 7.15, changes in the fetal heart rate characteristic of placental insufficiency occurred. Fetal arterial $PO_2$ is usually around 15mm Hg under these circumstances. Despite such a degree of asphyxia (lasting 2 to 3 hours in the monkey fetus), brain damage did not occur. However, if sufficient asphyxia was applied to bring the fetal pH below 7.0 for several hours, the newborn monkeys ultimately died of heart failure. Histologically, such animals exhibited severe brain edema with widespread cerebral necrosis. A few fetuses with asphyxia of intermediate severity and/or duration survived and manifested brain damage. This damage was generally cerebral and was characteristic of humans with cerebral palsy or epilepsy.

It is known that premature infants who sustain hypoxic injury generally exhibit changes in the deep cerebral structures within the walls of the ventricles where the germinal matrix resides. Such lesions are seen in individuals with cerebral palsy. Term infants sustaining hypoxic damage generally exhibit changes in the cerebral cortex. Such changes may serve as foci for seizures. Both these types of cerebral injury can be achieved in the primate fetus with partial hypoxia, but the vast majority of fetuses made hypoxic either die of cardiogenic shock or recover without any detectable sequelae.

## STUDIES CORRELATING ASPHYXIA WITH DEVELOPMENTAL DISABILITIES

Some prospective studies attempted to demonstrate relationships between intrapartum events and developmental disabilities. The Collaborative Perinatal Study (1972) was carried out at 12 teaching hospitals around the country and involved more than 50,000 pregnancies between 1959 and 1966. A large bank of data was assembled, and many of the studies referred to in this chapter make use of those data.

Niswander, Gordon, and Drage (1975) focused on a group of pregnancies believed to be at high risk for intrauterine hypoxia during labor—those mothers with abruptio, placenta previa, or prolapsed cord. Attesting to the severity of these problems is the fact that about one-fourth of these babies were perinatal deaths. A further subgroup of mothers were those 164 who suffered shock prenatally. Their 58 surviving babies make up the shock group. The study focused on long-term follow-up. At 4 years of age, babies in the study group were indistinguishable from matched controls in both low birth weight and mature birth weight categories (see Tables 10.4 and 10.5). Even more impressive is the fact that the same lack of difference exists when the shock subgroup is compared with matched controls (see Tables 10.6 and 10.7). It was impossible to demonstrate an effect of this catastrophic obstetric

Table 10.4. Four-year mean intelligence quotients of children who had been anoxic at time of delivery in comparison with a control group

| Babies | Case | Control |
|---|---|---|
| Mature birth weight: (334) | 99.1 | 100.2 |
| Low birth weight: (92) | 94.0 | 92.1 |

From Niswander, K. R., Gordon, M., & Drage, J. S. (1975). The effect of intrauterine hypoxia on the child surviving to 4 years. *Journal of Obstetrics and Gynecology, 121,* 892–899; reprinted by permission.

**Table 10.5.** Four-year fine motor performance of children who had been anoxic at time of delivery in comparison with a control group

| Babies | Case Number | Case Percentage | Control Number | Control Percentage |
|---|---|---|---|---|
| Mature birth weight: (341) | | | | |
| Normal | 263 | 77.1 | 272 | 79.8 |
| Suspect | 69 | | 64 | |
| Abnormal | 9 | | 5 | |
| Low birth weight: (90) | | | | |
| Normal | 59 | 65.6 | 60 | 66.7 |
| Suspect | 29 | | 28 | |
| Abnormal | 2 | | 2 | |

From Niswander, K. R., Gordon, M., & Drage, J. S. (1975). The effect of intrauterine hypoxia on the child surviving to 4 years. *Journal of Obstetrics and Gynecology, 121,* 892–899; reprinted by permission.

event on long-term mental or motor development in survivors. It must be remembered that many of these babies died; but those that survived did not do worse than babies whose mothers had normal labor and delivery.

The presence of abruptio, placenta previa, or prolapsed cord are only indirect markers for asphyxia. Mulligan et al. (1980) looked at 13,000 consecutive deliveries in which 1% of the infants were considered to be asphyxiated, as demonstrated by the need for more than 1 minute of positive pressure ventilation before the onset of spontaneous respiration. About half of the babies died in the newborn period. Sixty-five babies survived and were available for follow-up. Between ages 4 and 5, 18.5% of these babies had major sequelae and about 10% will never function independently. Surprisingly, 72.3% had no abnormalities whatsoever. IQ scores in the babies without neurologic abnormalities were more or less normally distributed, certainly without evidence for a detrimental effect (see Figure 10.1). The vast majority of asphyxiated infants either died or were normal, with about 20% of children having adverse sequelae regardless of gestational age.

**Table 10.6.** Four-year mean IQ score of children who had suffered shock prenatally in comparison with a control group

| Babies | Case | Control |
|---|---|---|
| Mature birth weight: (22) | 95.6 | 100.9 |
| Low birth weight: (13) | 100.9 | 95.0 |

From Niswander, K. R., Gordon, M., & Drage, J. S. (1975). The effect of intrauterine hypoxia on the child surviving to 4 years. *Journal of Obstetrics and Gynecology, 121,* 892–899; reprinted by permission.

**Table 10.7.** Four-year fine motor performance of children who had suffered shock prenatally in comparison with a control group

| Babies | Case | Control |
|---|---|---|
| Mature birth weight: (25) | | |
| Normal | 19 | 19 |
| Suspect | 6 | 6 |
| Abnormal | 0 | 0 |
| Low birth weight: (14) | | |
| Normal | 10 | 9 |
| Suspect | 4 | 5 |
| Abnormal | 0 | 0 |

From Niswander, K. R., Gordon, M., & Drage, J. S. (1975). The effect of intrauterine hypoxia on the child surviving to 4 years. *Journal of Obstetrics and Gynecology, 121,* 892–899; reprinted by permission.

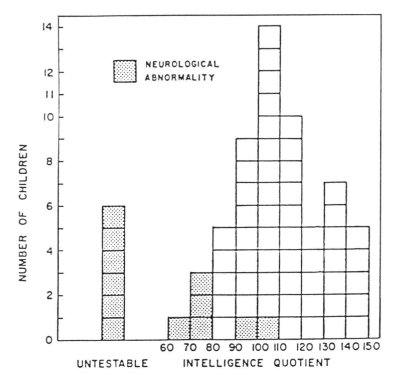

**Figure 10.1.** IQ distribution of survivors of asphyxia as determined by the Stanford-Binet Intelligence Scale. (From Mulligan, J. C., Painter, M. J., O'Donoghue, P. A., MacDonald, H. M., Allen, A. C., & Taylor, P. M. [1980]. Neonatal asphyxia: Vol. II. Neonatal mortality and long-term sequelae. *Journal of Pediatrics, 96,* 903–907; reprinted by permission.)

# THE APGAR SCORE AND DEVELOPMENTAL DISABILITIES

A commonly used marker for perinatal asphyxia is the low Apgar score. The Apgar score is composed of five categories, each with the possibility of 0, 1, or 2 point(s). An infant may thus have an Apgar score from 0–10. Scoring is done at 1 and 5 minutes. A score of 7 or more is considered normal, whereas a score of 0–3 requires urgent and intensive resuscitation.

Nelson and Ellenberg (1981) used the Collaborative Perinatal Study data to correlate Apgar scores with the ultimate development of disabling cerebral palsy. Of the 37,000 children followed up to 7 years, 120 had disabling cerebral palsy. The remainder of the children were used as the control group. Significantly more children with cerebral palsy had low Apgar scores than children without cerebral palsy. However, notice that more than half of the children with cerebral palsy had normal 1 minute Apgar scores, and three-fourths had 5 minute scores of 7–10 (see Table 10.8). These data were then examined in a different way. If a baby had a given Apgar score, what were the chances of developing cerebral palsy later in life? Table 10.9 shows that very low Apgar scores were strong predictors of neonatal death, as might be expected. However, of mature birth weight babies with a very low 1 minute Apgar score, only 1.5% developed cerebral palsy. If the low Apgar score persisted to 5 minutes, about 5% developed cerebral palsy—but 95% did not.

One possible explanation for the poor predictive value of low Apgar scores is the fact that Apgar scores are not a good measure of hypoxia and acidosis. For example, Sykes et al. (1982) obtained umbilical cord blood gases on 895 newborns. Of 34 babies with 1 minute Apgar scores of 0–3, only 10 were truly acidotic (pH less than 7, base deficit more than 12 mmol). Conversely, of 798 babies with 1 minute Apgar scores of 7–10, 56 were acidotic. Almost three-fourths of the acidotic babies were in the 90% with normal Apgar scores. Thus, Apgar scores may be a poor predictor of developmental disabilities because they are not valid measurements of fetal hypoxia and acidosis.

Table 10.8. Apgar scores in 120 children with disabling cerebral palsy in comparison with a control group

| | Apgar scores obtained at: | | | |
| | 1 minute | | 5 minutes | |
| Apgar score | Cerebral palsy | No cerebral palsy | Cerebral palsy | No cerebral palsy |
|---|---|---|---|---|
| 0–3 | 26% | 5% | 15% | 1% |
| 4–6 | 19% | 14% | 12% | 3% |
| 7–10 | 55% | 81% | 73% | 96% |

From Nelson, K. B., & Ellenberg, J. J. (1981). Apgar scores as predictors of chronic neurologic disability. *Pediatrics, 68,* 36–44; reprinted by permission.

**Table 10.9.** Outcome of babies with low (0–3) Apgar scores

|  | Apgar scores obtained at: | |
|---|---|---|
|  | 1 minute | 5 minutes |
| Less than 2500 g: | | |
| Death in first year | 48.2% | 74.5% |
| Cerebral palsy in survivors | 2.9% | 6.7% |
| More than 2500 g: | | |
| Death in first year | 5.6% | 15.5% |
| Cerebral palsy in survivors | 1.5% | 4.7% |

From Nelson, K. B., & Ellenberg, J. J. (1981). Apgar scores as predictors of chronic neurologic disability. *Pediatrics, 68,* 36–44; reprinted by permission.

In order to look at long-term prognosis in a group of very severely asphyxiated newborns, Scott (1976) followed 48 infants born with a 1 minute Apgar score of 0 and/or failure to establish spontaneous respiration within 20 minutes. About half of these babies died in the neonatal period. About one-fourth of the survivors developed cerebral palsy. IQ in the noncerebral palsy survivors were not very different from the normal population (see Figure 10.2). Scott (1976) then assessed the survivors on the basis of the type of stress endured at the time of delivery (see Table 10.10). "Prolonged stress" referred to babies who were small for dates or whose mothers had chronic illnesses that would be expected to impair placental perfusion. "Acute stress" included sudden events, such as prolapsed umbilical cord and breech delivery. Fetal distress included abnormal fetal heart rates in labor (greater than 160 or less than 100). It is interesting that the combination of prolonged stress plus fetal distress distinguished babies destined for cerebral palsy from those

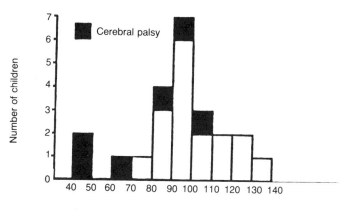

**Figure 10.2.** Severe birth asphyxia and later intelligence. [From Scott H. [1976]. Outcome of very severe birth asphyxia. *Archives of Disease in Childhood, 51,* 712–761; reprinted by permission.]

Table 10.10. Type of stress versus long-term outcome

|  | Cerebral palsy | Normal |
|---|---|---|
| Prolonged stress | 4 (66.7%) | 2 (11.8%) |
| Acute stress | 1 (16.7%) | 8 (47.0%) |
| Fetal distress | 5 (83.3%) | 7 (41.2%) |

From Scott, H. (1976). Outcome of very severe birth asphyxia. *Archives of Disease in Childhood, 51,* 712–716; reprinted by permission.

who were ultimately normal. This is reminiscent of Myers' (1972, 1975) work in primates. Acute anoxia was not associated with cerebral lesions, yet chronic hypoxia was. Most often it is not the normal fetus undergoing distress at delivery who develops cerebral palsy, but rather the fetus who is chronically in trouble long before labor.

## PREVENTION OF DEVELOPMENTAL DISABILITIES

What then can be done at labor and delivery to try to prevent developmental disabilities? In other chapters the importance of preventing prematurity and other prenatal problems is discussed. If babies who develop cerebral palsy or other disabilities are already in trouble long before labor, efforts ought to be directed toward detecting these chronically stressed fetuses and making labor and delivery as benign a process as possible. Since placental perfusion ceases whenever the intrauterine pressure exceeds 30 mm Hg, labor represents a series of hypoxic insults to every fetus. If the fetus has already been subject to chronic hypoxia in utero so that very little reserve exists, contractions may contribute the additional hypoxia that causes permanent damage. Thus, it becomes important to identify the fetus that can not tolerate contractions well.

### Electronic Fetal Monitoring

Fetal monitoring has become a standard means of assessing fetal condition. A computer counts the fetal heartbeats and continuously displays the rate. Uterine activity is also recorded. Three basic patterns of repetitive decelerations exist. Variable decelerations, occurring in up to 80% of all labors, represent a reflexive slowing of the heart, generally in response to even mild degrees of compression of the umbilical cord. These variable decelerations are considered benign except when severe and repetitive. Early decelerations are a reflex related to compression of the fetal head and are also generally felt to be benign. Late decelerations, however, represent uteroplacental insufficiency and are considered to be the most ominous fetal heart rate pattern.

Further refinement in interpretation of fetal heart rates came with the understanding that the normal fetus demonstrates beat-to-beat variability and that a sick fetus often loses this variability. Thus, Zanini, Paul, and Huey

(1980) showed that when scalp pH was measured during various types of fetal heart rate patterns, late and variable decelerations were associated with significant fetal acidosis when beat-to-beat variability was absent, and rarely when it was present (see Figure 10.3).

## Fetal pH Testing

Fetal heart rate monitoring would appear to be a good way to determine which fetuses are chronically stressed and least able to tolerate the hypoxia of uterine contractions. Unfortunately, virtually all investigators have found that at least 25%, and often 50%, of abnormal tracings are associated with a normal fetal condition. If all abnormal tracings were treated with immediate cesarean section, a large number of unnecessary operations would be performed. Therefore, it is necessary to confirm an abnormal fetal heart rate pattern with a fetal pH determination (done on a drop of scalp venous blood) before performing an urgent delivery. The combination of fetal heart rate monitoring and pH determination ought to be a potent way to select those fetuses at risk for developmental disabilities and keep them from the additional stress of labor. Perhaps these measures could prevent some of these babies from suffering brain damage. Unfortunately, data to support or refute this hypothesis are as yet unavailable.

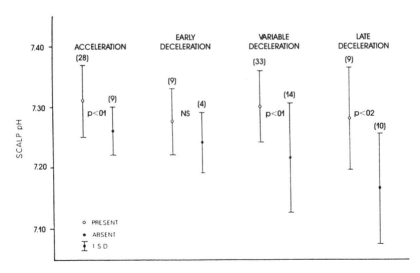

**Figure 10.3.** Various periodic fetal heart rate pattern groups. (From Zanini, B., Paul, R. H., & Huey, J. R. [1980]. Intrapartum fetal heart rate: Correlation with scalp pH in the preterm fetus. *American Journal of Obstetrics and Gynecology, 136,* 43–47; reprinted by permission.)

## Fetal Electroencephalography

Fetal electroencephalographic monitoring is one method being investigated. Borgstedt et al. (1975) reported a correlation between sharp wave activity on the fetal electroencephalogram and abnormal neurologic examination at 1 year of age. If this approach is proven to be valid, then it may be possible to identify those fetuses who have already sustained damage to the central nervous system before they are born, and thus, they may be delivered in such a way as not to worsen their condition.

## Prevention of Hyperglycemia

Myers' (1972) experimental work on the effects of asphyxia on the primate fetus has already been referred to above. Myers (1975) further refined these studies and found that the administration of moderate to large amounts of glucose to such animals just prior to the hypoxic insult leads to severe brain damage and death more rapidly than in fasted animals. Myers hypothesizes that the availability of glucose as a substrate leads to a greater local buildup of lactic acid in the brain under conditions of hypoxia, and this lactic acid causes edema and brain damage. If this hypothesis is proven, a possible means of preventing brain damage may be the avoidance of glucose infusion to the mother during labor, especially in the at-risk pregnancy.

In fact, a study from Philadelphia (Kenepp et al., 1982) showed such an effect in humans. Three groups of women about to undergo repeat cesarean section were pretreated with varying amounts of intravenous glucose before induction of anesthesia. Group A received 7.5 g of dextrose; group C, 25 g; and group B, 57.5 g. Incidentally, the 57.5 g represent 1,150 ml of a 5% dextrose solution and would not be a clinically unusual pretreatment. As shown in Table 10.11, there was a significant difference in umbilical glucose levels between groups A and B, and most important, a significant lowering of umbilical artery pH with the higher glucose load. Lawrence's group in Sheffield (Lawrence, Brown, Parsons, & Cooke, 1982) reported a similar lowering of fetal pH when 1,000 ml of a 10% glucose solution was given to laboring mothers over a 1 hour period (see Figure 10.4). Thus, it would seem that one way to prevent developmental disabilities might be to avoid administering large amounts of glucose to the laboring mother.

## Anesthesia and Analgesia

The use of anesthesia in childbirth is popularly considered to be detrimental to the well-being of the fetus and newborn. Various studies have shown measurable differences in attention span and habituation in newborns exposed to analgesic or anesthetic medications during labor when compared to those who have undergone a more "natural childbirth." Although the presence of a measurable difference in newborn behavior does not necessarily imply that the difference is "bad," it is reasonable to assume that, all other things being

**Table 10.11.** Umbilical venous and arterial blood values at birth

| | A | B | C | D |
|---|---|---|---|---|
| $PuvO_2$(kPa) | 4.3 ± 0.18 (14) | 4.4 ± 0.2(5) | 4.0 ± 0.28(5) | a.s. |
| $PusO_2$(kPa) | 2.4 ± 0.32(10) | 2.5 ± 0.21(16) | 2.0 ± 0.16(4) | a.s. |
| $PuvCO_2$(kPa) | 5.3 ± 0.14(15) | 5.7 ± 0.34(18) | 5.5 ± 0.09(5) | a.s. |
| $PusCO_2$(kPa) | 6.2 ± 0.26(10) | 7.2 ± 0.36(16) | 7.0 ± 0.32(4) | a.s. |
| uv pH* | 7.31 ± 0.007(16) | 7.28 ± 0.008(18) | 7.28 ± 0.010(5) | <0.01 |
| us pH | 7.25 ± 0.012(13) | 7.19 ± 0.015(18) | 7.20 ± 0.020(4) | <0.01 |
| uv glucose (mmol/l) | 3.8 ± 0.09(16) | 11.7 ± 0.66(19) | 4.3 ± 0.40(4) | <0.001 |
| us glucose (mmol/l) | 3.4 ± 0.20(13) | 11.0 ± 0.72(17) | 3.7 ± 0.15(4) | <0.001 |
| uv lactate (mmol/l) | 1.4 ± 0.16(12) | 2.2 ± 0.24(17) | 1.5 ± 0.11(4) | <0.05 |
| us lactate (mmol/l) | 1.6 ± 0.16(12) | 2.6 ± 0.32(16) | 2.2 ± 0.40(4) | <0.02 |

From Kenepp, N. B., Shelley, W. C., Gabbe, S. G., Kumar, S., Stanley, C. A., & Gutsche, B. B. (1982). Fetal and neonatal hazards of maternal hydration with 5% dextrose before cesarean section. *Lancet, i,* 1150–1152; reprinted by permission.

*p* measured by unpaired 2-tailed t-test between groups A and B

*a-v difference significantly greater in group A than in group B

Bracketed figures are number of births

Group A 7.5 gms of dextrose IV to the mother

Group B 57.5 gms of dextrose IV to the mother

Group C 25 gms of dextrose IV to the mother

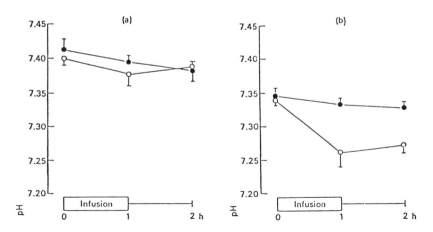

**Figure 10.4.** Whole blood pH (± SEM) in: a) maternal circulation and b) fetal circulation (O———O represents glucose infusion, and ●———● represents saline infusion). (From Lawrence, G. F., Brown, V. A., Parsons, R. J., & Cooke, I. D. [1982]. Fetomaternal consequences of high-dose glucose infusion during labor. *British Journal of Obstetrics and Gynaecology, 89,* 27–32; reprinted by permission.)

equal, the fewer drugs used the better. However, sometimes the choice is not between a happy, comfortable natural childbirth and one in which drugs are used. That is, drugs are used to relieve pain and anxiety. Though some mothers are well prepared and have relatively pain free and anxiety free labors, others are frightened or have particularly painful labors.

A number of primate studies have looked into the effect of maternal psychologic stress upon fetal physiology. Figure 10.5 depicts one such study in which the fetuses of rhesus monkeys had chronic arterial and venous catheters placed (Morishima, Pedersen, & Finster, 1978). Maternal psychologic stress consisted of the shining of a bright light in the mother's face. Both fetal pH and oxygen saturation fell during these periods of stress, and this was especially true with fetuses already somewhat hypoxic and acidotic. This effect has also been demonstrated with other types of maternal stress, such as noise, pain, even the ringing of the telephone. The effect appears to be related to a decrease in maternal uterine blood flow in response to stress, and may be catecholamine mediated. Thus, it is theoretically possible that *not* giving analgesic or anesthetic drugs to the anxious, stressed mother may be harmful to the fetus!

Even more provocative is the work of Myers (1972) in which pregnant rhesus monkeys about to be subjected to 12.5 minutes of total asphyxia were given barbiturate anesthesia. These monkeys were compared with monkeys delivered under local anesthesia. Those given barbiturates had a protective effect against asphyxia induced brain damage (see Figure 10.6). Other studies have confirmed this effect with moderate doses of barbiturates, although

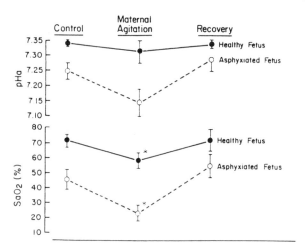

**Figure 10.5.** Mean (± SE) fetal pHa and $Sa_{O2}$ in the healthy and asphyxiated groups before, during, and after maternal excitement. (From Morishima, H. O., Pedersen, H., & Finster, M. [1978]. The influence of maternal psychological stress on the fetus. *American Journal of Obstetrics and Gynecology, 131,* 286–290; reprinted by permission.)

| Delivery | Degree of damage | | | |
|---|---|---|---|---|
| | 0 | + | ++ | +++ |
| Local | 0 | 0 | 3 | 4 |
| Barbiturate | 6 | 6 | 2 | 0 |
| Barbiturate (post delivery) | 0 | 0 | 3 | 1 |
| Barbiturate (acidotic) | 0 | 0 | 0 | 3 |

+ = Slight inferior colliculus injury. ++ = Severe inferior colliculus injury with several other loci involved. +++ = Severe inferior colliculi injury with extensive injury elsewhere.

**Figure 10.6.** Brain damage with 12.5 minutes of total asphyxia after delivery with the use of local and barbiturate anethesia. (From Myers, R. E. [1972]. Two patterns of perinatal brain damage and their conditions of occurrence. *American Journal of Obstetrics and Gynecology, 112,* 246–276; reprinted by permission.)

massive doses can have a harmful effect. Although no one is purposely administering barbiturates to mothers of asphyxiated fetuses, it is not reasonable to assume that fetuses born asphyxiated, whose mothers received barbiturates, were asphyxiated because of the drugs.

Another type of analgesia used in childbirth is paracervical block. A local anesthetic is injected into the nerve plexus at the junction of the cervix and vagina, effectively relieving the pain of the uterine contractions. It has now been demonstrated that paracervical block may cause slowing of the fetal heart, most likely because the local anesthetic causes vasoconstriction in the uterine arteries. In an already compromised fetus, this might increase the chances of neurologic damage. On this basis, paracervical block should probably be reserved for only the most normal situations.

## Mode of Delivery

Conventional wisdom has long held that traumatic forceps deliveries play a major role in causing brain damage. Although data linking difficult forceps delivery to increased perinatal mortality have long been available, similar data about long term neurologic follow-up are nonexistent.

The Collaborative Perinatal Study (1972) provided some information on this subject. As shown in Figure 10.7, this prospective study did not show any detrimental effect of forceps delivery on neurologic status at 1 year of age. The spontaneously delivered babies actually did less well than even the midforceps babies. However, these data may have been biased by confounding variables, such as gestational age and socioeconomic status, which might make forceps delivery less likely among higher risk groups.

Table 10.12 separates out forceps deliveries by degree of difficulty as judged by the obstetrician. There was clearly a higher prevalence of poor neurologic outcome with increasing difficulty of forceps delivery.

Friedman, Sachtleben, and Bresky (1977) found a small but significant difference in IQ related to midforceps in about 250 patients followed up to 4

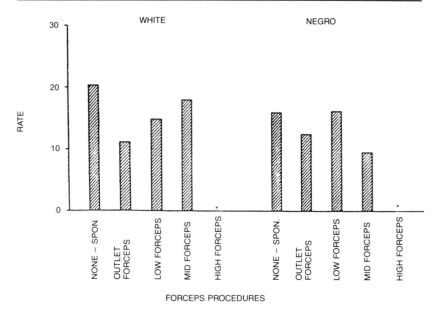

FORCEPS PROCEDURES

* RATE BASED ON LESS THAN 20 CASES.

**Figure 10.7.** Children neurologically abnormal at 1 year by procedure for vaginal delivery of vertex by race. (From Collaborative Perinatal Study. [1972]. *The women and their pregnancies* [DHEW Publication No. NIH 73–379]. Washington, DC: Department of Health, Education and Welfare.

years of age (see Table 10.13). Similar patterns emerged in speech, language, and hearing loss at 3 years of age. McBride et al. (1979), however, found no such IQ differences when more than 750 babies were similarly evaluated (see Figure 10.8).

**Table 10.12.** Children neurologically abnormal at 1 year by degree of difficulty of forceps usage according to race

| Degree of difficulty | White children | | | Black children | | |
|---|---|---|---|---|---|---|
| | 1-year exams | Abnormals | Rate | 1-year exams | Abnormals | Rate |
| None | 6,567 | 81 | 12.33 | 4,348 | 57 | 13.11 |
| Moderate | 669 | 12 | 17.94 | 406 | 3 | 7.39 |
| Severe | 187 | 10 | 53.48 | 163 | 5 | 30.67 |
| Failure | 26 | 0 | 0 | 51 | 0 | 0 |
| Total | 7,449 | 103 | 13.83 | 4,968 | 65 | 13.08 |
| No forceps | 5,521 | 112 | 20.29 | 10,435 | 167 | 16.00 |
| Unknown | 569 | · 7 | 12.30 | 534 | 8 | 14.98 |
| Total | 13,539 | 222 | 16.40 | 15,937 | 240 | 15.06 |

From Collaborative Perinatal Study. (1972). The women and their pregnancies (DHEW Publication No. NIH 73–379). Washington, DC: Department of Health, Education, and Welfare.

**Table 10.13.** Mean IQ by labor pattern and delivery type[a]

| Labor pattern | Spontaneous | Low forceps | Midforceps | Total |
|---|---|---|---|---|
| Normal | 107.6(18) | 106.1(21) | 101.3(19) | 105.0(58) |
| Prolonged latent phase | 103.9(7) | 107.8(5) | 101.0(1) | 105.2(13) |
| Protraction disorder | 105.9(8) | 101.4(7) | 100.6(16) | 102.2(31) |
| Arrest disorder | 98.0(1) | 100.6(16) | 98.6(36) | 99.2(53) |
| Total | 106.2(34) | 103.8(49) | 99.8(72) | 102.5(155) |

From Friedman, E. A., Sachtleben, M. R., & Bresky, P. A. (1977). Dysfunctional Labor: Vol. XII. Long-term effects on infant. *American Journal of Obstetrics and Gynecology, 127,* 779–783; reprinted by permission.

[a]Data limted to children with birth weights of 2,500 grams or more delivered of white nulliparas. ANOVA: delivery type, F = 5.8, $p < 0.01$; labor pattern, F = 3.9, $p = 0.01$; and delivery-labor, not significant.

Although some experts, such as Friedman et al. (1977), now advocate the total abandonment of midforceps deliveries, considerable controversy exists. Abandonment of all midforceps deliveries would be one solution to the difficulty of knowing which baby will suffer damage as a result of such a procedure. It would also add considerably to an already increasing cesarean section rate. That is because the option an obstetrician faces is not generally midforceps versus spontaneous delivery, but rather midforceps versus cesarean section. No one, however, would argue against the abandonment of difficult midforceps deliveries.

Breech delivery is another area of considerable controversy. In the earlier retrospective studies, breech delivery was always markedly more com-

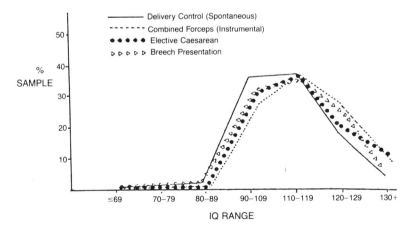

**Figure 10.8.** Distribution of total IQ scores. (From McBribe, W., Black, B., Brown, C., Dolby, R., Murray, A., & Thomas, D. [1979]. Method of delivery and developmental outcome at five years of age. *The Medical Journal of Australia, 1,* 303; reprinted by permission.)

mon in children with cerebral palsy than in the general population. Many other factors predisposing to developmental disability are also associated with breech presentation (Braun, Jones, & Smith, 1975). In a study of birth asphyxia at Magee Women's Hospital in Pittsburgh (MacDonald, Mulligan, Allen, & Taylor, 1980), babies born in breech position were significantly more likely to experience asphyxia than infants born in vertex position, even when prematurity was corrected for (see Table 10.14). Current trends, then, are to deliver premature breech babies by cesarean section, and to select term babies with breech presentation for vaginal delivery only if the clinical assessments of the fetus, the pelvis, and the labor are all favorable. As more data on long-term follow-up become available, practices will undoubtedly change.

Finally, it is valuable to describe the study of DeSouza and Richards (1978) in which 53 term babies with fetal distress diagnosed during labor plus severe neurologic abnormalities as newborns were matched with 53 normal controls and followed for 2 to 5 years. It was found that about 21% of the study group had neurologic abnormalities as opposed to none in the control group. Of those 21%, about 13% were of slight or doubtful significance, leaving about 8% with definite disabilities. Thus, in this group at what would be considered the highest risk for poor outcome, about 80% ended up perfectly normal and 92% had no real disabilities. The problem that remains, then, is to be better able to discriminate which patients are at the greatest risk and how to minimize that risk.

A large number of epidemiologic studies have been published confirming the lack of association between birth events and cerebral palsy. Nelson and Ellenberg (1981), applying multivariate analysis to the Collaborative Perinatal Study data base, found that labor and delivery events contributed little to account for cerebral palsy. Similarly, Naeye and Peters (1987) found little association between intrapartum factors and IQ at age 7 years. Painter, Scott, Hirsch, O'Donoghue, and Depp (1988) found no association between abnormal fetal heart rate patterns during labor and neurologic and cognitive status at 6 to 9 years of age. Also, descriptions of neurologic damage occur-

Table 10.14. Incidence of asphyxia

| Delivery | ≤ 36 weeks | > 36 weeks |
|---|---|---|
| Overall | 9.07% | 0.49% |
| Breech | 23.4% | 2.7% |
| | $p < 0.005$ | $p < 0.005$ |
| Vertex | 6.6% | 0.4% |

From MacDonald, H. M., Mulligan, J. C., Allen, A. C., & Taylor, P. M. (1980). Neonatal asphyxia: Vol. I. Relationship of obstetric and neonatal complications to neonatal mortality in 38,405 consecutive deliveries. *Journal of Pediatrics, 96,* 898–902; reprinted by permission.

ring in utero prior to delivery (Bejar et al., 1988; Paul et al., 1986) reinforce the concept that "fetal distress" during labor may be a result, rather than a cause, of neurologic damage.

One of the most important findings in the 1980s has been the observation that obstetric complications are not predictive of cerebral palsy or other neurologic damage in the absence of signs of neonatal compromise. For example, although low Apgar scores are a poor predictor of subsequent abnormality, obstetric complications were not associated with later cerebral palsy if high Apgar scores were present (Nelson & Ellenberg, 1981). The review of Perkins (1987) points out the poor correlation between birth events and later neurologic abnormality. In 1985, the National Institute of Child Health and Human Development and the National Institute of Neurological and Communicative Disorders and Stroke published a consensus report entitled "Prenatal and Perinatal Factors Associated with Brain Disorders" (Rosen & Hobel, 1986). A panel of experts reviewed the available data and concluded that the relationship between intrapartum events and brain disorders is poorly understood. They pointed out that neonates suffering perinatal hypoxicischemic encephalopathy and destined to be neurologically abnormal as a result, manifested neurologic symptoms during the first few days of life, most often within the first 12 hours. Thus, the child with cerebral palsy who had an entirely benign neonatal course is unlikely to have this disorder as a result of birth events.

## CONCLUSION

The study of the relationship between birth events and subsequent developmental disabilities is clearly in its infancy, despite many years of data collection. Nevertheless, given the current state of knowledge, it may be concluded that a normal fetal heart rate tracing, normal acid base balance in the fetus at birth, and a nontraumatic delivery are likely to be associated with a normal child. However, it must be remembered that the majority of abnormal children are not abnormal because of birth asphyxia or birth trauma. Similarly, the majority of asphyxic labors and traumatic deliveries result in normal children.

## REFERENCES

Adamsons, K., & Myers, R. E. (1977). Late decelerations and brain tolerance of the fetal monkey to intrapartum asphyxia. *American Journal of Obstetrics and Gynecology, 128*, 893–900.

Bejar, R., Wozniak, P., Allard, M., Benirschke, K., Vaucher, Y., Coen, R., Berry, C., Schragg, P., Villegas, I., & Resnik, R. (1988). Antenatal origin of neurologic damage in newborn infants: Vol. I. Preterm infants. *American Journal of Obstetrics and Gynecology, 159*, 357–363.

Bennett, F. C., Chandler, L. S., Robinson, N. M., & Sells, C. J. (1981). Spastic diplegia in premature infants. *American Journal of Diseases of Children, 135*, 732–737.

Borgstedt, A. D., Rosen, M. C., Chik, L., Sokol, R. J., Bachelder, L., & Leo, P. (1975). Fetal electroencephalography. *American Journal of Diseases of Children, 129*, 35–38.

Braun, F. H. T., Jones, K. L., & Smith, D. W. (1975). Breech presentation as an indicator of fetal abnormality. *Journal of Pediatrics, 86*, 419–421.

Collaborative Perinatal Study. (1972). *The women and their pregnancies* (DHEW Publication No. NIH 73–379). Washington, DC: Department of Health, Education and Welfare.

DeSouza, S. W., & Richards, B. (1978). Neurological sequelae in newborn babies after perinatal asphyxia. *Archives of Disease in Childhood, 53*, 564–569.

Eastman, N. J., Kohl, S. G., Maisel, J. E., & Kavaler, F. (1962). The obstretical background of 753 cases of cerebral palsy. *Obstretics and Gynecology Survey, 17*, 459–500.

Eastman, N. J., & DeLeon, M. (1955). The etiology of cerebral palsy. *American Journal of Obstretics and Gynecology, 69*, 950–961.

Friedman, E. A., Sachtleben, M. R., & Bresky, P. A. (1977). Dysfunctional labor: Vol. XII. Long-term effects on infant. *American Journal of Obstetrics and Gynecology, 127*, 779–783.

Holm, V. A. (1982). The causes of cerebral palsy: A contemporary perspective. *Journal of the American Medical Association, 247*, 1473–1477.

Kenepp, N. B., Shelley, W. C., Gabbe, S. G., Kumar, S., Stanley, C. A., & Gutsche, B. B. (1982). Fetal and neonatal hazards of maternal hydration with 5% dextrose before cesarean section. *Lancet, i*, 1150–1152.

Lawrence, G. F., Brown, V. A., Parsons, R. J., & Cooke, I. D. (1982). Feto-maternal consequences of high-dose glucose infusion during labour. *British Journal of Obstetrics and Gynaecology, 89*, 27–32.

Little, W. J. (1862). On the influence of abnormal parturition, difficult labours, premature birth, and asphyxia on the mental and physical condition of the child, especially in relation to deformities. *Transactions of the London Obstetrical Society, 3*, 293–298.

MacDonald, H. M., Mulligan, J. C., Allen, A. C., & Taylor, P. M. (1980). Neonatal asphyxia: Vol. I. Relationship of obstetric and neonatal complications to neonatal mortality in 38,405 consecutive deliveries. *Journal of Pediatrics, 96*, 898–902.

Mayer, P. S., & Wingate, M. B. (1978). Obstetric factors in cerebral palsy. *Obstretics and Gynecology, 51*, 399–406.

McBride, W. G., Black, B. P., Brown, C. J., Dolby, R. M., Murray, A. D., & Thomas, D. B. (1979). Method of delivery and developmental outcome at five years of age. *Medical Journal of Australia, 1*, 301–304.

Morishima, H. O., Pedersen, H., & Finster, M. (1978). The influence of maternal psychological stress on the fetus. *American Journal of Obstetrics and Gynecology, 131*, 286–290.

Mulligan, J. C., Painter, M. J., O'Donoghue, P. A., MacDonald, H. M., Allen, A. C., & Taylor, P. M. (1980). Neonatal asphyxia: Vol. II. Neonatal mortality and long-term sequelae. *Journal of Pediatrics, 96*, 903–907.

Myers, R. E. (1972). Two patterns of perinatal brain damage and their conditions of occurrence. *American Journal of Obstetrics and Gynecology, 112*, 246–276.

Myers, R. E. (1975). Four patterns of perinatal brain damage and their conditions of occurrence in primates. *Advances in Neurology, 10*, 223–234.

Naeye, R. L., & Peters, E. C. (1987). Antenotal hypoxia and low IQ values. *American Journal of Diseases of Children*, *141*, 50–54.

Nelson, K. B., & Ellenberg, J. J. (1981). Apgar scores as predictors of chronic neurologic disability. *Pediatrics*, *68*, 36–44.

Niswander, K. R., Gordon, M., & Drage, J. S. (1975). The effect of intrauterine hypoxia on the child surviving to 4 years. *Journal of Obstetrics and Gynecology*, *121*, 892–899.

Painter, M., Scott, M., Hirsch, R., O'Donoghue, P., & Depp, R. (1988). Fetal heart rate patterns during labor: Neurologic and cognitive development at 6 to 9 years of age. *American Journal of Obstetrics and Gynecology*, *159*, 854–858.

Paul, R. H., Yonekura, M. L., Cantrell, C. J., Turkel, S., Pavlova, Z., & Sipos, L. (1986). Fetal injury prior to labor: Does it happen? *American Journal of Obstetrics and Gynecology*, *154*, 1187–1193.

Perkins, R. P. (1987). Perspectives on perinatal brain damage. *Obstetrics and Gynecology*, *69*, 807–819.

Rosen, M. G., & Hobel, C. J. (1986). Prenatal and perinatal factors associated with brain disorders. *Obstetrics and Gynecology*, *68*, 416–421.

Scott, H. (1976). Outcome of very severe birth asphyxia. *Archives of Disease in Childhood*, *51*, 712–716.

Skatvedt, M. (1958). Cerebral palsy: A clinical study of 370 cases. *Acta Pediatrica*, *46*, 1–101.

Steer, C. M., & Bonney, W. (1962). Obstetric factors in cerebral palsy. *American Journal of Obstetrics and Gynecology*, *83*, 526–531.

Sykes, G. S., Johnson, P., Ashworth, F., Molloy, P. M., Gu, W., Stirrat, G. M., & Turnbull, A. C. (1982). Do Apgar scores indicate asphyxia? *Lancet*, *i*, 494–496.

Zanini, B., Paul, R. H., & Huey, J. R. (1980). Intrapartum fetal heart rate: Correlation with scalp pH in the preterm fetus. *American Journal of Obstetrics and Gynecology*, *136*, 43–47.

**11** | *Nancy B. Hansen*
*Richard E. McClead*

# ADVANCES IN NEONATAL INTENSIVE CARE TO IMPROVE LONG-TERM OUTCOME

Neonatal intensive care continues to evolve as a subspecialty in the field of pediatrics. The widespread availability of neonatal intensive care has dramatically decreased the birth weight-specific neonatal mortality rate since the 1970s. The mortality rate for infants with birth weights of 1,000 g to 1,500 g fell from 50% in the 1960s to less than 10% in the 1980s, while the mortality for infants less than 1,000 g birth weight fell from 90% to 50% during the same time period (Beuhler, Kleinman, Hugue, Strauss, & Smith, 1987).

These remarkable advances in survival for premature infants must, however, be put into perspective. In the United States, the rates of low birth weight (2,500 g and less) and very low birth weight (1,500 g and less) deliveries are significantly higher than in most Western industrialized countries, and statistics suggest that the rate of very low birth weight deliveries may be increasing (Institute of Medicine, 1985). Although low birth weight and prematurity are important predictors of neonatal mortality and childhood morbidity, improved survival rates for the critically ill neonate have not been associated with increased disability rates (Office of Technology Assessment, U.S. Congress, 1987). Thus, improvements in weight-specific neonatal survival has resulted in increased numbers of both normal and abnormal survivors. Overall, the cost of prematurity in this country remains extremely high whether measured in terms of excess neonatal mortality, long-term disabilities among neonatal intensive care unit survivors, or the economic costs of neonatal intensive care unit assistance.

Nonetheless, a brighter future for the critically ill newborn in the 1990s can be predicted due to important advances in the field of neonatology, several of which are reviewed in this chapter. These advances include: 1) management of the premature infant with respiratory distress syndrome as well as strategies to prevent chronic lung disease, including surfactant replacement therapy; 2) extracorporal membrane oxygenation for the full-term infant with persistent pulmonary hypertension; 3) cryotherapy for the treatment of retinopathy of prematurity; and 4) advances in the prevention and treatment of neonatal sepsis.

Other important medical concerns often observed in the neonatal intensive care unit, such as hyperbilirubinemia and intraventricular hemorrhage, are discussed in subsequent chapters (see Cashore, Chapter 12, and Volpe, Chapter 13, this volume).

## RESPIRATORY DISTRESS SYNDROME
## AND BRONCHOPULMONARY DYSPLASIA

Respiratory distress syndrome (RDS) or hyaline membrane disease remains the primary cause of infant mortality in premature infants. RDS at least doubles the length and cost of hospitalization compared to a premature infant without the disorder (Office of Technology Assessment, U.S. Congress, 1987). Furthermore, severe RDS is strongly correlated with many of the other major complications of prematurity, including intraventricular hemorrhage, bronchopulmonary dysplasia, retinopathy of prematurity (ROP), and necrotizing enterocolitis.

Simplistically, RDS develops because the premature infant lacks sufficient surfactant to coat the lungs' alveolar lining layer involving the air-water interface where gas exchange takes place. Without surfactant, premature infants are unable to keep their lungs inflated at low lung volumes. Thus, the premature infant with RDS develops respiratory failure and requires mechanical ventilation due to lung collapse and to tremendous difficulty involved in breathing.

Although advances in mechanical ventilatory techniques for the critically ill newborn are in part responsible for the improved survival rates of infants with RDS, widespread use of mechanical ventilation coupled with increased survival of very low birth weight infants has led to increasing numbers of neonatal intensive care unit survivors with the chronic lung disease, bronchopulmonary dysplasia. Bronchopulmonary dysplasia occurs in approximately one-third of infants who require mechanical ventilation at birth and is more frequent in very premature infants. The cause of bronchopulmonary dysplasia is multifactorial and is usually attributed to the combined effects of prematurity, lung damage from oxygen therapy, and mechanical ventilation. Bronchopulmonary dysplasia is the most common sequela of neonatal intensive care and a major cause of prolonged initial hospital stays, as well as the underlying cause of many rehospitalizations in an infant's first 2 years of life (Office of Technology Assessment, U.S. Congress, 1987). Infants with severe bronchopulmonary dysplasia have significantly increased post neonatal mortality rates as well as major problems with growth and development.

Although research efforts on bronchopulmonary dysplasia have increased understanding of this disease, the clinical impact of these efforts has been limited. Corticosteroid treatment of ventilator dependent infants with established bronchopulmonary dysplasia appears to improve short-term lung function and "weaning" from the ventilator, but this therapy has very serious potential side effects, including immunosuppression, hypertension, and gastrointestinal bleeding (Avery, Fletcher, Kaplan, & Brudno, 1985; Cummings, D'Eugenio, & Gross, 1989). Before corticosteroid therapy can be widely instituted, a long-term multicenter trial is needed to document the risks as well as the benefits of this powerful drug. Drug therapy to prevent bronchopulmonary dysplasia has focused on utilizing antioxidant agents to prevent oxygen toxicity. Unfortunately, little to no benefit has been observed with two antioxidants—vitamin E and superoxide dismutase (Sinkin & Phelps, 1987). Advances in ventilator management, including the introduction of high frequency oscillatory and jet ventilators, has shown some promise in reducing the lung trauma in infants with severe RDS, bronchopulmonary dysplasia, or both conditions. However, a multicenter controlled trial of high frequency ventilation failed to show any substantial benefit of these newer ventilatory techniques in uncomplicated RDS (HIFI Study Group, 1989).

The most significant advance in neonatal pulmonary care during the 1980s has been the development of artificial or natural (animal lung or amniotic fluid) surfactant extracts for the prevention of RDS. Dramatic improvements in pulmonary status have been seen in premature infants given exogenous artificial or natural surfactant immediately after birth (Merritt et al., 1986). The therapeutic potential of surfactant replacement therapy in neonatal RDS has been unequivocally documented in a number of well-designed, randomized controlled studies. Each of these studies demonstrate short-term improvements in respiratory function in premature infants. However, only one multicenter replacement trial (Morley, 1987) demonstrated that surfactant treatment significantly decreased the risk of death and bronchopulmonary dysplasia. Another well controlled, multicenter trial did not demonstrate any long-term differences in survival or major complications in newborns with bronchopulmonary dysplasia, patent ductus arteriosus, necrotizing enterocolitis, or periventricular/intraventricular hemorrhage (Hobar et al., 1989).

However, this latter study utilized a single dose regime. Multiple dose studies of surfactant replacement have documented improved survival and morbidity in treated infants. In some centers, as many as 90% of infants at 24–29 weeks gestation are surviving to discharge with surfactant treatment (Shapiro & Nutter, 1988). Thus, the effectiveness of exogenous surfactant replacement in ameliorating the short-term severity of initial RDS is well established. However, the effect of surfactant therapy on other complications of prematurity, such as bronchopulmonary dysplasia, intraventricular hemorrhage, and ROP, has not been clearly demonstrated.

Although exogenous surfactant replacement should become common practice following completion of more clinical trials and Food and Drug Administration approval, many unanswered questions remain: What is the efficacy of different surfactant preparations (human versus animal versus artificial)? When is the appropriate time and what is the appropriate method of administration? How many doses should be given? Which infants should be treated? Who should be followed for long-term effects? It is hoped that once surfactant is available to treat all premature infants at risk of developing severe RDS, the incidence of bronchopulmonary dysplasia will be reduced.

## EXTRACORPORAL MEMBRANE OXYGENATION

The most technically complicated and controversial therapy that has been introduced in the neonatal intensive care unit in the 1980s is extracorporal membrane oxygenation (Dworetz, Moya, Sabo, Gladstone, & Gross, 1989; Short, Miller, & Anderson, 1987). Extracorporal membrane oxygenation is used to treat persistent pulmonary hypertension of the full-term and near-term neonate. Previously called persistent fetal circulation, this disorder results from persistence of high pulmonary vascular resistance after birth. Infants with persistent pulmonary hypertension develop severe respiratory distress and respiratory failure, because the high pulmonary vascular resistance limits the amount of blood that can pass through the lungs to exchange oxygen and carbon dioxide. Contributing factors to an infant developing persistent pulmonary hypertension include asphyxia, meconium aspiration syndrome, group B streptococcal sepsis, and diaphragmatic hernia with lung hypoplasia. The hallmark of persistent pulmonary hypertension is intense cyanosis due to right to left shunting of the circulation away from the lungs. Standard medical management includes aggressive mechanical ventilation to induce hyperventilation, hyperoxygenation, and muscle paralysis with the use of vasodilating drugs to increase the pulmonary blood flow. Unfortunately, this form of management often results in barotrauma to the lungs and causes chronic lung disease. Furthermore, this disorder continues to have a 10%–20% mortality rate.

Extracorporal membrane oxygenation is basically a modified technique of cardiopulmonary bypass that is used for 7–10 days to support the infant's heart and lung functions. Catheters are placed in the carotid artery and jugular vein. Blood is removed from the venous circulation, passed through a membrane oxygenator, and returned to the baby. Anticoagulant therapy is required to prevent blood clots. In infants with reversible cardiac or pulmonary failure, this form of treatment allows the disease state, including sepsis, meconium aspiration, and/or elevated pulmonary vascular resistance, to subside, prevents the iatrogenic lung damage from aggressive mechanical ventilation, and lessens the chance of the infant developing bronchopulmonary dysplasia.

Extracorporal membrane oxygenation has several complications. These include serious bleeding complications secondary to the blood anticoagulation required by the technique, air embolism, and the risk of cerebral infarction due to ligation of one of the common carotid arteries. However, since 1975, close to 2,000 infants have been treated with extracorporal membrane oxygenation with an overall survival rate of 80% (Stork, 1988). It is important to note that most extracorporal membrane oxygenation centers do not place an infant on bypass unless they have failed vigorous trials of conventional therapy and meet a prognostic criteria of 80% mortality. This therapy is not used in the premature infant due to the overwhelming chance of fatal cerebral hemorrhage and technical difficulty of catheter placement.

## RETINOPATHY OF PREMATURITY

Retinopathy of prematurity (ROP), the disorder previously known as retrolental fibroplasia, remains an important cause of long term disability in the extremely premature infant. Here the developing blood vessels in the retina undergo pathologic changes in response to unknown stimuli to produce the disease entity ROP. Retinopathy of prematurity now has an international classification system (Silverman & Flynn, 1985). Stages I and II are most frequently observed and usually resolve without long-term sequelae. Stage III implies extraretinal fibrovascular proliferation of blood vessels and may cause retinal scarring or progress to retinal detachment (Stage IV) and blindness. Despite extensive research efforts aimed at prevention of this potentially blinding disorder, annually, approximately 500 infants suffer severe vision loss due to ROP (Phelps, 1981).

Although the epidemic of ROP that occurred in the late 1940s was clearly related to the routine administration of high concentrations of oxygen to treat RDS in the premature infant, the resurgence of ROP since the 1970s is most strongly linked to immaturity of the retina at birth and the increased survival of very premature infants (less than 28 to 30 weeks of gestation). Indeed, despite well-established standards of care that regulate the levels of inspired oxygen and blood oxygen levels (Bancalari et al., 1987), 40% of infants less than 1,000 g at birth will develop some stage of ROP, and from 10% to 15% will develop the scarring form of retinopathy. Thus, most neonatologists believe that the current form of ROP is largely unpreventable. An effective means for the prevention and treatment of ROP remains to be found. Vitamin E trials for prophylaxis and prevention of progression of ROP have produced conflicting results and major complications, including death from intravenous administration, have been associated with this form of therapy (Urrea & Rosenbaum, 1989). One large multicenter collaborative investigation documented that cryosurgery, a technique in which the proliferating ridge of blood vessels are destroyed in the retina, decreased the chances of retinal detachment by 50% in infants who have the more advanced stages of ROP (Cryotherapy for Retinopathy Cooperative Group, 1988). Thus, the incidence of blindness secondary to ROP should be decreased even though prevention and primary treatment of this disorder continues to elude neonatologists and ophthalmologists.

## NEW THERAPIES FOR NEONATAL SEPSIS

As many as 30% of neonatal deaths are in part attributed to neonatal sepsis, or blood poisoning. This is due to the multiple deficiencies in host defenses present in the newborn, as well as the complications of severe respiratory distress and hypotension that often accompany overwhelming bacterial infection in the newborn. The fetus makes only minimal amounts of immunoglobulins and must rely on maternally acquired IgG as the major source of host defense. The infant who is born prior to 32 weeks gestation will have received minimal amounts of maternal IgG, and this immunoglobulin deficiency increases with advancing postnatal age during the first few months of life (Ballow, Cates, Rowe, Goetz, & Desbonnet, 1986). Although antibiotic therapy and general supportive care remains the mainstays of therapy once infection has developed, several new approaches for prevention of sepsis in the at-risk infant have been introduced into the neonatal intensive care unit in the 1980s.

Group B streptococcal infection remains the major perinatal acquired bacterial pathogen in the neonatal intensive care unit. The most severe form of this infection, early onset disease, is usually acquired by intrauterine infection during labor and delivery. Several therapeutic approaches for prevention of perinatal acquired Group B streptoccocal infection have been studied, including active immunization of mothers (Baker et al., 1988), passive immunization of infants (Fischer, Hemming, Hunter, Wilson, & Baron, 1986), and chemoprophylaxis (Boyer & Gotoff, 1988). Active immunization of the mother would be the most specific form of prevention, yet the limited immunogenicity of current Group B streptococcal vaccines has resulted in disappointing clinical trials (Baker et al., 1988). Passive immunization of the infant poses problems in identification of the high-risk mother-infant pair before delivery, as well as the risks and costs of the large doses of immunoglobulin required if one chooses to treat the neonate by passive intrauterine transfusion (maternal transfusion) Unfortunately, treatment of the infant after birth by passive immunization with immunoglobulin transfusions does not prevent early onset disease due to intrauterine infection (Fisher et al., 1986).

Maternal chemoprophylaxis for Group B streptococcal infection has been extensively studied, and it is now proven that selective maternal-fetal intrapartum chemoprophylaxis with penicillin can prevent early onset Group B streptococcal infection (Boyer & Gotoff, 1986). In addition, postpartum administration of penicillin to infants born to mothers colonized with Group B streptococci provides some additional benefit (Siegel, McCracken, Thrilkeld, Milvenan, & Rosenfield, 1980). The major problem in this disorder remains the timely detection of the high-risk colonized woman to be treated perinatally without overtreatment of low-risk women, which increases the risk of adverse maternal penicillin reactions.

The other major type of neonatal sepsis that occurs in the neonatal intensive care unit is nosocomial infection in the form of staphylococcal epidermidis. Critically ill newborns with invasive venous or arterial catheters are particularly at risk. This population of infants is at high risk of acquired infection due to the developmental immaturity of their immune system.

The availability of intravenous immunoglobulin solutions has led to several studies of its use in the treatment of infection (Sidiropoulos, Boehme, von Muralt, Morell, & Barandun, 1986) and as a prophylactic treatment in premature infants at risk of infection (Chirico et al., 1987). The results of these studies are preliminary, but they do show a beneficial response to intravenous immunoglobulin, especially in the preterm infant. The results of the prophylactic studies are especially encouraging in view of the frequency of nosocomial infections in many neonatal intensive care units. However, as this form of therapy may potentially alter the developing immune system or cause other adverse effects, routine use of prophylactic intravenous immunoglobulin awaits further research documentation of the risks and benefits of this treatment.

## CONCLUSION

Innovations in the approach of care for the critically ill neonate have led to substantial improvements in neonatal mortality and morbidity since the 1970s. However, the history of neonatology has taught the painful lesson that new treatments should not become standard practice in the neonatal intensive care unit until subjected to rigorous clinical trials and careful analysis of the risks and benefits to the infant. Many of the new treatments this chapter reviews still await such critical analysis; but in the future these treatments may have a substantial impact on the outcome of many critically ill neonates.

## REFERENCES

Avery, G. B., Fletcher, A. B., Kaplan, M., & Brudno, D. S. (1985). Controlled trial of dexamethasone in respirator dependent infants with bronchopulmonary dysplasia. *Pediatrics, 75*, 106–111.

Baker, C. J., Rench, M. A., Edwards, M. S., Carpenter, R. J., Hays, B. M., & Kasper, D. L. (1988). Immunization of pregnant women with a polysaccharide vaccine of group B streptococcus. *New England Journal of Medicine, 319*, 1180–1185.

Ballow, M., Cates, K. L., Rowe, J. C., Goetz, C., & Desbonnet, C. (1986). Development of the immune system in very low birth weight infants: Concentrations of plasma immunoglobulins and patterns of infection. *Pediatric Research, 20*, 899–904.

Bancalari, E., Flynn, J., Goldberg, R. N., Bawol, R., Cassady, J., Schiffman, J., Feuer, W., Roberts, J., Gillings, D., & Sim, E. (1987). Influence of transcutaneous oxygen monitoring of the incidence of retinopathy of prematurity. *Pediatrics, 79*, 663–669.

Beuhler, J. W., Kleinman, J. C., Hogue, C. R. J., Strauss, L., & Smith, J. (1987). Birth weight-specific infant mortality, United States, 1960 to 1980. *Public Health Reports, 102*, 151–161.

Boyer, K. M., & Gotoff, S. P. (1986). Prevention of early onset neonatal group B streptococcal disease with selective intrapartum chemoprophylaxis. *New England Journal of Medicine, 314*, 1665–1669.

Boyer, K. M., & Gotoff, S. P. (1988). Antimicrobial prophylaxis of neonatal group B streptococcal sepsis. *Clinic of Perinatology, 15*, 831–851.

Chirico, G., Rondini, G., Plebani, A., Chiara, A., Massa, M., & Ugazio, A. G. (1987). Intravenous gammaglobulin therapy for prophylaxis of infecting high risk neonates. *Journal of Pediatrics, 110*, 437–442.

Cryotherapy for Retinopathy Cooperative Group. (1988). Multicenter trial of cryotherapy for retinopathy of prematurity: Preliminary results. *Archives of Ophthalmology, 106*, 471–479.

Cummings, J. J., D'Eugenio, D. B., & Gross, S. J. (1989). A controlled trial of dexamethasone in preterm infants at risk for bronchopulmonary dysplasia. *New England Journal of Medicine, 320*, 1505–1510.

Dworetz, A. R., Moya, F. R., Sabo, B., Gladstone, I., & Gross, I. (1989). Survival of infants with persistent pulmonary hypertension without extracorporeal membrane oxygenation. *Pediatrics, 84*, 1–6.

Fischer, G. W., Hemming, V. G., Hunter, K. W., Wilson, S. R., & Baron, P. A. (1986). Intravenous immunoglobulin in the treatment of neonatal sepsis. In A. Morell & U. E. Nydegger (Eds.), *Clinical use of intravenous immunoglobulins* (pp. 147–158). London: Academic Press.

HIFI Study Group, National Institute of Health. (1989). High-frequency oscillatory ventilation compared with conventional mechanical ventilation in the treatment of respiratory failure in preterm infants. *New England Journal of Medicine, 320*, 88–93.

Hobar, J., Soll, R., Sutherland, J., Kotagal, U., Philip, A., & Kessler, D. (1989). Multicenter randomized placebo controlled trial of surfactant. *New England Journal of Medicine, 320*, 959–965.

Institute of Medicine. (1985). *Preventing low birth weight*. Washington, DC: National Academy Press.

Merrit, T. A., Hallman, M., Bloom, B. T., Berry, C., Benirschke, K., Sahn, D., Key, T., Edwards, D., Jarvenpaa, A. L., Pohjavuori, M., Kankaanpaa, K., Kunnas, M., Paatero, H., Rapola, J., & Jaaskelainen, J. (1986). Prophylatic treatment of very premature infants with human surfactant. *New England Journal of Medicine, 315*, 785–790.

Morley, C. J. (1987). Ten centre trial of artificial surfactant in very premature babies. *British Medical Journal, 294*, 991–996.

Office of Technology Assessment, U. S. Congress. (1987). *Neonatal intensive care for low birth weight infants: Costs and effectiveness* (in OTA-HCS-38). Washington, DC: Author.

Phelps, D. L. (1981). Retinopathy of prematurity: An estimate of vision loss in the United States—1979. *Pediatrics, 67*, 924–927.

Shapiro, D., & Nutter, R. (1988). Controversies regarding surfactant replacement therapy. *Clinics in Perinatology, 15*, 891–901.

Short, B. L., Miller, M. K., & Anderson, K. D. (1987). Extracorporal membrane oxygenation in the management of respiratory failure in the newborn. *Clinics in Perinatology, 14*, 737–748.

Sidiropoulos, D., Boehme, U., von Muralt, R., Morell, A., & Barandun, D. (1986). Immunoglobulin supplementation in prevention or treatment of neonatal sepsis. *Pediatric Infectious Diseases, 5*, S193–S194.

Siegel, J. D., McCracken, G. H., Thrilkeld, N., Milvenan, B., & Rosenfield, C. (1980). Single dose penicillin prophylaxis against neonatal group B streptococcal infection. *New England Journal of Medicine, 303*, 769–773.

Silverman, W. A., & Flynn, J. J. (1985). *Contemporary issues in fetal and neonatal medicine: Vol. II. Retinopathy of prematurity*. Boston: Blackwell Scientific Publications.

Sinkin, R. A., & Phelps, D. (1987). New strategies for the prevention of bronchopulmonary dysplasia. *Clinics in Perinatology, 14*, 599–620.

Stork, E. (1988). Extracorporeal membrane oxygenation in the newborn and beyond. *Clinics in Perinatology, 15*, 815–829.

Urrea, P. T., & Rosenbaum, A. L. (1989). Retinopathy of prematurity: An ophthalmologist's perspective. In S. Isenberg (Ed.), *Eye in infancy* (pp. 428–456). Chicago: Yearbook Medical Publishers, Inc.

# 12 | William J. Cashore

# CONTRIBUTION OF HYPERBILIRUBINEMIA TO DEVELOPMENTAL DISABILITIES

The toxicity of bilirubin to the central nervous system has long been recognized. Previously, newborn infants with severe hyperbilirubinemia due to Rh erythroblastosis developed hypertonicity, opisthotonos, a high-pitched cry, a decreased sucking response, and seizures during the first few days after birth as their indirect bilirubin concentrations increased steadily to levels above 20 mg/dl and often above 30 mg/dl (van Praagh, 1961). Following a subsequent period of hypotonia, the infants would develop a syndrome of long-term neurologic disabilities. This syndrome was marked by choreoathetosis; high-tone hearing loss; disturbances of gait, balance, and eye muscle control; and, on rare occasion, severe mental retardation (Perlstein, 1960). The infants who died in the neonatal period showed a characteristic bright yellow staining of the central nervous system. The areas so stained include the basal ganglia, the hypothalamus, the auditory nucleus of the eighth nerve, and sometimes the brainstem and cerebellum. The stained areas showed evidence of intracellular bilirubin deposition and cell death, and the abnormal neurologic findings in surviving infants corresponded to injury in the stained areas (Gerrard, 1952).

Overt, or "classic," kernicterus is no longer observed as it was when Rh disease was a frequent occurrence. The target population has significantly changed. The infants at risk for bilirubin toxicity of the central nervous system tend to be low birth weight infants, and, occasionally, larger infants with asphyxia, sepsis, and/or severe respiratory distress. Very high levels of bilirubin that place previously asymptomatic infants at risk are relatively infrequent.

Autopsy findings from several centers make it clear that kernicterus does still occur. In one center at Women & Infants Hospital in Providence, Rhode Island, kernicterus was found in approximately 3% of the autopsy cases during the late 1970s, and in several other hospitals a similar frequency of kernicterus at autopsy was reported (Cashore, 1980; Gartner, Snyder, Chabon, & Bernstein, 1970). In many of the cases reported during the 1960s and 1970s, the finding of kernicterus was made without warning or without the typical symptomatology at bilirubin levels considerably lower than those that were found in the "classic" cases with Rh erythroblastosis (Gartner et al., 1970; Stern & Denton, 1965).

Although the exact mechanism of bilirubin toxicity is not known, it is toxic to a number of aspects of cell metabolism. The brain cells seem especially vulnerable. Bilirubin appears to interfere with biochemical reactions that initiate in or on cell membranes, including uncoupling of oxidative phosphorylation, overstimulation, and then suppression of cell respiration and inhibition of cyclic $3'5'$ adenosine monophosphate (Karp, 1979). Its action as a toxin may be nonspecific; it may choke or disrupt cell membranes on a physical basis.

Studies of bilirubin structure and chemical properties show that it is a weak acid and a weak polar compound, more soluble in polar than in nonpolar solutions, but poorly soluble in water. At a pH less than 7 in an aqueous medium, bilirubin acid forms internal hydrogen bonds and tends to precipitate. In this state, bilirubin appears to have a high affinity for membrane phospholipids and perhaps also for protein structures in membranes. It may therefore disrupt membrane functions in a number of ways, especially in the presence of acidosis (Brodersen, 1980).

## ENTRY OF BILIRUBIN INTO THE BRAIN

Normally, the blood-brain barrier, a combination of tight junctions and capillary transport mechanisms, excludes most of the bilirubin in the circulation from the central nervous system. Most bilirubin in the blood is bound to serum albumin, and most large molecules, including albumin, are excluded from the central nervous system by the blood-brain barrier. Small amounts of unbound bilirubin may diffuse from the plasma across the barrier, but small amounts of bilirubin entering in this way under normal conditions may be detoxified by endogenous mechanisms in the brain cells. Larger amounts of bilirubin may be deposited in the brain by: 1) injury to the barrier, such as a circulatory or osmotic insult, which allows tight junctions to open; 2) a marked increase in unbound or diffusible bilirubin, such as might be produced by introduction of a displacing drug; or 3) damage to the target tissues themselves. Whether the entry of bilirubin occurs by a breakdown in the barrier to albumin bound bilirubin, or by an increase in the diffusion of unbound bilirubin, when in contact with the cells, bilirubin appears to be more toxic in its unbound than in its bound form, possibly because it is the unbound bilirubin that precipitates as the acid (Brodersen, 1980).

The role of predisposing factors in producing this effect appears clinically and experimentally well established, but the mode of action of the predisposing factors, such as acidosis or hypoxia, is not clearly understood. The relative lack of specific abnormal findings in low birth weight infants, later found to have kernicterus at autopsy, may be due either to the relative state of immaturity of the basal ganglia in these infants or to the masking effect of other clinical complications, such as intracranial hemorrhage, which is accompanied by more dramatic physical findings in the neonatal period.

Experimental evidence has demonstrated several conditions relevant to clinical settings in which brain uptake of bilirubin increases. Hyperosmolarity increases the entry of albumin and bilirubin into the brain, even when the increase in plasma osmolarity is not abrupt (Bratlid, Cashore, & Oh, 1983; Burgess, Stonestreet, Cashore, & Oh, 1985). Hypercarbia also increases albumin and bilirubin uptake in the brain, probably via carbon dioxide mediated hyperperfusion and hypertension (Bratlid, Cashore, & Oh, 1984; Burgess, Oh, et al., 1985). In piglets, the blood-brain barrier is equally impermeable to albumin at 2 days and 2 weeks of age, but it is more permeable to bilirubin at 2 days than at 2 weeks, with a greater uptake of bilirubin in the midbrain and basal ganglia than in the cortex (Lee, Stonestreet, Oh, & Cashore, 1989). Therefore, there appears to be an age-related maturation of the blood-brain barrier to bilirubin, with greater vulnerability at younger ages and preferential uptake of bilirubin in subcortical areas. Even when the blood-brain barrier is opened to albumin, unbound bilirubin appears to be more toxic to brain function than bound bilirubin (Wennberg & Hance, 1986). This observation is consistent with the models proposed by Brodersen (1980) and other investigators for the toxicity of free bilirubin.

## BILIRUBIN AND CHRONIC DYSFUNCTION IN THE CENTRAL NERVOUS SYSTEM

Since early studies (Gerrard, 1952), it has been clear that bilirubin encephalopathy syndrome represents a spectrum of central nervous system abnormalities. A number of studies of the patient population susceptible to Rh disease showed diminished IQ and motor dysfunction to be more prevalent in an untreated population than in a population of infants later treated by exchange transfusions (Johnston et al., 1967). Studies of the effects of bilirubin on mental and motor functions in large unselected populations without Rh erythroblastosis have tended to yield ambiguous results. However, as reported in several early studies, central nervous system dysfunction associated with elevated plasma bilirubin levels among infants participating in the Collaborative Perinatal Study (1972) has demonstrated that the possible relationship between bilirubin and subtle forms of central nervous system dysfunction is cause for concern.

Boggs, Hardy, and Frazier (1967) and Scheidt, Mellits, Hardy, Drage, and Boggs (1977) reported psychomotor delay during the first year in infants with a history of elevated serum bilirubin concentration. The risks in such infants of psychomotor delay appear to be incremental, with increasing bilirubin concentrations beginning at 8 mg/dl to 9 mg/dl in low birth weight infants and at 16 mg/dl to 19 mg/dl in term infants. Although bilirubin itself was found to be a risk factor in these studies, the risk of psychomotor delay during the first year associated with bilirubin was considerably potentiated by such factors as low birth weight, shortened gestation, and low Apgar scores. In both studies, preterm infants appeared definitely to be more vulnerable. The incremental risk of psychomotor delay in preterm infants appeared to increase by 1.8% for each mg/dl of serum indirect bilirubin above 9 mg/dl, whereas the incremental risk for term infants appeared to increase by about 0.3% for each mg/dl of serum indirect bilirubin above 15 mg/dl.

However, longitudinal studies of several populations of children extending beyond the fourth year suggest that the overall risk of serious central nervous system disabilities appears to be less than predicted by the results of a first year analysis. In a study of term infants, followed by multiple diagnostic measures, Rubin, Balow, and Fisch (1979) found no significant differences in verbal and performance IQs, neurologic findings, or school readiness in 240 children with previous jaundice and 125 controls studied between the ages of 4 and 7 years. It is interesting to note that the infants with jaundice in this study showed similar degrees of minor psychomotor delay at 8 and 12 months as did the infants in the studies by Boggs et al. (1967) and Scheidt et al. (1977).

In the studies by Rubin et al. (1979), there were slight but significant decreases in the mean birth weight and gestational age of the group having the highest bilirubin levels. The effect of immaturity in producing apparent mild psychomotor delay during the first year may have to be considered in the evaluation of these studies. It is, however, encouraging to note that at age 4 to 7 years, all groups segregated according to bilirubin level showed similar performance and similar school readiness on an extensive battery of tests for mental and motor functions. Similarly, a longitudinal study of carefully followed infants born in Sweden during the 1960s and 1970s, and later analyzed according to peak bilirubin levels, showed that there was no significant difference in neurologic or cognitive performance among term infants segregated according to bilirubin levels but controlled for other variables until the serum bilirubin levels exceeded 24 mg/dl to 25 mg/dl (Bengtsson & Verneholt, 1974). Finally, Naeye (1978) reported a statistical association among amniotic fluid infections, elevated bilirubin levels during neonatal life, and later psychomotor impairment. In this group, as well as others, the effect of low birth weight appeared to combine with the risk of infection and that of increased bilirubin to produce a greater overall risk of bilirubin related psychomotor impairment in preterm infants than in otherwise asymptomatic term infants.

Epidemiologic evidence shows that bilirubin has both independent and additive effects contributing to early signs of psychomotor impairment, but in neonatal follow-up clinics for high-risk infants, specific abnormal findings due to bilirubin alone seem comparatively uncommon. The extremely complicated clinical histories of very low birth weight infants appear to make bilirubin effects difficult to separate from the effects of other neonatal insults. It can be stated that typical cases of "classic" bilirubin encephalopathy are not often encountered in follow-up clinics in the 1980s and 1990s. Perhaps the full syndrome of kernicterus in very low birth weight infants is a fatal lesion when it occurs.

It appears that moderate elevations of serum bilirubin in asymptomatic term infants do not present a major risk of long-term cognitive or neurologic disabilities. However, there is some evidence to support the concept that transient neurobehavioral changes or short-term psychomotor delay may result from exposure to bilirubin levels at 16 mg/dl to 20 mg/dl in apparently healthy infants. Transient and reversible changes in brainstem auditory evoked responses have been reported in term infants (Nakamura et al., 1985; Perlman & Frank, 1988). Jaundiced newborns with bilirubin levels between 10 mg/dl and 20 mg/dl also show other behavior changes, including cry instability and decreased auditory orienting responsiveness (Rapisardi, Vohr, Cashore, Peucker, & Lester, 1989; Vohr, Rapisardi, et al., 1989). The observed slight increase in brainstem conduction time, instability in cry variables, and decreased auditory orientation appear to correlate with increasing serum bilirubin. Clinically, these may sometimes be observed as subtle behavioral changes and appear to resolve without obvious residual neurologic abnormalities (Vohr, Lester, et al., 1989).

For preterm infants, there is some indication that an elevated bilirubin level is an additive factor influencing at least short-term outcome, in combination with such factors as low birth weight, low gestation, and amniotic fluid infections (van de Bor, van Zeben-Vander Aa, Verloove-Vanhorick, Brand, & Ruys, 1989). It is encouraging to find that "classic" bilirubin encephalopathy does not frequently appear later in low birth weight infants seen in follow-up clinics. However, the specific contribution of bilirubin to disabilities that are seen in low birth weight survivors with complicated clinical histories is still not clear. The use of such assessment modalities as brainstem auditory evoked potentials may help to clarify this issue further.

## PREVENTION AND TREATMENT OF HYPERBILIRUBINEMIA

The obvious choice of treatment for elevated serum indirect bilirubin that has already risen to unacceptable levels is a whole blood exchange transfusion. This has remained the treatment of choice for such a condition since it was first introduced in the late 1940s. More important is the ability to recognize infants at risk for significant hyperbilirubinemia and to intervene effectively in a preventive manner. Such infants include those with maternal fetal blood group incompatibilities, whether of the Rh or ABO variety (immunization of Rh negative women is discussed by Hinman, Chapter 18, this volume); infants at risk for significant perinatal infections; and low birth weight preterm infants who, in addition to their risks of immaturity, have lower plasma albumin levels, diminished bilirubin binding to albumin, and possibly an immature or injured blood-brain barrier.

The first line of prevention and management in these infants is an awareness of the potential for hyperbilirubinemia. Close observation often permits the use of an early exchange transfusion where indicated to prevent the serum bilirubin from rising to unacceptable levels. In many infants, the early institution of phototherapy is used as a preventive treatment to stabilize bilirubin at acceptable low levels.

The risk of severe central nervous system injury from moderately elevated bilirubin levels in thriving infants with breast milk jaundice appears to be low. No cases of kernicterus have been reported in healthy breast-fed infants, even at relatively high serum bilirubin levels (15 mg/dl to 25 mg/dl). Nevertheless, the development of breast milk jaundice should oblige the physician to follow such an infant closely and to intervene preventively if the bilirubin level exceeds 15 mg/dl. For less mature infants, the threshold for treatment is lowered, whether it is phototherapy or exchange transfusion, to levels of 10 mg/dl to 15 mg/dl, depending on the maturity and clinical condition of the infant.

Future prospective and follow-up studies, perhaps using more sensitive instruments and focusing on more specific findings, may help further clarify the magnitude of risk posed to newborn infants, particularly immature newborn infants, by elevated serum bilirubin levels.

## CONCLUSION

In conclusion, the "classic" bilirubin encephalopathy syndrome is now a rare clinical occurrence, but kernicterus is still found at autopsy in low birth weight infants. In combination with other factors, especially low birth weight and amniotic fluid infections, moderate hyperbilirubinemia appears to be associated with an increased prevalence of developmental delay in the first year. The risk for developmental delay increases in a linear fashion with increases in maximum indirect (unconjugated) bilirubin concentration, and is greater in preterm than in term infants. Follow-up studies, although on small cohorts of infants, have failed to demonstrate significant cognitive or motor disabilities at age 4–7 years in moderately jaundiced term infants, some of whom did have evidence of mild psychomotor delay at 2 years of age.

Evaluation of the long-term effects of hyperbilirubinemia in preterm infants is confounded by other clinical variables presenting independent and perhaps greater risks of long-term disabilities than jaundice. In such patients, accurate evaluation of the effects of hyperbilirubinemia on outcome may require development of more specific and sensitive ways to identify the specific lesions and disabilities most likely to be caused by increased bilirubin.

## REFERENCES

Bengtsson, B., & Verneholt, J. (1974). A follow-up study of hyperbilirubinemia in healthy, full-term infants without isoimmunization. *Acta Paediatrica Scandinavica, 63*, 70–80.

Boggs, T. R., Hardy, J., & Frazier, T. (1967). Correlation of neonatal total bilirubin concentrations and developmental status at age 8 months. *Journal of Pediatrics, 71*, 553–560.

Bratlid, D., Cashore, W. J., & Oh, W. (1983). Effect of serum hyperosmolality on opening of the blood-brain barrier for bilirubin in rat brain. *Pediatrics, 71*, 909–912.

Bratlid, D., Cashore, W. J., & Oh, W. (1984). Effect of acidosis on bilirubin deposition in rat brain. *Pediatrics, 73*, 431–434.

Brodersen, R. (1980). Bilirubin transport in the newborn infant, reviewed with relation to kernicterus. *Journal of Pediatrics, 96*, 349–356.

Burgess, G. H., Oh, W., Bratlid, D., Brubakk, A. M., Cashore, W. J., & Stonestreet, B. S. (1985). The effects of brain blood flow on brain bilirubin deposition in newborn piglets. *Pediatric Research, 19*, 691–696.

Burgess, G. H., Stonestreet, B. S., Cashore, W. J., & Oh, W. (1985). Brain bilirubin deposition and brain blood flow during acute urea-induced hyperosmolarity in newborn piglets. *Pediatric Research, 19*, 537–542.

Cashore, W. J. (1980). Free bilirubin concentrations and bilirubin binding affinity in term and pre-term infants. *Journal of Pediatrics, 96*, 521–527.

Collaborative Perinatal Study. (1972). *The women and their pregnancies* (DHEW Publication No. NIH 73–379). Washington, DC: Department of Health, Education and Welfare.

Gartner, L. M., Snyder, R. N., Chabon, R. S., & Bernstein, J. (1970). Kernicterus: High incidence in premature infants with low serum bilirubin concentrations. *Pediatrics, 45*, 906–917.

Gerrard, J. (1952). Kernicterus. *Brain, 75*, 526–570.

Johnston, W., Angara, V., Baulmal, R., Hawke, W. A., Johnson, R. H., Keet, S., &

Wood, M. (1967). Erythroblastosis fetalis and hyperbilirubinemia: A five-year follow-up with neurological, psychological, and audiological evaluation. *Pediatrics, 39*, 88–92.

Karp, W. (1979). Biochemical alterations in neonatal hyperbilirubinemia and bilirubin encephalopathy: A review. *Pediatrics, 64*, 361–368.

Lee, C., Stonestreet, B. S., Oh, W., & Cashore, W. J. (1989). Permeability of the blood-brain barrier to $^{125}$I albumin-bound bilirubin in newborn piglets. *Pediatric Research, 25*, 452–456.

Naeye, R. L. (1978). Amniotic fluid infections, neonatal hyperbilirubinemia, and psychomotor impairment. *Pediatrics, 62*, 497–503.

Nakamura, H., Takada, S., Shimabuku, R., Matsuo, M., Matsuo, T., & Negishi, H. (1985). Auditory nerve and brainstem responses in newborn infants with hyperbilirubinemia. *Pediatrics, 75*, 703–708.

Perlman, M., & Frank, J. W. (1988). Bilirubin beyond the blood-brain barrier. *Pediatrics, 81*, 304–315.

Perlstein, M. A. (1960). The late clinical syndrome of posticteric encephalopathy. *Pediatric Clinics of North America, 7*, 665–687.

Rapisardi, G., Vohr, B., Cashore, W. J., Peucker, M., & Lester, B. (1989). Assessment of infant cry variability in high-risk infants. *International Journal of Pediatric Otorhinolaryngology, 17*, 19–29.

Rubin, R. A., Balow, B., & Fisch, R. O. (1979). Neonatal serum bilirubin levels related to cognitive development at ages 4 through 7 years. *Journal of Pediatrics, 94*, 601–604.

Scheidt, P. C., Mellits, E. D., Hardy, J. B., Drage, J. S., & Boggs, T. R. (1977). Toxicity to bilirubin in neonates: Infant development during the first year in relation to maximum neonatal serum bilirubin concentration. *Journal of Pediatrics, 91*, 292–297.

Stern, L., & Denton, R. L. (1965). Kernicterus in small premature infants. *Pediatrics, 35*, 483–485.

van de Bor, M., van Zeben-Vander Aa, T. M., Verloove-Vanhorick, S. P., Brand, R., & Ruys, J. H. (1989). Hyperbilirubinemia in preterm infants and neurodevelopmental outcome at 2 years of age. *Pediatrics, 83*, 915–920.

van Praagh, R. (1961). Diagnosis of kernicterus in the neonatal period. *Pediatrics, 28*, 870–876.

Vohr, B. R., Lester, B., Rapisardi, G., O'Dea, C., Brown, L., Peucker, M., Cashore, W., & Oh, W. (1989). Abnormal brainstem function (BAER) correlates with acoustic cry features in term infants with hyperbilirubinemia. *Journal of Pediatrics.*

Vohr, B. R., Rapisardi, G., Karp, D., O'Dea, C., Lester, B., Garcia-Coll, C. T., Brown, L., Oh, W., & Cashore, W. J. (1989). Behavioral changes correlated with cry characteristics and brainstem auditory evoked responses (BAER) in term infants with moderate hyperbilirubinemia. *Pediatric Research, 25*, 19A.

Wennberg, R. P., & Hance, A. J. (1986). Experimental bilirubin encephalopathy: Importance of total protein, protein binding, and blood-brain barrier. *Pediatric Research, 20*, 789–792.

# 13 | Joseph J. Volpe

# INTRAVENTRICULAR HEMORRHAGE IN THE PREMATURE INFANT

Periventricular-intraventricular hemorrhage is the most common serious neurologic event of the neonatal period (Volpe, 1981). This lesion has achieved its prominence, in large part, because of the remarkable improvements in both neonatal intensive care and survival rate for premature infants since the 1980s.

The high incidence of this lesion has been demonstrated by studies in which premature infants were subjected to routine computerized tomography (CT) or ultrasound scans in the first week of life (Ahmann, Lazzara, Dykes, Brann, & Schwartz, 1980; Holt & Allan, 1981; Levene & Starte, 1981; Papile, Burstein, Burstein, & Koffler, 1978) (see Table 13.1). Approximately 35%–45% of all infants born weighing less than 1,500 g, or are at less than 35 weeks gestation, have been found to exhibit periventricular-intraventricular hemorrhage. The incidence is highest among infants born at less than 32 weeks gestation. The high incidence and essential gravity of this lesion make it the most important determinant of neurologic morbidity in most neonatal intensive care units.

## NEUROPATHOLOGY

### Primary Lesion

The primary lesion in periventricular-intraventricular hemorrhage is bleeding, principally from small vessels, into the periventricular germinal matrix (Volpe, 1981). In most infants, the hemorrhage originates in the germinal matrix over-

---

This chapter was prepared by Dr. Volpe in 1982 and was updated for this book by Dr. Pueschel.

197

Table 13.1 Incidence of periventricular-intraventricular hemorrhage in premature infants

| Criteria for inclusion | Total number studied | Imaging technique | Incidence of periventricular-intraventricular hemorrhage |
|---|---|---|---|
| <1,500 g | 46 | Computerized tomography | 43% |
| <35 weeks | 191 | Computerized tomography | 40% |
| <35 weeks | 264 | Ultrasound | 34% |
| <35 weeks | 124 | Ultrasound | 43% |

Sources: Ahmann, Lazzara, Dykes, Brann, and Schwartz (1980); Holt and Allan (1981); Levene and Starte (1981); Papile, Burstein, Burstein, and Koffler (1978).

lying the head of the caudate nucleus at the level of the foramen of Monro. In infants born at less than 28 weeks gestation, however, the hemorrhage often originates in the germinal matrix overlying the body of the caudate nucleus in the territory of the anterior choroidal artery and the deep lateral striate arteries. Beyond 32 weeks gestation, periventricular-intraventricular hemorrhage emanating from the germinal matrix becomes distinctly less common; in mature infants, intraventricular hemorrhage, albeit uncommon, may emanate from the choroid plexus.

## Intraventricular Hemorrhage

At autopsy, intraventricular hemorrhage presents a striking appearance. In the majority of cases, the germinal matrix hemorrhage ruptures through the ependyma into the ventricular system. Blood typically spreads throughout the ventricles, then passes through the outflow foramina of the fourth ventricle to collect in the basilar cisterns of the posterior fossa. Particular characteristic findings include large clots in the occipital horns of the lateral ventricles and within the subarachnoid space of the cisterna magna (Larroche, 1977; Pape & Wigglesworth, 1979).

## Obstruction of
## Cerebrospinal Fluid Flow and Hydrocephalus

Subsequent to the initial hemorrhage, an obliterating fibrosing arachnoiditis may develop and cause the obstruction of cerebrospinal fluid (CSF) flow that results in chronic posthemorrhagic hydrocephalus. Moreover, obstruction of CSF pathways by blood clot and debris may occur prior to the development of the obliterative arachnoiditis, virtually anywhere along the path of CSF flow, and cause more acutely evolving hydrocephalus.

## Intraparenchymal "Extension"

In particularly severe lesions, the periventricular hemorrhage appears to extend into the cerebral parenchyma. In such cases the development of a porencephalic cyst is a frequent sequela. However, it should be recognized that the nature of this intraparenchymal hemorrhage coexisting with intraventricular hemorrhage has not been clearly defined. Such a lesion is usually described as an intraparenchymal "extension," implying a dissecting process from blood in the matrix or ventricles with the production of an intraparenchymal hematoma. However, neuropathologic observations suggest that intraparenchymal hemorrhage most commonly is concurrent with hemorrhagic infarction rather than simple extension of matrix hemorrhage (Flodmark et al., 1980).

## PATHOGENESIS

The pathogenesis of periventricular-intraventricular hemorrhage remains the subject of intense investigation. Elucidating the pathogenesis is necessary in order to accomplish the ultimate goal of preventing the hemorrhage and its sequelae. An analysis of the pathogenesis of periventricular-intraventricular hemorrhage must consider several factors relating to: 1) the anatomic and physiologic determinants of the distribution and regulation of cerebral blood flow and pressure within the germinal matrix, 2) the nature of the germinal matrix vasculature itself, and 3) the extravascular factors.

### Anatomic and Physiologic
### Determinants of Cerebral Blood Flow and Pressure

**Pressure-Passive Cerebral Blood Flow**  Studies of cerebral blood flow in premature newborn infants after only modest perinatal asphyxia suggest that cerebral circulation under such circumstances is pressure-passive (Lou, Lassen, & Friis-Hansen, 1979). This implies that arterial hypertension could be a critical pathogenetic factor for periventricular-intraventricular hemorrhage (Volpe, 1978). Experimental observations with newborn beagle puppies support this contention (Goddard, Lewis, Armstrong, & Zeller, 1980). Thus, the latter demonstration of pressure-passive cerebral blood flow in the human infant has obvious pathogenetic significance, and the controversy over whether this state reflects impaired cerebrovascular autoregulation detracts from the particular importance of events that will cause elevations of arterial blood pressure in the small infant. Indeed, elevations in arterial blood pressure comparable in magnitude to those used in the experimental models of intraventricular hemorrhage have been observed in the first minutes of life during apneic episodes, spontaneous or handling-induced motor activity, seizures, rapid eye movement sleep, exchange transfusions, rapid colloid infusions, and as a consequence of asphyxia (Volpe, 1981).

    **Asphyxia**  The interaction of various systemic and intracranial factors in increasing cerebral blood flow, and the possibility of hemorrhage, may be most pronounced in the premature infant with asphyxia. In this case, three factors combine initially to cause an increase in cerebral blood flow: 1) hypercapnia with its attendant perivascular acidosis, 2) the "diving reflex," which preferentially shunts blood to the brain, and 3) arterial hypertension. There may be marked changes in cerebral blood flow secondary to therapeutic maneuvers superimposed on these physiologic responses. For example, the rapid infusion of volume expanders (Goldberg, Chung, Goldman, & Bancalari, 1980) and the use of hyperosmolar solutions or pressor agents all may cause sudden increases in perfusion pressure that, because of pressure-passive cerebral blood flow, might be transmitted directly to the cerebral capillary bed.

**Cerebral Venous Pressure and Flow** In addition to alterations in capillary pressure produced by arterial factors, increased venous pressure in certain circumstances may cause or exacerbate the increased pressure within the periventricular capillaries. Elevations of venous pressure may occur with asphyxia, particularly when associated with hypoxic cardiac failure, and in hyaline membrane disease, especially in association with positive pressure ventilation (Vert, Nomin, & Sibout, 1975). Deformations of the compliant skull in the premature infant may cause obstruction of venous sinuses with a secondary increase in venous pressure. Such deformations could occur during vaginal delivery.

Elevated pressure may be more likely to occur in the small veins in the periventricular region sites most vulnerable to hemorrhage because of this region's distinctive venous anatomy. Thus, there is a U-turn in the direction of venous flow as the internal cerebral veins are formed at the level of the foramen of Monro and at the head of the caudate nucleus.

### Germinal Matrix Vasculature

Vascular factors of significance in the genesis of periventricular-intraventricular hemorrhage include the nature of the periventricular capillaries in the germinal matrix. Pape and Wigglesworth (1979) characterized the anatomic appearance of the periventricular capillary bed as "a persisting immature vascular rete which is only remodeled into a definite capillary bed when the germinal matrix disappears" (p. 18). Indeed, the vessels themselves cannot be categorized clearly by light microscopic features, such as arterioles, capillaries, or venules (Hambleton & Wigglesworth, 1976; Haruda & Blanc, 1981). The vessel walls in premature infants of less than 30 weeks gestation consist of a layer of endothelium without smooth muscle, collagen, or elastin. Even at term, simple endothelium lined channels persist in the remnants of the germinal matrix. In addition to these structural considerations, the metabolic activity of brain capillary endothelial cells suggests that they are particularly dependent on oxidative metabolism (Goldstein, 1979; Oldendorf, Cornford, & Brown, 1977). Thus, they may be readily injured by hypoxic insult, which, as emphasized above, often occurs in the setting of periventricular-intraventricular hemorrhage.

## Extravascular Factors

Extravascular factors that may be involved in the genesis of periventricular-intraventricular hemorrhage include elements of the periventricular region itself. The periventricular germinal matrix is a gelatinous region that appears to provide poor support for the many small vessels that course through it, although careful documentation of this notion is lacking. In addition, the periventricular germinal matrix of the human premature infant has been shown to contain a high level of fibrinolytic activity (Gilles, Price, Kevy, & Berenberg, 1971). This factor may explain why a capillary hemorrhage has the capacity to enlarge into a massive lesion that may extend into the ventricular system or dissect into brain parenchyma or both. Finally, it has been suggested that a decreased tissue pressure (DeCourten & Rabinowicz, 1981) or a subatmospheric CSF pressure (Welch, 1980) may contribute to the occurrence of periventricular-intraventricular hemorrhage.

## CLINICAL FEATURES

### Time of Occurrence

The clinical features of periventricular-intraventricular hemorrhage vary from a catastrophic neurologic event to an extremely subtle, perhaps even silent, occurrence. The time of onset of the lesion is not known with great precision, but is most often in the first 2 days of life. In an autopsy study in which the hemorrhage was timed by the use of Chromium-50-labeled red blood cells, the median age of onset was 38 hours (Tsiantos et al., 1974). In other studies of living infants by serial ultrasonography, periventricular-intraventricular hemorrhage has been detected frequently in the first 12 hours of life. Based on a population of infants studied prospectively by ultrasonography, experience tends to support this earlier occurrence of the initial lesion in the majority of infants. Approximately 50% of affected infants exhibited their periventricular-intraventricular hemorrhage in the first 24 hours of life (Perlman & Volpe, 1982). It should be emphasized, however, that progression of the initial lesion is common. This is particularly true in premature infants with an initial subpendymal hemorrhage who experience a secondary hypoxic insult. Such a clinical course has been demonstrated with pneumothorax (Hill, Perlman, & Volpe, 1982). In 15 infants with tension pneumothorax, major intraventricular hemorrhage was documented shortly after the occurrence of the pneumothorax.

### Catastrophic Syndrome

The occurrence of periventricular-intraventricular hemorrhage may be accompanied by either of two basic clinical syndromes (Volpe, 1981). The first is the classic presentation of a major hemorrhage; that is, a catastrophic neurologic deterioration that usually evolves in minutes to hours and consists of deep stupor or coma, respiratory abnormalities, generalized tonic seizures, unreactive pupils, absence of extraocular movements, and flaccid quadriparesis. This neurologic syndrome is often accompanied by a falling hematocrit, bulging anterior fontanel, systemic hypotension, bradycardia, temperature instability, metabolic acidosis, and abnormalities of glucose and water homeostasis. Acute hydrocephalus may occur. Many infants fail to survive this catastrophic event.

### Saltatory Syndrome

The second clinical syndrome is a more subtle deterioration that occurs usually, but not exclusively, in the infant with a smaller hemorrhage (Volpe, 1974). This syndrome tends to evolve over hours to days, often in a saltatory fashion, and is characterized by a change in level of alertness (either stupor or an irritable, apparently alert state); a decrease in spontaneous and elicited movements; hypotonia; and subtle abnormalities of eye position and movement, including skew deviation, vertical drift of eyes (usually downward), and incomplete horizontal movements to oculocephalic maneuver (doll's head maneuver). The more subtle abnormalities of this second syndrome may be missed easily in an infant who is already compromised by the nonneurologic disorders of prematurity or affected by other neurologic disorders.

### "Silent" Hemorrhage

It has been argued that clinically silent intraventricular hemorrhage is common, and it is certainly true that clinically undetected intraventricular hemorrhage is a frequent occurrence. In a prospective study of premature infants subjected to routine CT scans in the first week of life, only about half of the cases of periventricular-intraventricular hemorrhage were correctly predicted on the basis of clinical criteria (Lazzara, Ahmann, Dykes, Brann, & Schwartz, 1980). The most reliable sign was an unexplained fall in hematocrit or a failure of the hematocrit to rise following transfusion. In contrast, careful neurologic evaluation was performed in parallel with ultrasonographic examination of the head in a consecutive series of 100 newborn infants (Dubowitz, Levene, Morante, Palmer, & Dubowitz, 1981). Impaired visual tracking, later development of roving eye movements, and an abnormal popliteal angle were correlated with intraventricular hemorrhage in infants of less than 36 weeks gestation. In infants of 32–35 weeks gestation, hypotonia and poor mobility were also noted. Thus, careful sequential neurologic examination may be a sensitive means of detecting the development of intraventricular hemorrhage in the premature infant.

## PROGNOSIS

Since the early 1980s, it has become clear that the outcome of neonatal intraventricular hemorrhage is not uniformly grim. This change in prognosis relates in considerable part to the detection by CT or ultrasound of small lesions that in the past would have gone undetected. This changing prognosis appears to parallel the improved outlook for sick premature infants in general and appears to relate to the improved supportive care provided by neonatal intensive care units.

## Short-Term Outcome

There is a direct (though somewhat variable) relationship between the severity of the hemorrhage, as assessed by CT scan or ultrasonography, and the prognosis. With mild hemorrhage, survival is the rule and progressive posthemorrhagic ventricular dilatation is rare. Even with moderate lesions, mortality rates are low, approximately 10%, and the incidence of progressive posthemorrhagic ventricular dilatation is approximately 20%. Severe lesions, however, still carry a poor prognosis. The majority of infants with such lesions die and most of the survivors develop progressive posthemorrhagic ventricular dilatation. Those infants with hemorrhagic intraparenchymal involvement, as well as intraventricular hemorrhage, have the worst outlook; the large majority die and essentially all survivors are left with neurologic deficits.

## Long-Term Outcome

Because definitive diagnosis of intraventricular hemorrhage has been accomplished readily only since the 1980s, detailed information on long-term neurologic outcome is not available. Initial data with follow up for 12–36 months indicate a direct relationship of outcome to the severity of the hemorrhage (Krishnamoorthy, Shannon, DeLong, Todres, & Davis, 1979; Papile, Munsick, Weaver, & Pecha, 1979; Shankaran, Slovis, Bedard, & Poland, 1982). As might be predicted, severe motor and intellectual deficits have been the rule in infants with severe hemorrhage. Such deficits are rare in infants with lesions limited to periventricular hemorrhage or small intraventricular hemorrhage. The prognosis for infants with moderate degrees of hemorrhage might be expected to lie between these two extremes. Nevertheless, it should be recognized that the determinants of neurologic outcome in sick, small premature babies are diverse and a relationship to severity of hemorrhage is by no means invariable. Indeed, the individual infant's prognosis is related to one or more of the mechanisms of brain injury observed in association with intraventricular hemorrhage, as discussed below.

## MECHANISMS OF BRAIN INJURY

The recognized mechanisms of brain injury associated with periventricular-intraventricular hemorrhage include: preceding or concurrent hypoxic-ischemic insult(s), increased intracranial pressure and decreased cerebral perfusion, destruction of periventricular white matter, destruction of glial precursors in the germinal matrix, focal cerebral ischemia, and posthemorrhagic hydrocephalus. The precise importance of each of these factors varies with each case.

## Preceding Hypoxic-Ischemic Insult(s)

Since intraventricular hemorrhage is often preceded by hypoxic-ischemic insult(s), lesions caused by such insults (Volpe, 1981) may be expected to be important in determining long-term prognosis. Thus, periventricular leukomalacia and selective neuronal injury to brainstem nuclei (as well as to cerebral and cerebellar cortices) have been identified in association with periventricular-intraventricular hemorrhage. Unfortunately, no systematic analysis of these hypoxic-ischemic lesions and their association with periventricular-intraventricular hemorrhage has yet been performed.

## Increased Intracranial Pressure

Marked intracranial hypertension and impaired cerebral perfusion may be important determinants of long-term brain injury following severe intraventricular hemorrhage. Cerebral perfusion pressure is determined by the mean arterial blood pressure minus the intracranial pressure. In severe intraventricular hemorrhage, intracranial pressures in the range of 200 mm to 250 mm water may occur. Moreover, in seriously ill, premature infants, the systemic blood pressure may fall precipitously. Therefore, in the infant with a severe intraventricular hemorrhage and marginal arterial blood pressure, even a relatively small increase in intracranial pressure may impair cerebral perfusion seriously.

## Destruction of Periventricular White Matter

Destruction of periventricular white matter by intraparenchymal hematoma may be a cause of focal cerebral deficits following periventricular-intraventricular hemorrhage. Intracerebral hemorrhage, commonly described as intraparenchymal extension, is not unusual. Major lesions of this type have been observed in at least one-third of severe hemorrhages. These intraparenchymal lesions are associated with tissue destruction and cyst formation (Pasternak, Mantovani, & Volpe, 1980), and their evolution is readily followed by CT scan or ultrasonography.

## Destruction of Glial Precursors

The periventricular germinal matrix in the human premature infant gives rise to glial precursors. Focal destruction of the germinal matrix by periventricular hemorrhage might lead to deficits in cerebral glial and consequent deficits in myelination. This suggestion requires direct study.

## Focal Cerebral Ischemia

Focal brain ischemia secondary to arterial vasospasm is a frequent concomitant of intracranial hemorrhage in adults. The possibility that a similar sequence of events might occur with neonatal intraventricular hemorrhage was suggested by a study of cerebral blood flow velocity in the anterior cerebral arteries in a group of infants with intraventricular hemorrhage (Bada, Hajjar, Chua, & Sumner, 1979). A later prospective study involving 100 patients weighing less than 1,500 g failed to confirm these observations (Perlman & Volpe, 1982).

## Posthemorrhagic Hydrocephalus

Hydrocephalus, or progressive posthemorrhagic ventricular dilatation, is a frequent consequence of intraventricular hemorrhage. As might be expected, there is a good correlation between the severity of the intraventricular hemorrhage and the probability of developing hydrocephalus. Ventricular dilatation may begin with the initial lesion. This is especially true if the intraventricular hemorrhage is severe. More commonly, however, progressive posthemorrhagic ventricular dilatation begins approximately 1–3 weeks after the hemorrhage. The rapidity with which the hydrocephalus develops, in general, also is correlated with the severity of the initial lesion. Traditional clinical criteria (i.e., a rapidly enlarging head, a full anterior fontanel, separated cranial sutures) are not adequate to detect progressive posthemorrhagic ventricular dilatation in infants. These signs do not appear for days to weeks after ventricular dilatation has commenced. The development of infantile hydrocephalus prior to rapid head growth was suggested initially by neuropathologic (Larroche, 1972) and clinical (Korobkin, 1975) studies. In a subsequent study utilizing serial CT scans, ventricular dilatation prior to rapid head growth was documented (Volpe, Pasternak, & Allen, 1977). The delay before the onset of rapid head growth was shown to be variable and to range from a few days to weeks.

The precise relation between ventricular dilatation per se and the genesis of brain injury remains unknown. Of particular importance is whether ventricular dilatation at relatively low pressures (i.e., prior to rapid head growth) causes brain injury. Ventricular dilatation has been shown to result in deleterious anatomic changes; that is, axonal stretching and, eventually, axonal loss and gliosis (Milhorat, Clark, Hammock, & McGrath, 1970; Rubin, Hochwald, Tiell, Mizutani, & Ghatak, 1976; Weller & Shulman, 1972). There is a simultaneous attenuation of the caliber of major cerebral vessels and a decrease in number of secondary and tertiary vessels (Wozniak, McLone, & Raimondi, 1975). This is particularly true in periventricular white matter. Periventricular edema has also been demonstrated. These anatomic changes are reversible with shunting, at least in experimental animals and probably in infants as well. Adverse physiologic changes, including decreased blood flow in the anterior cerebral artery (Hill & Volpe, 1982) and increased latency of visual evoked potentials (Ehle & Sklar, 1979), also accompany ventricular dilatation and are similarly reversible with shunting. Such effects have been seen even in normal pressure hydrocephalus. Important topics for future research include delineation of the factors that cause these adverse effects to become irreversible and the means by which these effects can be prevented.

## DIAGNOSIS

### Ultrasound Scanning

Of the diagnostic techniques available, the most valuable is ultrasound scanning of the head via the anterior fontanel. Initial work with real-time ultrasound scanners used transducers containing a linear array of detectors applied to the side of the head (Pape et al., 1979). Improved resolution became apparent when the anterior fontanel was utilized as the acoustic window (Allan, Roveto, Sawyer, & Courtney, 1980). The advent of sector-scan ultrasound imaging through the anterior fontanel resulted in scan quality and resolution that approached that of CT scanning. This technique is adequate for the detection of even small hemorrhages. Imaging in both coronal and sagittal planes is possible. Intraventricular blood is detected readily and generally is distinguishable from the choroid plexus. Alterations in periventricular structure associated with intraparenchymal echogenicity and the subsequent development of cystic structures are also detected easily. Ventricular configuration and size can be visualized and, through the use of cursors, quantified.

The portable capability and ease of use of the instrument has permitted the documentation of important pathogenetic factors. For example, pneumothorax (Hill & Volpe, 1982) has better defined the temporal window in which the bulk of periventricular-intraventricular hemorrhages occur and permitted the evaluation of therapeutic interventions in acute hemorrhage and progressive posthemorrhagic ventricular dilatation (Hill, Taylor, & Volpe, 1981). The advantages over CT scanning relate not only to the instrument's portability but also to the apparent safety of the ultrasonic beam versus the ionizing radiation of CT. The principal limitations of the technique have related to the difficulty of detection of relatively small quantities of blood in normal-sized ventricles, and primary subarachnoid hemorrhage.

### Computerized Tomographic Scanning

Until 1979–1980, the CT scan had been considered the definitive means of characterizing the site and extent of periventricular-intraventricular hemorrhage in the living premature infant. As indicated above, ultrasound scanning must now be considered to have preempted this role. As the hazards associated with transporting small premature infants for CT scanning are well known, and the long-term effects of radiation from multiple CT scans over short periods of time during early development are unknown, CT scanning must now be relegated to a secondary place in the routine detection and evaluation of periventricular-intraventricular hemorrhage. Nevertheless, the CT scan does demonstrate the site and extent of periventricular-intraventricular hemorrhage quite clearly. The size and pattern of ventricular dilatation is also seen well. Moreover, CT probably remains the preferred technique for identification of certain parenchymal lesions, such as periventricular leukomalacia or cerebral infarcts, and extracerebral lesions, such as subdural hematoma. Of course, CT remains the definitive technique for evaluating ventricular size and parenchymal structure after closure of the anterior fontanel.

## MANAGEMENT OF INTRAVENTRICULAR HEMORRHAGE

Management of intraventricular hemorrhage will be considered here in terms of prevention of the lesion and acute management thereof. Prevention measures include: prevention of premature birth, prenatal medical intervention, delivery at high-risk perinatal centers, postnatal medical intervention, and avoidance of cerebral hyperperfusion. Acute management of periventricular-intraventricular hemorrhage includes: the ethical question of treatment, maintenance of cerebral perfusion, and detection of posthemorrhagic hydrocephalus.

### Prevention

**Prevention of Premature Birth**  The ultimate goal in the management of intraventricular hemorrhage is prevention. The most direct way to prevent this devastating lesion would be to prevent premature birth. This topic is addressed by Cetrulo, D'Alton, and Newton, Chapter 9, this volume.

**Prenatal Medical Intervention**  Certain drugs administered prenatally may play a role in decreasing the incidence of periventricular-intraventricular hemorrhage. Preliminary data suggest that administration of tocolytic agents during premature labor is associated with a decreased incidence of intraventricular hemorrhage (Horbar, Leahy, & Lucey, 1981). In addition, the use of steroids (specifically betamethasone) in premature labor may reduce the severity of hyaline membrane disease in offspring of treated mothers. As a result of this effect, this therapy may decrease the likelihood of intraventricular hemorrhage (Clark et al., 1981). Clearly, these issues require further study.

**Delivery at Perinatal Centers**  If premature delivery cannot be prevented, the patient should, if possible, be moved prior to delivery to a perinatal center specializing in high-risk deliveries. Studies have shown that infants born outside such centers and then transported to neonatal intensive care units have a higher incidence of intraventricular hemorrhage than apparently similar infants born at a high-risk perinatal center (Clark et al., 1981). Whether these differences relate to parturitional factors, resuscitation factors, subsequent neonatal intensive care, or a combination of these requires further study.

**Postnatal Medical Intervention** Specific postnatal interventions designed to prevent intraventricular hemorrhage have included administration of phenobarbital or ethamsylate. Donn, Roloff, and Goldstein (1981) reported on their experience with 60 infants with a birth weight less than 1,500 g who were assigned randomly either to a group given phenobarbital or to a control group. Two loading doses of 10 mg/kg each were administered intravenously 12 hours apart and were followed by maintenance doses of 2.5 mg/kg every 12 hours. In the control group, periventricular-intraventricular hemorrhage occurred in 14 of 30 infants, or 47%, an incidence consistent with previously reported figures. By contrast, periventricular-intraventricular hemorrhage occurred in only 4 of the 30 infants in the phenobarbital group—an incidence of 13%. It should be noted, however, that if grade I hemorrhages (i.e., subependymal hemorrhages only) are excluded, the incidences of hemorrhage were 10 of 30, or 33%, in the control group; and 4 of 30, or 13%, in the phenobarbital group. However, a role for phenobarbital in the prevention of intraventricular hemorrhage is not supported by a similar, though not identical, study from Great Britain (Morgan, Benson, & Cooke, 1982) where the incidences of intraventricular hemorrhage were 16 of 30 (51%) in untreated infants and 14 of 30 (47%) in phenobarbital treated infants. Also, Kuban et al. (1986) reported a higher prevalence of intraventricular hemorrhage in the phenobarbital treated infants than in the control infants.

The effect of ethamsylate, a capillary stabilizing drug, on periventricular-intraventricular hemorrhage has also been evaluated (Morgan, Benson, & Cooke, 1981). Ethamsylate is thought to reduce bleeding from capillaries by reinforcement of basement membrane through its action on the polymerization of hyaluronic acid and by increasing platelet adhesiveness. The drug or a placebo was assigned in a double blind fashion to a group of 70 infants. Periventricular-intraventricular hemorrhage developed in 9 of the 35 infants (26%) administered ethamsylate and in 18 of the 35 infants (51%) given a placebo. However, the incidence of severe hemorrhage was not different between the two groups (ethmasylate, 14%, placebo, 17%). Again more data are needed to determine the value of this agent in prevention of clinically significant periventricular-intraventricular hemorrhage.

The administration of indomethacin has been studied as well. Ment et al. (1985, 1987) reported that indomethacin had a positive effect in so far as there was a lower overall prevalence of intraventricular hemorrhage in the indomethacin treated group. Bandstra et al. (1987) studied 199 premature infants and also found a lower overall prevalence of intraventricular hemorrhage in the indomethacin treated infants. Yet, these authors did not observe any differences in the prevalence of severe hemorrhages or in the mortality rate. Other investigators (Green, Bada & Leffler, 1987; Hanigan et al., 1987) failed to show a decrease in the prevalence or severity of intraventricular hemorrhage after the administration of indomethacin in prematurely born infants.

Vitamin E has also been studied in the prevention of intraventricular hemorrhage. In their initial studies, Chiswick et al. (1983) reported that vitamin E administration to prematurely born infants resulted in no effect on the overall prevalence of intraventricular hemorrhage but had a threefold lower frequency of severe intraventricular hemorrhage. Speer et al. (1984) investigated 134 prematurely born infants and found a lower prevalence of intraventricular hemorrhage in vitamin E treated infants compared with a control population. Sinha, Davies, Toner, Bogle, and Chiswick (1987) studied 210 premature infants and observed a lower overall prevalence of all hemorrhages and of severe hemorrhages in vitamin E treated infants. In another study, Phelps, Rosenbaum, Isenberg, Leake, and Dorey (1987) administered vitamin E to 287 premature infants. These investigators reported that vitamin E did not prevent retinopathy of prematurity (ROP), and there even was a higher prevalence of severe intraventricular hemorrhage in the treated infants.

The mechanism of any beneficial effect of vitamin E relates to its potent antioxidant property. Vitamin E probably operates as a free radical scavenger to protect matrix capillary endothelial cells from hypoxic injury (Volpe, 1989).

**Maintenance of Cerebral Perfusion** Of major importance in postnatal prevention of the occurrence of intraventricular hemorrhage is careful attention to cerebral perfusion and, particularly, avoidance of events that lead to sudden increases in cerebral perfusion. Because available data suggest that cerebral blood flow in the sick newborn is pressure-passive (Lou et al., 1979), events that cause sharp increases in blood pressure are potentially dangerous. Experimental studies support the importance of hypertension in pathogenesis (see Pathogenesis section, p. 199). A growing body of data obtained with human premature infants supports this notion. For example, the clinical observations of Fujimura et al. (1979) indicated that fluctuations in systemic blood pressure after initial low levels are important in the genesis of intraventricular hemorrhage. Goldberg et al. (1980) demonstrated a clear relationship between rapid volume expansion and intraventricular hemorrhage. Furthermore, Milligan (1980) utilized jugular venous occlusion plethysmography to demonstrate that transfusion induced increases in blood pressure resulted in striking increases in cerebral blood flow and, then, intraventricular hemorrhage within 12 hours of these increases. Similarly, other studies (Hill & Volpe, 1982) documented a causative relationship between pneumothorax and intraventricular hemorrhage. The mechanism of this relation appeared to be a striking increase in cerebral blood flow velocity caused by a sharp increase in blood pressure at the time of the pneumothorax. Since spikes of blood pressure have been well documented in premature infants with simple motor activity or handling as well as with seizures and apnea, potential causative events for intraventricular hemorrhage (and fertile topics for future investigation) should be apparent.

## Acute Management of Intraventricular Hemorrhage

In many instances, all efforts to stop premature labor are unsuccessful and postnatal efforts of intraventricular hemorrhage cannot be prevented. The physician is then faced with the task of managing the infant who has been subjected to this serious intracranial insult.

**Ethical Question** The first question that must be answered following periventricular-intraventricular hemorrhage is, "Should this infant be treated at all?" If the infant has sustained a severe hemorrhage with massive intraventricular and intraparenchymal clotting visible on ultrasound or CT scan and, in addition, has had a catastrophic clinical deterioration, the prognosis is grim. In such cases, an ethical question arises that deserves detailed consideration beyond the scope of this chapter. Such issues have been raised (Hemphill & Freeman, 1977) and deserve review by all who care for small premature infants. Clinical criteria alone are usually inadequate to make a judgment of a hopeless prognosis in an infant with severe intraventricular hemorrhage. A catastrophic clinical deterioration can be seen in the absence of massive hemorrhage and vice versa. For example, one clinical picture of an infant with intraventricular hemorrhage showed a total brainstem failure; however, the infant survived and was nearly normal at the 1 year follow-up (Pasternak & Volpe, 1979). Such cases emphasize the importance of utilizing all available information in critical decision-making, but should not be used to rationalize aggressive and unrealistic support in infants with truly massive hemorrhages. The best estimate of prognosis is obtained by a combined assessment of the extent of the hemorrhage, as determined by ultrasound or CT scan; the details of the clinical picture; and assessment of the extent of any prior hypoxic-ischemic insult.

**Maintenance of Cerebral Perfusion** Once the decision to treat has been made, the essential initial task is the maintenance of cerebral perfusion. Cerebral perfusion pressure is determined by the mean arterial blood pressure minus the intracranial pressure. As has been emphasized above, severe intraventricular hemorrhage may cause elevated intracranial pressure and may be associated with low arterial blood pressure. Arterial blood pressure must be maintained at adequate levels, but this must be done judiciously because the cerebral circulation is likely to be pressure-passive in the sick premature infant. Aggressive therapy may convert a small lesion into a severe one. Intracranial pressure, when significantly increased in relation to arterial blood pressure, should be lowered. In order to do this, one must first know that the pressure is elevated. Unfortunately, this vital bit of information is often not obtained during lumbar puncture in the premature infant. Once the presence of seriously increased intracranial pressure has been established, two principal methods are available for lowering it: lumbar or ventricular puncture. Lumbar puncture is perhaps the less dangerous of the two techniques and is often quite effective. During the acute period following the hemorrhage, communication usually exists between the ventricular system and the lumbar subarachnoid space. Experience has shown that there is little danger to this approach, although caution should be exercised, especially in the presence of a large unilateral intracerebral hematoma.

**Detection of Posthemorrhagic Hydrocephalus** Serial ultrasound scans are necessary to detect the evolution of posthemorrhagic hydrocephalus. These are critical because the clinical concomitants of progressive ventricular dilatation do not appear for days to weeks after the development of the hydrocephalic state. Once hydrocephalus is detected, a new series of therapeutic issues (discussed in detail by Volpe, 1981) requires consideration.

## CONCLUSION

Periventricular-intraventricular hemorrhage is a very important adverse neurologic event of the neonatal period. It is common and can be very severe. Such hemorrhage begins in the germinal matrix but may spread into and throughout the ventricular system. It may be accompanied by hemorrhage within the brain parenchyma. The pathogenesis of periventricular-intraventricular hemorrhage is still imperfectly understood, but relates principally to the anatomy and physiology of the developing cerebral vasculature, the germinal matrix, and cerebral blood flow.

Periventricular-intraventricular hemorrhage may be marked clinically by a catastrophic neurologic deterioration, but is more commonly accompanied by a saltatory progression that may be difficult to detect. Both concomitant neonatal disease and therapeutic interventions for such disease have been implicated in the initiation and exacerbation of periventricular-intraventricular hemorrhage.

Real-time ultrasound scanning with portable instruments is now the preferred procedure for identifying periventricular-intraventricular hemorrhage and for assessing its sequelae. Prognosis relates principally to the severity of the lesion, especially concomitant parenchymal involvement.

Early management must be particularly directed to the maintenance of cerebral perfusion. Later management is predominantly the therapy of posthemorrhagic hydrocephalus. In either case, effective management is useful in the prevention and amelioration of developmental disabilities that too commonly complicate the subsequent course of infants with intraventricular hemorrhage or posthemorrhage hydrocephalus.

## REFERENCES

Ahmann, P. A., Lazzara, A., Dykes, F. D., Brann, A. W., Jr., & Schwartz, J. F. (1980). Intraventricular hemorrhage in the high-risk preterm infant: Incidence and outcome. *Annals of Neurology, 7*, 118–124.

Allan, W. C., Roveto, C. A., Sawyer, L. R., & Courtney, S. E. (1980). Sector scan ultrasound imaging through the anterior fontanelle: Its use in diagnosing neonatal periventricular-intraventricular hemorrhage. *American Journal of Diseases of Children, 134*, 1028–1034.

Bada, H. S., Hajjar, W., Chua, C., & Sumner, D. S. (1979). Noninvasive diagnosis of neonatal asphyxia and intraventricular hemorrhage by Doppler ultrasound. *Journal of Pediatrics, 95*, 775–779.

Bandstra, E. S., Montalvo, B. M., Goldberg, R. N., Pacheco, I., Ferrer, P. L., Flynn, J., Gregorios, J. B., & Bancalari, E. (1988). Prophylactic indomethacin for prevention of intraventricular hemorrhage in premature infants. *Pediatrics, 82*, 533–542.

Chiswick, M. L., Johnson, M., Woodhall, C., Gowland, M., Davies, J., Toner, N., & Sims, D. G. (1983). Protective effect of vitamin E (DL alpha tocopherol) against intraventricular haemorrhage in premature babies. *British Medical Journal, 287*, 81–84.

Clark, C. E., Clyman, R. I., Roth, R. S., Sniderman, S. H., Lane, B., & Ballard, R. A. (1981). Risk factor analysis of intraventricular hemorrhage in low birth weight infants. *Journal of Pediatrics, 99*, 625–628.

DeCourten, G. M., & Rabinowicz, T. (1981). Intraventricular hemorrhage in premature infants: Reappraisal and new hypothesis. *Developmental Medicine and Child Neurology, 23*, 389–403.

Donn, S. M., Roloff, D. W., & Goldstein, G. W. (1981). Prevention of intraventricular hemorrhage in preterm infants by phenobarbitone: A controlled trial. *Lancet, i*, 215–217.

Dubowitz, L. M. S., Levene, M. I., Morante, A., Palmer, P., & Dubowitz, V. (1981). Neurologic signs in neonatal intraventricular hemorrhage: A correlation with real-time ultrasound. *Journal of Pediatrics, 99*, 127–133.

Ehle, A., & Sklar, F. (1979). Visual evoked potentials in infants with hydrocephalus. *Neurology, 29*, 1541–1544.

Flodmark, O., Becker, L. E., Harwood-Nash, D. C., Fitzhardinge, P. M., Fitz, C. R., & Chuang, S. H. (1980). Correlation between computed tomography and autopsy in premature and full-term neonates that have suffered perinatal asphyxia. *Radiology, 137*, 93–103.

Fujimura, M., Salisbury, D. M., Robinson, R. O., Howat, P., Emerson, P. M., Keeling, J. W., & Tizard, J. P. M. (1979). Clinical events relating to intraventricular hemorrhage in the newborn. *Archives of Disease in Childhood, 54*, 409–414.

Gilles, F. H., Price, R. A., Kevy, S. V., & Berenberg, W. (1971). Fibrinolytic activity in the ganglionic eminence of the premature human brain. *Biology of the Neonate, 18*, 426–432.

Goddard, J., Lewis, R. M., Armstrong, D. L., & Zeller, R. S. (1980). Moderate rapidly induced hypertension as a cause of intraventricular hemorrhage in the newborn beagle model. *Journal of Pediatrics, 96*, 1057–1060.

Goldberg, R. N., Chung, D., Goldman, S. L., & Bancalari, E. (1980). The association of rapid volume expansion and intraventricular hemorrhage in the preterm infant. *Journal of Pediatrics, 96*, 1060–1063.

Goldstein, G. W. (1979). Pathogenesis of brain edema and hemorrhage: Role of the brain capillary. *Pediatrics, 64*, 357–360.

Green, R. S., Bada, H. S., & Leffler, C. W. (1987). Controlled trial of indomethacin (IND) prevention of neonatal intraventricular/periventricular hemorrhage (IVH/PVH). *Pediatric Research, 21*, 362A.

Hambleton, G., & Wigglesworth, J. S. (1976). Origin of intraventricular hemorrhage in the preterm infant. *Archives of Disease in Childhood, 51*, 651–659.

Hanigan, W. C., Kennedy, G., Roemisch, F., Anderson, R., Cusack, T., & Miller, T. (1987). Prophylactic indomethacin for the prevention of periventricular hemorrhage. *Pediatric Research, 21*, 491A.

Haruda, F., & Blanc, W. A. (1981). The structure of intracerebral arteries in premature infants and the autoregulation of cerebral blood flow. *Annals of Neurology, 10*, 303.

Hemphill, M., & Freeman, J. M. (1977). Ethical aspects of care of the newborn with serious neurological disease. *Clinics in Perinatology, 4*, 201–209.

Hill, A., Perlman, J. M., & Volpe, J. J. (1982). Relationship of pneumothorax to occurrence of intraventricular hemorrhage in the premature newborn. *Pediatrics, 69*, 144–149.

Hill, A., Taylor, D. A., & Volpe, J. J. (1981). Treatment of posthemorrhagic hydrocephalus by serial lumbar puncture: Factors that account for success or failure. *Annals of Neurology, 10*, 284.

Hill, A., & Volpe, J. J. (1982). Decrease in pulsatile flow in the anterior cerebral arteries in infantile hydrocephalus. *Pediatrics, 60*, 4–7.

Holt, P. J., & Allan, W. F. (1981). The natural history of ventricular dilatation in neonatal intraventricular hemorrhage and its therapeutic implication. *Annals of Neurology, 10*, 293.

Horbar, J. D., Leahy, K., & Lucey, J. F. (1981). The incidence of perinatal intracranial hemorrhage (ICH) following maternal administration of isoxsuprine and betamethasone. *Pediatric Research, 15*, 664.

Korobkin, R. (1975). The relationship between head circumference and the development of communicating hydrocephalus following intraventricular hemorrhage. *Pediatrics, 56*, 74–77.

Krishnamoorthy, K. S., Shannon, D. C., DeLong, G. R., Todres, I. D., & Davis, K. R. (1979). Neurologic sequelae in the survivors of neonatal intraventricular hemorrhage. *Pediatrics, 64*, 233–237.

Kuban, K. C., Leviton, A., Krishnamoorthy, K. S., Brown, E. R., Teele, R. L., Baglivo, J. A., Sullivan, K. F., Huff, K. R., White, S., Cleveland, R. H., Allred, E. N., Spritzer, K. L., Skouteli, H. N., Cayea, P., & Epstein, M. F. (1986). Neonatal intracranial hemorrhage and phenobarbital. *Pediatrics, 77*, 443–450.

Larroche, J. C. (1972). Posthemorrhagic hydrocephalus in infancy: Anatomical study. *Biology of the Neonate, 20*, 289–299.

Larroche, J. C. (1977). *Developmental pathology of the neonate*. New York: Excerpta Medica.

Lazzara, A., Ahmann, P., Dykes, F., Brann, A. W., Jr., & Schwartz, J. (1980). Clinical predictability of intraventricular hemorrhage in preterm infants. *Pediatrics, 65*, 30–34.

Levene, M. I., & Starte, D. R. (1981). A longitudinal study of posthemorrhagic ventricular dilatation in the newborn. *Archives of Disease in Childhood*, *56*, 905–910.

Lou, H. C., Lassen, N. A., & Friis-Hansen, B. (1979). Impaired autoregulation of cerebral blood flow in the distressed newborn infant. *Journal of Pediatrics*, *94*, 118–121.

Ment, L. R., Duncan, C. C., Ehrenkranz, R. A., Kleinman, C. S., Pitt, B. R., Taylor, K. J., Scott, D. T., Stewart, W. B., & Gettner, P. (1985). Randomized indomethacin trial for the prevention of intraventricular hemorrhage in very low birth weight infants. *Journal of Pediatrics*, *107*, 937–943.

Ment, L. R., Duncan, C. C., Ehrenkranz, R. A., Kleinman, C. S., Taylor, K. J., Scott, D. T., Gettner, P., Sherwonit, E., & Williams, J. (1987). Randomized low dose indomethacin trial for the prevention of intraventricular hemorrhage in very low birth weight neonates. *Annals of Neurology*, *22*, 406–407.

Milhorat, T. H., Clark, R. G., Hammock, M. K., & McGrath, P. P. (1970). Structural, ultrastructural, and permeability changes in the ependyma and surrounding brain favoring equilibrium in progressive hydrocephalus. *Archives of Neurology*, *22*, 397–407.

Milligan, D. W. A. (1980). Failure of autoregulation and intraventricular hemorrhage in preterm infants. *Lancet*, *i*, 896–898.

Morgan, M. E. I., Benson, J. W. T., & Cooke, R. W. I. (1981). Ethamsylate reduces the incidence of periventricular hemorrhage in very low birth weight babies. *Lancet*, *i*, 830–831.

Morgan, M. E. I., Benson, J. W. T., & Cooke, R. W. I. (1982). Does phenobarbitone prevent periventricular hemorrhage in very low birth weight babies? A controlled trial. *Pediatrics*, *70*, 186–189.

Oldendorf, W. H., Cornford, M. E., & Brown, W. J. (1977). The large apparent work capability of the blood brain carrier: A study of the mitochondrial content of capillary endothelial cells in brain and other tissues of the rat. *Annals of Neurology*, *1*, 409–417.

Pape, K. E., Gusick, G., Houang, M. T. W., Blackwell, R. J., Sherwood, A., Thorburn, R. J., & Reynolds, E. O. R. (1979). Ultrasound detection of brain damage in preterm infants. *Lancet*, *i*, 1261–1264.

Pape, K. E., & Wigglesworth, J. S. (1979). *Hemorrhage, ischaemia, and the perinatal brain*. Philadelphia: J. P. Lippincott.

Papile, L. A., Burstein, J., Burstein, R., & Koffler, H. (1978). Incidence and evolution of subependymal and intraventricular hemorrhage: A study of infants with birth weights less than 1,500 g. *Journal of Pediatrics*, *92*, 529–534.

Papile, L. A., Munsick, G., Weaver, N., & Pecha, S. (1979). Cerebral intraventricular hemorrhage (CVH) in infants 1,500 grams: Developmental follow-up at one year. *Pediatric Research*, *13*, 528.

Pasternak, J. F., Mantovani, J. F., & Volpe, J. J. (1980). Porencephaly from periventricular-intracerebral hemorrhage in a premature infant. *American Journal of Diseases of Children*, *134*, 673–675.

Pasternak, J. F., & Volpe, J. J. (1979). Full recovery from prolonged brainstem failure following intraventricular hemorrhage. *Journal of Pediatrics*, *95*, 1046–1049.

Perlman, J. M., & Volpe, J. J. (1982). Cerebral blood flow velocity in relation to intraventricular hemorrhage in the premature newborn. *Journal of Pediatrics*, *100*, 956–959.

Phelps, D. L., Rosenbaum, A. L., Isenberg, S. J., Leake, R. D., & Dorey, F. J.

(1987). Tocopherol efficacy and safety for preventing retinopathy of prematurity: A randomized, controlled, double-masked trial. *Pediatrics, 79*, 489–500.

Rubin, R. C., Hochwald, G. M., Tiell, M., Mizutani, H., & Ghatak, N. (1976). Hydrocephalus: Vol. I. Histological and ultrastructural changes in the preshunted cortical mantle. *Surgical Neurology, 5*, 109–114.

Shankaran, S., Slovis, T. L., Bedard, M. P., & Poland, R. L. (1982). Sonographic classification of intracranial hemorrhage: A prognostic indicator of mortality, morbidity, and short-term neurologic outcome. *Journal of Pediatrics, 100*, 469–475.

Sinha, S., Davies, J., Toner, N., Bogle, S., & Chiswick, M. (1987). Vitamin E supplementation reduces frequency of periventricular haemorrhage in very preterm babies. *Lancet, i*, 466–470.

Speer, M. E., Blifeld, C., Rudolph, A. J., Chadda, P., Holbein, M. E., & Hittner, H. M. (1984). Intraventricular hemorrhage and vitamin E in the very low birth weight infant: Evidence for efficacy of early intramuscular vitamin E administration. *Pediatrics, 74*, 1107–1112.

Tsiantos, A., Victorin, L., Relier, J. P., Dyer, N., Sundell, H., Brill, A. B., & Stahlman, M. (1974). Intracranial hemorrhage in the prematurely born infant: Timing of clots and evaluation of clinical signs and symptoms. *Journal of Pediatrics, 85*, 854–859.

Vert, P., Nomin, P., & Sibout, M. (1975). Intracranial venous pressure in newborns: Variation in physiologic state and in neurologic and respiratory disorders. In L. Stern (Ed.), *Intensive care in the newborn* (pp. 133–147). New York: Masson.

Volpe, J. J. (1974). Neonatal intracranial hemorrhage: Iatrogenic etiology? *New England Journal of Medicine, 291*, 43–45.

Volpe, J. J. (1978). Neonatal periventricular hemorrhage: Past, present and future. *Pediatrics, 92*, 693–696.

Volpe, J. J. (1981). *Neurology of the newborn.* Philadelphia: W. B. Saunders.

Volpe, J. J. (1989). Intraventricular hemorrhage in the premature infant—current concepts: Part II. *Annals of Neurology, 25*, 109–116.

Volpe, J. J., Pasternak, J. F., & Allan, W. C. (1977). Ventricular dilatation preceding rapid head growth following neonatal intracranial hemorrhage. *American Journal of Diseases of Children, 131*, 1212–1215.

Welch, K. (1980). The intracranial pressure in infants. *Journal of Neurosurgery, 52*, 693–699.

Weller, R. O., & Shulman, K. (1972). Infantile hydrocephalus: Clinical, histological, and ultrastructural study of brain damage. *Journal of Neurosurgery, 36*, 255–265.

Wozniak, M., McLone, D. G., & Raimondi, A. J. (1975). Micro- and macrovascular changes as the direct cause of parenchymal destruction in congenital murine hydrocephalus. *Journal of Neurosurgery, 43*, 535–545.

# 14 | Harvey L. Levy

# NEONATAL SCREENING FOR METABOLIC DISORDERS

The opportunity to prevent developmental disabilities is perhaps no better illustrated than in the screening of newborns for metabolic disorders. This type of screening identifies biochemical conditions that may produce mental retardation or other disabilities, but for which clinical abnormalities can be prevented by neonatal diagnosis and specific treatment.

The most well-known example of screening and early treatment is phenylketonuria (PKU). In 1934, this disease was discovered to be a cause of mental retardation (Fölling, 1934). In subsequent years the genetic pattern of PKU was elucidated, and its biochemical basis became known (Jervis, Block, Bolling, & Kanze, 1940). In the early 1950s, Bickel, Gerrard, and Hickmans (1953) found that early dietary treatment could prevent mental retardation in patients with PKU. The challenge was to detect infants with PKU before clinical signs of brain damage appeared.

This challenge was met in the early 1960s when Guthrie and Susi (1963) developed a simple bacterial inhibition assay for phenylalanine that could be applied to blood impregnated filter paper. Using this blood test, infants in newborn nurseries could be routinely evaluated for PKU from blood specimens obtained by sticking the heel with a lancet and blotting a filter paper card with a few drops of blood. This filter paper blood specimen would be

This chapter was supported in part by grant #HSMHA-MCH 01-H-000111 from the Bureau of Health Care, Delivery, and Assistance, U.S. Department of HHS, Maternal and Child Health Research grant #MCJ-250501, and grant #NS 05096 from the National Institute of Neurological and Communicative Disorders and Stroke.

mailed to a central laboratory for phenylketonuria testing. A significantly increased phenylalanine concentration in the blood specimen indicated that the infant had phenylketonuria.

By the mid-1960s, many states had begun routine newborn PKU screening programs. Infants with PKU were identified in larger numbers than had been anticipated and were showing normal development while on treatment. The success of PKU screening led to the addition of tests for other metabolic disorders that were similar in principle to phenylketonuria. These tests could be applied to the same filter paper specimen that was obtained for PKU screening. Thus, in a number of states, infants were also routinely screened for galactosemia, maple syrup urine disease (MSUD), and homocystinuria (Levy, 1973). A test for congenital hypothyroidism has been added to most newborn screening programs (Dussault et al., 1975), and has been the most valuable addition since screening began.

## NEWBORN SCREENING PROGRAMS

In the United States, screening of newborn blood for PKU is legally mandated in more than 40 states and comprehensively conducted on a voluntary basis in the others. PKU screening is also carried out in Canada, most European countries, Australia, New Zealand, Japan, several South American countries, Israel, and other Asian nations. Newborn screening for congenital hypothyroidism is almost as widespread. Screening for galactosemia is practiced by about one-third of the programs in the United States and by most of those in other countries. Screening for maple syrup urine disease and homocystinuria is less often included.

### Regionalization

Screening for hypothyroidism has had a major impact upon the organization of newborn screening programs. The radioimmunoassay for this screening requires considerable technical skill and expertise, unlike the relatively simple bacterial inhibition assays for PKU and other inborn errors of metabolism. In addition, the capital outlay for equipment to perform radioimmunoassays and the cost of maintaining this equipment are also much greater than expenses necessary to support the Guthrie bacterial inhibition assays. These considerations were strong arguments for the establishment of regional centers in which a state with an adequately equipped and staffed laboratory would perform tests on newborn blood specimens from adjacent states as well as from its own state. Expenses would be shared through contractual arrangements. Regionalization began in the northwestern part of the United States when Oregon agreed to screen specimens from Alaska and Montana. New England followed shortly thereafter with Massachusetts being the central screening facility for specimens from Connecticut, Maine, New Hampshire, Rhode Island,

and Vermont (Figure 14.1). Regionalized newborn screening also exists in the Rocky Mountains and in the middle Atlantic areas (Levy & Mitchell, 1982).

## Newborn Urine Screening

Many metabolic disorders in newborn infants are not identifiable by blood screening but are readily detectable in urine. The late Mary Efron recognized this and in 1966 initiated routine newborn urine screening in Massachusetts. Urine specimens are similar to newborn blood specimens except that a filter paper card is impregnated with urine instead of blood. The parent obtains the specimen when the infant is 3–4 weeks old by pressing a wet portion of the diaper onto the card. A specimen kit is usually supplied when the infant leaves the hospital.

The specimen is mailed to the Massachusetts laboratory where it is tested by paper chromatography for amino acids and certain organic acids, such as methylmalonic acid (Levy, Coulombe, & Shih, 1980). Only Massachusetts and Rhode Island in the United States and Quebec in Canada conduct this type of newborn urine screening.

Urine screening has resulted in the identification of such disorders as cystinuria, Hartnup disease, histidinemia, methylmalonic aciduria, cystathioninemia, argininosuccinicaciduria, and others (Levy, Madigan, & Shih, 1972) not identified by blood screening. Some of these disorders are clinically important, but many are probably benign. Thus, newborn urine screening probably does have a role in the prevention of developmental disabilities, but one that is much more limited than newborn blood screening (Levy et al., 1980).

## RESULTS OF SCREENING

### Phenylketonuria

Since newborn screening began, tens of thousands of infants with PKU have been identified throughout the world. These infants have received early dietary therapy, and as a result, mental retardation from PKU has virtually been eliminated in areas that conduct newborn screening for phenylketonuria (Williamson, Koch, Azen, & Chang, 1981).

Though these early treated children have normal intelligence (and some even have superior intelligence), Koff and her co-workers found that many have visual perceptual deficits (Koff, Boyle, & Pueschel, 1977). This observation has since been confirmed by many groups, and it is now recognize that these children can have substantial learning difficulties (Levy, 1986).

One concern regarding treatment of PKU raises the question: Must the phenylalanine restricted diet for PKU be continued throughout life or can it be discontinued during childhood? This matter is not yet settled. Until the 1970s,

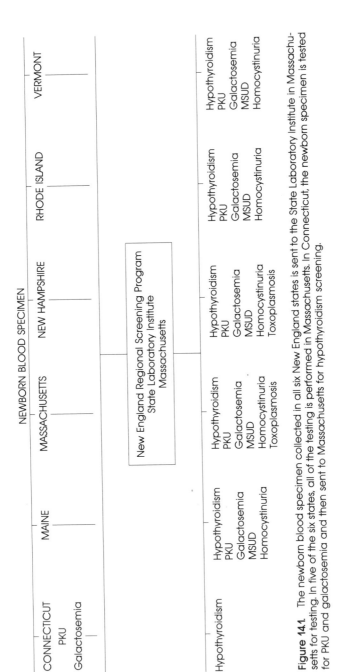

**NEWBORN BLOOD SPECIMEN**

| CONNECTICUT | MAINE | MASSACHUSETTS | NEW HAMPSHIRE | RHODE ISLAND | VERMONT |
|---|---|---|---|---|---|
| PKU<br>Galactosemia | Hypothyroidism<br>PKU<br>Galactosemia<br>MSUD<br>Homocystinuria | Hypothyroidism<br>PKU<br>Galactosemia<br>MSUD<br>Homocystinuria<br>Toxoplasmosis | Hypothyroidism<br>PKU<br>Galactosemia<br>MSUD<br>Homocystinuria<br>Toxoplasmosis | Hypothyroidism<br>PKU<br>Galactosemia<br>MSUD<br>Homocystinuria | Hypothyroidism<br>PKU<br>Galactosemia<br>MSUD<br>Homocystinuria |

New England Regional Screening Program
State Laboratory Institute
Massachusetts

Hypothyroidism

**Figure 14.1.** The newborn blood specimen collected in all six New England states is sent to the State Laboratory Institute in Massachusetts. In five of the six states, all of the testing is performed in Massachusetts. In Connecticut, the newborn specimen is tested for PKU and galactosemia and then sent to Massachusetts for hypothyroidism screening.

many treatment centers, especially in the United States, recommended diet termination when the child was 5 or 6 years old. This practice has been questioned, however, on the basis of observations suggesting IQ reductions in children with PKU who resumed a normal diet (Waisbren, Schnell, & Levy, 1980). It now seems quite clear that some children with early treated PKU, especially those whose blood phenylalanine level exceeds 16 mg/dl suffer a reduction in IQ if treatment is discontinued at age 5 years (Waisbren, Mahon, Schnell, & Levy, 1987). Accordingly, most clinics now recommend continuation of the diet (Schuett & Brown, 1984).

A major issue is maternal PKU. This issue considers mental retardation, microcephaly, congenital heart disease, and low birth weight among offspring of women with PKU who did not have a phenylalanine restricted diet during pregnancy (Lenke & Levy, 1980). Before newborn screening for PKU, this was not a major problem because most women with PKU were severely mentally retarded and only infrequently bore children. With newborn screening and early treatment, many young women with PKU have normal or, at least, near normal intelligence and will likely wish to bear children. Thus, the question raised: Will all of their children be mentally retarded? There is hope that treatment during pregnancy, especially if begun prior to conception, will protect the fetus and result in normal offspring (Levy, 1987). Specific dietary treatment for maternal PKU during pregnancy has been established (Pueschel, Hum, & Andrews, 1977).

## Congenital Hypothyroidism

The frequency of congenital hypothyroidism, as determined by routine newborn screening, is about three times that of PKU (Fisher et al., 1979). Thus, in just a few years of screening, many infants with hypothyroidism have been identified and treated with thyroid hormone.

The IQs of these treated children at 4 years of age have been normal and comparable to their euthyroid siblings (New England Congenital Hypothyroidism Collaborative Study, 1981). At later ages, however, they are found to have learning difficulties and visual motor deficits similar to those in early treated children with PKU (Glorieux, Dussault, Letarte, Guyda, & Morissette, 1983; Rovet, Ehrlich, & Sorbara, 1987). In addition, those children treated may also have a high frequency of behavioral difficulties (Rovet, Ehrlich, & Sorbara, 1989).

## Galactosemia

The frequency of galactosemia from newborn screening varies between 1 : 30,000 to 1 : 100,000 (Levy & Hammersen, 1978). Newborn screening and early dietary intervention with milk restriction have certainly prevented neonatal death from Gram negative sepsis in many infants (Levy, Sepe, Shih, Vawter, & Klein, 1977). Growth and development in galactosemic infants identified by routine screening may be somewhat delayed in some children (Buist, Waggoner, Donnell, & Levy, 1988). Speech and language deficits have also been noted in many of these children (Waisbren, Norman, Schnell, & Levy, 1983), and the girls usually develop ovarian failure (Kaufman, Donnell, Roe, & Kogut, 1986).

## Maple Syrup Urine Disease

Maple syrup urine disease (MSUD) is an autosomal recessively inherited disorder in branched-chain amino acid degradation. Affected infants develop marked elevations of leucine, isoleucine, and valine as well as their branched-chain ketoacid analogues. Profound ketoacidosis ensues, often beginning during the first week of life. This is characterized by lethargy, hypotonia or hypertonia, and seizures. If intensive care is not initiated at this time, neonatal death occurs. Treatment of the acute condition includes peritoneal dialysis or hemodialysis, intravenous fluid support, and anticonvulsant medication. Following recovery from the acute episode, metabolic control is required for the prevention of mental retardation. This includes a special diet restricted in leucine and other branched-chain amino acids.

About 1 in 225,000 infants is found to have MSUD (Naylor & Guthrie, 1978). The results of treatment are somewhat mixed, but many children are thriving and have normal intelligence. Prompt treatment and careful follow-up can lead to a successful outcome in MSUD, as clearly demonstrated by the Montreal group (Clow, Reade, & Scriver, 1981).

## Homocystinuria

Homocystinuria is an autosomal recessive defect in methionine metabolism, at the point where homocysteine is converted to cystathionine. This defect results in increased homocystine in blood and urine as well as increased methionine. As expected, cystathionine is reduced, most prominently in the brain where it normally is present in large quantity. The clinical complications of homocystinuria include dislocated ocular lenses (ectopia lentis), mental retardation, skeletal abnormalities, and propensity for thromboembolism. Treatment consists of a special diet restricted in methionine.

Homocystinuria has a frequency similar to that of MSUD, about 1 in 200,000 (Mudd, Levy, & Skovby, 1989). Identification by newborn screening and early dietary treatment seem to prevent mental retardation and perhaps skeletal abnormalities. Dislocation of the ocular lenses occurs in many patients with homocystinuria, however, despite good dietary control (Pullon, 1980).

## FUTURE SCREENING TESTS

Several tests now available could be applied to the filter paper blood specimen. Muscular dystrophy can be identified by a spot assay that will record increased activity of creatine kinase (Zellweger & Antonik, 1975). The absence of therapy that will prevent the clinical manifestations of this disease, however, seems to militate against its use in routine newborn screening. Cystic fibrosis can also be identified in the newborn blood specimen through a radioimmunoassay for trypsinogen (Crossley, Elliott, & Smith, 1979) and may be a valuable addition in that mortality and morbidity seems to be reduced by newborn screening detection (Wilcken & Chalmers, 1985).

A radioimmunoassay for hydroxyprogesterone can be used to identify infants with congenital adrenal hyperplasia in the newborn period (Pang, Hotchkiss, Drash, Levine, & New, 1977). Here the argument for newborn screening is quite strong since there is effective preventive therapy that can be lifesaving. Neonatal diagnosis can lead to prompt identification of the sex, and this can have important lifetime implications for the infant. Pilot screening has been successfully performed in a number of countries, including the United States (Pang et al., 1988).

## CONCLUSION

It is clear that routine newborn screening for a number of metabolic disorders is an effective and important measure in preventing developmental disabilities. Already the vast majority of newborns in most developed nations are routinely screened for PKU. A growing number of infants are also being screened for congenital hypothyroidism, galactosemia, maple syrup urine disease, homocystinuria, and other disorders. Many of these infants will develop into healthy and intellectually normal children, so very different from the children with these disorders with mental retardation and developmental disabilities who previously, unfortunately, were not screened in infancy. All of this, a veritable revolution in the care and prognosis of metabolic disorders, became possible because of Guthrie's simple but profoundly important blood test.

## REFERENCES

Bickel, H., Gerrard, J., & Hickmans, E. M. (1953). Influence of phenylalanine intake on phenylketonuria. *Lancet, ii,* 812–813.

Buist, N., Waggoner, D., Donnell, G., & Levy, H. (1988). The effect of newborn screening on prognosis in galactosemia: Results of an international survey. *American Journal of Human Genetics, 43,* A3.

Clow, C. L., Reade, T. M., & Scriver, C. R. (1981). Outcome of early and long-term management of maple syrup urine disease. *Pediatrics, 68,* 856–862.

Crossley, J. R., Elliott, R. B., & Smith, P. A. (1979). Dried blood spot screening for cystic fibrosis in the newborn. *Lancet, i,* 472.

Dussault, J. H., Coulombe, P., Laberge, C., Letarte, J., Guyda, H., & Khoury, K. (1975). Preliminary report on a mass screening program for neonatal hypothyroidism. *Journal of Pediatrics, 86,* 670–674.

Fisher, D. A., Dussault, J. H., Foley, T. P., Jr., Klein, A. H., LaFranchi, S., Larsen, P. R., Mitchell, M. L., Murphey, W. H., & Walfish, P. G. (1979). Screening for congenital hypothyroidism: Results of screening. *Journal of Pediatrics, 94,* 700–705.

Fölling, A. (1934). Über Ausscheidung von Phenylbrenztraubensäure in den Harn als Stoffwechselanomalie in Verbindung mit Imbezillität [About the excretion of phenylpyruvic acid in the urine as an inborn error of metabolism including mental retardation]. *Hoppe-Seyler's Zeitschrift für Physiologische Chemie, 227,* 169–176.

Glorieux, J., Dussault, J. H., Letarte, J., Guyda, H., & Morissette, J. (1983). Preliminary results on the mental development of hypothyroid infants detected by the Quebec screening program. *Journal of Pediatrics, 102,* 19–22.

Guthrie, R., & Susi, A. (1963). A simple phenylalanine method for detecting phenylketonuria in large populations of newborn infants. *Pediatrics, 32,* 338–343.

Jervis, G. A., Block, R. J., Bolling, D., & Kanze, E. (1940). Chemical and metabolic studies on phenylalanine: II. The phenylalanine content of the blood and spinal fluid in phenylpyruvic oligophrenia. *Journal of Biological Chemistry, 134,* 105–113.

Kaufman, F. R., Donnell, G. N., Roe, T. F., & Kogut, M. D. (1986). Gonadal function in patients with galactosemia. *Journal of Inherited Metabolic Disease, 9,* 140–146.

Koff, E., Boyle, P., & Pueschel, S. M. (1977). Perceptual motor functioning in children with phenylketonuria. *American Journal of Diseases of Children, 131,* 1084–1087.

Lenke, R. R., & Levy, H. L. (1980). Maternal phenylketonuria and hyperphenylalaninemia: An international survey of the outcome of untreated and treated pregnancies. *New England Journal of Medicine, 303,* 1202–1208.

Levy, H. L. (1973). Genetic screening. In H. Harris & K. Hirschhorn (Eds.), *Advances in human genetics* (Vol. 4, pp. 1–104). New York: Plenum.

Levy, H. L. (1986). Phenylketonuria—1986. *Pediatrics in Review, 7,* 269–275.

Levy, H. L. (1987). Maternal phenylketonuria: Review with emphasis on pathogenesis. *Enzyme, 38,* 312–320.

Levy, H. L., Coulombe, J. T., & Shih, V. E. (1980). Newborn urine screening. In H. Bickel, R. Guthrie, & G. Hammersen (Eds.), *Neonatal screening for inborn errors of metabolism* (pp. 89–103). New York: Springer-Verlag.

Levy, H. L., & Hammersen, G. (1978). Newborn screening for galactosemia and other galactose metabolic defects. *Journal of Pediatrics, 92,* 871–877.

Levy, H. L., Madigan, P. M., & Shih, V. E. (1972). Massachusetts metabolic disorders screening program: I. Techniques and results of urine screening. *Pediatrics, 49,* 825–836.

Levy, H. L., & Mitchell, M. L. (1982). The current status of newborn screening. *Hospital Practice, 17,* 89–97.

Levy, H. L., Sepe, S. J., Shih, V. E., Vawter, G. F., & Klein, J. O. (1977). Sepsis due to *Escherichia coli* in neonates with galactosemia. *New England Journal of Medicine, 297,* 823–825.

Mudd, S. H., Levy, H. L., & Skovby, F. (1989). Disorders of transsulfuration. In C. R. Scriver, A. L. Beaudet, W. S. Sly, & D. Valle (Eds.), *The metabolic basis of inherited disease* (6th ed., pp. 693–734). New York: McGraw-Hill.

Naylor, E. W., & Guthrie, R. (1978). Newborn screening for maple syrup urine disease. *Pediatrics, 61,* 262–266.

New England Congenital Hypothyroidism Collaborative. (1981). Effects of neonatal screening for hypothyroidism: Prevention of mental retardation by treatment before clinical manifestations. *Lancet, ii,* 1095–1098.

Pang, S., Hotchkiss, J., Drash, A. L., Levine, L. S., & New, M. I. (1977). Microfilter paper method for 17 alpha hydroxyprogesterone radioimmunoassay: Its application for rapid screening for congenital adrenal hyperplasia. *Journal of Clinical Endocrinology and Metabolism*, 45, 1003–1008.

Pang, S., Wallace, M. A., Hofman, L., Thuline, H. C., Dorche, C., Lyon, I. C. T., Dobbins, R. H., Kling, S., Fujieda, K., & Suwa, S. (1988). Worldwide experience in newborn screening for classical congenital adrenal hyperplasia due to 21-hydroxylase deficiency. *Pediatrics*, 81, 866–874.

Pueschel, S. M., Hum, C., & Andrews, M. (1977). Nutritional management of the female with phenylketonuria during pregnancy. *American Journal of Clinical Nutrition*, 30, 1153–1161.

Pullon, D. H. H. (1980). Homocystinuria and other methioninemias. In H. Bickel, R. Guthrie, & G. Hammersen (Eds.), *Neonatal screening for inborn errors of metabolism* (pp. 29–44). New York: Springer-Verlag.

Rovet, J., Ehrlich, R., & Sorbara, D. (1987). Intellectual outcome in children with fetal hypothyroidism. *Journal of Pediatrics*, 110, 700–704.

Rovet, J., Ehrlich, R. M., & Sorbara, D. L. (1989). Effect of thyroid hormone level on temperament in infants with congenital hypothyroidism detected by screening of neonates. *Journal of Pediatrics*, 114, 63–68.

Schuett, V. E., & Brown, E. S. (1984). Diet policies of PKU clinics in the United States. *American Journal of Public Health*, 74, 501–503.

Waisbren, S. E., Mahon, B. E., Schnell, R. R., & Levy, H. L. (1987). Predictors of intelligence quotient and intelligence quotient in persons treated for phenylketonuria early in life. *Pediatrics*, 79, 351–355.

Waisbren, S. E., Norman, T. R., Schnell, R. R., & Levy, H. L. (1983). Speech and language deficits in early treated children with galactosemia. *Journal of Pediatrics*, 102, 75–77.

Waisbren, S. E., Schnell, R. R., & Levy, H. L. (1980). Diet termination in children with phenylketonuria: A review of psychological assessments used to determine outcome. *Journal of Inherited Metabolic Disease*, 3, 149–153.

Wilcken, B., & Chalmers, G. (1985). Reduced morbidity in patients with cystic fibrosis detected by neonatal screening. *Lancet*, ii, 1319–1321.

Williamson, M. L., Koch, R., Azen, C., & Chang, C. (1981). Correlates of intelligence test results in treated phenylketonuric children. *Pediatrics*, 68, 161–167.

Zellweger, H., & Antonik, A. (1975). Newborn screening for Duchenne muscular dystrophy. *Pediatrics*, 55, 30–34.

# 15 | Betty R. Vohr

# SCREENING THE YOUNG INFANT FOR NEUROLOGIC AND DEVELOPMENTAL DISABILITIES

The diagnosis of neurodevelopmental disabilities at the earliest possible age allows the primary physician to establish a sound framework for a comprehensive support system for the infant with disabilities and his or her family with appropriate medical and educational advice. Early identification, however, is dependent upon the targeting of high-risk populations and the implementation of diagnostic screening programs for that risk population.

## HISTORICAL CONSIDERATIONS

Infants cared for in a neonatal intensive care unit represent a contemporary risk population. A review of the history of specialized care for premature infants indicates that there were few high-risk premature survivors in the first few decades of this century, and minimal follow-up data were collected on them. The earliest long-term follow-up studies of low birth weight infants were done in the preintensive care era of the 1940s and 1950s. These studies identified an incidence of major sequelae in 50% to 70% of low birth weight survivors (Drillien, 1967; Lubchenco et al., 1963). Subsequently, with the evolution of the intensive care era in the 1960s, maternal and infant transport systems, and extended regionalization programs, survival of low birth weight infants steadily improved (Fitzhardinge & Ramsey, 1973; Hack, Merkatz, Jones, & Fanaroff, 1980; Rawlings, Reynolds, Stewart, & Strang, 1971;

Stewart & Reynolds, 1974; Stewart, Turcan, Rawlings, & Reynolds, 1977). Therapy and management became more sophisticated through the combined efforts of the obstetrician, the neonatologist, and the perinatologist. Many factors have led to improved survival among low birth weight infants, including advances in perinatal monitoring, improved nutrition, hyperalimentation, treatment of hyperbilirubinemia with phototherapy and exchange transfusion, new approaches to asphyxia through intrauterine monitoring and assessment, and the use of assisted ventilation and surfactant.

## HIGH-RISK FOLLOW-UP

Survival statistics spanning a 10-year period (1975–1985) for the Neonatal Intensive Care Unit at Women and Infants Hospital of Providence, Rhode Island, indicate a steady improvement in survival of infants with a birth weight less than 1,500 g from 57% to 72% (Table 15.1). For infants weighing 1,000 g–1,500 g, the survival rate is 85%, and for infants weighing under 1,000 g, the survival rate has more than tripled from 16% to 57%.

The improved survival of the smallest premature infants in perinatal centers throughout the country was followed by the realization that there was a need to assess the quality of life of these survivors. During the 1970s, most of the major neonatal centers began to develop follow-up programs to assess the neonatal and long-term outcomes of specific risk populations. Professionals working with mothers and infants voiced the concern that the survival of these tiny infants would result in an increase in the number of children with disabilities. It was no longer good enough merely to state that an infant had survived the newborn period and had been discharged from the hospital. Since improved survival in the past has not always been associated with improved morbidity, the concern was a real one. A classic example was the initial use of oxygen for respiratory distress in prematures, which resulted in large numbers of infants with visual impairments, such as secondary retrolental fibroplasia (Kinsey, 1956; Phelps, 1981; Terry, 1942). This possibility of iatrogenic sequelae resulting from new technology was yet another incentive for developing follow-up programs.

A comprehensive follow-up program has service, educational, and research goals. The primary service-oriented goals related to the screening

Table 15.1. Neonatal survival statistics

| Birth weight in grams | 1975 | 1980 | 1985 |
| --- | --- | --- | --- |
| <1,500 | 70/121 (57%) | 97/133 (73%) | 110/152 (72%) |
| >1,000 to ≤1,500 | 64/84 (76%) | 81/91 (89%) | 70/82 (85%) |
| ≤1,00 | 6/37 (16%) | 16/42 (38%) | 40/70 (57%) |

These data include inborn and outborn infants from the Women & Infants Hospital Neonatal Intensive Care Unit, Providence, Rhode Island.

process include the identification of infants with medical, neurologic, sensory, developmental, and psychosocial disabilities, and the referral of identified infants to appropriate community resources, such as an early intervention program. The education-oriented goal of the follow-up program is to serve as a source of teaching material for house officers by providing them with ready access to both normal and atypical models of growth and development. Furthermore, with the increasing complexity of medical problems of many neonatal intensive care unit survivors, parent education becomes an additional important component. Finally, research-oriented goals for an effective screening process must include both retrospective and prospective data collection and analyses to ultimately assess cause and effect relationships, provide valid statistics to substantiate changes in procedure, and thereby function as a quality control mechanism for the special care nursery.

Because of the large number of infants cared for in an individual tertiary care center and the inability to follow all these infants comprehensively in a follow-up program, specific criteria must be established to identify and evaluate sequentially those infants at greatest risk. Criteria are determined by each center in part by the type of population served, that is, low versus high socioeconomic status, adolescent versus older mother, and rural versus metropolitan living environments. In addition, specific criteria for enrollment into a follow-up program continue to change in conjunction with the introduction of new diagnostic procedures and treatment modalities. Neonatal follow-up program risk criteria that are used at Women and Infants Hospital of Rhode Island include:

1. Low birth weight ($\leq$ 1,250 g)
2. Asphyxia: 5 minute Apgar score $\leq$ 3
3. Respiratory morbidities, including infants with bronchopulmonary dysplasia, oxygen dependent infants, and infants on a home apnea monitor
4. Neonatal seizures, intracranial hemorrhage, hydrocephalus, microcephaly, abnormal neurologic examination
5. Meningitis and/or sepsis documented by positive culture or torch titers
6. Hyperbilirubinemia requiring exchange transfusion
7. Intrauterine growth retardation
8. Dysmorphism and/or genetic abnormalities
9. Serious unresolved psychosocial problems

Very low birth weight continues to be an important risk factor with the risk of sequelae inversely related to birth weight in infants less than 1,250 g. Infants born between 22 and 28 weeks gestation are at greatest risk for severe respiratory distress syndrome (RDS), bronchopulmonary dysplasia (BPD), intracerebral hemorrhage, and retinopathy of prematurity (ROP). Infants with perinatal asphyxia are surviving in increasing numbers and are at risk for seizure disorders and neurologic sequelae (Brown & Purves, 1974).

Infants with RDS requiring assisted ventilation have a higher incidence of neurodevelopmental morbidity than healthy controls (Fitzhardinge, 1978). Infants at great risk are those with BPD, a chronic lung disease related to positive pressure ventilation and/or elevated levels of inspired oxygen (Northway, Rosan, & Porter, 1967). Northway (1979) reported a 34% prevalence of cerebral palsy, mental retardation, deafness, and blindness in BPD survivors. Follow-up studies of BPD infants at Women & Infants Hospital identified a 52% incidence of major neurologic abnormalities (Vohr, Bell, & Oh, 1982). Meningitis, sepsis, and hyperbilirubinemia requiring exchange transfusion are all related to an increased incidence of sequelae (Fitzhardinge, Kazemi, Ramsey, & Stern, 1974; Gartner, Snyder, Chabon, & Bernstein, 1970; Papile, Burstein, Burstein, & Koffler, 1978).

The neonatal course of the small for gestational age (SGA) infants is characterized by more frequent occurrence of asphyxia, polycythemia, hyperviscosity, hypoglycemia, and hypocalcemia (Bard, 1978). The prevalence of neurodevelopmental sequelae in the preterm SGA infant, however, continues to be a controversial subject because of the heterogeneity of the population studied. Differences in degree of growth retardation, gestational age, perinatal care, neonatal complications, and socioeconomic status among studies leads to difficulties in comparing outcomes (Fitzhardinge & Steven, 1972; Lugo & Cassady, 1971; Vohr, Cowett, Rosenfield, & Oh, 1979; Vohr & Oh, 1983). It has been demonstrated, however, that SGA infants with genetic or congenital abnormalities or specific syndromes, especially those with small heads (symmetric growth retardation), have the poorest outcome (Clarren & Smith, 1978).

## NEONATAL ASSESSMENT

A detailed, systematic, and sensitive parent interview must be included in the neonatal assessment to identify all important environmental and social risk factors in order to facilitate comprehensive management and referral. Psychosocial problems requiring monitoring include maternal drug or alcohol abuse, psychiatric disorders, teenage pregnancy, and family dysfunction (Escalona, 1982).

Major congenital stigmata that particularly fit a syndrome pattern are invariably identified by clinical evaluation and at times confirmed by laboratory testing during the neonatal period (Cooper, 1975). Infants with identifiable syndromes known to be associated with developmental problems are referred during the neonatal period to the appropriate facility within the community for early intervention, genetic counseling, and management. The presence of a single defect, such as epicanthic fold, however, may have no significance. Yet, the presence of several minor defects that do not fit a known syndrome may be a signpost indicating a first trimester insult and a need for ongoing developmental monitoring.

The neurologic examination of the newborn has tended to be a lengthy evaluation that includes multiple methods to assess alertness, muscle tone, posture, and reflexes (Amiel-Tison, 1968; Brazelton, 1984). A shortened version is often more practical. Clinical neurologic signs that place the infant at risk for neurodevelopmental sequelae include abnormal muscle tone or posture patterns; asymmetry of muscle tone, posture, or reflexes; abnormal head growth; seizures; oculomotor disturbances; and disturbed suck-swallow mechanism. The neonatal evaluation in the low birth weight infant should include a neurologic examination at 6–8 weeks postnatal age, just prior to discharge, with ophthalmologic and hearing screens completed (depending on the presence of specific sensory risk factors). Since the vast majority of developmental disabilities are not identified in the newborn period by neurologic examination, infants with high-risk status require a series of evaluations to monitor changing patterns of motor functions, to assess developmental levels, and to identify malfunctioning sensory systems (Vohr & Garcia-Coll, 1985a, 1985b; Vohr et al., 1989; Vohr, Garcia-Coll, & Oh, 1988).

Major abnormalities that can be identified during the first year are those that require comprehensive medical, neurologic, and educational support services. These include:

1. Major motor deficits, particularly cerebral palsy
2. Seizure disorders
3. Sensorineural deafness
4. Blindness, particularly retrolental fibroplasia in the low birth weight infant
5. Head growth abnormalities, congenital malformations, syndromes, and mental retardation

Repeated neurologic assessments during the first year of life, in combination with an infant developmental assessment, simplify the identification process. The Bayley Scales of Infant Development (Bayley, 1969) is a well standardized infant assessment instrument with cognitive, motor, and behavior components. If time and finances are restricted, the Denver Developmental Assessment (Frankenberg & Dodds, 1967) is a developmental screening option.

Abnormal neurologic signs identified early in the first year of life are often transient and are no longer observed at 18 months to 2 years, reflecting the biologic plasticity of the neonate. In contrast, some infants with mildly suspect findings in the neonatal period progress to more serious neurologic sequelae or manifest subsequent learning difficulties related to language, attention deficit, and visual perceptual motor performance.

## PERIODIC ASSESSMENT IN EARLY CHILDHOOD

After the first year of life, milder and more subtle neurodevelopmental abnormalities can be identified by systematic neurologic and developmental assessments. These abnormalities include:

1. Fine and gross motor impairments
2. Visual-perceptual motor inefficiencies
3. Minor motor deficits and balancing difficulties
4. Myopia or strabismus
5. Mild hearing loss
6. Receptive or expressive language deficiencies
7. Behavioral abnormalities, such as hyperkinetic or anxiety states

Although early follow-up studies focused primarily on major disabilities, the trend has been to look further at more minor abnormalities with the classification of the patient into normal, suspect, and abnormal categories, depending on neurologic and developmental findings.

Between 3 and 5 years of age, neurologic assessment is expanded to include more refined gross and fine motor assessment. The Stanford Binet Intelligence Test (Terman & Merrill, 1973) and the McCarthy Scales of Children's Abilities (McCarthy, 1972) are options for assessing levels of developmental functioning. Additional developmental tests that have been found helpful in making educational recommendations for children 5 years and older include the Beery Visual Motor Index (Beery, 1967) and the Wide Range Achievement Test.

Data from the collaborative perinatal project identified the magnitude of the risk for developing cerebral palsy for infants under 1,500 g (Nelson & Ellenberg, 1978). A 7 year follow-up of 54,000 children born from 1959–1966 identified the risk to be 90.4/1,000 for infants less than 1,500 g as compared to 3.3/1,000 for infants weighing more than 2,500 g (p < 0.001). This relationship between very low birth weight and motor disabilities is now well accepted.

It is fortunate that clinical signs of cerebral palsy in some children (identified during the first year of life) may diminish steadily during childhood and in some cases resolve completely. This finding was demonstrated in a 7 year follow-up of 37,000 children who had serial neurologic examinations in the National Collaborative Perinatal Project (Nelson & Ellenberg, 1982). Of 229 1-year-old children (with a diagnosis of cerebral palsy) enrolled in the longitudinal study, 118 (52%) demonstrated no motor disabilities by 7 years of age. The children with mild disabilities at 1 year of age were more likely to have a complete resolution of their abnormalities.

## FOLLOW-UP MORBIDITY TRENDS

Many reports have focused on the survival and reduced morbidity of infants under 1,000 g birth weight (Bier, Garcia-Coll, Oh, & Vohr, 1988; Nickel, Bennett, & Lamson, 1982; Pape, Buncie, & Fitzhardinge, 1978). These studies are in sharp contrast to the first follow-up report of infants under 1,000 g born from 1947 to 1950 (Lubcheno et al., 1963). Survival was rare and 100% of survivors had a major disability. A paper by Nickel et al. (1982) on infants less than 1,000 g born from 1960 to 1972 reported survival at 16.9%. Some centers are even publishing survival at 47%–48% (Driscoll et al., 1982; Pape et al., 1978). Some investigators are, in addition, evaluating the presence of school difficulties, the level of developmental functioning in an academic setting, and requirements for special education. Nickel et al. (1982) identified a 64% prevalence of developmental problems in infants with a birth weight less than 1,000 g at a mean age of 10.6 years. Major disabilities were present in 28% of the population evaluated. These outcome data demonstrate three specific trends: 1) increasing survival of infants under 1,000 g, 2) decreasing prevalence of major disabilities, and 3) increasing identification of developmental abnormalities. This information stresses the importance of long-term follow-up to school age and repeated diagnostic evaluations of the low birth weight survivors.

Premature children with or without motor abnormalities may have associated visual abnormalities (Vohr & Garcia-Coll, 1985b; Vohr et al., 1989). Retrolental fibroplasia (RLF) was first described as a disorder or prematurity by Terry in 1942. However, the relationship between RLF and oxygen was not confirmed until the 1950s. Factors determined to be related include prematurity, multiple birth, and exchange transfusion. Despite the fact that improved oxygen monitoring, including microblood techniques and transcutaneous oxygen monitoring that have permitted much more accurate blood oxygen monitoring, the increased survival of less mature infants has made this disorder a continuing cause of childhood blindness. Contemporary studies indicate a 2%–4% incidence of stage III-IV RLF, which is scarring with severe blindness or myopia. The incidence of stage I-II is 20%–30% (Bauer, 1978; Phelps, 1981). Fortunately, stage I-II findings are transient in most infants. More minor ophthalmologic problems have been reported in ranges of 4% to 40% of children and are more common in youngsters with cerebral palsy. These findings indicate a continued need for meticulous ophthalmologic monitoring of these tiny infants (Palma, 1981).

Hearing loss is identified more commonly in the neonatal intensive care unit graduate and is an important diagnosis because it is a significant contributing factor to language, cognitive, and behavioral abnormalities. Multiple factors have been implicated as etiologic factors resulting in sensorineural hearing loss in low birth weight infants and range from hyperbilirubinemia to low birth weight (Table 15.2). Sensorineural hearing loss in low birth weight infants is presently in the range of 2% to 4%. Follow-up studies at Women and Infants Hospital have shown a higher than expected prevalence of conductive hearing loss in low birth weight survivors. This conductive hearing loss was related to recurrent respiratory morbidities in the first year of life (Vohr, Regan, Daniel, & Oh, 1981). Audiometric screening has three compo-

Table 15.2. Risk criteria for sensorineural hearing loss

1. Family history of childhood hearing impairment
2. Prenatal infections (e.g., cytomegalovirus, rubella, herpes, toxoplasmosis, syphilis)
3. Anatomic malformations involving the head or neck (e.g., dysmorphic appearance, including syndromal and nonsyndromal abnormalities, overt or submucous cleft palate, morphologic abnormalities of the pinna)
4. Birth weight less than 1,500 g
5. Hyperbilirubinemia level exceeding criterion level for exchange transfusion
6. Bacterial meningitis, especially Haemophilus influenza meningitis
7. Severe asphyxia, which may include infants with Apgar scores from 0 to 3 or infants who fail to start breathing spontaneous respiration by 10 minutes

1982 Statement of the Joint Committee on Infant Hearing Screening (American Academy of Pediatrics, Academy of Otolarynogology, Head and Neck Surgery, American Nurses Association, and the American Speech, Language and Hearing Association).

nents: pure tone hearing assessment, tympanometry, and brainstem evoked response evaluation. Infants without a history of risk criteria can be screened clinically by observing responses to auditory stimuli and monitoring receptive expressive language development. Infants with positive risk criteria should have a detailed audiometric evaluation.

## MANAGEMENT

Management of the impaired infant and his or her family after discharge can be critical. Early identification of neurologic, sensory, or other developmental abnormalities is only the first step. The infant and his or her family must be referred to the most appropriate supportive and comprehensive therapy or educational program within their community. In many communities, early intervention programs are available to infants immediately after their discharge from the hospital. An early intervention program is an organized program of environmental enrichment that provides developmentally appropriate activities to infants and toddlers who have, or who are at risk, for a variety of developmental disabilities. The program also provides support and guidance to the family. In addition to referrals of infants and toddlers between birth and 3 years to early intervention programs or speech and language intervention programs, referral is also indicated for children with disabilities of 3–5 years of age and older to special education programs.

The Education for All Handicapped Children Act, PL 94-142, was enacted in 1975. This legislation ensures the right of education to all handicapped children, at no charge to their families. It is still up to physicians and educators to identify eligible children, inform the families of the availability of the educational programs, and make the referrals.

## CONCLUSION

The etiology of developmental abnormalities in high-risk infant survivors is multifactorial. A variety of perinatal and genetic variables in combination with social and environmental factors are involved. Only through continued perinatal center follow-up, with meticulous data collection and analysis, will the primary physician be able to arrive at a better understanding of the etiologic factors involved. It is clear, however, that greater numbers of at-risk infants are surviving. Therefore, a continued focus on identification of abnormalities at the earliest possible age is indicated in order to provide support and to initiate appropriate therapeutic and educational options. This approach to high-risk infant follow-up can alleviate family disruption and prevent or modify specific developmental disabilities.

## REFERENCES

Amiel-Tison, C. (1968). Neurological examination of the maturity of newborn infants. *Archives of Disease in Childhood, 43*, 89–93.

Bard, H. (1978). Neonatal problems of infants with intrauterine growth retardation. *Journal of Reproductive Medicine, 21*, 359–364.

Bauer, C. R. (1978). The occurrence of retrolental fibroplasia in infants of birth weight 1,000 g and less. *Clinical Research, 26*, 824.

Bayley, N. (1969). *Bayley Scales of Infant Development*. New York: Psychological Corporation.

Beery, K. E. (1967). *Developmental test of visual motor integration*. Chicago: Follett.

Bier, J. B., Garcia-Coll, C., Oh, W., & Vohr, B. R. (1988). The impact of maternal transport on outcome in infants with a birth weight < 750 grams. *Pediatric Research, 23*, 1440A.

Brazelton, T. B. (1984). Neonatal behavioral assessment scale. In M. C. O. Bax (Ed.), *Clinics in developmental medicine* (2nd ed., pp. 1–25). London: Spastics International Medical Publications, Ltd.

Brown, J., & Purves, R. J. (1974). Neurologic aspects of perinatal asphyxia. *Developmental Medicine and Child Neurology, 16*, 567–580.

Clarren, S.K., & Smith, D. N. (1978). The fetal alcohol syndrome. *New England Journal of Medicine, 298*, 1063–1067.

Cooper, L. Z. (1975). Congenital rubella in the United States. In S. Krugman (Ed.), *Infections of the fetus and newborn infant* (pp. 1–22). Chicago: Yearbook Medical Publishers, Inc.

Drillien, C. M. (1967). The incidence of mental and physical handicaps in school age children of very low birth weight. *Pediatrics, 39*, 238–247.

Driscoll, J. M., Driscoll, Y. T., Steir, M. E., Stark, R. I., Dangman, B. C., Perez, A., Wung, J., & Kritz, P. (1982). Mortality and morbidity of infants less than 1,001 g birth weight. *Pediatrics, 69*, 21–26.

Escalona, S. K. (1982). Babies at double hazard: Early development of infants at biologic and social risk. *Pediatrics, 70*, 670–676.

Fitzhardinge, P. M. (1978). Follow-up studies in infants treated by mechanical ventilation. *Clinics in Perinatology, 5*, 452–461.

Fitzhardinge, P. M., Kazemi, M., Ramsey, M., & Stern, L. (1974). Long-term sequelae of neonatal meningitis. *Developmental Medicine and Child Neurology, 16*, 3–9.

Fitzhardinge, P. M., & Ramsey, M. (1973). The improving outlook for the small prematurely born infant. *Developmental Medicine and Child Neurology, 15*, 447–459.

Fitzhardinge, P. M., & Steven, E. M. (1972). The small-for-date infant: Neurological and intellectual sequelae. *Pediatrics, 50*, 50–57.

Frankenberg, W. K., & Dodds, J. B. (1967). The Denver Developmental Screening Test. *Journal of Pediatrics*, *71*, 181.

Gartner, L. M., Synder, B. N., Chabon, R. S., & Bernstein, S. (1970). Kernicterus: High incidence in premature infants with low serum bilirubin concentrations. *Pediatrics*, *45*, 906–917.

Gunn, T. R., Aranda, J. V., & Little, J. (1978). Incidence of retrolental fibroplasia. *Lancet*, *i*, 216–217.

Gunn, T. R., Easdown, J., & Outerbridge, E. W. (1980). Risk factors in retrolental fibroplasia. *Pediatrics*, *65*, 1096–1100.

Hack, M., Merkatz, I., Jones, P., & Fanaroff, A. (1980). Changing trends of neonatal and postneonatal deaths in very low birth weight infants. *American Journal of Obstetrics and Gynecology*, *137*, 797–800.

Kinsey, V. E. (1956). Retrolental fibroplasia: Cooperative study of retrolental fibroplasia and the use of oxygen. *Archives of Ophthalmology*, *56*, 481–543.

Lubchenco, L. O., Horner, F. A., Reed, L. H., Hix, I. E., Metcalf, D., Cohig, R., Elliot, H. C., & Bourg, M. (1963). Sequelae of premature birth. *American Journal of Diseases of Children*, *106*, 101–115.

Lugo, G., & Cassady, G. (1971). Intrauterine growth retardation. *American Journal of Obstetrics and Gynecology*, *109*, 615–622.

McCarthy, M. (1972). McCarthy scales of children's abilities. New York: Psychological Corporation.

Nelson, K. B., & Ellenberg, J. H. (1978). Epidemiology of cerebral palsy. In B. S. Schoenberg (Ed.), *Advances in neurology* (pp. 150–177). New York: Raven Press.

Nelson, K. B., & Ellenberg, J. H. (1982). Children who "outgrew" cerebral palsy. *Pediatrics*, *69*, 529–536.

Nickel, R. E., Bennett, F. C., & Lamson, F. N. (1982). School performance of children with birth weights of 1,000 g or less. *American Journal of Diseases of Children*, *136*, 105–110.

Northway, W. H. (1979). Observations on bronchopulmonary dysplasia. *Journal of Pediatrics*, *95*, 815–818.

Northway, W. H., Rosan, R. C., & Porter, D. Y. (1967). Pulmonary disease following respirator therapy by hyaline membrane disease: Bronchopulmonary dysplasia. *New England Journal of Medicine*, *276*, 357–368.

Palma, E. A. (1981). Optimal timing of examination for acute retrolental fibroplasia. *Ophthalmology*, *88*, 662.

Pape, K. E., Buncie, R. J., & Fitzhardinge, P. M. (1978). The status at two years of low-birth-weight infants born in 1974 with birth weights less than 1,001 g. *Journal of Pediatrics*, *92*, 253–260.

Papile, L., Burstein, J., Burstein, R., & Koffler, H. (1978). Incidence and evolution of subependymal hemorrhage: A study of infants with birth weights less than 1,500 g. *Journal of Pediatrics*, *92*, 529–534.

Phelps, D. L. (1981). Retinopathy of prematurity: An estimate of vision loss in the United States. *Pediatrics*, *67*, 924–926.

PL 94-142 (Education of All Handicapped Children Act of 1975). To USC 1401 et seq. *Federal Register*, *42*, (163), 42474–42518.

Rawlings, G., Reynolds, E. O. R., Stewart, A., & Strang, L. B. (1971). Changing prognosis for infants of very low birth weight. *Lancet*, *i*, 516–519.

Stewart, A. L., & Reynolds, E. O. R. (1974). Improved prognosis for infants of very low birth weight. *Pediatrics*, *54*, 724–735.

Stewart, A. L., Turcan, D. M., Rawlings, G., & Reynolds, E. O. R. (1977). Prognosis for infants weighing 1,000 g or less at birth. *Archives of Disease in Childhood*, *52*, 97–104.

Terman, L. M., & Merrill, M. A. (1973). *Stanford Binet Intelligence Scale.* Boston: Houghton Mifflin.

Terry, T. L. (1942). Extreme prematurity and fibroblastic overgrowth of persistent vascular sheath behind each crystalline lens: Vol. I. Preliminary Report. *American Journal of Ophthalmology, 25,* 203–204.

Vohr, B. R., Bell, E., & Oh, W. (1982). Follow-up of infants with bronchopulmonary dysplasia (1500 g). *American Journal of Diseases of Children, 136,* 443–447.

Vohr, B. R., Cowett, R. M., Rosenfield, A. G., & Oh, W. (1979). The preterm small for gestational age infants: A two year follow-up study. *American Journal of Obstetrics and Gynecology, 133,* 425–431.

Vohr, B. R., & Garcia-Coll, C. (1985a). Increased morbidity in low birth weight survivors with severe retrolental fibroplasia. *Journal of Pediatrics, 106*(2), 287.

Vohr, B. R., & Garcia-Coll, C. (1985b). Neurodevelopmental and school performance of very low birth weight infants: A seven year longitudinal study. *Pediatrics, 76*(3), 345–350.

Vohr, B. R., Garcia-Coll, C., Mayfield, S., Brann, B., Shaul, P., & Oh, W. (1989). Neurologic and developmental status related to the evolution of visual-motor abnormalities from birth to 2 years of age in preterm infants with intraventricular hemorrhage (IVH). *Journal of Pediatrics, 115,* 296–302.

Vohr, B. R., Garcia-Coll, C., & Oh, W. (1988). Language development at 2 years of age in low birth weight infants. *Developmental Medicine and Child Neurology, 30,* 608–615.

Vohr, B. R., & Oh, W. (1983). Growth and development of preterm small for gestational age infants. *Journal of Pediatrics, 103,* 941–945.

Vohr, B. R., Regan, B., Daniel, P., & Oh, W. (1981). Hearing impairment in low birth weight (LBW) children. *Pediatric Research, 15,* 456A.

# V

# PREVENTION OF DEVELOPMENTAL DISABILITIES DURING EARLY CHILDHOOD

# 16 | Nancy M. Johnson-Martin

# EARLY
# INTERVENTION
# AS A PREVENTIVE
# STRATEGY

The lead article in the March 1980 issue of *Pediatrics*, "Early Intervention for Infants with Down Syndrome: A Controlled Trial" (Piper & Pless, 1980), presented data on 37 infants assigned to either an intervention or a control group. These data led the authors to conclude:

> The failure to demonstrate benefits for the treated group in this study is disappointing for those who believe such therapy is an effective method for minimizing the retardation in Down syndrome. Although other possible explanations exist for these results, the findings clearly suggest that the efficacy of this form of early intervention is doubtful. (p. 467)

At that time, this event sent shock waves through the early intervention community, not because the study was a definitive one challenging the effectiveness of early intervention in general, but because it appeared in a first-class journal widely read by physicians who are among the strongest critics of early intervention. Also, it is a well-known phenomenon that people are much less critical in their evaluation of information that agrees with their perception than of that which disagrees. Thus, it was feared that unwarranted conclusions would be drawn from this study, disregarding two important factors: 1) "intervention" for Piper and Pless (1980) consisted only of 12 sessions of demonstrating stimulation activities to parents over a 6 month period, with no effort to assess parental follow through, much less intervention that is normally included in an intervention program; and 2) "effectiveness" was determined only by scores on one instrument, the Griffiths Mental Development Scales.

The publication of this article prompted a flurry of discussion beginning with somewhat defensive articles from interventionists pointing out the flaws in the Piper and Pless study, reviewing other evidence of effectiveness, and discussing values of intervention not tapped by the usual measures of developmental progress (Bricker, Carlson, & Schwarz, 1981; Denhoff, 1981). The defensiveness gave way to a serious discussion about the difficulty of demonstrating intervention effectiveness given the lack of well-designed and executed scientific studies (Casto & Mastropieri, 1986; Dunst, 1985; Shonkoff & Hauser-Cram, 1987; Simeonsson, Cooper, & Scheiner, 1982).

The Piper and Pless article and the aftermath highlight two major, unresolved issues that have plagued the early intervention movement since its beginning in the late 1950s and early 1960s. Although early intervention has been conceived broadly to be a strategy for preventing or remediating developmental disabilities, there has been little agreement as to what constitutes early intervention. Moreover, the specific remediation expected for clearly atypical children has been poorly articulated.

To ask the question, "Is early intervention effective in preventing developmental disabilities?" is analogous to asking, "Is medicine effective in curing sick people?" The question is too general to be answered within a scientific framework. In the case of the early intervention question, "early" may mean under 1 year of age or as late as 3 or 4 years of age; "intervention" may consist of extra handling or rocking in the neonatal intensive care nursery or may be an extensive home training program for both infant and parents; "effective" may be interpreted as keeping the child within normal developmental norms, increasing the child's developmental rate, preventing secondary effects of a disability, keeping a child out of an institution, or helping a family function more adequately. In order to begin to evaluate early intervention efforts, it is necessary to ask in each instance: "Who is doing what to whom and for what purpose?"

## DEFINING THE PARAMETERS

### Who: Service Providers

In the preface to the book emanating from the meeting of the President's Committee on Mental Retardation in 1974, Tjossem and Stephens (1976) noted that the major professions with the responsibility and capability to deliver early intervention services were education, nursing, and medicine. In the ensuing years, early intervention has continued to rely on these disciplines but has expanded to include physical and occupational therapists, psychologists, speech clinicians, social workers, and child development specialists. Regardless of the extent to which a setting is interdisciplinary or transdisciplinary in orientation, early intervention is apt to have a different character when provided by physical therapists than when provided by an educator or a speech clinician. Likewise, there will be a difference when it is provided by two educators, one trained in behavioral methodology and the other in neurodevelopmental theory. Any careful study of intervention programs should include a specification of the characteristics of the intervenors, a practice that is ignored in most literature.

## What: Content of Intervention

Apart from the impact of professional orientation, there are other important variables that determine what constitutes intervention. Some of these are: the role the parents play in intervention, the setting of the intervention, and the basic orientation of the intervention program. In some programs intervention consists primarily of specific therapies for the child, therapies that are provided by trained professionals. In others, the parents are seen as the primary agents of change. Professionals train the parents to become teachers and therapists for their children. If the intervention takes place in a highly structured center, there may be a daily log of the child's performance on a variety of specific activities. The amount of time spent on the various activities is carefully documented. If the intervention takes place in the home, records may or may not be kept. The amount of time spent on each activity is at the parent's discretion. In some programs, intervention is basically "educational," that is, skills are task analyzed into small steps and each step is taught to the child. In others, intervention is considered to be "therapy," that is, efforts are made to work on underlying developmental processes rather than on teaching specific skills. In still others, intervention is considered to be "stimulation," the child is provided with toys and experiences appropriate to normal children of the same developmental level with the assumption that as the child is ready, he or she will incorporate these experiences.

Each of these variables could be expected to have a major effect on the outcome of intervention. Without a careful description of what is being done and for how long, it is difficult to assess either positive or negative outcomes.

## To Whom: Targets of Intervention

The characteristics of the children who are the focus of intervention are vitally important in determining an appropriate content of intervention as well as the goals for intervention. Children who are at risk for developmental problems because of the socioeconomic status of their parents are biologically quite different than children who are at risk because of prematurity or other medical complication early in life. Even more different are children with known genetic, neurologic, or sensory impairments. It is unreasonable to assume that all will benefit from the same educational or therapeutic program; nor is it reasonable to expect that parents will be equally motivated or effective in doing their part in an intervention program (Browder, 1981). Scientifically sound studies of early intervention are made particularly difficult by the fact that many early intervention programs serve a range of children, varying both on the dimension of the nature and severity of disability (from high risk to profoundly multiply handicapped) and on the dimension of available resources within the family. Combining data from such diverse subjects would make the effectiveness of any particular intervention approach difficult to demonstrate simply because of the variability in all measures. Furthermore, no one intervention is appropriate for all children, a fact that further exacerbates the problem. Each program must be individually tailored, thus requiring single subject designs or system, such as Goal Attainment Scaling suggested by Simeonsson, Cooper, et al. (1982).

### For What Purpose: Goals of Intervention

Effectiveness can be assessed only in terms of how well intervention produces a desired outcome. A review of the literature on early intervention could readily lead one to conclude that the only, or at least the primary, goal of intervention programs is to improve mental development, since the primary outcome measures are indices of mental development. Yet, a visit to almost any intervention program would convince the visitor that a great deal is going on besides the promotion of cognitive development. Parents are receiving support and counseling, attention is paid to facilitating a positive interaction between the parent and the child, efforts are made to improve the ease with which physical care can be provided to the child, and at times the child is simply entertained. Clearly, quality of life for both children and families is an implicit if not explicit goal of intervention. Yet, little effort has been made to examine the effectiveness of intervention in meeting these goals.

## MEASURES OF PROGRESS

### IQ Fixation

Although using IQ as a primary outcome measure may have been appropriate for the initial studies of intervention for young children at risk for mental retardation because of socioeconomic conditions, its appropriateness as the primary measure for other populations must be questioned. Not only do these populations have characteristics that may preclude valid estimates of intellectual functioning, mental retardation is only one of the handicapping conditions early intervention is designed to remediate.

### Nature of Infant Mental Tests

One reason for questioning the appropriateness of IQ outcome measures is the nature of the measures themselves. Infant tests consist almost entirely of sensory and motor items. They have been shown repeatedly to be poor predictors of later intellectual development in the normal population (Kagan, Kearsley, & Zelazo, 1978; Thomas, 1970; Zelazo, 1977). For the population with developmental disabilities, such tests are reportedly more accurate predictors, but there is evidence that they may be better at predicting a continuing disability than at predicting mental development per se (Johnson, 1982). This should be expected, as many children with serious developmental disabilities have specific sensory and/or motor impairments that preclude normal interactions with the materials included in infant tests. Accurate estimates of their cognitive ability may not be possible until they mature sufficiently to interact with tests that make fewer demands on their deficient systems. For example, it is not uncommon in diagnostic clinics to see individuals with moderate to severe cerebral palsy who have been described as severely or profoundly mentally retarded in the preschool years but who demonstrate normal and even above normal intellectual ability once they have learned to communicate through speech or have developed an indicator response that allows assessment through a test such as the Pictorial Intelligence Test (French, 1964).

There is also evidence that infant mental tests measure different skills at different ages within the infancy period, as well as different skills than are found on tests of cognitive function in later childhood and adulthood. McCall (1979) has discussed this issue as discontinuity in development, suggesting that: 1) there are stages of development with different tasks being developmentally important at each stage and 2) the relationship between the skills important at one stage and those important at another is often unclear. Thus, if one infant is much better than another at visual tracking and auditory localization at 2 months of age, one cannot necessarily expect him or her to also be better at putting blocks in a cup or ringing a bell purposely at 6 months of age. Likewise, the child who is better with the sensorimotor tasks at 6 months may not be better with the language items that become increasingly prevalent on the tests after 18 months. Intervention that is effective in improving a child's acquisition of sensorimotor skills may not have lasting effects on IQ at a later stage when language is more critical in the score. However, intervention may have lasting effects on the child's ability to manipulate objects in the environment, certainly a critical factor in long-term adaptation to the external world.

Finally, because of the nature of their construction, intelligence tests may be among the least sensitive indicators of the changes that might be expected as a result of intervention. Items for most infant and preschool scales were chosen because they differentiated the performance of older and younger children. It is likely, therefore, that neurologic maturation plays an important role in many of them. In fact, some of them may be much more a function of maturation than of experience. One could not expect environmental interventions to have a major impact on such items.

## IQ Versus Adaptation

A second reason for questioning the reliance on mental tests as primary outcome measures is the apparent assumption that IQ or Mental Development Index (MDI) is the only factor in mental retardation. According to the definition from the American Association on Mental Retardation, individuals with mental retardation are those whose performance is two or more standard deviations below the mean on standardized intelligence tests *and* who show concurrent deficits in adaptive behavior (Grossman, 1973).

Secondary and tertiary prevention efforts through early intervention, therefore, should focus both on cognitive performance and on adaptive behavior. Likewise, the assessment of effectiveness should include both areas.

In addition, there is good reason to believe that efforts to assess intervention effectiveness will be more successful if they focus on adaptive behaviors than if they continue to focus on cognitive status. Information available from long-term follow-up of intervention efforts aimed at high-risk infants and preschoolers (Lazar & Darlington, 1982) suggests that some of the major effects of early intervention will be seen in changes in interpersonal skills, self-esteem, mastery motivation, activities of daily living (feeding, dressing, etc.), and all components of adaptive behavior.

Unfortunately, however, there are major limitations in the instruments available for measuring adaptive behavior. In the infancy period, published tests of adaptive behavior rely primarily on gross motor milestones and on the same fine motor and sensorimotor items that are included in the mental tests. Children with cerebral palsy or other disorders that interfere with performance are again at a disadvantage. Likewise, programs that try to document the effectiveness of intervention for these children will have a difficult time doing so with the most commonly used instruments. Instruments may need to be developed that focus on factors such as ease of care, responsiveness, ability to initiate the reinforced social interactions, and so forth. Some progress is being made in this area by developers of parent questionnaires (Abidin, 1983) and of rating scales for children (Simeonsson, Huntington, Short, & Ware, 1982).

Even in populations where it may be possible to document progress by commonly used adaptive behavior scales, these scales may be missing the most significant accomplishments of the program. In a visit to the Experimental Education Unit of the University of Washington in 1976, this author had the privilege of observing both the preschool program for children with Down syndrome and the vocational training program that included a number of teenagers and young adults with Down syndrome. A comparison of the students in the two programs dramatically illustrated the effects of early intervention, although these effects were not being systematically measured. The 5-year-olds in the preschool program clearly demonstrated better language, social, and prevocational skills than did the adolescents and young adults.

Undoubtedly, IQs were different in the preschool and vocational populations. IQ frequently decreases over time in individuals with Down syndrome. However, decreases in IQ are a result of tests requiring more abstract thinking in order to maintain scores, not a result of skills being lost. Regardless of the follow-up IQs of the children in the preschool program, they are assured of a brighter future than the cohort of Down syndrome individuals a half generation older. Measures of prevocational and social competence not tapped by most adaptive behavior scales may be more stable indicators of successful intervention for this population than IQ or adaptive behavior scales.

## CONSIDERING THE EVIDENCE

### Socioeconomic High-Risk Populations

Probably the best data available on the effects of early intervention come from the study of populations at risk for mental retardation because of socioeconomic conditions. This is, in part, because the availability and characteristics of this population have made it relatively easy to adopt good scientific methodology (i.e., having experimental and control groups randomly assigned or matched on critical variables) and, in part, because the goal for intervention is related to established measures. That is, the goal is to promote normal mental development, and there are a variety of well-standardized instruments for measuring mental development (albeit with the limitations noted above). In a review in *Pediatric Annals*, Haskins, Finkelstein, and Stedman (1978) concluded that early education or stimulation programs for socioeconomically high-risk children have been shown to be effective in maintaining near normal intellectual growth in the preschool years. Many gains in IQ appear to be lost after school entry, and there is some evidence that including mothers in the intervention program yields longer lasting results. They also noted that in addition to IQ change, some authors reported differences between experimental and control groups in other behaviors that might relate to success, such as task persistence, resistance to distraction, and curiosity (Miller & Dyer, 1975).

A report by Lazar and Darlington (1982) presented follow-up data on 12 independently designed and implemented preschool programs of the 1960s. Graduates of these preschool programs were evaluated; some were as young as 9 years of age and some as old as 19 years at the time of the follow-up. In addition to IQ, the investigators compared these children to control or comparable nonintervention groups on achievement test scores, other indicators of school competence (e.g., assignment to special education or repetition of a grade), and the attitudes and values of both the children and their families. The data indicate that:

1. Controlling for family background and initial ability, program graduates were significantly less likely to be assigned to special education or to be retained than were controls. This was true regardless of sex, ethnic background, initial ability level, or early family background factors.
2. Program graduates retained higher IQs for several years after the program ended. Actual school achievement was better, but not significantly so.
3. Program graduates were more likely to give achievement related reasons for being proud of themselves.
4. Mothers of program graduates had higher vocational aspirations for their children and more positive attitudes toward school performance. (Lazar & Darlington, 1982)

One of the important aspects to emerge from this follow-up study is the need to measure variables other than mental ability, even in this population where mental retardation was the specific target of intervention. It was clear in this study that assignment to special education (and thus the label "mentally retarded" in school) is determined not only by IQ but by other factors as well. The authors pointed out that the data indicate that there are two paths to avoid placement in special education. One path is to have a normal IQ at age 6 (a factor that is strongly influenced by participation in early intervention) and a mother with a higher educational level. This path is also significantly affected by having a father present and by having fewer siblings. The second path is to participate in early intervention, independent of the background factors, and IQ by age 6. This strongly suggests that early intervention promotes some adaptive skills, such as motivation, good conduct, and task persistence, that serve as important indicators of effectiveness and make a child appear more competent.

## Medically High-Risk Populations

The earliest studies on medically high-risk populations were done in hospital special care nurseries. In a review of early intervention literature prepared by The National Committee for Services to Very Young Children with Special Needs and Their Families (INTER-ACT), Garland, Swanson, Stone, and Woodruff (1981) pointed out that there has been a theoretical difference among researchers regarding the specific environmental factors in intensive care nurseries that might contribute to subsequent developmental delay. Operating on the hypothesis that nurseries are deprived environments, some investigators have provided additional stimulation. Others have attempted to intervene by reducing or altering what is felt to be the overstimulation or inappropriate stimulation of around-the-clock bright lights and the bustling activity of the nursery personnel.

In the 1960s, data were published demonstrating the effectiveness of extra holding (Hasselmeyer, 1966), stroking (Solkoff, Yaffe, Weintraub, &

Blase, 1969), rocking (Freedman & Boverman, 1966), and vestibular stimulation (Neal, 1968) in producing weight gain and more competent responses in high-risk infants, even showing effects lasting as long as 8 months in higher Bayley motor scores (Solkoff et al., 1969). These studies were followed in the 1970s with studies of auditory stimulation (Barnard, 1972; Katz, 1971), kinesthetic stimulation (Barnard, 1972), visual stimulation (Scarr-Salapatek & Williams, 1973), and maternal handling (Powell, 1974), with data showing effects at follow-up for as long as 1 year on the Cattell and Bayley Scales. Such studies have had a major impact on the way intensive care nurseries are run and how the parents of the infants in those nurseries are involved in the early lives of their infants. In fact, it is probably fair to say that some of what was once described as early intervention is now simply considered good nursery management in many intensive care nurseries.

Intervention for medically high-risk infants after they leave the hospital has been more difficult to study, in part, because it is impossible to control environmental variables other than those under study and, in part, because the mobility of society makes longitudinal studies problematic. Perhaps because of improvements in the technology for dealing with high-risk infants, it now appears that most medical problems at birth are less powerful indicators of outcome than are socioeconomic conditions (Caputo, Goldstein, & Taub, 1981). Most medically high-risk infants who survive will be normal at 12 months of age without significant intervention beyond the nursery (Campbell & Wilhelm, 1982). These data suggest: 1) that intervention for infants at risk because of socioeconomic factors is warranted, particularly if the infants are also at-risk medically; 2) that appropriate stimulation of medically high-risk infants during their nursery stay is probably helpful; and 3) that it may be unnecessary to provide intervention for other medically high-risk infants except as evidence accumulates that specific risk factors merit special attention or as problems are noted in follow-up care.

## Populations with Known Disorders

Evaluating the data on ameliorating the effects of handicapping conditions for children with known genetic, sensory, or neurologic defects is a difficult task. Research in this area is beset with both ethical and practical problems. The ethical problems revolve around the issue of denying or delaying treatment that might be effective in order to have a control group. This is a particularly critical issue in infant intervention, because it is generally believed that the plasticity of the organism decreases with age. The practical problems relate to difficulties in matching samples for experimental and control groups, identifying adequate measures to assess whether the intervention is making a difference on the desired parameters, identifying samples of adequate size, dealing with the increased variance produced by health conditions, and finding financial support for the longitudinal studies that are necessary to document long-term effects. In a review of such studies since 1975, Simeonsson, Cooper, et al. (1982) concluded that few studies met the criteria for scientific research, such as specification of inclusion criteria, documentation of reliability, random assignment, and/or the use of control/contrast groups.

**Down Syndrome**   Perhaps the most widely studied group with disabilities in early intervention is that of children with Down syndrome. In the 1970s, a number of studies were published documenting the effectiveness of early intervention in helping infants with Down syndrome reach mental, motor, and language milestones at a more normal rate than untreated but home-reared infants with Down syndrome (Bricker & Bricker, 1976; Clunies-Ross, 1979; Hanson, 1977; Hayden & Haring, 1976; Zausmer, Pueschel, & Shea, 1972). However, adequate control groups have rarely been available. Most investigators have compared the progress of treated children with the available literature on infants raised at home. Hanson (1977), for example, presented graphs comparing the achievement of milestones by normal children, children with Down syndrome in the University of Oregon program, and reported data on children with Down syndrome raised at home without intervention. Although the nonintervention comparison group was not a control group in the usual sense, the graphs are instructive. They show that not only were the mean attainment levels of children in the early intervention group nearer the means of normal children than those of the comparison group, but the variability of the children in the intervention group (ages between which 50% of the children accomplished the skill) was similar to the variability of normal children.

In contrast, the variability of the nonintervention group was much greater in the case of every milestone passed. For example, there is approximately a 5 month range within which normal children and the Down syndrome intervention group say "dada" and "mama" with almost identical means, whereas the range reported for nonintervention Down syndrome children is 55 months (a mean only about 5 months greater). A more typical example is "walks with support." The mean for normal children is around 10 months, for children with Down syndrome who had early intervention it is around 15 months, and for children with Down syndrome in the nonintervention group it is around 21 months. The variability is 5, 10, and 40 months respectively. What this may suggest is that some children with Down syndrome raised at home will progress as well with intervention as without, but that there are some who will be very delayed without intervention. There has as yet been no effort to identify the factors in the home that have an impact on the development of children with Down syndrome. On the basis of data in other areas, one would have to suspect that socioeconomic factors play a major role.

Although Piper and Pless (1980) had more scientifically respectable experimental and control groups, their data are not a convincing refutation of the data presented by other early intervention programs that have young children with Down syndrome. As noted above, their intervention was truly minimal. The projects showing the most success have involved weekly or daily contact with the children and their families over one or more years of intervention.

**Sensory Impairments**   Data are more scarce and less persuasive when children with other sorts of biological impairments are considered, largely because of the practical problems associated with collecting such data. There have been few published reports on children with sensory impairments. Horton (1976) demonstrated significant differences on measures of language complexity and achievement test scores between children with hearing impairments who entered intervention before and after age 3 years. Early intervention with this group has also been reported to prevent the development of maladaptive behavior that contributes to poor integration into society (Northcott, 1971). In a longitudinal study of children with visual impairments, Adelson and Fraiberg (1975) found that intervention children did better than nonintervention children in neuromuscular maturation and postural achievement, with treated children remaining within the range expected for normal children. These children performed better in self-initiated locomotion and mobility, but did not remain within normal expectations, probably because of the necessity of substituting sound for sight as an incentive for moving.

**Mixed Groups with Disabilities**   With mixed groups of infants with disabilities, data have often been reported in terms of changes in rate of development rather than by comparing experimental and control groups. That is, if a child is assessed at 6 months and is functioning at the 3 month level, the child is assumed to be developing at half the normal rate. If at 9 months the child is functioning like a 6 month old, development is at two-thirds the normal rate. Thus, the rate of development has increased, presumably as a result of intervention. As noted above, this is a problematic approach because of the nature of both the instruments for measuring development and the discontinuity of development itself. Nevertheless, it has been one of the few strategies available to investigators.

In their review, Garland et al. (1981) cited the work of Elder (1976), who reported significant gains in the development of infants with multihandicaps after 2 years of parent/infant education and therapy. The children continued learning at improved rates when retested at ages 3 and 5 years. Similarly, Wider and Hicks (1970) found that infants with neurological impairments from 9 to 44 months made significant gains in the areas of physical, social, and intellectual growth in a United Cerebral Palsy project. These findings are also supported by the data collected by Meisel (1976) as part of the National Collaborative Infant Project. She found that across programs and within handicapping conditions, the earlier a child entered an intervention program, the better the child was functioning at age 3 years, except in the case of severe and profound disabilities where either little progress was made or the instruments used for measurement were insensitive to progress.

Using a meta-analysis to statistically integrate findings from 74 research studies on the efficacy of early intervention with infants and preschoolers with disabilities, Casto and Mastropieri (1986) concluded that early intervention produces a positive effect and that longer, more intense programs are associated with efficacy. From the same data base, Shonkoff and Hauser-Cram (1987) selected 31 studies in which the children were under 36 months and had biological disabilities and in which there were a control or contrast group and no major validity threats to the study. This meta-analysis revealed differential effects for kinds of outcome, for disability group, and for kinds of program, indicating a need for much more careful studies in which the variables of interest are well-defined.

There have been two reports assessing the effectiveness of intervention through modified multiple baseline techniques. Barrerra et al. (1976) and Johnson-Martin, Jens, and Attermeier (1985) used a technique that involved assessing mixed groups of children with disabilities in all areas of development, targeting only a selected number of those areas for intervention for a given period of time, and then reassessing them to compare the progress made in areas targeted and nontargeted for intervention. In the latter study, intervention was continued through a second phase in which the targeted and nontargeted areas were reversed after the second assessment, and progress was again compared at a third assessment point. Both of these studies demonstrated greater progress in the areas targeted for intervention. In the Johnson-Martin et al. (1985) study there were sufficient subjects to also show that the greatest evidence of intervention effectiveness was seen in the children with mild and moderate disabilities.

In evaluating intervention for infants with severe and multiple disabilities, one must particularly question the usefulness of measures based on development in normal infants. These children with multiple disabilities may never move through some normal sequences of development regardless of the intensity of intervention efforts. Yet, early intervention may have important effects. In some cases it may be appropriate to consider not getting worse as an important indicator of effectiveness, although this is rarely discussed. In other cases it may be appropriate to evaluate whether the child is able to live a less restricted life (e.g., at home rather than in an institution), even if the life is not just like that of other people.

Scheifelbusch (1978) and Bricker and Dow (1980), in reporting data on children with severe and profound disabilities, have suggested that early intervention ameliorates the effects of these handicaps. Progress can be assessed in these children on skills that are significant in determining subsequent school or institutional placement. Simeonsson, Cooper, et al. (1982) reported that only 48% of the studies on early intervention since 1975 provide empirical evidence for effectiveness, but propose that this may be an underestimate for several possible reasons: 1) statistical significance could not be obtained because of limited sample sizes, 2) children may have made progress in developmental domains not measured, 3) children may have made progress in management areas not measured, and 4) there may have been significant changes in the family or other dimensions not specific to the child. These investigators argue for a broader utilization of measures of child characteristics and family adjustment.

## OTHER EFFECTS OF EARLY INTERVENTION

There have been attempts to focus attention on measures other than simple indicators of developmental progress, particularly in an effort to weigh the costs of early intervention against the long-range benefits. A survey of 32 Handicapped Children's Early Education Program (HCEEP) projects by the Bureau of Education for the Handicapped found that: 1) the greatest effect of the program had been on personal social behavior and the least on motor behavior, 2) two-thirds of the graduates with disabilities were in regular school classrooms, and 3) those in regular classrooms were judged as more advanced by their teachers than children with similar disabilities not served in early intervention programs (Stock et al., 1976). Similarly, a follow-up of graduates from the University of Washington's Model Preschool Program (with various levels of mental retardation and other disabilities) showed fewer special education placements at school age than similar children who did not have early intervention (Hayden, Morris, & Bailey, 1977). Both of these studies suggest that within the clearly handicapped population, as well as within the at-risk population, IQ is but one factor influencing special class placement; other factors include the expense and stigma associated with such placements.

### Cost-Benefit Analyses

In another examination of HCEEP projects, De Weerd (1981) completed a cost-benefit analysis. She determined that the cost of early education for each child in the projects averaged $5,984, whereas projected benefits were $14,819, based on: 1) evidence that the children went into less restrictive and less expensive programs ($3,353), 2) the potential for greater lifetime earning power for the child because of more normal educational experiences ($10,798), and 3) the increased earning power of the mother as a result of having a child in the program ($668).

A somewhat different analysis was done by Garland et al. (1981) based on 940 children from a variety of early intervention programs. They compared the cost of early intervention with the savings accrued by less restrictive placement during the school years, particularly focusing on the ages at which intervention begins. Their data indicate that there are substantial savings when intervention begins at age 2 and maximum savings when intervention is initiated during the first 2 years of life. "Compared to a beginning intervention at age 6, these preschool programs resulted in a savings from $9,000 to $10,000 per child for the cost of education to age 18" (Garland et al., 1981, p. 15, 19).

Others argue that such cost-benefit studies are seriously flawed. They conclude that despite beliefs to the contrary, there is not yet sound empirical evidence to support the hypothesis that early intervention reduces later education costs or to confirm the notion that "earlier is better" (Barnett & Escobar, 1988). Yet, the belief remains strong and has been translated into public policy. A number of states already have free public education programs for all citizens with disabilities from birth to age 21. Under PL 99-457 (Education of the Handicapped Act Amendments of 1986), 3–5-year-olds with disabilities will be entitled to free public education services in 1991, and incentives will be provided to states to assume responsibility for providing intervention services for infants and toddlers with disabilities. Given the many demands on both state and federal dollars, the need for better empirical research on the costs and benefits of such education is evident.

## Impact on Families

In the studies reported thus far, it is clear that most efforts to justify intervention have been based on what happens to the child, usually only in terms of what happens to the child's specific skills. Very little attention is paid to what might be described as quality of life issues for the child and family. Studies are now beginning to focus on the extent to which early intervention provides parents with coping skills to allow them to keep children at home for longer periods of time, provides a better life for that child, promotes greater feelings of competence for parents, and results in great savings to taxpayers. Cullari and Redmon (1982), in a study in Michigan, surveyed families receiving extensive intervention for their children with disabilities and families that had institutionalized their children with disabilities. Of those receiving intervention, 19% said they planned to keep their children at home and 45% said that the services were instrumental in making that decision. Those who had institutionalized their children cited care problems and family disruption as deciding factors.

It is obvious that a child with disabilities has an impact on the entire family and that the effectiveness of intervention must be viewed within this context. Studies of siblings of children with disabilities suggest that they have more adjustment problems than those of normal children (Adams, 1969; Grossman, 1972; Poznanski, 1969). Parents of children with disabilities are reported to have more restricted social contacts and to suffer more stress (Farber & Ryckman, 1965; Hutt & Gibby, 1976). Until 1984, few data have been reported on the effects of early intervention on these important variables. A few studies are cited in the INTER-ACT report (Garland et al., 1981). For example, Lillie (1975) found that parents in intervention programs reported increased emotional support. Parents in a study by Hess, Block, Costello, Knowles, and Largary (1971) reported increased satisfaction, self-esteem, competence, and a positive effect on their friendships and outside activities.

In order to investigate the nature of stress and social isolation of parents of children with disabilities, Saur (1981) compared the family network, family interaction patterns, and stress in families with young children with disabilities to a matched sample of families with normal children of the same ages. His data do not show significant differences between the groups, contrary to the data and clinical impressions reported for other groups of families of children with disabilities.

Similarly, in a longitudinal study of families of infants between 6 and 27 months of age, Gowen, Johnson-Martin, Goldman, and Appelbaum (1989) found no significant differences between mothers of infants with and without disabilities in the number of depressive symptoms reported, nor in the stability of such symptoms. One explanation for these findings is that, contrary to other studies of parental distress, the children included in these studies were all under 3 years of age. Another important factor, however, is that all of the children with disabilities included in these studies were enrolled in early intervention programs. Professionals, including early intervention specialists, were represented significantly more in the social support networks of families with infants with disabilities than in the families with infants without disabilities. One effect of early intervention programs may be to buffer the family against the stress and isolation that have been reported to characterize families of children with disabilities in other studies.

## CONCLUSION

The early intervention movement, beginning in the late 1950s and early 1960s, has passed through the enthusiasm and rapid growth of infancy, the naive optimism of childhood, and the hardheadedness, self-doubt, and defensiveness of a prolonged adolescence. It is now ready to begin the pursuits of adulthood, having confidence in its purposes and a willingness to engage in constructive self-evaluation. These are some signs of its directions for the next few years:

1.  There appears to be an acknowledgment that educational intervention, regardless of how early it is begun or how carefully it is programmed, cannot "cure" developmental disabilities. There is, however, a concomitant recognition that enhancing the quality of life for the person with developmental disabilities is both a worthy humanitarian goal and a means of saving grief for families and money for society.

2. A growing emphasis on the needs of families has evolved out of the recognition that persons with disabilities both influence and are influenced by their environment. It is noteworthy that this emphasis is not only being initiated by frontline service programs, but has become a major governmental objective. PL 99-457, passed in 1987, established a new state grant program for infants and toddlers, ages birth through 2 years. This law requires that an Individualized Family Service Plan (IFSP) be developed for each family served.

3. Cooperation is beginning to occur between developmentalists, who are involved in basic research, and interventionists, who are paving the way for better methodology in early intervention research and a better understanding of atypical developmental processes. Some investigators who began their careers with the study of cognitive processes in normal childhood are now focusing on assessing these processes in the hard to assess atypical child (Fagan & Singer, 1983; Mundy, Seibert, Hogan, & Fagan, 1983; Zelazo, 1977). Others are considering the effects that specific disorders may have on particular aspects of cognitive development; for example, how movement disorders may be detrimental to the development of spatial concepts (Campos, Svedja, Campos, & Berthenal, 1982).

4. There is a recognition in the intervention community of the need for sound effectiveness studies, studies that carefully examine outcomes other than (or in addition to) simple measures of developmental progress. Better designed and executed studies along with meta-analyses and other statistical procedures for combining data sets will make it possible to extract more meaningful information from early intervention studies, studies that, individually, may be limited by their small sample sizes.

5. New techniques for measuring change through single subject designs are being developed that may eventually provide the best mechanisms for evaluating the effectiveness of early intervention without resorting to experimental control groups.

Thus, it appears that the adulthood of the early intervention movement will be an exciting time, both in terms of an expansion of knowledge and expertise and in terms of providing better services to infants and young children with disabilities and their families.

## REFERENCES

Abidin, R. R. (1983). *Parenting stress index*. Charlottesville, VA: Pediatric Psychology Press.

Adams, M. (1969). Siblings of the retarded: Their problems and treatment. In W. Wolfensberger & R. Kurth (Eds.), *Management of the family of the mentally retarded* (pp. 444–452). Chicago: Follett.

Adelson, E., & Fraiberg, S. (1975). Gross motor development in infants blind from birth. In B. Friedlander, B. G. Steritt, & G. Kirk (Eds.), *Exceptional infant: Assessment and intervention* (Vol. 3, pp. 63–83). New York: Brunner/Mazel.

Barnard, K. (1972). *The effects of stimulation on the duration and the amount of sleep and wakefulness in the premature infant.* Unpublished doctoral dissertation, University of Washington, Seattle.

Barnett, W. S., & Escobar, C. (1988). The economics of early intervention for handicapped children: What do we really know? *Journal of Division of Early Childhood, 12*, 169–181.

Barrerra, M., Routh, D., Johnson, N., Parr, C., Goolsby, E., & Schroeder, S. (1976). Early intervention with biologically handicapped infants and young children: A preliminary study using multiple baseline procedures. In T. Tjossem (Ed.), *Intervention strategies for high risk infants and young children* (pp. 609–627). Baltimore: University Park Press.

Bricker, D., Carlson, L., & Schwarz, R. (1981). A discussion of early intervention for infants with Down syndrome. *Pediatrics, 67*, 45–46.

Bricker, D., & Dow, M. (1980). Early intervention with the young severely handicapped child. *Journal of The Association for Persons with Severe Handicaps, 5* (3), 130–142.

Bricker, W., & Bricker, D. (1976). The infant, toddler and preschool research and intervention project. In T. Tjossem (Ed.), *Intervention strategies for high risk infants and young children* (pp. 545–572). Baltimore: University Park Press.

Browder, J. (1981). The pediatrician's orientation to infant stimulation programs. *Pediatrics, 67*, 42–52.

Campbell, S., & Wilhelm, I. (1982). Developmental sequences in infants at high risk for central nervous system dysfunction: The recovery process in the first year of life. In J. Stack (Ed.), *An interdisciplinary approach to the optimal development of infants: The special child* (pp. 90–153). New York: Human Services Press.

Campos, J., Svedja, M., Campos, R., & Berthenal, B. (1982). The emergence of self-produced locomotion: Its importance for psychological development in infants. In D. Bricker (Ed.), *Intervention with at risk and handicapped infants: From research to application* (pp. 195–216). Baltimore: University Park Press.

Caput, D., Goldstein, K., & Taub, H. (1981). Neonatal compromise and later psychological development: A ten-year longitudinal study. In S. Friedman & M. Sigmon (Eds.), *Preterm birth and psychological development* (pp. 353–386). New York: Academic Press.

Casto, G., & Mastropieri, M. (1986). The efficacy of early intervention programs: A meta-analysis. *Exceptional Children, 52*(5), 417–424.

Clunies-Ross, G. (1979). Accelerating the development of Down's syndrome infants and young children. *Journal of Special Education, 13*(2), 169–177.

Cullari, S., & Redmon, W. (1982, September). *A need assessment of supportive service for parents of developmentally disabled infants.* Paper presented at the meeting of the American Psychological Association, Washington, DC.

Denhoff, E. (1981). Current status of infant stimulation or enrichment programs for children with developmental disabilities. *Pediatrics, 67*, 32–37.

De Weerd, J. (1981). Early education services for children with handicaps: Where have we been, where are we now, and where are we going? *Journal Division of Early Childhood, 2*, 15–24.

Dunst, C. (1985). Rethinking early intervention. *Annals of Intervention Developmental Disability, 5*, 165–201.

Elder, W. (1976). *Final report: EMI project.* Washington, DC: Bureau of Education for the Handicapped.

Fagan, J., & Singer, L. (1983). Infant recognition memory as a measure of intelligence. In L. Lipsitt (Ed.), *Advance in infancy research* (Vol. 2, pp. 31–78). Norwood, NJ: Ablex.

Farber, B., & Ryckman, D. (1965). Effects of severely mentally retarded children on family relationships. *Mental Retardation Abstracts*, 2(1), 7–17.

Freedman, D., & Boverman, H. (1966). The effects of kinesthetic stimulation on certain aspects of development in premature infants. *Journal of Orthopsychiatry*, *36*, 223–224.

French, J. (1964). *Pictorial test of intelligence*. Boston: Houghton Mifflin.

Garland, C., Swanson, J., Stone, N., & Woodruff, G. (Eds.). (1981). *Early intervention for children with special needs and their families: Findings and recommendations* (Paper # 11). Monmouth, OR: Westar Series.

Gowen, J., Johnson-Martin, N., Goldman, B., & Appelbaum, M. (1989). Feelings of depression and feelings of parenting competence in mothers of handicapped and nonhandicapped infants: A longitudinal study. *American Journal on Mental Retardation*, *94*(3), 259–271.

Grossman, F. (1972). *Brothers and sisters of retarded children*. Syracuse: Syracuse University Press.

Grossman, H. (Ed.). (1973). *Manual on terminology and classification in mental retardation* (American Association on Mental Deficiency, Special Publication Series No. 2). Baltimore: Garamond/Pridemark Press.

Hanson, M. (1977). *Teaching your Down's syndrome infants: A guide for parents*. Baltimore: University Park Press.

Haskins, R., Finkelstein, N., & Stedman, D. (1978). Infant stimulation programs and their effects. *Pediatric Annals*, *7*, 123–143.

Hasselmeyer, E. (1966). The premature infant's response to handling. *American Journal of Orthopsychiatry*, *36*, 223–224.

Hayden, A., & Haring, N. (1976). Early intervention for high-risk infants and young children: Programs for Down's syndrome children. In T. Tjossem (Ed.), *Intervention strategies for high-risk infants and young children* (pp. 573–607). Baltimore: University Park Press.

Hayden, A., Morris, K., & Bailey, D. (1977). *Final report: Effectiveness of early education for handicapped children* (pp. 573–607). Washington, DC: Bureau of Education for the Handicapped.

Hess, R., Block, M., Costello, J., Knowles, R., & Largary, D. (1971). Parent involvement in early education. In E. Grothberg (Ed.), *Day care: Resources for decisions* (pp. 265–298). Washington, DC: Office of Economic Opportunity.

Horton, K. (1976). Early intervention for hearing-impaired infants and young children. In T. Tjossem (Ed.), *Intervention strategies for high-risk infants and young children* (pp. 371–380). Baltimore: University Park Press.

Hutt, M., & Gibby, R. (1976). *The mentally retarded child: Development, education and treatment*. Boston: Allyn & Bacon.

Johnson, N. (1982). Assessment paradigms and atypical infants: An interventionist's perspective. In D. Bricker (Ed.), *Intervention with at-risk and handicapped infants: From research to application* (pp. 63–76). Baltimore: University Park Press.

Johnson-Martin, N., Jens, K., & Attermeier, S. (1985). *The Carolina curriculum for handicapped infants and infants at risk*. Baltimore: Paul H. Brookes Publishing Co.

Kagan, J., Kearsley, R., & Zelazo, P. (1978). *Infancy: Its place in human development*. Cambridge: Harvard University Press.

Katz, V. (1971). Auditory stimulation and developmental behavior of the premature infant. *Nursing Research*, *20*, 196–201.

Lazar, I., & Darlington, R. (1982). Lasting effects of early education: A report from the consortium for longitudinal studies. *Monographs of the Society for Research in Child Development*, *47* (2–3, Serial No. 195).

Lillie, D. (1975). The parent in early childhood education. *Journal of Research and Development in Education*, *8*(2), 7–13.

McCall, R. (1979). The development of intellectual functioning in infancy and the prediction of later IQ. In J. Osofsky (Ed.), *Handbook of infant development* (pp. 707–741). New York: John Wiley & Sons.

Meisel, J. (1976). *A nationally organized collaborative project to provide comprehensive services for atypical infants and their families: Evaluation report*. Unpublished manuscript, United Cerebral Palsy Association, Inc., New York.

Miller, L., & Dyer, J. (1975). Four preschool programs: Their dimensions and effects. *Monographs of the Society for Research in Child Development*, *40* (5–6, Serial No. 162).

Mundy, P., Seibert, J., Hogan, A., & Fagan, J. (1983). Novelty responding and behavioral development in young, developmentally delayed children. *Intelligence*, *7*, 163–174.

Neal, M. (1968). Vestibular stimulation and developmental behavior of the small premature infant. *Nursing Research*, *3*, 2–5.

Northcott, W. (1971). The integration of young deaf children into ordinary educational programs. *Exceptional Children*, *38*, 29–32.

Piper, M., & Pless, I. (1980). Early intervention for infants with Down syndrome: A controlled trial. *Pediatrics*, *65*, 463–467.

PL 99-457, *Education of the Handicapped Act Amendments*, 1986.

Powell, L. (1974). The effect of extra stimulation and maternal involvement on the development of low birth weight infants and on maternal behavior. *Child Development*, *45*, 106–113.

Poznanski, E. (1969). Psychiatric difficulties in siblings of handicapped children. *Clinical Pediatrics*, *8*(4), 232–234.

Saur, W. (1981). *Social networks and family environments of mothers of multiply, severely handicapped children*. Unpublished doctoral dissertation, Florida State University, Tallahassee.

Scarr-Salapatek, S., & Williams, M. (1973). The effects of early stimulation on low birth weight infants. *Child Development*, *44*, 94–101.

Scheifelbusch, R. (Ed.). (1978). *Bases of language intervention*. Baltimore: University Park Press.

Shonkoff, J. P., & Hauser-Cram, P. (1987). Early intervention for disabled infants and their families: A quantitative analysis. *Pediatrics*, *80*, 650–658.

Simeonsson, R., Cooper, D., & Scheiner, A. (1982). A review and analysis of the effectiveness of early intervention programs. *Pediatrics*, *69*, 635–641.

Simeonsson, R., Huntington, G., Short, R., & Ware, W. (1982). Carolina record for individual behavior: Characteristics of handicapped infants and children. *Topics in Early Childhood Special Education*, *2*(2), 43–55.

Solkoff, N., Yaffe, S., Weintraub, D., & Blase, R. (1969). Effects on handling on the subsequent development of premature infants. *Developmental Psychology*, *1*, 765–768.

Stock, J., Newborg, J., Whek, L., Schenck, E., Gabel, J., Spurgeon, M., & Ray, H. (1976). *Evaluation of handicapped children's early education program (HCEEP): Final report*. Columbus, OH: Battelle Center for Improved Education.

Thomas, H. (1970). Psychological assessment instruments for use with human infants. *Merrill-Palmer Quarterly of Behavioral Development*, *16*, 179–223.

Tjossem, T., & Stephens, B. (1976). Preface. In T. Tjossem (Ed.), *Intervention strategies for high-risk infants and young children* (pp. xxiii–xxx). Baltimore: University Park Press.

Wider, D., & Hicks, J. (1970). *Evaluation of an early intervention program for neurologically impaired children and their families.* Unpublished manuscript, United Cerbral Palsy (UCP) of Queens, New York.

Zausmer, E., Pueschel, S., & Shea, A. (1972). A sensory-motor stimulation for the young child with Down's syndrome: Preliminary report. *MCH Exchange, 2,* 1–4.

Zelazo, P. (1977). Reactivity to perceptual-cognitive events: Application for infant assessment. In R. Kearsley and I. Siegel (Eds.), *Infants at risk: The assessment of cognitive functioning* (pp. 49–83). Hillsdale, NJ: Lawrence Erlbaum Associates.

# 17 | Brian L. G. Morgan

# NUTRITION AND BRAIN DEVELOPMENT

Growth of the brain follows a sigmoidal pattern (Davison & Dobbing, 1966). The transient period of rapid development represented by such curves is known as the brain growth spurt. It is at this period that the brain is most vulnerable to factors that adversely affect growth. In addition to this critical anatomical period of growth, the brain also has critical periods in the development of physiological, biochemical, and psychological functions when these are maturing at their most rapid rate. Within each aspect of growth, there are additional critical periods. For instance, within the anatomical growth period, the timing of most rapid cellular division is not the same as that for the most rapid rate of myelination or that when dendritic arborization is maximal. In addition, different regions of the brain may be characterized by a different critical period for a similar function. For example, the maturation of a particular enzyme may occur earlier in the cerebrum than in the cerebellum. All of these critical phases of growth occur during intrauterine life or in the early postnatal period. Once the chronological time has passed for a particular aspect of growth, nothing can be done to restart it.

## CELLULAR GROWTH

Brain growth occurs by increasing cell numbers (hyperplasia) and by increasing cell size (hypertrophy). The diploid nuclei of any one species contain a constant amount of DNA that is different from that for any other species (Bolvin, Vendrely, & Vendrely, 1948; Enesco & Leblond, 1962). In the human this is 6.0 picograms (pg). With the exception of a few tetraploid

Purkinje cells in the cortices of the cerebrum and cerebellum, all cells in the human brain are diploid (Lapham, 1968). Thus, by dividing total brain DNA content by the amount per cell, the number of cells can be calculated. Estimations of cell numbers in different brain regions may be similarly calculated. The small number of tetraploid cells present in the human brain is unlikely to affect these calculations significantly. Brain RNA content increases in proportion to the increase in DNA throughout the growing period (Winick & Noble, 1965).

Although total DNA content gives an accurate assessment of cell numbers, it does not differentiate among different cell types. The nervous system has many different cell types that can be broadly categorized into glial cells and neurons. The cells within each of these categories have different dimensions and probably have different protein and RNA contents (Winick, 1976).

In humans, brain wet weight increases until about 6 years of age (Dobbing & Sands, 1973). Before birth, there is a decline in the rate of cell division but division continues to occur until at least 6 years of age and possibly longer. Two peaks of DNA synthesis can be distinguished during the development of the human brain (Figure 17.1). The first occurs at about 18 weeks of gestation, which corresponds to the maximal rate of neuronal synthesis, and the second peak occurs around birth, which represents the time of most rapid glial cell division (Dobbing & Sands, 1973).

The forebrain and brainstem DNA levels reach 70% of mature levels by 2 years of life and gradually increase from that point to reach a maximum at 6

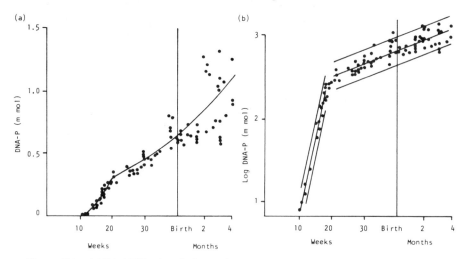

**Figure 17.1.** (a) Total DNA phosphate, equivalent to total cell number, in the forebrain of human fetuses and infants; (b) a semilogarithmic plot of the same data as shown in (a). In (b) regression lines with 95% confidence limits are shown. (From Dobbing, J., & Sands, J. [1973]. The quantitative growth and development of the human brain. *Archives of Disease in Childhood, 48*, 757–767; reprinted by permission.)

years of age. In the cerebellum, DNA content proceeds more rapidly to reach adult levels by 2 years of age. Cellularity is heavily weighted in favor of the cerebellum that represents only 10% of the total brain weight but contains 30% of total brain DNA. Extensive microneuron proliferation occurs postnatally in the cerebellum (Raaf & Kernohan, 1944) and possibly in other areas until about 20 months of age (Figure 17.2).

Winick (1976) has proposed a theory (Figure 17.3) to account for growth in the body. He maintains that any organ growth can be divided into three phases. In the first phase, there is a rapid division of cells with cell size remaining constant. In the second phase, DNA synthesis continues at a slower rate and protein synthesis continues at the same rate resulting in an increase in cell size and a smaller increase in cell numbers. In the third phase, there is an increase in cell size as DNA synthesis stops and protein continues to be produced. Growth finally stops when protein synthesis equals protein degradation, which is at maturity. Winick emphasizes that there is a gradual change from one phase to another in this scheme and a good deal of overlap exists.

Sands, Dobbing, and Gratrix (1979) criticized this theory based on their data from rats that showed that mean cell size increases at an earlier stage than proposed by Winick and quickly reaches a constant level. In addition, their

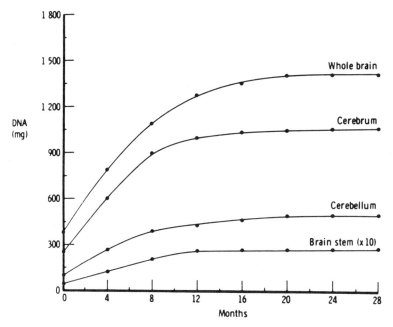

**Figure 17.2.** Total DNA content in the different regions of the human brain during development. (From Winick, M. [1976]. *Malnutrition and brain development* [p. 53]. New York: Oxford University Press; reprinted by permission.)

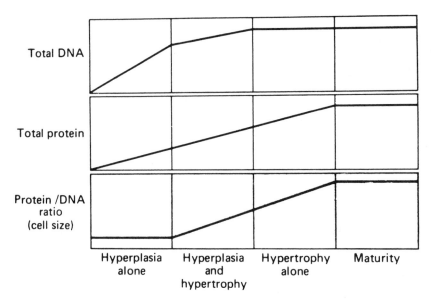

**Figure 17.3.** Changes in brain DNA, protein, and protein/DNA ratios during the periods of cellular growth. (From Winick, M. [1976]. *Malnutrition and brain development* [p. 54]. New York: Oxford University Press; reprinted by permission.)

results indicate that cell multiplication continues unabated throughout tissue growth until growth comes to an end. These studies were carried out using kidney, liver, and heart tissue and results have not as yet been reported for the brain. The control of both the rate of DNA synthesis and its period of synthesis are largely unknown.

## Brain Lipids

The brain lipid content increases gradually during development. The major increase in lipid concentration occurs in myelin, which accounts for most of the brain lipid (Davison & Dobbing, 1966). The rate of myelin synthesis in the postnatal period is greater than that of DNA synthesis, which accounts for increased cholesterol/DNA and phospholipid/DNA ratios (Rosso, Hormazabal, & Winick, 1970).

In the central nervous system, myelin is formed from the membranes of oligodendroglial cells, and myelination begins after these cells have completed division (Altman, 1969). These glial cells then surround the nerve axons in a spiral fashion, and a progressive deposition of lipids occurs within the developing myelin sheath (Bunge, 1968), resulting in the transformation of oligodendroglial cell membranes into the specialized adult myelin with its lamellar structure.

Various markers have been used to plot the development of myelin. Several substances found in high concentration in myelin have been used, including cholesterol and cerebroside sulphatide. Cholesterol is found in high concentrations in other cell membranes (Kritchevsky & Holmes, 1962), whereas cerebroside sulphatide is only present in myelin. Using cerebroside sulphatide as a marker, myelin has been shown to increase by 300% to 400% between 34 weeks of gestation and birth. The most rapid rate of increase occurs between 12 and 24 weeks of postnatal life, by which time the brain contains 50% of its adult level of myelin. By 4 years of age, a full complement of myelin has developed. An impediment to the oligodendroglial cell proliferation or to the accumulation of myelin at this early stage of development will lead to a permanent deficit in brain myelin content (Chase, Dorsey, & McKhann, 1967; Dobbing, 1964; Ghittoni & Raveglia, 1973).

The principal glycolipids in the brain are the cerebrosides in myelin and gangliosides. A number of different species of gangliosides have been isolated from the brain. The four species depicted in Table 17.1 constitute 95% of the gangliosides of the normal human brain. In the mammalian, brain

**Table 17.1.** Major gangliosides of normal human brain

| Name | Symbol | Proposed structure |
|---|---|---|
| Monosialoganglioside | $G_{M1}$ | Gal(1 → 3)GalNAc(1 → 4)Gal(1 → 4)Glu(1 ↑ 1)Cer<br>3<br>↑<br>2<br>NeuNAC |
| Disialoganglioside | $G_{D1a}$ | Gal(1 → 3)GalNAc(1 → 4)Gal(1 → 4)Glu(1 ↑ 1)Cer<br>3       3<br>↑       ↑<br>2       2<br>NeuNAC   NeuNAC |
| Disialoganglioside | $G_{D1b}$ | Gal(1 → 3)GalNAc(1 → 4)Gal(1 → 4)Glu(1 ↑ 1)Cer<br>3<br>↑<br>2<br>NeuNAC(8 ← 2)NeuNAC |
| Trisialoganglioside | $G_{T1}$ | Gal(1 → 3)GalNAc(1 → 4)Gal(1 → 4)Glu(1 ↑ 1)Cer<br>3       3<br>↑       ↑<br>2       2<br>NeuNAC   NeuNAC(8 ← 2)NeuNAC |

From Dickerson, J. W. T., & McGurk, H. (1982). *Brain and behavioral development* (p. 58). Surrey, England: Surrey Univeristy Press; reprinted by permission.

*Key:*
Gal = galactose
GalNAc = *N*-acetylgalactosamine
Glu = glucose
Cer = ceramide
NeuNAC = *N*-acetylneuraminic acid

gangliosides contain 65% and glycoproteins 32% of the total $N$-acetyl-neuraminic acid (NeuNAC), and the remainder is found in the free form (Brunngraber, Whitting, Haberland, & Brown, 1972). The brain has the highest concentration of gangliosides of any tissue in the body and represents 5%–10% of the total lipid content of some nerve tissue cell membranes (Ledeen, 1978).

Small quantities of gangliosides are found in all cellular and subcellular brain fractions, but the major portion is found in the neurons (Ledeen, 1978; Suzuki, 1967). Similarly, the bulk of the glycoproteins are bound to neurons (Dekirmenjian, Brunngraber, Lemkey-Johnston, & Larremendi, 1969).

By far, the largest fraction of the gangliosides present in the brain's complement of 10 neurons is located in the dendritic and axonal plexuses (Hamberger & Svennerholm, 1971; Hess, Bass, Thalheimer, & Devarakon-da, 1976; Norton & Poduslo, 1971); specifically, the synaptic plasma membranes are their major loci (Dekirmenjian et al., 1969; Lapetina, Soto, & DeRobertis, 1968; Morgan & Winick, 1981). The microsomal disialoganglio-side $G_{DIa}$ has been put forward as a marker for dendritic arborization (Dickerson, Merat, & Yusuf, 1982).

It has been widely suggested that gangliosides play an important role in behavior (Dunn & Hogan, 1975; Irwin & Samson, 1971; Morgan & Winick, 1980b). Theoretical models have been proposed in which sialocompounds are viewed as important constituents in the functional units of neuronal membranes in that they exert an ion binding and releasing function (Morgan & Sinai, 1983; Schengrund & Nelson, 1975).

Synaptogenesis includes the growth of the presynaptic axon, contact with and "recognition" of the appropriate postsynaptic neuron, replacement of growth cone organelles, and assembly at the active zone of presynaptic and postsynaptic dense material, complete with ion channels and transmitter receptor molecules. In the recognition process, there is some evidence to implicate surface glycoproteins that are incorporated into the synaptic membrane (Rees, 1978).

## BRAIN METABOLISM

Energy metabolism of the brain varies considerably from birth to old age, as does blood flow. Cerebral oxygen consumption is low at birth, rises rapidly with cerebral growth, and reaches its maximum level when maturation is completed (Himwich & Fazekas, 1941; Kennedy, Grave, Jehle, & Sokoloff, 1972). Several enzymes of oxidative metabolism in the brain show a similar rise in level of activity (Sokoloff, 1974).

Blood flow reaches its peak at different times in different regions of the brain in accordance with the speed of maturation of each region (Sokoloff, 1974). Those regions with large amounts of white matter have their highest blood flow when myelination is at its peak. Thereafter, blood flow gradually declines to its mature value with changes in blood flow possibly matching the changes in metabolic rate.

At 6 years of age, a child has its maximum cerebral blood flow and an accompanying oxygen consumption of 5.2 ml $O_2$/100 g/min or 60 ml/min per whole brain, which amounts to half the total body basal oxygen consumption. This is much higher than in the adult and may account for extra energy needed for brain growth and development (Kennedy & Sokoloff, 1957; Sokoloff, 1966).

As well as cerebral energy metabolism changing with age, the brain's metabolic fuels also change. Just after birth a baby is hypoglycemic and its blood ketone levels are low (Krebs, Williamson, Bates, Page, & Hawkins, 1971). Milk is high in fat, and so an infant is in a ketogenic state. Ketones form an important cerebral fuel for energy metabolism at this time (Persson, Settergren, & Dahlquist, 1972). The enzymes involved in ketone utilization are most active during the early postnatal period and least active in adult life. Hence, the developing brain has a much greater ability to extract and utilize ketones from the blood. After weaning, when ketosis subsides, these enzymes become less active and glucose becomes the major substrate for cerebral energy metabolism (see Figure 17.4) (Carney-Crane & Morgan, 1983; Krebs et al., 1971). Inadequate fat intake during the sucking period is a suspected cause of impaired cholesterol synthesis and hence diminished myelination (Carney-Crane & Morgan, 1983).

The newborn human brain will withstand hypoxia for a longer period of time than the adult brain (Winick, 1976), which is indicative of the predominance of glycolysis during the early stages of brain development. After birth, respiration becomes increasingly more important until it assumes the dominant role in glucose metabolism. This change is gradual and proceeds in a caudocephalic direction from the spinal cord to the cerebral cortex (Porcellati, 1972). Glycogen has a fairly high rate of turnover and is an important part of both neurons and glial cells (Porcellati, 1972), but exactly what role it fulfills in development has yet to be defined.

The unique position of glucose in brain metabolism in the adult is partly due to the blood-brain barrier that impedes entry into the brain of most substrates. Little is known of the development of the blood-brain barrier. It is not known if the barrier develops at the same time for all substrates or whether it develops permeability at different times for different substrates.

There is a high influx of amino acids into the neonatal brain (Seta, Sershen, & Laijtha, 1972), believed to be due to the absence of a blood-brain barrier (Sessa & Perez, 1975). During development, the brain levels of glutamine and the acidic amino acids gradually increase and the levels of the basic and neutral amino acids decrease (Agrawal, Davis, & Himwich, 1966; Machiyama, Balazs, & Julian, 1965). This differential effect on transporta-

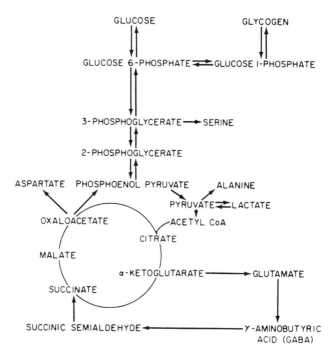

**Figure 17.4.** Some important pathways of glucose metabolism in the mammalian brain. (From Dickerson, J. W. T., & McGurk, H. [1982]. *Brain and behavioural development* [p. 63]. Surrey, England: Surrey University Press; reprinted by permission.)

tion of amino acids with maturation is probably due to the development of amino acid transport systems within the blood-brain barrier, each of which transports a specific group of amino acids to cater to the brain's needs for that group independent of the other systems. This change in amino acid transport capacity is one mechanism by which amino acid supply of the maturing brain may be lowered. The similarity in timing of protein synthesis and amino acid transport suggests an important role of amino acid supply in controlling protein synthesis in the neonatal brain (Winick, 1976).

The accumulation of protein in the human brain is probably linear from the 6th month of gestation until the 2nd postnatal year and subsequently decreases. Proteins are closely involved in metabolism as enzymes, in transport, and as structural components. In association with lipids, proteins regulate the properties of membranes and the interchange of ions and molecules both within cells and between cellular and extracellular fluid. Many proteins are formed continually throughout life and rapid alterations occur within a single day. Winick (1976) has estimated that the half life of human brain proteins is 14 days, which gives a daily synthesis of 4 g of protein per day.

One theory of memory involves changes in protein synthesis (Hyden & Egyhazi, 1964). Because of the complexity of brain proteins, it is not possible to envisage a "critical" or "vulnerable" period in brain protein development.

## EFFECTS OF MALNUTRITION ON BRAIN GROWTH AND DEVELOPMENT

It was once thought that the brain was "spared" the consequences of malnutrition. However, although its growth is affected less than body weight by nutritional deprivation, even moderate malnutrition at the period of maximum cell division will lead to growth retardation of the brain (Cravioto & Delicardie, 1979).

More than 30 nutritional factors are needed for the normal growth of brain cells (Balazs, Lewis, & Patel, 1979). Reduced levels of a single nutrient can delay mitosis for many days. For instance, during the early proliferative stages of brain growth, a drop in the level of a single amino acid in the intracellular pool below a critical level (usually 10 to 40 picomoles) will result in the cessation of protein synthesis and arrested cell growth. If the missing substance is provided at a later date, although cell proliferation may be reinstituted, interference with normal brain growth may be irreversible.

Brain growth is time dependent, and any nutritional insult throughout the period of growth will lead to a permanent deficit in brain size. Nutritional rehabilitation after that time will not lead to catch-up growth. If undernutrition is of a shorter duration, and the infant is rehabilitated before the end of the growth period, those phases of growth that were ongoing at the time of the insult will be the affected ones. If, for instance, the brain is undersupplied with nutrients from the third to the fifth fetal month, neuronal division will be reduced. Conversely, undernutrition during the period of the fifth fetal to the third postnatal month will mainly affect the glial cells (Dobbing, 1974).

Because of the complex programming of brain growth and development, interference with one part of the growth may interfere with all subsequent steps that are dependent on the first one. For example, malnutrition in the first 8 to 9 months of postnatal life inhibits lipid synthesis and the growth of oligondendroglia, which in turn result in retarded myelination (Winick, 1976).

### Brain Size

Mean body weight and mean brain weight are significantly lower in malnourished than in well-fed children (Brown, 1966). However, brain-to-body weight ratios of malnourished children are often higher than for well-fed infants. This can partly be explained by a sparing effect, but is also partly due to edema (Engsner, 1974).

Malnutrition occurring in utero may also result in small-for-date babies with small head circumference and reduced brain weight (Gruenwald, 1963), although these brain variables are usually normal for body weight (McLean & Usher, 1970). Children with head circumferences less than the 10th percentile at birth have poor growth, later microcephaly, and neurologic deficits.

Pediatricians routinely measure the head circumference of young children and use such values as an indicator of brain growth. Winick and Rosso (1969) have been able to correlate head circumference values with brain cell numbers. Undernourished children often have a reduced head circumference (Stoch & Smythe, 1963; Winick & Rosso, 1969). However, they do not always show intellectual impairment (Winick, 1976). The reason often given is that environmental stimulation can overcome the learning deficits resulting from a small brain size (Morgan & Winick, 1980b; Winick, Meyer, & Harris, 1975). In environmental stimulation studies with animals, the only significant change in brain chemistry occurring is an elevated NeuNAC content (Morgan & Winick, 1980a). Thus, Morgan, Boris, and Winick (1982) hypothesized that brain NeuNAC levels are a better measure of brain function than is brain size. They have further shown that serum NeuNAC levels correlate with brain NeuNAC levels and proposed that serum NeuNAC levels be used as an in vivo measure of functional brain development.

## Brain Composition and Cellular Growth

**Effects of Intrauterine Undernutrition**    Intrauterine undernutrition most often results from placental insufficiency and the resulting decrease in flow of nutrients to the fetus. It can also arise from maternal undernutrition. The most common nutritional problem encountered by the human fetus is inadequate intake of energy and protein. The condition is quite common and can arise from depleted maternal nutrient stores as a result of poor dietary intake before and during pregnancy, serious illness, or frequent pregnancies. The maternal manifestation of the syndrome is inadequate weight gain, which is exacerbated if the mother is underweight before pregnancy (Rosso, 1981).

In the human brain, the number of neurons is only reduced when undernutrition is imposed early in gestation, as rapid neuronal division is completed by about 26 weeks of gestation. If it is imposed late in gestation, only glial cell numbers are affected. A reduction in glial cells does not affect intelligence as much as loss of neurons (Chase, 1976; Fancourt, Campbell, Harvey, & Norman, 1976; Low et al., 1978). Impaired proliferation of glial cells is associated only with a decrease in the amount of myelin in the brain. A loss of cells from the cerebrum is more detrimental to intelligence than a loss of cells from the cerebellum. Dow (1970) showed that the loss of cells from the cerebellum results in impaired movement but not in impairment to intellect, perception, or sensory functions.

**Effects of Postnatal Malnutrition**   We have little data on the effects of protein energy malnutrition (PEM) on the cellularity of the human brain. The brains of children severely malnourished in early life are small for their age, although their head size is often larger than normal for their body weight (Figure 17.5). Brain cell numbers (as measured by DNA content) are much reduced in malnourished children (Figure 17.6) but DNA concentrations are often normal (Figure 17.7).

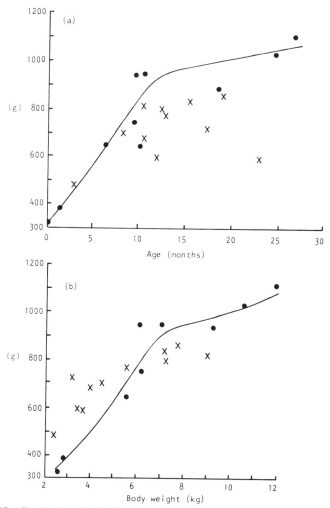

**Figure 17.5.**   The brain weights of malnourished (x) and control (●) Jamaican children plotted (a) against age and (b) against body weight. (From Merat, A. [1971]. *Effects of protein-calorie malnutrition on brain gangliosides.* Doctoral dissertation, University of Surrey, Surrey, England; reprinted by permission.)

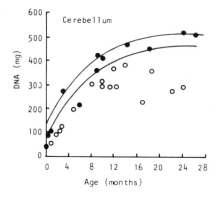

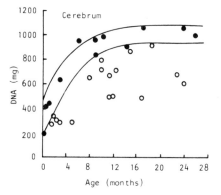

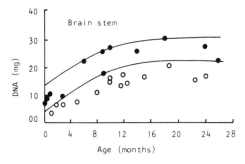

**Figure 17.6.** The effect of protein-energy malnourishment on the DNA content of the human cerebellum, cerebrum and brain stem. Values for malnourished children shown (O) and those for normal children shown (●). (From Winick, M., Rosso, P., & Waterlow, J. [1970]. Cellular growth on cerebrum, cerebellum and brain stem in normal and marasmic children. *Experimental Neurology, 26,* 393–400; reprinted by permission.)

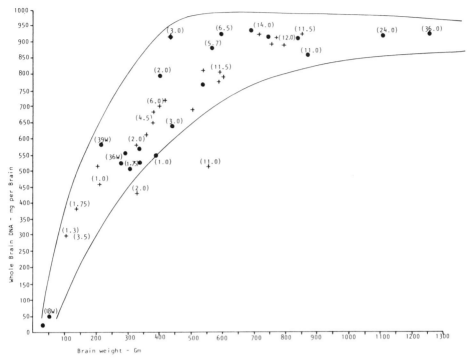

**Figure 17.7.** The DNA content of the human brain plotted against the brain weight. Values of malnourished children shown (+) and those for controls shown (●). Age of fetuses is in weeks (w), all others in months. (From Dickerson, J. W. T. [1981]. Nutrition, brain growth and environment. In K. J. Connolly & H. F. R. Prechtl [Eds.], *Maturation and development* [pp. 110–130]. London: Spastics International Medical Publishers, Heinemann; reprinted by permission.)

There are two broad clinical classifications of severe malnutrition in young children: marasmus and kwashiorkor. Often they overlap in the same child and occur as a mixed syndrome. Marasmus occurs during the first year of life and is seen in the infant who is starved, often as a result of early weaning or not being properly fed. It also occurs as a result of prolonged diarrhea. This condition is more threatening to brain development than kwashiorkor because it occurs at an earlier critical age (Winick, Rosso, & Waterlow, 1970). Kwashiorkor occurs in children of 2–3 years of age, who have been weaned onto low protein diets providing an abundance of calories as starch (Chase, 1976; Chase, Canosa, Dabiere, Welch, & O'Brien, 1974).

## Myelin Lipids and Myelination

**Effects of Intrauterine Undernutrition** Small-for-gestational-age (SGA) babies have reduced brain levels of the myelin lipids cerebroside sulphatide (Chase, Welch, Dabiere, Vasan, & Butterfield, 1972) and galactose cerebroside (Sarma & Rao, 1974). They also have low activities of the rate limiting enzyme of sulphatide synthesis, namely galactolipid sulphotransferase (Chase et al., 1972).

**Effects of Postnatal Undernutrition** Whether cerebroside sulphatide (Chase et al., 1974) or cholesterol (Rosso et al., 1970) is used as a marker, there is a good deal of evidence to show that chronically malnourished children have low brain myelin levels for their chronologic age. However, cholesterol concentration in the forebrain, and presumably in other brain areas too, remains the same (Dickerson, 1975).

## Malnutrition and Synaptic Development

During the hyperplastic phase of neuronal development from 12 to 26 weeks of pregnancy, neurons are created at the rate of 250,000 per minute (Dobbing, 1974). Most neurons in the brain are formed during the second trimester (Cowan, 1979). At birth, the infant brain contains about 100 billion neurons, which is the full complement of neurons found in the adult brain (Hubel, 1979). Of the 100 billion neurons, no two are identical. In the entire central nervous system, only 2 or 3 million neurons are motor neurons (Nauta & Feirtag, 1979). Most of the 100 billion neurons are neither motor nor sensory in function, instead forming a vast network to store (memory) and transmit messages (Morgane et al., 1978).

Each neuron is composed of a round body surrounded by a network of fine tube like extensions, the dendrites, that provide the main physical surface on which the neuron receives incoming messages. The axon is a fine extension of the cell body, thinner and longer than the dendrites. Coordinated brain activity is produced by the passage of electrical impulses from the cell body to other parts of the brain via the axon. At the axon terminal, a synaptic gap separates the axon from the cell membrane of the adjoining neuron. A typical neuron may have anywhere from 1,000 to 10,000 synapses and may receive information from about 1,000 other neurons. Synapses are usually between the axon of one cell and the dendrite of another, but can also be axon to axon and axon to cell body (Stevens, 1979).

When a nerve impulse reaches the terminal of the axon, it causes calcium ions to release either an excitatory or inhibitory transmitter. The transmitter crosses the synaptic gap and binds to the receptor sites on the adjacent neuron's cell membrane. In this way either an excitatory or inhibitory message is passed on to the neuron. The major portion of the neurotransmitter bound to the cell members dissociates, and then is taken up again by the axon of origin. Some portion is broken down by enzymes outside the axon terminal in the synaptic cleft. One such enzyme is acetylcholinesterase, which can cleave 25,000 molecules of acetylcholine per second (Ulus, 1977).

Each neuron synthesizes a characteristic transmitter from precursor molecules inside its own axon. This is stored in vesicles within the synaptosome. There may be thousands of synaptic vesicles in a single terminal, each of which contains between 10,000 and 100,000 molecules of the transmitter (Iversen, 1979). About 20 substances have been identified as transmitters, including serotonin, acetylcholine, catecholamines, histamine, gamma-aminobutyric acid, glycine, glutamate, and aspartate. Certain parts of the brain may release serotonin, affecting particular kinds of nerve cells, whereas in other areas it may be norepinephrine. It is not clear whether each nerve cell releases only one sort of neurotransmitter or whether some cells release a mixture.

Obviously, for proper brain function, the structural framework of the brain neurons, dendrites, and axons must be intact as well as the enzyme systems involved in the synthesis and degradation of chemical transmitters. All that is known with confidence is that dendritic arborization is predominantly postnatal (Dobbing, 1981).

Gangliosides seem to be a good marker for dendritic arborization, as they are located in high concentration in gray matter. Children dying from malnutrition in Jamaica were shown to have a deficit in total ganglioside Neu-NAC in the forebrain (Figure 17.8). This deficit was found to be entirely in the disialoganglioside fraction or $G_{DIa}$ fraction (Dickerson, 1980; Merat, 1971). $G_{DIa}$ is found mainly in dendrites in animals (Dickerson et al., 1982), and so this may indicate a retarded dendritic development. $G_{DIa}$ levels in the brains of the Jamaican children were too low for the weight of the forebrains but DNA and cholesterol levels were correct for forebrain weight. Hence, it would seem that dendritic development, and hence transmission of information throughout the brain, was most affected.

As mentioned earlier, gangliosides may be the link between biochemistry and behavior in the brain of nutritionally deprived children and animals in ways other than simply as structural components of membranes (Dunn & Hogan, 1975; Irwin & Samson, 1971; Schengrund & Nelson, 1975). Additional evidence to support this view has come from experiments in which undernourished rat pups were subjected to early environmental stimulation (Morgan & Winick, 1980b). Stimulation of pups during the first 21 days of life reduced the change in open field behavior caused by undernutrition. This change was associated with a significantly higher ganglioside and glycoprotein NeuNAC content in the brain. This was a permanent effect because at age 6 months, after the rats had been nutritionally rehabilitated, the effects of early stimulation were shown in an improved ability to learn a Y maze. In another experiment (Morgan & Winick, 1980b), NeuNAC given intraperitoneally was shown to cause a rise in brain ganglioside and glycoprotein

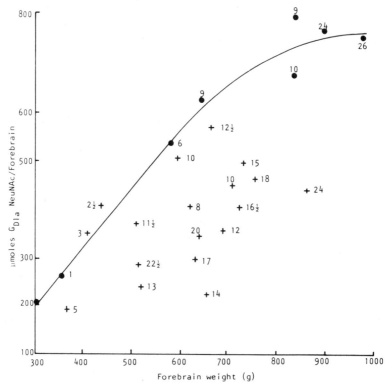

**Figure 17.8.** The effect of protein-energy malnutrition on the amount of the disialo-ganglioside in the human forebrain. Values for malnourished children shown (+) and those for controls shown (●). Age of children given in months. (From Dickerson, J. W. T. [1980]. Protein deficiency and the brain. In G. G. Birch & K. J. Parker [Eds.], *Food and health: Science and technology*. London: Elsevier Applied Science Publishers; reprinted by permission.)

NeuNAC. Treatment from 14 to 21 days after birth of rat pups undernourished for the first 21 days of life brought about these changes without altering brain weight, cell size, and cell number. Changes in behavior identical to those resulting from early stimulation were seen.

As both environmental stimulation and administration of NeuNAC caused the same changes in brain NeuNAC and behavior, it is suggested that brain NeuNAC is a determining factor in the expression of behavior. Morgan and Sinai (1983) have further shown that this might be explained by a role of NeuNAC in neurotransmission. Ganglioside NeuNAC is involved in the uptake of neurotransmitter molecules at the synaptic membrane. Under-nourished animals have a lower level of ganglioside in their synaptic membranes that leads to an inefficient uptake process and, hence, to inefficient use of neurotransmitter substances. Morgan and Naismith (1982) have shown that undernutrition delays the development of enzymes involved in glyco compound synthesis. In addition, nutritionally deprived animals have lower brain contents of such enzymes.

## Malnutrition and Energy Metabolism

Fetal malnutrition resulting in intrauterine growth retardation often involves vascular insufficiency that leads to anoxia. Anoxia, even for short periods, can reduce the rate of cell division in the brain (Winick, 1976). Furthermore, anoxia at birth in a full-term baby occurs at a period when brain growth and cell division are taking place at a rapid rate.

## Fatty Acids and Brain Development

The brain contains very little triglyceride. Its high fatty acid content is due to the presence of phospholipids, glycolipids, and sphingolipids in the brain cell membranes. Fatty acids are categorized as saturated or unsaturated with the latter containing one or more double bonds. The unsaturated fatty acids in the brain are derived from linoleic acid, which is the only fatty acid present in cerebral tissue that cannot be made by the human body (Collins et al., 1971; Holmann, 1973). This biosynthetic process is one of chain elongation and desaturation into the long chain polyunsaturated fatty acids necessary for normal brain development.

The spectrum of polyunsaturated fatty acids in the human brain changes with age. As the gray matter increases, so does the long chain polyunsaturated fatty acid content. This primarily occurs in utero. Long chain polyunsaturated fatty acids are not readily made from linoleic acid during this period of rapid development (Cowey, Owen, Adron, & Middleton, 1976). Because they are not present in vegetable foods, it has been hypothesized that animal fat is necessary in the diet for normal development of the human brain (Crawford, Sinclair, Msuya, & Munhambo, 1973). This has definitely been shown to be the case in rats (Carney-Crane & Morgan, 1983).

## Malnutrition and Brain Protein

There are few data available that concern the impact of undernutrition on human brain protein. Phenylketonuria does represent one inborn error of metabolism that provides some relevant information. In this disorder, there is a deficiency of the enzyme phenylalanine hydroxylase leading to an impairment of phenylalanine metabolism. If this disorder is not diagnosed early in life and the child is not given a low phenylalanine diet, the growth and development of the brain is impaired due to the accumulation in the blood and brain of high levels of phenylalanine. This is a good example of how an excess of one amino acid can decrease the levels of other amino acids and limit protein synthesis in the brain.

## Amino Acids and Neurotransmitters

The intracellular free amino acids in the brain provide the substrate for protein synthesis and neurotransmitter synthesis. Such amino acids are either obtained from the plasma or produced locally from precursors. In the adult human brain four amino acids are present at concentrations in excess of 1 mM/g. These are taurine (1.25 mM/g), glutamic acid (7.19 mM/g), aspartic acid (1.10 mM/g), and glutamine (5.55 mM/g) (Hansen, Perry, Wada, & Sokol, 1973). A reduction in the supply of protein would be expected to limit both neurotransmitter synthesis and protein synthesis. Such measurements are difficult to make in children. A number of experiments on the effects of malnutrition on brain amino acids have been done on other species, including monkeys (Enwonwu & Worthington, 1973, 1974). The results of these studies show that in young animals the plasma levels of certain amino acids (especially the branched chain amino acids and tryptophan) are reduced by protein energy malnutrition, and particularly in kwashiorkor. These changes are reflected in the amino acid pools in the brain. In older animals subjected to protein energy malnutrition, the changes in the plasma and brain amino acids are less severe (Nowak & Munro, 1977).

## Iron Deficiency

Brain iron is present as part of prosthetic groups (heme or flavin) for a number of enzymes as well as in a storage form that is bound to a protein similar to ferritin. With increasing age, all areas of the brain except the medulla show an increase in nonheme iron (Leibel, Greenfield, & Pollitt, 1979). There is a great deal of variation from one part of the brain to another, but, in general, levels of nonheme iron are at about 10% of adult values at birth, 50% by 10 years of age, and at a maximal level at 20 to 50 years (4–5 mg per 100 g wet weight of tissue). Iron containing brain cytochromes rise rapidly to maximal levels at the same rate as the accretion of myelin (Dallman, 1974).

Iron plays an important role in many metabolic processes, including its role as a cofactor for a number of enzymes critical to oxidative and neurotransmitter metabolisms. Studies have shown that changes in activity of these enzymes occur relatively early in the course of iron deficiency (Dallman, Refino, & Yland, 1982). Such changes may account for the behavioral changes that have been associated with even mild iron deficiency (Pollitt & Leibel, 1982). In children, mild iron deficiency affects attentional processes. Such children are less attentive to those environmental clues that aid problem solving. In iron deficient infants, remedial deficits in attention related behaviors have been described (Oski & Honig, 1977). These iron-related changes in cognitive function are quite small and may not carry clinical relevance (Pollitt & Leibel, 1982).

## Brain Function: Behavior and Intelligence

A review of the literature on human subjects shows that malnutrition in early life alters the chemical composition of the brain. There are several reports of catch-up growth in children. Engsner (1974) has reported that some catch-up of head circumference occurs in children with kwashiorkor during rehabilitation. Although catch-up growth occurs also in children with marasmus, it is less complete.

Evidence shows that intrauterine undernutrition may not necessarily permanently hinder catch-up (Davies, 1980). However, in all of these studies catch up growth is measured in terms of increase in head circumference, which tells nothing of what is going on at the cellular level. The question that must be answered is whether or not undernutrition in early life has long-term effects on intellectual performance. This question has yet to be resolved as there are some studies in the literature that attest to a long-term effect and others that do not. This apparent contradiction may be explained by other environmental factors that go along with poverty (Cravioto & Delicardie, 1979; Pollitt & Thomson, 1977).

There is just one study of prenatal undernutrition in which many of the confounding variables were adequately controlled. This study examined the effects of the famine in Holland during World War II (Stein, Susser, Saenger, & Marolla, 1975). These observations indicated that infants exposed to undernutrition in utero had normal mental functioning later in life. However, this study was not very representative of typical prenatal undernutrition, as the infants in question had normal head circumference despite a 10% loss in body weight.

Studies of small-for-date infants, who are comparatively as growth retarded as those infants affected by parental malnutrition, indicate that the function of the central nervous system may be permanently impaired. This is shown by the fact that large numbers of these children have low IQ scores, poor school performance, behavioral problems, and other signs of minimal brain damage (Fitzhardinge & Stevens, 1972). Observations of twins sometimes confirm these observations (Babson & Phillips, 1973; Fujikura & Froehlich, 1974; Pereira, Sundararaj, & Begum, 1979).

Several studies have shown that postnatal undernutrition can be partially overcome by environmental stimulation. Children who have been malnourished as a result of pediatric disease in affluent societies tend not to suffer from permanent behavioral deficits (Lloyd-Still, 1976). The rule seems to be that the older the child, the less likely there will be a behavioral deficit. This is not surprising because older children have more complete brain growth.

Lien, Meyer, and Winick (1977) and Winick et al. (1975) selected two groups of Korean female children from a population of children that had been taken into the Holt adoption agency either before the age of 24 months or after the age of 2 years. Each group was subdivided into 3 groups: 1) severely malnourished before adoption (below the 3rd percentile for height and weight), 2) moderately malnourished (from the 3rd through the 24th percentile for height and weight), and 3) well-fed (at or above the 25th percentile for height and weight). All children were rehabilitated at the agency before being brought to the United States and placed in middle-class American families. To be included in the study, the first group of children had to have been adopted by Americans before the end of their brain growth period (1.5–3 years) and the second after the normal period of brain growth (3–5 years of age).

When examined after 6 years in the United States and after a good deal of environmental stimulation, the early adopted children were found to have IQ and achievement scores that not only surpassed those of the average Korean child of the same age, but also of the average American child. However, the severely malnourished group still scored significantly less well than the other two groups.

In those children adopted at an older age, it was found that, although the well nourished and moderately malnourished girls reached and surpassed the American average, the severely malnourished children fell short of it. Comparison of the results for this group with those for the early adopted group showed that in every case the early adopted group scored better than the late adopted group.

This study supports the view that malnourished children rehabilitated after the age of active brain growth do not perform as well as those rehabilitated before this time. Of course, one might argue that their environment prior to adoption and rehabilitation was more important to their future development than their plan of nutrition. However, there is no doubt whatsoever that given a stimulating environment all children performed beyond expectation. Thus, environmental stimulation would seem to partially overcome the effects of nutritional deprivation and is, in fact, the only therapy available for children who have been malnourished during the period of their brain growth spurt.

## CONCLUSION

Investigations provide evidence that optimal brain development and functioning is dependent on adequate nutrition. Undernutrition may affect adversely both intrauterine and postnatal brain growth. In particular, protein malnutrition may have deleterious effects on brain maturation and brain function as detailed in this chapter.

## REFERENCES

Agrawal, H. C., Davis, J. M., & Himwich, W. A. (1966). Postnatal changes in free amino acid pool of rat brain. *Journal of Neurochemistry, 13*, 607–615.

Altman, J. (1969). DNA metabolism and cell proliferation. In A. Lajtha (Ed.), *Handbook of neurochemistry* (Vol. 2, pp. 137–182). New York: Plenum.

Babson, G. S., & Phillips, D. S. (1973). Growth and development of twins of dissimilar size at birth. *New England Journal of Medicine, 289,* 937–940.

Balazs, R., Lewis, P. D., & Patel, A. J. (1979). Nutritional deficiencies and brain development. In F. Falkner & J. M. Tanner (Eds.), *Human growth 3: Neurobiology and nutrition.* New York: Plenum.

Bolvin, A., Vendrely, R., & Vendrely, C. (1948). L'acide desoxyribonucléique du noyau cellulaire dépositaire des caractères héréditaires: Arguments d'ordre analytique. [Desoxyribonucleic acid of the cellular nucleus as transporting agent of hereditary characteristics: Analytical summary]. *C. R. Acad. Sci., 226,* 1061–1063.

Brown, R. E. (1966). Organ weight in malnutrition with special reference to brain weight. *Developmental Medicine and Child Neurology, 8,* 512–522.

Brunngraber, E. G., Whitting, L. A., Haberland, C., & Brown, B. (1972). Glycoproteins in Tay-Sachs disease: Isolation and carbohydrate composition of glycopeptides. *Brain Research, 38,* 151–162.

Bunge, R. P. (1968). Glial cells and the central myelin sheath. *Physiological Reviews, 48,* 197–251.

Carney-Crane, S., & Morgan, B. L. G. (1983). The effect of alterations in ketone body availability in the utilization of beta-hydroxybutyrate by developing rat brain. *Journal of Nutrition, 113,* 1063–1072.

Chase, H. P. (1976). Undernutrition and growth and development of the human brain. In J. D. Lloyd-Still (Ed.), *Malnutrition and intellectual development* (pp. 13–38). Lancaster: MTP.

Chase, H. P., Canosa, C. A., Dabiere, C. S., Welch, N. N., & O'Brien, D. (1974). Postnatal undernutrition and human brain development. *Journal of Mental Deficiency Research, 18,* 355–366.

Chase, H. P., Dorsey, J., & McKhann, G. (1967). The effect of malnutrition on the synthesis of myelin lipid. *Pediatrics, 40,* 551–559.

Chase, H. P., Welch, N. N., Dabiere, C. S., Vasan, N. S., & Butterfield, L. J. (1972). Alterations in human brain biochemistry following intrauterine growth retardation. *Pediatrics, 50,* 403–411.

Collins, F. D., Sinclair, A. J., Royle, J. P., Coats, D. A., Maynard, A. T., & Leonard, R. F. (1971). Plasma lipids in human linoleic acid deficiency. *Nutrition and Metabolism, 13,* 150–167.

Cowan, N. M. (1979). The development of the brain. *Scientific American, 241,* 112–113.

Cowey, C. B., Owen, J. M., Adron, J. W., & Middleton, C. (1976). Studies on the nutrition of flat fish: The effect of different dietary fatty acids on the growth and fatty acid composition of turbot (Scophtholamus maximus). *British Journal of Nutrition, 36,* 479–486.

Cravioto, J., & Delicardie, E. R. (1979). Nutrition, mental development and learning. In F. Falkner & J. M. Tanner (Eds.), *Human growth 3: Neurobiology and nutrition.* New York: Plenum.

Crawford, M. A., Sinclair, A. J., Msuya, P. M., & Munhambo, A. (1973). Structural lipids and their polyenoic constituents in human milk. In C. Galli, G. Jacini, & A. Pecile (Eds.), *Dietary lipids and postnatal development.* New York: Raven Press.

Dallman, P. R. (1974). Tissue effects of iron deficiency. In A. Jacobs & M. Norwood (Eds.), *Iron in biochemistry and medicine* (pp. 437–475). New York: Academic Press.

Dallman, P. R., Refino, C., & Yland, M. J. (1982). Sequence of development of iron deficiency in the rat. *American Journal of Clinical Nutrition, 35*, 671–677.

Davies, D. P. (1980). Some aspects of "catch-up" growth in "light-for-dates babies." In B. Wharton (Ed.), *Topics in pediatrics: Vol. 2. Nutrition in childhood.* Tunbridge Wells, England: Pitman Medical.

Davison, A. N., & Dobbing, J. (1966). Myelination as a vulnerable period in brain development. *British Medical Bulletin, 22*, 40–44.

Dekirmenjian, H., Brunngraber, E. G., Lemkey-Johnston, N., & Larremendi, L. M. H. (1969). Distribution of gangliosides, glycoprotein-NANA and acetylcholinesterase in axonal and synaptosomal fractions of cat cerebellum. *Experimental Brain Research, 8*, 97–104.

Dickerson, J. W. T. (1975). Effect of growth and undernutrition on the chemical composition of the brain. In A. Chavez, H. Bourges, & S. Basta (Eds.), *Proceedings of the Ninth International Congress on Nutrition (Mexico).* Basel: Karger.

Dickerson, J. W. T. (1980). Protein deficiency and the brain. In G. G. Birch & K. J. Parker (Eds.), *Food and health: Science and technology.* London: Elsevier Applied Science Publishers.

Dickerson, J. W. T. (1981). Nutrition, brain growth and environment. In K. J. Connolly & H. F. R. Prechtl (Eds.), *Maturation and development* (pp. 110–130). London: Spastics International Medical Publishers, Heinemann.

Dickerson, J. W. T., & McGurk, H. (1982). *Brain and behavioral development.* Surrey, England: Surrey University Press.

Dickerson, J. W. T., Merat, A., & Yusuf, H. K. M. (1982). The effects of malnutrition on the developing nervous system. In J. W. T. Dickerson & H. McGurk (Eds.), *Brain and behavioural development* (pp. 73–108). Surrey, England: Surrey University Press.

Dobbing, J. (1964). The influence of early nutrition on the development and myelination of the brain. *Proceedings of the Royal Society of London. Series B: Biological Sciences, 159*, 503–509.

Dobbing, J. (1974). The later development of the brain and its vulnerability. In J. A. Davis & J. Dobbing (Eds.), *Scientific foundations in pediatrics* (pp. 565–576). London: Heineman.

Dobbing, J. (1981). Nutritional growth restriction and the nervous system. In R. H. S. Thompson & A. W. Davison (Eds.), *The molecular basis of neuropathology.* London: Arnold.

Dobbing, J., & Sands, J. (1973). The quantitative growth and development of the human brain. *Archives of Disease in Childhood, 48*, 757–767.

Dow, R. S. (1970). Historical review of cerebellar investigations. In W. S. Fields & W. D. Willis (Eds.), *The cerebellum in health and disease* (pp. 5–13). St. Louis, MO: Warren H. Green, Inc.

Dunn, A. J., & Hogan, E. L. (1975). Brain gangliosides: Increased incorporation of 1-3H glucosamine during training. *Pharmacology, Biochemistry and Behavior, 3*, 605–612.

Enesco, M., & Leblond, C. P. (1962). Increase in cell number as a factor in the growth of the organs of the young male rat. *Journal of Embryology and Experimental Morphology, 10*, 530–562.

Engsner, G. (1974). Brain growth and motor nerve conduction velocity in children with protein calorie malnutrition. *Acta University Upsala, 180*, 1–60.

Enwonwu, C. O., & Worthington, B. S. (1973). Accumulation of histidine, 3-methylhistidine, and homocarnosine in the brains of protein-calorie deficient monkeys. *Journal of Neurochemistry, 21*, 799–807.

Enwonwu, C. O., & Worthington, B. S. (1974). Regional distribution of homocarnosine and other ninhydrinpositive substances in brains of malnourished monkeys. *Journal of Neurochemistry*, *22*, 1045–1052.

Fancourt, R., Campbell, S., Harvey, D., & Norman, A. P. (1976). Follow up study of small for date babies. *British Medical Journal*, *1* (6023), 1435–1437.

Fitzhardinge, P. M., & Stevens, E. M. (1972). The small for date infant: Vol. II. Neurological and intellectual sequelae. *Pediatrics*, *50*, 50–54.

Fujikura, T., & Froehlich, L. A. (1974). Mental and motor development in monozygotic twins with dissimilar birthweights. *Pediatrics*, *53*, 884–889.

Ghittoni, N. E., & Raveglia, F. (1973). Effects of malnutrition on the lipid composition of cerebral cortex and cerebellum in the rat. *Journal of Neurochemistry*, *21*, 983–987.

Gruenwald, P. (1963). Chronic fetal distress and placental insufficiency. *Biology of the Neonate*, *5*, 215–268.

Hamberger, A., & Svennerholm, L. (1971). Composition of gangliosides and phospholipids of neuronal and glial cell enriched fractions. *Journal of Neurochemistry*, *18*, 1821–1829.

Hansen, S., Perry, T. L., Wada, J. A., & Sokol, M. (1973). Brain amino acids in baboons with light-induced epilepsy. *Brain Research*, *50*, 480–483.

Hess, H. H., Bass, N. H., Thalheimer, C., & Devarakonda, R. (1976). Gangliosides and the architecture of human frontal and rat somatosensory isocortex. *Journal of Neurochemistry*, *26*, 1115–1121.

Himwich, H. E., & Fazekas, J. F. (1941). Comparative studies of the metabolism of the brain of infant and adult dogs. *American Journal of Physiology*, *132*, 454–459.

Holmann, R. T. (1973). Essential fatty acid deficiency in humans. In C. Galli, G. Jacini, & A. Pecile (Eds.), *Dietary lipids and postnatal development*. New York: Raven Press.

Hubel, D. H. (1979). The brain. *Scientific American*, *241*, 45–53.

Hyden, H., & Egyhazi, E. (1964). Changes in RNA content and base composition in cortical neurons of rats in a learning experiment involving transfer of handedness. *Proceedings of the National Academy of Sciences of the United States of America*, *52*, 1030–1035.

Irwin, L. N., & Samson, F. E. (1971). Content and turnover of gangliosides in rat brain following behavioral stimulation. *Journal of Neurochemistry*, *18*, 203–211.

Iversen, L. L. (1979). The chemistry of the brain. *Scientific American*, *241*, 134–149.

Kennedy, C., Grave, G. D., Jehle, J. W., & Sokoloff, L. (1972). Changes in blood flow in the component structures of the dog brain during postnatal maturation. *Journal of Neurochemistry*, *19*, 2423–2433.

Kennedy, C., & Sokoloff, L. (1957). An adaptation of the nitrous oxide method to the study of cerebral circulation in children: Normal values for cerebral blood flow and cerebral metabolic rate in childhood. *Journal of Clinical Investigation*, *36*, 1130–1137.

Krebs, H. A., Williamson, D. H., Bates, M. W., Page, M. A., & Hawkins, R. A. (1971). The role of ketone bodies in caloric homeostasis. *Advances in Enzyme Regulation*, *9*, 387–409.

Kritchevsky, D., & Holmes, W. L. (1962). Occurrence of desmosterol in developing rat brain. *Biochemical and Biophysical Research Communications*, *7*, 128–131.

Lapetina, E. G., Soto, E. F., & DeRobertis, E. (1968). Lipids and proteolipids in isolated subcellular membranes of rat brain cortex. *Journal of Neurochemistry*, *15*, 437–445.

Lapham, L. W. (1968). Tetraploid DNA content of Purkinje neurons of human cerebellar cortex. *Science*, *159*, 310–312.

Ledeen, R. W. (1978). Ganglioside structure and distribution: Are they localized at the nerve endings? *Journal of Supramolecular Structure*, *8*, 1–17.

Leibel, R. L., Greenfield, D. B., & Pollitt, E. (1979). Iron deficiency: Behavior and brain biochemistry. In M. Winick (Ed.), *Nutrition: Pre- and postnatal development* (pp. 383–439). New York: Plenum.

Lien, N. M., Meyer, K. K., & Winick, M. (1977). Early malnutrition and late adoption: A study of their effects on the development of Korean orphans adopted into American families. *American Journal of Clinical Nutrition*, *30*, 1734.

Lloyd-Still, J. D. (1976). Clinical studies on the effects of malnutrition during infancy on subsequent physical and intellectual development. In J. D. Lloyd-Still (Ed.), *Malnutrition and intellectual development* (pp. 103–121). Lancaster: MTP.

Low, J. A., Galbraith, R. S., Muir, D., Killen, H., Karchmar, J., & Campbell, D. (1978). Intrauterine growth retardation: A preliminary report of long term morbidity. *American Journal of Obstetrics and Gynecology*, *130*, 534–545.

Machiyama, Y., Balazs, R., & Julian, T. (1965). Oxidation of glucose through the gamma-aminobutyrate pathway in brain. *Biochemical Journal*, *96*, 68–79.

McLean, F., & Usher, R. (1970). Measurement of liveborn fetal malnutrition infants compared with similar gestation and similar birth weight controls. *Biology of the Neonate*, *16*, 215–221.

Merat, A. (1971). *Effects of protein-calorie malnutrition on brain gangliosides*. Doctoral dissertation, University of Surrey, Surrey, England.

Morgan, B. L. G., Boris, G. L., & Winick, M. (1982). A useful correlation between blood and brain *N*-acetylneuraminic acid contents. *Biology of the Neonate*, *42*, 299–303.

Morgan, B. L. G., & Naismith, D. J. (1982). The effect of early postnatal undernutrition on the growth and development of the rat brain. *British Journal of Nutrition*, *48*, 15–23.

Morgan, B. L. G., & Sinai, J. (1983). *The role of N-acetylneuraminic acid in neurotransmission*. Unpublished manuscript, Columbia University, Institute of Human Nutrition, New York.

Morgan, B. L. G., & Winick, M. (1980a). Effects of administration of *N*-acetylneuraminic acid (NANA) on brain NANA content and behavior. *Journal of Nutrition*, *110*, 416–424.

Morgan, B. L. G., & Winick, M. (1980b). Effects of environmental stimulation on brain *N*-acetylneuraminic acid content and behavior. *Journal of Nutrition*, *110*, 425–432.

Morgan, B. L. G., & Winick, M. (1981). The subcellular localizatin of administered *N*-acetylneuraminic acid in the brains of well-fed protein restricted rats. *British Journal of Nutrition*, *46*, 231–238.

Morgane, P. J., Miller, M., Kempner, T., Stern, W., Farbes, W., Hall, R., Bronzino, J., Kissane, J., Hawrylewicz, E., & Resnick, O. (1978). The effects of protein malnutrition on the developing central nervous system in the rat. *Neuroscience and Biobehavioral Reviews*, *3*, 139–230.

Nauta, W. J. H., & Feirtag, M. (1979). The organization of the brain. *Scientific American*, *241*, 88–111.

Norton, W. T., & Poduslo, J. F. (1971). Neuronal perikarya and rat brain: Chemical composition during myelination. *Journal of Lipid Research*, *12*, 84–90.

Nowak, T. S., & Munro, H. N. (1977). Effects of protein calorie malnutrition on biochemical aspects of brain development. In R. J. Wurtman & J. J. Wurtman (Eds.), *Nutrition and the brain* (Vol. 2.). New York: Raven Press.

Oski, F. A., & Honig, A. M. (1977). The effects of therapy on the developmental scores of iron deficient infants. *Journal of Pediatrics*, *92*, 21–25.

Pereira, S. M., Sundararaj, R., & Begum, A. (1979). Physical growth and neurointegrative performance of survivors of protein energy malnutrition. *British Journal of Nutrition*, *42*, 165–171.

Persson, B., Settergren, G., & Dahlquist, G. (1972). Cerebral arteriovenous difference of acetoacetate and D-beta-hydroxybutyrate in children. *Acta Paediatrica Scandinavica*, *61*, 273–278.

Pollitt, E., & Leibel, R. L. (1982). Functional aspects of iron deficiency. In E. Pollitt & R. L. Leibel (Eds.), *Iron deficiency: Brain biochemistry and behavior* (pp. 93–208). New York: Raven Press.

Pollitt, E., & Thomson, C. (1977). Protein calorie malnutrition and behavior: A review from psychology. In R. J. Wurtman & J. J. Wurtman (Eds.), *Nutrition and the brain* (Vol. 2.). New York: Raven Press.

Porcellati, G. (1972). Biochemical processes in brain and nervous tissue. *Bibliotheca Nutritio et Dieta*, *17*, 16–35.

Raaf, J., & Kernohan, J. W. (1944). A study of the external granular layer in the cerebellum: The disappearance of the external granular and the growth of the molecular and internal granular layers in the cerebellum. *American Journal of Anatomy*, *75*, 151–172.

Rees, R. P. (1978). The morphology of interneuronal synaptogenesis: A review. *Federation Proceedings*, *37*, 2000–2009.

Rosso, P. (1981). Nutrition and maternal-fetal exchange. *American Journal of Clinical Nutrition*, *34*, 744–755.

Rosso, P., Hormazabal, J., & Winick, M. (1970). Changes in brain weight, cholesterol, phospholipid and DNA content in marasmic children. *American Journal of Clinical Nutrition*, *23*, 1275–1279.

Sands, J., Dobbing, J., & Gratrix, C. A. (1979). Cell number and cell size: Organ growth and development and the control of catch-up growth in rats. *Lancet*, *ii*, 503–505.

Sarma, M. K. J., & Rao, K. S. (1974). Biochemical composition of different regions in brains of small for date infants. *Journal of Neurochemistry*, *22*, 671–677.

Schengrund, C. L., & Nelson, J. T. (1975). Influence of cation concentration on the sialidase activity of neuronal synaptic membranes. *Biochemical and Biophysical Research Communications*, *63*, 217–223.

Sessa, G., & Perez, M. M. (1975). Biochemical changes in rat brain associated with development of the blood brain barrier. *Journal of Neurochemistry*, *25*, 779–782.

Seta, K., Sershen, H., & Laijtha, A. (1972). Cerebral amino acid uptake in vivo in newborn mice. *Brain Research*, *47*, 415–425.

Sokoloff, L. (1966). Cerebral circulatory and metabolic changes associated with aging. *Research Publications—Association for Research in Nervous and Mental Disease*, *41*, 237–251.

Sokoloff, L. (1974). Changes in enzyme activities in neural tissues with maturation and development of the nervous system. In F. O. Schmitt & F. G. Worden (Eds.), *The neurosciences: Third study program* (pp. 885–898). Cambridge: M.I.T. Press.

Stein, Z., Susser, M., Saenger, G., & Marolla, F. (1975). *Famine and human development: The Dutch hunger winter of 1944–45*. New York: Oxford University Press.

Stevens, C. E. (1979). The neuron. In M. Winick (Ed.), *Scientific American book: The brain*. Oxford: W. H. Freeman.

Stoch, M. B., & Smythe, P. M. (1963). Does undernutrition during infancy inhibit brain growth and subsequent intellectual development? *Archives of Disease in Childhood*, *38*, 546–552.

Suzuki, K. (1967). Formation and turnover of the major brain gangliosides during development. *Journal of Neurochemistry, 14*, 917–925.

Ulus, I. H. (1977). The effect of choline on cholinergic function. In D. J. Jenden (Ed.), *Cholinergic mechanisms and psychopharmacology*. New York: Plenum.

Winick, M. (1976). *Malnutrition and brain development*. New York: Oxford University Press.

Winick, M. (1976). Nutrition and cellular growth of the brain. In M. Winick (Ed.), *Malnutrition and brain development* (pp. 63–97). New York: Oxford University Press.

Winick, M., Meyer, K. K., & Harris, R. C. (1975). Malnutrition and environmental enrichment by early adoption. *Science, 190*, 1173–1175.

Winick, M., & Noble, A. (1965). Quantitative changes in DNA, RNA, and protein during prenatal and postnatal growth. *Developmental Biology, 12*, 451–466.

Winick, M., & Rosso, P. (1969). Head circumference and cellular growth of the brain in normal and marasmic children. *Journal of Pediatrics, 74*, 774–778.

Winick, M., Rosso, P., & Waterlow, J. (1970). Cellular growth on cerebrum, cerebellum and brain stem in normal and marasmic children. *Experimental Neurology, 26*, 393–400.

# 18 | *Alan R. Hinman*

# IMMUNO-
# PROPHYLAXIS OF
# DEVELOPMENTAL
# DISABILITIES

Immunoprophylaxis plays a role in preventing developmental disabilities in each of the three areas in which they are produced: genetic, acquired in utero, and acquired after delivery. The genetic cause of developmental disabilities that can be prevented through immunization is Rh incompatibility; its consequences can be prevented with passive immunization. Those acquired disabilities preventable by immunoprophylaxis are caused by certain infections; these can be prevented by active immunization.

## IMMUNOPROPHYLAXIS OF
## GENETICALLY DETERMINED DISABILITIES

In 1970, Rh incompatibility was responsible for an estimated 3,800 instances of Rh hemolytic disease of the newborn (Wysowski, Flynt, Goldberg, & Connell, 1979). Some of these cases resulted in death, others in mental retardation or deafness. The development and introduction of Rh immune globulin in 1968 provided a specific means of preventing Rh sensitization of the mother, which has a strong likelihood of producing damage to subsequent infants. During the 1970s, there was a 65% decline in the reported incidence of Rh hemolytic disease of the newborn. Several factors were responsible for this decline, including changing trends in fertility. However, it is estimated that 60%–70% of the decline was due to the use of Rh immunoglobulin (Adams, Marks, Gustafson, & Oakley, 1981). Unfortunately, use of this extremely effective product has not been as widespread as hoped, and the problem remains at a low level, approximately 14 cases/10,000 live births. Further reductions in incidence will only be brought about by more widespread use of Rh immunoglobulin in Rh negative women following abortion, amniocentesis, or delivery. There is also discussion about the practicality of administering the product to Rh negative women before delivery (see also von Oeyen, Chapter 5; Hoyme, Chapter 7, this volume).

## IMMUNOPROPHYLAXIS OF PRENATAL CAUSES OF DISABILITIES

Intrauterine infection with both measles and mumps viruses has been reported to cause congenital abnormalities that could impede normal development, and measles infection in pregnancy may also lead to premature delivery (Jespersen, Littauer, & Saglild, 1977; Siegel, 1973; Young, 1976). However, these infections do not appear to play a major role in causing developmental disabilities.

Rubella is the major cause of congenital infection (leading to developmental disability) that can be prevented by active vaccination. Table 18.1

**Table 18.1.** Developmental disabilities associated with congenital rubella infection

| | |
|---|---|
| Bone lesions | |
| Cardiac defects | —Myocardial necrosis |
| | —Patent ductus arteriosus |
| | —Pulmonary stenosis and coarctation |
| | —Ventricular septal defect |
| Central nervous system defects | —Encephalitis |
| | —Mental retardation |
| | —Microcephaly |
| | —Progressive panencephalitis |
| | —Psychomotor retardation |
| | —Spastic quadriparesis |
| Deafness | |
| Diabetes mellitus | |
| Eye defects | —Cataracts |
| | —Glaucoma |
| | —Microphthalmia |
| | —Retinopathy of prematurity |
| Growth retardation | |
| Hepatitis | |
| Interstitial pneumonitis | |
| Precocious puberty | |
| Psychiatric disorders | |
| Thrombocytopenic purpura | |
| Thyroid disorders | |

Adapted by permission from Krugman, S., Katz, S. L., Gershon, A. A., & Wilfert, C. M.: *Infectious diseases of children,* ed. 8, St. Louis, 1985, The C. V. Mosby Co.

includes a partial list of the developmental disabilities that may be associated with congenital rubella infection. The last major epidemic of rubella in the United States, 1964–1965, resulted in congenital anomalies in an estimated 20,000 infants. Table 18.2 summarizes the morbidity associated with this epidemic. A substantial proportion of these infants had multiple defects that further limited their ability to develop normally.

Deafness is certainly one of the most common abnormalities associated with congenital rubella infection. Congenital rubella infection has been described as "the cause which is identifiable as responsible for the greatest proportion of deafness in children" (Martin, 1982). It has been estimated that in 1980 there were more than 6,000 students in educational programs for the hearing impaired in the United States who were deaf because of congenital rubella infection (Stuckless, 1980). In the 1970 census of persons who are deaf, congenital rubella infection was reported to be responsible for 5.2% of all deafness in the United States, and the cause of deafness in 31.85% of those who were born deaf (Schein & Delk, 1974). Fisch (1973) has estimated that congenital rubella infection is responsible for approximately 6% of congenital deafness in the absence of major rubella epidemics and up to 24% following a major rubella epidemic.

In addition to the physical disabilities associated with congenital rubella infection, profound alterations have been seen in the mental and behavioral functions of children with congenital rubella syndrome (CRS). Chess, Fernandez, and Korn (1978) reported that 37.0% of 243 children age 2.5 to 5 years with documented congenital rubella infection had mental retardation, 18.3% had behavior disorders, and 7.4% had autism. Of 210 children age 8 to 9 years with documented congenital rubella infection, 25.7% had mental retardation, 32.9% had behavior disorders, and 6.2% had autism.

**Table 18.2.** Estimated morbidity associated with the 1964–1965 rubella epidemic in the United States

| | |
|---|---|
| Acquired rubella | |
| Rubella cases | 12,500,000 |
| Encephalitis | 2,084 |
| Congenital rubella syndrome | |
| Excess fetal wastage | 6,250 |
| Therapeutic abortions | 5,000 |
| Total | 11,250 |
| Deaf children | 8,055 |
| Deaf-blind children | 3,580 |
| Children with mental retardation | 1,790 |
| Other congenital rubella syndrome | 6,575 |
| Total | 20,000 |
| Excess neonatal deaths | 2,100 |

The introduction of live attenuated rubella vaccines in 1969 gave promise that the tragic consequences of congenital rubella infection could be averted. However, for a variety of reasons, the strategy developed for prevention of CRS was different from the typical vaccination strategy in which vaccine is given to the population at highest risk, in this case, women of childbearing age. One of the major factors having to do with adoption of indirect strategies was uncertainty as to whether the vaccine virus itself might have teratogenic potential. Two major approaches to vaccination were undertaken (Preblud, Serdula, Frank, Brandling-Bennett, & Hinman, 1980). In the United States, school children were vaccinated, and a program of routine vaccination of children at 12 months of age was carried out. This strategy was designed to interrupt the circulation of rubella virus and thus reduce the likelihood that a pregnant woman would come in contact with that virus. Additionally, it was anticipated that vaccine induced immunity would be permanent, thus protecting girls when they subsequently entered the childbearing period. An alternative policy was adopted in Great Britain and in some other countries. This approach was aimed at providing individual protection to girls as they entered the childbearing age, and involved vaccination only of girls at ages 12 to 14 years. In this approach, rubella virus would continue to circulate in the population.

The results of the strategies have been different. In the United States, the historic 6- to 9-year epidemic cycle of rubella has been interrupted and no epidemics have occurred since 1964 (Figure 18.1). The reported incidence of

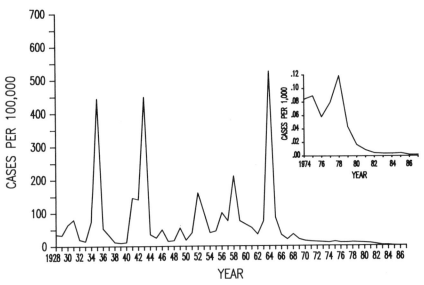

Figure 18.1. Rubella incidence in 10 selected areas—Maine, Rhode Island, Connecticut, New York City, Ohio, Illinois, Wisconsin, Maryland, Washington, DC, Massachusetts—from 1928 to 1987.

CRS has also declined substantially, as shown in Figure 18.2. The decline in incidence of CRS parallels the decline in reported incidence of rubella in individuals 15 years of age and older. This accelerated decline in the incidence in individuals in this age group is likely due to two factors. The first factor is maturation (in the over 15-year age group) of children initially vaccinated as school children; the second factor is the increased efforts made to immunize teenagers with rubella (and measles) vaccines during intensive immunization efforts in the United States. It can thus be seen that the approach in the United States has had a major impact on the occurrence of CRS by preventing epidemics, even though it has not completely prevented the condition.

By contrast, in the United Kingdom, the epidemic cycle of rubella infection has continued unabated, as expected. Two epidemics have been reported in Great Britain in the period between 1969 and 1982. Compliance with the vaccination program has been variable, but data indicate that a decreasing

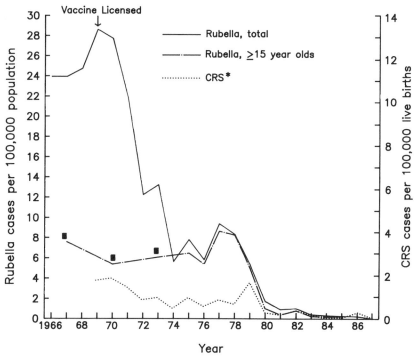

Figure 18.2.   Incidence rate of reported cases of rubella and congenital rubella syndrom (CRS) in the United States from 1966 to 1987. (∅ represents confirmed and compatible cases by year of birth; provisional data due to delayed diagnosis and reporting. ■ represents average annual United States estimate based on data from Illinois, Massachusetts, and New York City for the 3-year periods 1966–1968, 1969–1971, and 1972–1974.)

proportion of the childbearing-age women are susceptible to rubella, suggesting that the UK approach may finally demonstrate some impact on the occurrence of CRS (Banatvala, 1982). It seems clear that the most dramatic impact on the occurrence of CRS will come through a combined approach involving direct protection of women of childbearing age as well as interruption of transmission of rubella virus through vaccination (Hinman, Bart, Orenstein, & Preblud, 1983). Authorities in the United Kingdom have now established a goal of elimination of rubella, measles, and mumps. This will be accomplished by a program of universal vaccination of young children of both sexes using combined measles-mumps-rubella (MMR) vaccine (Miller, 1988). Vaccination of adult women is now feasible because of the demonstrated low (negligible) risk of teratogenicity from vaccine virus (Centers for Disease Control, 1987). (See also Von Oeyen, Chapter 5, and Pueschel, Scola, & McConnell, Chapter 6, this volume.)

## IMMUNOPROPHYLAXIS OF
## POSTNATALLY ACQUIRED CAUSES OF DISABILITIES

Table 18.3 lists some of the developmental disabilities that may be associated with infectious diseases against which all children in the United States are

Table 18.3. Developmental disabilities associated with postnatally acquired vaccine-preventable diseases

| Infectious disease | Developmental disability |
|---|---|
| Diphtheria | Death |
| | Myocarditis |
| | Paralysis |
| | Ocular paralysis |
| Measles | Death |
| | Blindness |
| | Deafness |
| | Encephalitis |
| | Mental retardation |
| | Subacute sclerosing panencephalitis |
| Mumps | Deafness |
| Pertussis | Death |
| | Brain damage |
| | Bronchiectasis/emphysema |
| Poliomyelitis | Death |
| | Paralysis |
| Rubella | Encephalitis |
| Tetanus | Death |

now supposed to be vaccinated: diphtheria, measles, mumps, pertussis, poliomyelitis, rubella, and tetanus. Death is included as the "ultimate" developmental disability. Some of these conditions are of varying importance in different parts of the world and the true frequency of virtually all of these complications is not well documented. Measles is the most common cause of blindness in some African countries, whereas it is only a minor cause of blindness in the industrialized nations (Benezra & Chirambo, 1977; McGlashan, 1969; Sandford-Smith & Whittle, 1979). In the 1970 census of persons who were deaf (Schein & Delk, 1974), measles was reported as the cause in 4.3% and pertussis as the cause in 2.6% of individuals who are deaf; mumps has been described as the cause of deafness in 0.6% of students enrolled in special education programs for the hearing impaired (Jensema, 1974). The occurrence of each of these diseases and subsequent developmental disabilities has been markedly reduced by the widespread use of vaccines.

## Diphtheria

In the first few decades of this century, diphtheria was one of the leading causes of death in young children. The reported number of cases reached a peak of more than 200,000 in the early 1920s and then began a rapid decline, which was accelerated by the introduction and use of diphtheria toxoid beginning in the 1930s. Since 1979, the number of reported cases has dropped even further, in part, as a result of discontinuation of reporting of cutaneous diphtheria (Figure 18.3). In 1987, only three cases of diphtheria were reported in the United States.

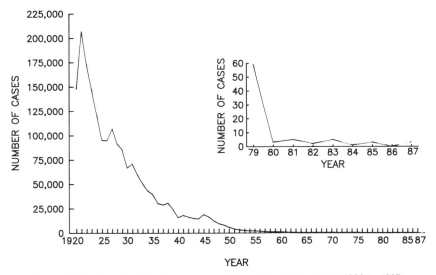

Figure 18.3. Reported diphtheria cases in the United States from 1920 to 1987.

## Measles

Early in the twentieth century, measles killed thousands of children each year in this country, and virtually everyone had been infected by the age of 15. Even after the antibiotic era began in the 1950s, the average number of cases was more than 500,000 with nearly 500 deaths each year. The introduction of measles vaccine in 1963 and its subsequent widespread use has brought about a dramatic decline in incidence (Figure 18.4). Progress has been so striking that a goal has been established to eliminate indigenous measles entirely from this country. Although the initial target date of 1982 was not met, considerable progress has been made (Markowitz et al., 1989). In 1987, 3,655 cases of measles were reported.

## Mumps

Mumps has also been essentially a universal disease and its incidence has fallen dramatically following the 1967 introduction of live mumps virus (Figure 18.5). In 1987, 12,848 cases were reported.

## Pertussis

Pertussis (whooping cough) incidence reached a peak in 1934, when more than 265,000 cases were reported and thousands of deaths were recorded. The reported incidence of pertussis began to decline even before vaccines were put into wide use in the 1940s, but the rate of decline was accelerated by the widespread use of pertussis vaccine (Figure 18.6). In 1987, 2,823 cases of pertussis were reported.

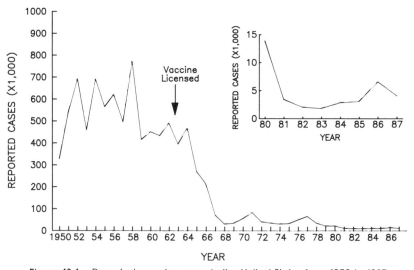

**Figure 18.4.** Reported measles cases in the United States from 1950 to 1987.

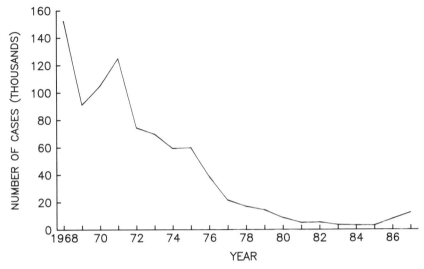

**Figure 18.5.** Reported mumps cases in the United States from 1968 to 1987.

Reports indicate that pertussis vaccine is associated with the development of acute encephalopathy in some infants, with residual damage in a few. One estimate of the frequency of this occurrence is 1 in 110,000 doses for acute encephalopathy and 1 in 310,000 doses for acute encephalopathy with residual damage 1 year later (Miller, Ross, Alderslade, Bellman, & Rawson,

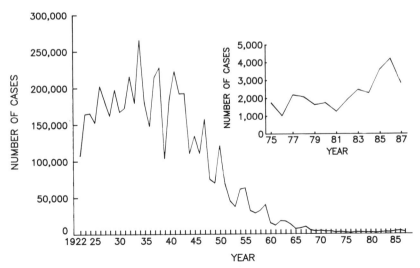

**Figure 18.6.** Reported pertussis cases in the United States from 1922 (the first year of report) to 1987.

1981). Concern about these adverse reactions to pertussis vaccine led to a marked decline in pertussis immunization in Great Britain beginning in 1974. The result of this decline in vaccination coverage was a major epidemic of pertussis in the period from 1977 to 1979 with more than 100,000 cases and 36 deaths (Joint Committee on Vaccination and Immunization, 1981). Even taking into account the adverse events associated with pertussis vaccination, the benefits of pertussis immunization clearly outweigh the risks (Hinman & Koplan, 1984; Koplan, Schoenbaum, Weinstein, & Fraser, 1979).

## Poliomyelitis

Summer epidemics of paralytic poliomyelitis increased in intensity in this country during the 1940s and reached a peak in 1952 when more than 20,000 cases of the paralytic disease were reported (Figure 18.7). The introduction of inactivated polio vaccine in 1956 and oral polio vaccine in 1961 had a dramatic impact on the occurrence of polio in this country (Figure 18.8). Since 1980, fewer than 10 cases of paralytic polio have been reported each year, on average, in the United States.

## Tetanus

Tetanus only became notifiable in 1947, and the maximum number of cases reported was 601, in 1948. However, it was much more common in the past, with 1,253 tetanus deaths recorded in this country in 1933. The incidence of tetanus also has undergone a marked decline since tetanus toxoid came into

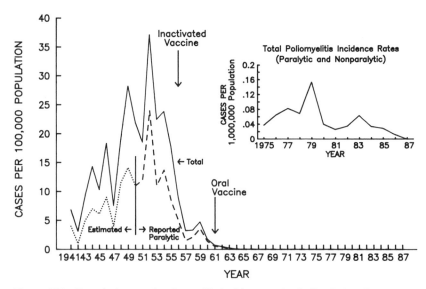

Figure 18.7. Reported annual poliomyelitis incidence rates in the United States from 1941 to 1987.

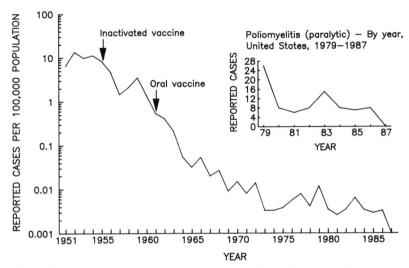

**Figure 18.8.** Reported paralytic poliomyelitis in the United States from 1951 to 1987.

wide use in the 1940s (Figure 18.9). In 1987, there were 48 cases of tetanus reported in this country, and the median age of cases was more than 50 years.

Table 18.4 summarizes the maximum reported morbidity and mortality for each of the conditions discussed (along with the year in which the maximum was reported). All have undergone declines of greater than 90% and three conditions (diphtheria, measles, polio) have been reduced almost to the

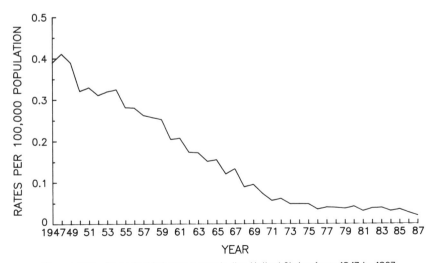

**Figure 18.9.** Reported tetanus cases in the United States from 1947 to 1987.

**Table 18.4.** Comparison of maximum and current morbidity with the percent of change in vaccine-preventable diseases

| Disease | Maximum cases (year) | | 1987 | Percent change | 1990 objectives |
|---|---|---|---|---|---|
| Diphtheria | 206,939 | (1921) | 3 | −99.999 | 50 |
| Measles | 894,134 | (1941) | 3,655 | −99.59 | 500[a] |
| Mumps[b] | 152,209 | (1968) | 12,848 | −91.56 | 1,000 |
| Pertussis | 265,269 | (1934) | 2,823 | −98.94 | 1,000 |
| Polio (paralytic) | 21,269 | (1952) | 0[c] | −100.00 | 10 |
| Rubella[d] | 57,686 | (1969) | 306 | −99.47 | 1,000 |
| Congenital rubella syndrome (CRS) | 20,000[d] | (1964–1965) | 5 | −99.98 | 10 |
| Tetanus[e] | 601 | (1948) | 48 | −92.01 | 50 |

[a]All imported or import-related.
[b]First reportable in 1968.
[c]Suspect cases under evaluation.
[d]First reportable in 1966.
[e]First reportable in 1947.

vanishing point (Centers for Disease Control, 1982). Immunization levels in children are now at their highest levels ever. More than 95% of children entering school for the first time in 1987 had received the recommended vaccines.

Precise figures are not available on either the current or the former occurrence of developmental disabilities associated with the above mentioned infectious diseases. However, some data are available on deaths due to measles and the reported occurrence of two complications of measles, namely acute encephalitis and subacute sclerosing panencephalitis (SSPE). These figures are shown in Table 18.5. There has been more than a 99% reduction in the reported occurrence of measles and measles associated deaths in the 20 years since the vaccine was introduced. Measles encephalitis has undergone a similar reduction, and SSPE rates have also fallen dramatically, paralleling the decline in measles incidence but occurring approximately 7 years later (Figure 18.10). It is reasonable to assume that the incidence of severe consequences of the other diseases has similarly paralleled the reported occurrence of morbidity and mortality.

It must also be acknowledged that on rare occasions, the vaccines themselves may cause damage that can result in developmental disabilities. These unfortunate occurrences may become more prominent as the incidence of certain infectious diseases declines to the vanishing point. For example, oral polio vaccine (OPV) is associated with paralysis in vaccine recipients or their contacts at an approximate rate of 1 in 2.6 million doses distributed (Nkowane et al., 1987). As there are approximately 22 million doses of OPV distributed in this country each year, this gives an annual average of approximately 6

Table 18.5. Reported incidence of measles cases and deaths, measles encephalitis, and subacute sclerosing panencephalitis (SSPE) in the United States from 1960 to 1981

| Year | Cases | Deaths | Encephalitis | SSPE |
|------|-------|--------|--------------|------|
| 1960 | 441,703 | 380 | — | 2 |
| 1961 | 423,919 | 434 | — | 6 |
| 1962 | 481,530 | 408 | — | 1 |
| 1963 | 385,156 | 364 | 239 | 12 |
| 1964 | 458,083 | 421 | 300 | 9 |
| 1965 | 261,904 | 276 | 171 | 22 |
| 1966 | 204,136 | 261 | 219 | 28 |
| 1967 | 62,705 | 81 | 62 | 45 |
| 1968 | 22,231 | 24 | 19 | 47 |
| 1969 | 25,826 | 41 | 35 | 51 |
| 1970 | 47,351 | 89 | 27 | 47 |
| 1971 | 75,290 | 90 | 69 | 52 |
| 1972 | 32,275 | 24 | 26 | 41 |
| 1973 | 26,690 | 23 | 37 | 44 |
| 1974 | 22,094 | 20 | 14 | 27 |
| 1975 | 24,374 | 20 | 17 | 26 |
| 1976 | 41,126 | 12 | 44 | 24 |
| 1977 | 57,345 | 15 | 32 | 18 |
| 1978 | 26,871 | 11 | 13 | 14 |
| 1979 | 13,597 | 6[a] | 3 | 10[a] |
| 1980 | 13,506 | 6[a] | 3[a] | 7[a] |
| 1981 | 3,032 | 2[a] | 1[a] | 7[a] |

[a]Provisional data.

cases of vaccine associated paralysis. If this number is compared to the more than 20,000 cases of paralytic disease that occurred in a year in this country before the vaccine was available, it would clearly be an insignificant number. However, polio has been so successfully controlled that vaccine associated cases now account for the majority of all polio cases reported. To the casual observer this might suggest that the risk of vaccine is greater than the risk of disease. However, this suggestion ignores the fact that current disease levels have been reached and can only be maintained by continuing use of the vaccine. Debate continues about the appropriate role of inactivated polio vaccine (IPV), which has no known risk of vaccine associated paralysis.

## CONCLUSION

Infectious diseases have been prominent causes of developmental disabilities in children in the past. Rh incompatibility has also been responsible for a significant number of deaths and developmental disabilities. To date, immunoprophylaxis has been one of the most effective means of preventing devel-

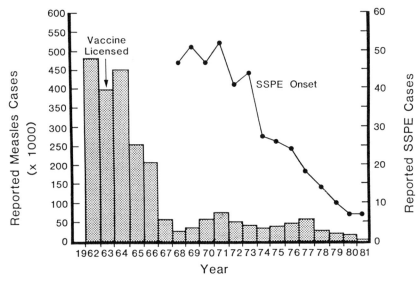

**Figure 18.10.** Reported measles and subacute sclerosing panencephalitis (SSPE) cases in the United States from 1962 to 1981.

opmental disabilities, and future developments should bring about even further accomplishments.

Many other infections may be associated with subsequent developmental disability, including infections due to cytomegalovirus, hepatitis B virus, herpes virus, and varicella-zoster virus. A vaccine has already been licensed to protect against hepatitis B, and there are research efforts underway to develop vaccines for the others. Future presentations on "immunoprophylaxis of developmental disabilities" will doubtless encompass a much longer list than given here.

## REFERENCES

Adams, M. M., Marks, J. S., Gustafson, J., & Oakley, G. P., Jr. (1981). Rh hemolytic disease of the newborn: Using incidence observations to evaluate the use of Rh immune globulin. *American Journal of Public Health, 71*, 1031–1035.

Banatvala, J. E. (1982). Rubella vaccination: Remaining problems. *British Medical Journal, 284*, 1285–1286.

Benezra, D., & Chirambo, M.D. (1977). Incidence and causes of blindness among the under 5 age group in Malawi. *British Journal of Ophthalmology, 61*, 154–157.

Centers for Disease Control. (1982). Childhood immunization initiative: United States, 5 year follow up. *Morbidity and Mortality Weekly Report, 31*, 232–232.

Centers for Disease Control. (1987). Rubella vaccination during pregnancy: United States, 1984–1986. *Morbidity and Mortality Weekly Report, 36*, 664–666.

Chess, S., Fernandez, P., & Korn, S. (1978). Behavioral consequences of congenital rubella. *Journal of Pediatrics*, *93*, 699–703.

Fisch, L. (1973). Epidemiology of congenital hearing loss. *Audiology*, *12*, 411–425.

Hinman, A. R., Bart, K. J., Orenstein, W. A., & Preblud, S. R. (1983). Rational strategy for rubella vaccination. *Lancet*, *i*, 39–41.

Hinman, A. R., & Koplan, J. P. (1984). Pertussis and pertussis vaccine: Reanalysis of benefits, risks, and costs. *Journal of the American Medical Association*, *251*, 3109–3113.

Jensema, C. (1974). Children in educational programs for the hearing impaired whose impairment was caused by mumps. *Journal of Speech and Hearing Disorders*, *40*, 164–169.

Jespersen, C. S., Littauer, J., & Saglild, U. (1977). Measles as a cause of fetal defects: A retrospective study of ten measles epidemics in Greenland. *Acta Paediatrica Scandinavica*, *66*, 367–372.

Joint Committee on Vaccination and Immunization. (1981). The whooping cough epidemic 1977–1979. *Department of Health and Social Security: Whooping cough.* London: Her Majesty's Stationery Office.

Koplan, J. P., Schoenbaum, S. C., Weinstein, M. C., & Fraser, D. W. (1979). Pertussis vaccine: An analysis of benefits, risks, and costs. *English Journal of Medicine*, *301*, 906–911.

Krugman, S., Katz, S.L., Greshon, A.A., &Wilfert, C. M. (1985). *Infectious diseases of children* (8th ed.). St. Louis: C. V. Mosby Co.

Markowitz, L. E., Preblud, S. R., Orenstein, W. A., Rovira, E. Z., Adams, N. C., Hawkins, C. E., & Hinman, A. R. (1989). Patterns of transmission in measles outbreaks in the United States, 1985–1986. *New England Journal of Medicine*, *320*, 75–81.

Martin, J. A. M. (1982). Aetiological factors relating to childhood deafness in the European community. *Audiology*, *21*, 149–158.

McGlashan, N. D. (1969). Measles, malnutrition and blindness in Wapula Province, Zambia. *Tropical and Geographical Medicine*, *21*, 157–162.

Miller, C. (1988). Introduction of measles-mumps-rubella vaccine. *Health Visitor*, *61*, 116–117.

Miller, D. L., Ross, E. M., Alderslade, R., Bellman, M. H., & Rawson, N. S. B. (1981). Pertussis immunization and serious acute neurological illness in children. *British Medical Journal*, *282*, 1595–1599.

Nkowane, B. M., Wassilak, S. G. F., Orenstein, W. A., Bart, K. J., Schonberger, L. B., Hinman, A. R., & Kew, O. M. (1987). Vaccine-associated paralytic poliomyelitis: United States, 1973 through 1984. *Journal of the American Medical Association*, *257*, 1335–1340.

Preblud, S. R., Serdula, M. K., Frank, J. A., Jr., Brandling-Bennett, A. D., & Hinman, A. R. (1980). Rubella vaccination in the United States: A ten-year review. *Epidemiologic Reviews*, *2*, 171–194.

Sandford-Smith, J. H., & Whittle, H. C. (1979). Corneal ulceration following measles in Negerian children. *British Journal of Ophthalmology*, *63*, 720–724.

Schein, J. D., & Delk, M. T., Jr. (1974). *The deaf population of the United States.* Silver Spring, MD: National Association of the Deaf.

Siegel, M. (1973). Congenital malformations following chickenpox, measles, mumps, and hepatitis: Results of a cohort study. *Journal of the American Medical Association*, *226*, 1521–1524.

Stuckless, E. R. (1980). Projections for deaf students with maternal rubella: College and other alternatives. *American Annals of the Deaf*, *125*, 985–992.

Wysowski, D. K., Flynt, J. W., Jr., Goldberg, M. F., & Connell, F. A. (1979). Rh-hemolytic disease: Epidemiologic surveillance in the United States, 1968 to 1975. *JAMA*, *242*, 1376–1379.

Young, N. A. (1976). Chickenpox, measles, and mumps. In J. S. Remington & J. O. Klein (Eds.), *Infectious diseases of the fetus and newborn*. Philadelphia: W. B. Saunders.

# 19 | John S. O'Shea

# PREVENTING ACCIDENTS IN CHILDREN

New advances are being made in the prevention of accidents involving young children. Keeping children, adolescents, and young adults away from as much harm as possible is a concern of pediatricians, families, and others involved with children's health. Over the years there has been a gradual accumulation of information about preventing accidents, and although much important information is still missing, it is encouraging to reflect on what is now fairly well established.

Some prefer not to use the word "accidents" in describing injuries, stressing that accidents occur somewhat predictably and should therefore be preventable (Pearn, 1985). In fact, a study of London mothers indicated that children under age 16 living at home with mothers who either were depressed or had a history of two or more years of poor health, shortage of money, or marital tensions had four times the number of accidents than did a control group whose mothers did not have these difficulties but who were otherwise socioeconomically similar (Brown & Davidson, 1978). Parental knowledge of and attention to childhood safety has been found to be directly correlated with their educational attainment (Haaga, 1986; Rivara & Howard, 1982), and child activity and parental perception of the need for reprimand have been shown to be directly related to the frequency of childhood injury (Langley, McGee, Silva, & Williams, 1983). Furthermore, the occurrence of injuries in young children seems to be correlated with injuries in later years (Bijur, Gold-

Portions of what is presented in this chapter are based on material in O'Shea (1986) and O'Shea, Collins, and Butler (1982).

ing, & Haslum, 1988). Behavioral characteristics also seem to be predictive (Bijur, Golding, Haslum, & Kurzon, 1988).

Whether called accidents or injuries, trauma remains the main cause of death in children over 1 year of age as well as the cause of much morbidity. Data concerning long-term morbidity are scarce, but it seems reasonable to assume that the prevalence of long-term morbidity is sizable. It includes physical and emotional suffering by children and financial strain for both the family and society. Short-term morbidity is better recorded. In Great Britain, trauma accounts for one-fifth of all hospital admissions of people 1–15 years of age and results in one-third of all hospital emergency facility visits (Jackson, 1978).

Accident or injury mortality is fairly well documented, especially compared to morbidity. Each year about 112,000 people under the age of 25 die, about 37,000 of whom die because of accidents. Some 23,000 of these 37,000 deaths are due to moving vehicles, 4,000 are caused by water mishaps, 2,000 occur in fires, 1,900 are due to poisoning, and 600 are due to falls. During the time period from 1980 to 1985, almost 10,000 children up to 14 years of age died each year from injuries. Injuries were responsible for about 44% of the deaths in children age 1–4 years, 51% age 5–9 years, and 58% age 10–14 years (National Center for Health Statistics, 1985).

Since 1920, there has been a gradual decline in the total number of deaths of people under the age of 25, as well as a decline of about 50% in the number of accidental deaths. However, little or no progress has been demonstrated in the prevention of accidental deaths since 1960, although the total number of annual traffic fatalities had fallen by 1984 to 43,500, the lowest since the 1960s (Cerelli, 1984). In general, accidental deaths in moving vehicles have remained constant since the mid-1920s. Similarly, accident mortality statistics in Sweden have declined by about 40% since the 1960s, but with very little change in moving vehicle deaths (Berfenstam, 1979). Evidence from Britain indicates a decline in vehicle deaths, probably due to occupant restraint use (Sheerman, 1984).

Most European countries now have nationwide committees on childhood accident prevention, including representatives of government, industry, insurance companies, health care providers, and consumers. In North America, various medical groups (e.g., the Physicians for Automotive Safety, the American Academy of Pediatrics, the Ambulatory Pediatric Association, State Health Departments) have also become concerned with accident prevention but are just beginning to work directly with other intimately involved groups, such as manufacturers and insurance companies. Avoiding injuries and minimizing the impact of those that do occur requires ongoing collaborative educational and legislative efforts aimed at consumers and manufacturers.

## MOVING VEHICLE ACCIDENTS

Moving vehicle accidents, the most common cause of accidental death in young people, involve primarily automobile and school bus drivers and passengers, cycle drivers and passengers, airline passengers, pedestrians, skateboard riders, lawnmower victims, and baby walker users.

### Automobile and School Bus Injuries

Most children involved in automobile accidents are passengers, not pedestrians. In the United States, passenger deaths are about 2.3 times as numerous as pedestrian.

**Age-Specific Information on Automobile Accidents**  Even though infants are generally more apt to die from nonaccidental than accidental causes, a Baltimore study noted that children in the first year of life were about twice as likely to be killed while riding in automobiles as other children (Karwacki & Baker, 1979). In this report, only 1 of 13 victims under the age of 1 was restrained, and 8 were held on the laps of adult passengers. Overall, about 40% of all infants under the age of 1 traveling in cars are carried on adult laps (Williams, 1976b). People 15–25 years of age are also at special risk for severe automobile injury. In a study of 99 patients whose average age was 16.5 years, 18 reported that they always used safety belts, 40 sometimes, and 41 never (Litt & Steinerman, 1981). Moreover, several surveys have indicated that people of all ages are not apt to be restrained adequately. Usually less than 20% are restrained in a manner found by the Consumer Union to be safe in frontal accidents at 30 miles per hour and in sideways collisions at 20 miles per hour (Consumer Union, 1982).

**Prevention of Automobile Accidents**  In addition to secure vehicle construction, restraining people within automobiles remains a promising way to decrease severe injuries. Passive restraint systems (involving automatic belting for the occupants or air bags that inflate upon impact) are not as widespread as systems requiring some degree of active participation by the occupants. Among the effective active restraints available in the United States are infant seats made to accommodate children of up to 20 pounds or 26 inches in height. Toddler seats are suitable for larger children up to about age 4, and seat belts for older children.

Infant seats are usually installed in the front seat of automobiles, with the infant facing rearwards, and secured by built-in seat belts. Some infant seats are convertible to toddler seats. These are usually positioned so that the child sits in the rear seat facing forwards restrained either by a five-point harness (both shoulders, both hips, and crotch), by a shield placed before the child, or by a combination of belts and shield. As with infant seats, toddler seats require built-in belts. Some require a special belt connecting the top of the back of the toddler seat with the rear of the vehicle, often necessitating special drilling into the automobile's metal frame. Children over the age of 4 are usually restrained by built-in belt systems that ideally should include lap and shoulder belts. Booster seats prevent young children from having the shoulder belt cross in front of their necks and also elevate them for better vision. These seats must be carefully secured by the automobile's built-in belts to prevent them from dislodging on impact. Although occupants over the age of 4 sitting in the rear seat of an automobile should be restrained by both lap and shoulder belts, most rear seats contain only lap belts.

So far, consumer education has not been shown to be particularly effective in preventing automobile accidents. In the United States, such efforts have been primarily sponsored by insurance companies and by health care providers in an attempt to persuade parents to restrain their children adequately. Since 1968, Physicians for Automotive Safety have attempted to encourage other physicians to stress automobile safety to their patients and their parents. A survey in 1976 from southern California indicated, however, that of 192 board certified pediatricians, only 3% discussed automobile safety at each visit and only 39% annually for each family in their practices (Liberman, Emmet, & Coulson, 1976). Yet, a study from Washington, D.C. (Greenberg & Coleman, 1981) found that 70% of pediatricians provided regular counseling about automobile safety. A report from St. Louis in 1977 noted that only 5% of parents recalled their physicians mentioning automobile restraints at any time in the past (Simons, 1977).

However, there are other efforts that seem promising. In 1979, the United States Department of Transportation's National Highway Traffic Safety Administration sponsored nine workshops on child automobile safety held in various areas of the country, with the cooperation of the University of North Carolina's Highway Safety Research Center and the American Academy of Pediatrics. Since 1980, the American Academy of Pediatrics and the National Safety Council have had campaigns designed to increase physician awareness of automobile safety issues. The efforts of the American Academy of Pediatrics have included the "First Ride . . . Safe Ride" and "Make It Click . . . Buckle Up" programs for which more information is available direct from the American Academy of Pediatrics, 141 Northwest Point Road, Elk Grove Village, IL 60007, (800)433-9016. Pediatricians' success with seat belt discussions with school children has been encouraging (Macknin, Gustafson, Gassman, & Barich, 1987).

Those health care providers who make actual efforts to persuade parents to restrain their children have not achieved impressive success as of 1989. It is likely that parents are not really as convinced by what they hear from health care providers as the providers suppose. Perhaps the providers have not developed the necessary expertise in educational methods or other methods of persuasion used so successfully by advertising firms (Pless, 1978). Some pediatricians have been shown, however, to be able to increase automobile restraint use by 50%–100% in their infant patients by counseling parents. Data concerning counseling parents of older children are scanty, as are studies in which follow-up has been longer than several months (Allen & Bergman, 1976; Kanthor, 1976). A study from the University of Pittsburgh and the Insurance Institute for Highway Safety indicates that only about one-fourth of infants are adequately restrained in automobiles when observed at 2–4 months of life, with little difference noted between those infants whose mothers received various attempts at education while immediately postpartum. In fact, only 28% of the 180 patients whose mothers received automobile safety literature and a free infant seat actually were adequately restrained at follow-up, compared with 21% of 174 patients whose mothers had received neither attempts at education nor a seat (Reisinger & Williams, 1978).

Attempts at decreasing childhood automobile deaths by legislation appear more promising, perhaps because they are not dependent on convincing individual parents or other people that automobile restraints are worthwhile (Williams & Lund, 1986). Discrete groups of legislators and law enforcement officers need to be persuaded not only that restraints are useful, but also that it is proper to require by law that citizens use them (Pearn, 1985).

These points are still considered controversial by some. After several years of effort, Dr. Robert S. Sanders, Chairman of the Tennessee chapter of the American Academy of Pediatrics' Accident Prevention and Poison Control Committee, led a successful effort to have his state pass a law effective in 1978 requiring that all children under the age of 4 riding in private automobiles be restrained. Although the number of restrained children under the age of 4 increased within 2 years from 12% to 31% in the cities and from 6% to 15% in rural areas, several difficulties were noted with the Tennessee legislation: First, young children were covered only when riding in private automobiles but not in vans or taxis; second, children were initially not required to be restrained if held on an adult's lap; and third, local law enforcement officers were not particularly enthusiastic about enforcing the law until given much in-service education and supplied with car seats to lend parents found to be in violation of the law. Since the law went into effect very few children under the age of 4 have been killed, the number of all children killed has progressively fallen, and children not restrained were found many times more apt to be killed than those restrained (Decker, Dewey, Hutcheson, & Schaffner, 1984).

In 1980, Rhode Island became the second state with a restraint law for children. In April of 1981, the Rhode Island law was amended first to include children under the age of 4 riding in the front or rear of any motor vehicle and second to specify that restraints meet the January 1981 crash test requirements established by the United States Department of Transportation. As of late 1988, all states had enacted child restraint legislation. In most states, a fine of approximately $15 or proof of purchase of a restraint seat within 7 days after a violation is required. Generally, however, failure to use restraints is not allowed to be considered as contributory negligence.

Another legislative approach has been the development of standards for child automobile restraint devices, a process that has taken many years. In 1966, the United States Congress authorized the Department of Transportation to set safety standards for the design of "motor vehicles and related equipment." In 1971, the Department of Transportation passed Standard No. 213 for "child seating systems." The 1971 standard did not, however, apply to infants unable to sit up without support and, furthermore, did not require that restraint systems be tested in simulated crashes, only that they be shown to withstand static forces (Shelness & Charles, 1975). Since January 1981, all child restraint systems have been required to be dynamically tested in crashes.

Car restraint legislation has fared differently outside the United States. Following the passage of legislation in Ontario in 1976 that required all healthy people over 5 years of age be restrained and that reduced speed limits, there has been a decline of about 15% in the number of deaths and injuries in automobile accidents (MacKillop, 1978).

More impressive results have come from Victoria, Australia. In 1970, a law was enacted that required all people over the age of 8 to wear seat belts, with the exception of milk and bread delivery people. This law has been extended to those under the age of 8 who are now required to wear either belts or other approved child restraints. Since the enactment of this legislation, the number of persons killed per vehicle has declined by more than 50%, from 8.1 per 10,000 vehicles in 1970 to 3.4 in 1980 (Joubert, 1981) and with good persistence of these figures through 1987.

However, there is still an obvious need (notably in the United States) for more legislative involvement in child automobile safety, including more severe penalties for drunken drivers (Margolis, Kotch, & Lacey, 1986). Federal funding has encouraged many states to raise their drinking ages to 21 years of age and to consider other approaches to discourage driving while intoxicated. Student and parent groups, such as S.A.D.D. (Students Against Driving Drunk) and M.A.D.D. (Mothers Against Drunk Driving), have also become quite active on the national level.

Attention has also focused on the design of automobiles in meeting certain safety standards. Vehicle improvements have consisted primarily of strengthening the roofs and doors, especially in United States made automobiles. The National Highway Traffic Safety Administration and the American Academy of Pediatrics have tried to encourage vehicle manufacturers to install child restraint systems (at least five-point harnesses) in all new vehicles, including taxicabs. Air bags designed to inflate upon collision continue to be studied and have reached the status of being safe for people of all ages. Their expense, as well as the fact that most require the use of a lap belt, have made them unpopular enough that they are practically unavailable for new automobiles made in the United States, although their use is supported by the American Academy of Pediatrics (1984) and other organizations concerned with automobile safety.

**School Bus Accidents**  About 150 children, mostly between the ages of 5 and 14, die annually in the United States in school bus accidents. Although many of these deaths continue to occur at railroad crossings, it seems possible that some could be prevented if seat backs in school buses were raised to decrease whiplash injuries after collision and if roof hatches were provided to allow children to escape more rapidly when buses are overturned. Other possibilities to be explored include requiring passengers to be seated and adequately restrained.

**All Terrain Vehicles**  The danger of all terrain vehicles, especially those with three wheels used by young children, has been emphasized in the late 1980s (American Academy of Pediatrics, 1987; Sneed, Stover, & Fine, 1986). Legislation and public education are both now being developed.

## Cycle Accidents

**Bicycle Accidents**  About 500 children between the ages of 5 and 14 die each year while riding bicycles, with almost all of these deaths involving collision with another vehicle (National Safety Council, 1976). This annual rate has remained fairly constant during the 1970s and early 1980s, in spite of a doubling in the rate for adults (Faigel, 1977). About 90% of all children under the age of 12 who die in bicycle accidents are considered responsible for their injury (e.g., children darting into traffic from a driveway or failing to obey a stop sign) (Williams, 1976a).

Various approaches to decrease these bicycle-related deaths have not been critically evaluated. It would seem potentially fruitful to teach children to adjust their bicycle size as they grow and to ride carefully; for example, avoiding rough riding surfaces, wearing helmets, and obeying traffic rules. Parent education should emphasize the need to teach children traffic laws and to buy bicycles that are not too large or too mechanically complicated. Most children under the age of 7 cannot manage a bicycle with wheels greater than 20 inches in diameter. Most children under the age of 10 need bicycles with wheels 24 inches or less, while children over 10 years of age can usually ride well with adult-size bicycles (26- or 27-inch wheels). "High rise" and "light weight" or "racing" bicycles place the rider's center of gravity higher than the traditional, more stable "middle weight" bicycles. "High rise" bicycles also tend to place the rider's center of gravity toward the back, whereas "lightweight" bicycles have the center of gravity more toward the front.

**Motorcycle Accidents**  About 400 adolescents die in motorcycle accidents in this country annually. Adolescents who ride motorcycles have a 2% chance of being killed or seriously injured for each year they own a motorcycle. Ninety percent of all motorcycle accidents result in injury or death, compared to 9% of all other moving vehicle accidents (Doolittle, Brown, & Boshell, 1979; Rivara, Dicker, Bergman, Dacey, & Herman, 1988). Helmets seem to be helpful in reducing head injuries without increasing the risk of neck injuries or decreasing vision or hearing appreciably. After head injury, the next most common severe injury is to the lower legs, with motorcycle accidents frequently found to be the most common cause of hospitalization for lower leg trauma (Balcerak, Pancione, & States, 1978).

The most important approach to preventing motorcycle accidents appears to be legislation. Perhaps these morbidity figures should encourage extensive review of the overall acceptability of motorcycle use. At the least, helmets with face protection are imperative. This is demonstrated by the experience in the United States after helmets were no longer legally required (Losee & Sturner, 1978; McSwain & Petrucelli, 1984; Russo, 1978). Legislation requiring helmets for motorcyclists has begun to be reintroduced in some states, but this has not met with as much success as the legislation raising the drinking age to 21.

## Airplane Injuries

Although very few children die or are severely injured in airplanes, attention has focused on child restraints as well as on improving impact resistance of airplane seats themselves. Recent anecdotal reports seem to indicate that the improvement in airplane crash survival is possible with these two approaches.

## Pedestrian Injuries

As noted earlier, annually about 1,500 young people die as pedestrians in the United States. Pedestrian education programs have not been sufficiently developed or evaluated, and other approaches to this problem, such as walkways separated from roads by barriers or the prohibition of pedestrian traffic in poorly lighted areas at night are often quite complicated. Much additional effort should be directed to develop educational and physical methods to decrease this large number of deaths and the even larger number of injuries.

## Skateboard Accidents

Although not usually fatal, there are about 100,000 injuries annually to children using skateboards that require hospital emergency facility visits in the United States. About one-third of the injuries are fractures of the forearm or lower leg, another third involve contusions or abrasions, and the rest are mostly head and abdominal injuries. The most promising way to avoid at least some of these injuries would appear to be to require that all skateboarding be done on clear, smooth surfaces not accessible to motor vehicles or other pedestrians (American Academy of Pediatrics, 1979; Jacobs & Keller, 1977).

## Lawnmower Accidents

Like skateboard injuries, lawnmower accidents are rarely fatal. They are usually due to contact with blades or from thrown objects and frequently result in toe or finger amputations. Many of these accidents appear preventable if grasscatchers are always used, if the areas to be mowed are cleaned beforehand of debris, and if hand controls are mounted on mowers to allow them to be turned off quickly. Another possibility might be keeping the blades sharp so that a machine's speed could be kept as low as possible (Letts & Mardirosian, 1977).

## Baby Walker Injuries

As many as 42% of all accidental head injuries in children under 1 year are due to the use of a walker (Stoffman, Bass, & Fox, 1984). The lack of demonstrated efficacy of walkers as aids to development would seem to make their risk difficult to justify. Furthermore, they do not succeed as substitute play pens.

## WATER MISHAPS

The importance of water mishaps is stressed by the fact that more boys between the ages of 5 and 14 die from drowning than from any other accidental cause. Especially in older children, some drownings are due to voluntary hyperventilation that many swimmers perform before submerging to allow them to hold their breaths longer under water. Hyperventilation appears to allow swimming for longer periods primarily by decreasing carbon dioxide tension, which in turn decreases cerebral blood flow, making swimmers less conscious of evolving hypoxia. An occasional swimmer will dull his or her consciousness so much by hyperventilation that drowning ensues. Since the 1970s, hyperventilation before swimming has been discouraged by the United States National Collegiate Athletic Association and various other groups that monitor swimming contests. It is presently discouraged by increasing numbers of swimming coaches, and in fact there are now many fewer deaths during swimming contests.

However, as might be expected, most drownings or near drownings occur not among children in swimming contests, but among poorly supervised children who cannot swim (O'Carroll, Elkon, & Weiss, 1988). More than 95% of all reported drownings or near drownings occur in swimming pools, swimming holes, bathtubs, or at beaches when the children were not being closely observed. Infant water instruction can make adult supervisors over confident, and forced submersion can lead to water intoxication (Pearn, 1985). Although fencing in swimming pools, providing trained lifeguards at public swimming areas, and teaching children to swim early in life all sound promising, there is much more to learn about preventing drownings or near drownings.

A report from Honolulu concerns seven children drowned in bathtubs. The oldest child was a boy 2 years 4 months old who appeared to have been a victim of child abuse, but the other six children were quite similar to each other and apparently were not victims of child abuse. Each of these six had been left in a bathtub under the supervision of a sibling less than 4 years of age (Pearn, Brown, Wong, & Bart, 1979). One 10-month-old drowned and two other 10-month-olds nearly drowned in buckets of water in their homes (Scott & Eigen, 1980). Bathtub electrocutions from hair dryers, especially involving young children under age 5, have also become a menace (Budnick, 1984a).

## THERMAL INJURIES

Scalds are the most common cause of thermal injuries, accounting for about 40% of all burned children who receive medical attention and for 75% of all burned children under the age of 4. About three-fourths of all scalds occur in kitchens, usually from water heated on stoves. Most other scalds occur in bathtubs. As in the prevention of many accidents, close supervision of children is important.

One method to prevent scalds is to lower thermostats on hot water heaters. Based on adult data, it would appear that keeping hot water heaters at less than 125° F (51° C) prevents some accidental scalds (Feldman, Schaller, Feldman, & McMillion, 1980). It is not known, however, whether young people's skin differs in susceptibility to thermal injuries compared to adults'. Electric hot water heaters, moreover, are quite difficult to adjust, and decreasing hot water heater thermostat settings obviously has no effect on the incidence of scalds from liquids being heated on kitchen stoves or inflicted in child abuse. Furthermore, even though bathing and laundering can be adequately accomplished at 125° F, dishwashers require higher temperatures to avoid glassware spotting.

Another approach to preventing heat-related injuries is the development of flame resistant sleepwear. Even though scalds are the most common heat-related injury found in children, fire is apt to result in severe burns, especially when clothing is ignited by open flames. Although considered potentially carcinogenic, tris (2,3 dibromopropyl) phosphate appears quite effective in making sleepwear flame resistant. Severely burned children treated at the Shriner's Burn Institute in Boston have less frequently been victims of sleepwear burns since the United States Department of Commerce required the use of flame-resistant coating in 1973. About half of all burned children referred to the Institute have flame burns, with about 25% involving sleepwear before 1973 and less then 10% since then (McLaughlin, Clarke, Stahly, & Crawford, 1977).

Another preventive measure is the use of fire and smoke detectors. Three types of fire and smoke detectors are available in the United States: heat detectors, photoelectric smoke detectors, and ionization smoke detectors. Usually set to sound an alarm when ambient temperature rises above 135° F (57° C), heat detectors require no electric power. They are especially effective in monitoring furnaces and garages. Photoelectric detectors used to require alternating current, but are now available with battery power. They are especially effective in detecting smoldering fires, because they are relatively insensitive to small particles emitted during cooking. Ionization smoke detectors account for most sales of fire and smoke detectors in the United States. They require only battery power, but frequently produce false alarms, especially when they are installed near places where cooking is done or where warm pieces of equipment are kept. Detectors of any type should be placed near the ceiling, where heat and smoke are found in greater quantities and should be installed on each level of a house (Reisinger, 1982). It has been demonstrated that it is feasible to provide detectors free of charge in neighborhoods having a relatively high risk of fire (Gorman, Charney, Holtzman, & Roberts, 1985; Shaw, McCormick, Kustra, Ruddy, & Casey, 1988).

## POISONING

Another type of childhood accident that seems most readily avoided by close supervision is poisoning. Most accidental poisoning occurs in the late afternoon and early evening, when children are frequently less well supervised than at other times, and parents or guardians are apt to be tired and preoccupied with discussing the events of the day and preparing meals. Although not yet subjected to careful scrutiny, it would seem that various attempts to increase parental vigilance might be helpful in preventing accidental poisoning.

Two approaches have been developed to complement observation in the prevention of poisoning. The first of these is the child resistant packaging of drugs, required for most drugs in the United States since 1972 and in Great Britain since 1976. There has been a 63% decrease in hospital admissions for accidental salicylate poisoning reported in England, and a similar reduction in the United States, following the introduction of such packaging (Sibert, Craft, & Jackson, 1977). The second advance is the development of child resistant locks for cabinets, in accordance with regulations established by the Food and Drug Administration of the United States Department of Health and Human Services. Several of these locks have been evaluated (Godwin, 1978). Developing such locks for kitchen and medicine cabinets appears especially promising, with childhood poisoning occurring about as frequently in the kitchen as in the bathroom. The major ongoing challenge in developing child-resistant closing devices is consumer acceptance. Locks must be easy enough for adults to open so that they are not tempted to leave them unlocked.

When accidental poisoning occurs, prompt information can expedite treatment and is often reassuring to the parent. Since the 1960s, a variety of poison information centers have been established in the United States and around the world. These centers usually provide trained pharmacists or nurses to answer all telephone inquiries, supported by a collection of references. Often they are staffed by local internists, pediatricians, veterinarians, botanists, and sometimes by regional toxicology specialists. It is essential that poison centers provide enough public and medical awareness activities to ensure that the center is promptly notified of a poisoning episode, especially as most inquiries require nothing more than reassurance and syrup of ipecac (if indicated), both of which should be offered as quickly as possible. The advisability of having a supply of syrup of ipecac in homes with young children needs to be more effectively emphasized. Assessments of public and medical knowledge of strategies in poison prevention and acute management should be conducted periodically, and morbidity and mortality statistics monitored to assess the efficacy of a particular poison center.

## FALLS

It appears that a large proportion of severe falls suffered by children between 5 and 10 years of age in the United States occur on playgrounds. Swings account for 43% of playground injuries, various types of climbing apparatus account for about 27%, and sliding boards account for about 15%. The Franklin Institute Research Laboratories in Philadelphia have studied the ability of various types of ground surfaces to cushion falls. Concrete or asphalt, most commonly used in surfacing playgrounds, provide inadequate cushioning. Sand of 10 or more inches in depth absorbs impacts from a height of up to 10 feet, the height of many playground sliding boards (Reichelderfer, Overbach, & Greensher, 1979).

Other injuries include falls from trampolines. Trampoline injuries can be severe, even resulting in quadriplegia, but their incidence remains unclear (American Academy of Pediatrics, 1981; Torg & Das, 1984).

Although playground falls and trampoline injuries are frequently severe, it is reassuring to note that most falls of children from their beds are not, as indicated in a study from Detroit. None of the 246 children brought to medical attention after reportedly falling from their beds was seriously injured, although three had linear skull fractures without neurologic signs (Helfer, Slovis, & Black, 1977).

## OTHER ACCIDENTS

Toys frequently injure children, especially by inflicting eye trauma, being aspirated (Southard & Arena, 1976), or causing falls or fires (Centers for Disease Control, 1984). Even hair can be dangerous, occasionally causing strangulation if caught in machinery (Kindley & Todd, 1978). Adverse responses to drugs (whether prescribed or not) are not uncommon, as observed in children premedicated for computed tomographic scans (Mitchell et al., 1982). Electrical (Thompson & Ashwal, 1983), fireworks (McFarland, Harris, Kobayashi, & Dicker, 1984), and toothpick (Budnick, 1984b) injuries are relatively rarely encountered in children, but farm injuries (American Academy of Pediatrics, 1988; Cogbill, Busch, & Stiers, 1985; Rivara et al., 1988) and firearm mishaps (Keck, Istre, Coury, Jordan, & Eaton, 1988; Ordog et al, 1988) are now receiving increasing attention. Most of these hazards are best avoided by supervision and product improvements, but firearms should probably be totally excluded from children's environments.

## CONCLUSION

Accidents remain the most common cause of death in young children over 1 year of age, with no changes in overall statistics noted since the 1960s. Automobile accidents are the most frequent cause of serious injury in young people, especially infants under the age of 1 and people 15–24 years old. Many of these accidents result in developmental disabilities with their accompanying disappointment and decreased potential. To date, the most successful approaches to accident prevention have tended to be legislation, with much future work needed.

## REFERENCES

Allen, D. B., & Bergman, A. G. (1976). Social learning approaches to health education: Utilization of infant auto restraint devices. *Pediatrics, 58*, 323–328.

American Academy of Pediatrics. (1979). Skateboard policy statement. *Pediatrics, 63*, 924–925.

American Academy of Pediatrics. (1981). Trampolines II. *Pediatrics, 67*, 438.

American Academy of Pediatrics. (1984). Automatic passenger protection systems. *Pediatrics, 74*, 146–147.

American Academy of Pediatrics. (1987). All-terrain vehicles: Two, three, and four-wheeled unlicensed motorized vehicles. *Pediatrics, 79*, 306–308.

American Academy of Pediatrics. (1988). Rural injuries. *Pediatrics, 81*, 902–903.

Balcerak, J. C., Pancione, K. L., & States, J. D. (1978). Moped, mini-bike, and motorcycle accidents: Associated injury problems. *New York State Journal of Medicine, 78*, 628–633.

Berfenstam, R. (1979). Prevention of childhood accidents in Sweden: With special attention to the work of The Joint Committee for Prevention of Accidents. *Acta Paediatrica Scandinavica, 275* (Suppl.), 88–95.

Bijur, P. E., Golding, J., & Haslum, M. (1988). Persistence of occurrence of injury: Can injuries of preschool children predict injuries of school-aged children? *Pediatrics, 82*, 707–717.

Bijur, P. E., Golding, J., Haslum, M., & Kurzon, M. (1988). Behavioral predictions of injury in school-age children. *American Journal of Diseases of Children, 142*, 1,307–1,312.

Brown, G. W., & Davidson, S. (1978). Social class, psychiatric disorder of mother, and accidents to children. *Lancet, i*, 378–381.

Budnick, L. D. (1984a). Bathtub-related electrocutions in the United States, 1979 to 1982. *Journal of the American Medical Association, 252*, 918–920.

Budnick, L. D. (1984b). Toothpick-related injuries in the United States, 1979 through 1982. *Journal of the American Medical Association, 252*, 796–797.

Centers for Disease Control. (1984). Toy safety: United States, 1983. *Morbidity and Mortality Weekly Report, 33*, 697–698.

Cerelli, E. C. (1984). Preliminary report, 1984 traffic fatalities. *Research Notes.* Washington DC: National Center for Statistics and Analysis.

Cogbill, T. H., Busch, H. M., Jr., & Stiers, G. R. (1985). Farm accidents in children. *Pediatrics, 76*, 562–566.

Consumer Union. (1982, March). Child safety seats. *Consumer Reports, 3*, 171–175.

Decker, M. D., Dewey, M. J., Hutcheson, R. H., Jr., & Schaffner, W. (1984). The use and efficacy of child restraint devices: The Tennessee experience, 1982 and 1983. *Journal of the American Medical Association, 252*, 2571–2575.

Doolittle, R. P., Brown, R. T., & Boshell, A. (1979). Adolescents and motorcycle safety: The case for health advocacy. *Pediatrics, 64*, 963–965.

Faigel, H. C. (1977). Bicycles and safety, revisited. *Clinical Pediatrics, 16*, 597–598.

Feldman, K. W., Schaller, R. T., Feldman, J. A., & McMillion, M. (1980). Tap water scald burns in children. *Pediatrics, 62*, 1–7.

Godwin, R. H. (1978). Child-resistant locks in poison control. *Pediatrics, 61*, 750–752.

Gorman, R. L., Charney, E., Holtzman, N. A., & Roberts, K. B. (1985). A successful city-wide smoke detector giveaway program. *Pediatrics, 75*, 14–18.

Greenberg, L. W., & Coleman, A. B. (1981). Seat belt use and automobile safety counseling by pediatricians. *Southern Medical Journal, 74*, 1172–1174.

Haaga, J. (1986). Children's seat belt usage: Evidence from the National Health Interview Survey. *American Journal of Public Health, 76*, 1425–1427.

Helfer, R. E., Slovis, T. L., & Black, M. (1977). Injuries resulting when small children fall out of bed. *Pediatrics, 60*, 533–535.

Jackson, R. H. (1978). Hazards to children in traffic: A pediatrician's look at road accidents. *Archives of Disease in Childhood, 53*, 807–813.

Jacobs, R. A., & Keller, E. L. (1977). Skateboard accidents. *Pediatrics, 59*, 939–942.

Joubert, P. N. (1981). Development and effects of seat belt laws in Australia. In R. N. Green & E. Petrucelli (Eds.), *Proceedings of the International Symposium on Occupant Restraint* (pp. 111–118). Morton Grove, IL: American Association for Automotive Medicine.

Kanthor, H. A. (1976). Car safety for infants: Effectiveness of prenatal counseling. *Pediatrics, 58*, 320–322.

Karwacki, J. J., Jr., & Baker, S. P. (1979). Children in motor vehicles: Never too young to die. *Journal of the American Medical Association, 242*, 2848–2851.

Keck, N. J., Istre, G. R., Coury, D. L., Jordan, F., & Eaton, A. P. (1988). Characteristics of fatal gunshot wounds in the home in Oklahoma, 1982–1983. *American Journal of Diseases of Children, 142*, 623–626.

Kindley, A. D., & Todd, R. M. (1978). Accidental strangulation by mother's hair. *Lancet, i*, 565.

Langley, J., McGee, R., Silva, P., & Williams, S. (1983). Child behavior and accidents. *Journal of Pediatric Psychology, 8*, 181–189.

Letts, R. M., & Mardirosian, A. (1977). Lawnmower injuries in children. *Canadian Medical Association Journal, 116*, 1151–1153.

Liberman, H. M., Emmet, W. L., II, & Coulson, A. H. (1976). Pediatric automobile restraints, pediatricians, and the Academy. *Pediatrics, 58*, 316–319.

Litt, I. F., & Steinerman, P. R. (1981). Compliance with automobile safety devices among adolescents. *Journal of Pediatrics, 99*, 484–486.

Losee, J. M., & Sturner, W. Q. (1978). A survey of Rhode Island motorcycle fatalities during 1975 and 1976. *Rhode Island Medical Journal, 61*, 333–340.

MacKillop, H. I. (1978). Effects of seat belt legislation and reduction of highway speed limits in Ontario. *Canadian Medical Association Journal, 119*, 1154–1158.

Macknin, M. L., Gustafson, C., Gassman, J., & Barich, D. (1987). Office education by pediatricians to increase seat-belt use. *American Journal of Diseases of Children, 141*, 1305–1307.

Margolis, L. H., Kotch, J., & Lacey, J. H. (1986). Children in alcohol-related motor vehicle crashes. *Pediatrics, 77*, 870–875.

McFarland, L. V., Harris, J. R., Kobayashi, J. M., & Dicker, R. C. (1984). Risk factors for fireworks related injury in Washington State. *Journal of the American Medical Association, 251*, 3251–3254.

McLaughlin, E., Clarke, N., Stahly, K., & Crawford, J. D. (1977). One pediatric burn unit's experience with sleepwear-related injuries. *Pediatrics, 60*, 405–409.

McSwain, N. E., Jr., & Petrucelli, E. (1984). Medical consequences of motorcycle helmet nonusage. *Journal of Trauma, 24*, 233–236.

Mitchell, A. A., Louik, C., Lacouture, P., Slone, D., Goldman, P., & Shapiro, S. (1982). Risks to children from computed tomographic scans. *Journal of the American Medical Association, 247*, 2358–2388.

National Center for Health Statistics, Public Health Service. (1985). *U.S. Department of Health and Human Services final mortality statistics*. Washington, DC: Author.

National Safety Council. (1976). *Accident facts*. Chicago: Author.

O'Carroll, P. W., Elkon, F., & Weiss, B. (1988). Drowning mortality in Los Angeles County, 1976–1984. *Journal of the American Medical Association, 260*, 380–383.

Ordog, J. G., Wasserberger, J., Schatz, I., Owens-Collins, D., English, K., Balasubramanian, S., & Schlater, T. (1988). Gunshot wounds in children under 10 years of age. *American Journal of Diseases of Children, 142*, 618–622.

O'Shea, J. S. (1986). Childhood accident prevention strategies. *Forensic Science International, 30*, 99–111.

O'Shea, J. S., Collins, E. W., & Butler, C. B. (1982). Pediatric accident convention. *Clinical Pediatrics, 2*, 290–297.

Pearn, J. H. (1985). Current controversies in child accident prevention. *Australia and New Zealand Journal of Medicine, 15*, 782–786.

Pearn, J. H., Brown, J., III, Wong, R., & Bart, R. (1979). Bathtub drownings: Report of seven cases. *Pediatrics, 64*, 68–70.

Pless, I. B. (1978). Accident prevention and health education: Back to the drawing board? *Pediatrics*, *62*, 431–435.

Reichelderfer, T. E., Overbach, A., & Greensher, J. (1979). Unsafe playgrounds. *Pediatrics*, *64*, 962–963.

Reisinger, K. S. (1982). Preventing deaths due to fire. *Preventing childhood injuries*. Columbus, OH: Ross Laboratories.

Reisinger, K. S., & Williams, A. F. (1978). Evaluation of programs designed to increase the protection of infants in cars. *Pediatrics*, *62*, 280–287.

Rivara, F. P., Dicker, B. G., Bergman, A. B., Dacey, R., & Herman, C. (1988). The public cost of motorcycle trauma. *Journal of the American Medical Association*, *260*, 221–223.

Rivara, F. P., & Howard, D. (1982). Parental knowledge of child development and injury risks. *Developmental and Behavioral Pediatrics*, *2*, 103–105.

Russo, P. K. (1978). Easy rider—hard facts: Motorcycle helmet laws. *New England Journal of Medicine*, *299*, 1074–1076.

Scott, P. H., & Eigen, H. (1980). Immersion accidents involving pails of water in the home. *Journal of Pediatrics*, *96*, 282–283.

Shaw, K. N., McCormick, M. C., Kustra, S. L., Ruddy, P. M., & Casey, R. D. (1988). Correlates of smoke detector usage in an innercity population: Participants in a smoke detector give away program. *American Journal of Public Health*, *78*, 650–653.

Sheerman, B. (1984). *Seat belt use laws: The British experience*. Washington, DC: Highway Users Federation and Automobile Safety Foundation.

Shelness, A., & Charles, S. (1975). Children as passengers in automobiles: The neglected minority on the nation's highways. *Pediatrics*, *56*, 271–284.

Sibert, J. R., Craft, A. W., & Jackson, R. H. (1977). Child-resistant packaging and accidental child poisoning. *Lancet*, *ii*, 289–290.

Simons, P. S. (1977). Failure of pediatricians to provide automobile restraint information to parents. *Pediatrics*, *60*, 646–648.

Sneed, R. C., Stover, S. L., & Fine, P. R. (1986). Spinal cord injury associated with all-terrain vehicle accidents. *Pediatrics*, *77*, 271–274.

Southard, S. C., & Arena, J. M. (1976). A comprehensive protocol for evaluating the safety of toys for preschool children. *Clinical Pediatrics*, *15*, 1107–1109.

Stoffman, J. M., Bass, M. J., & Fox, A. M. (1984). Head injuries related to the use of baby walkers. *Canadian Medical Association Journal*, *131*, 573–575.

Thompson, J. C., & Ashwal, S. (1983). Electrical injuries in children. *American Journal of Diseases of Children*, *137*, 231–235.

Torg, J. S., & Das, M. (1984). Trampoline related quadriplegia. *Pediatrics*, *74*, 804–812.

Williams, A. F. (1976a). Factors in the initiation of bicycle-motor vehicle collisions. *American Journal of Diseases of Children*, *130*, 370–377.

Williams, A. F. (1976b). Observed child restraint use in automobiles. *American Journal of Diseases of Children*, *130*, 1311–1317.

Williams, A., F., & Lund, A. K. (1986). Seat belt use laws and occupant crash protection in the United States. *American Journal of Public Health*, *76*, 1438–1442.

# 20
## Karen E. Senft
## Siegfried M. Pueschel

# LEAD POISONING IN CHILDHOOD

Although lead has been known to have an adverse influence on human physiologic function for many centuries (Felton, 1965), only since the late 1960s has lead poisoning in childhood been recognized as a serious public health problem (Lin-Fu, 1970; Needleman, 1988).

In many other countries legislation concerning lead poisoning has been enacted since the early part of this century, and childhood lead poisoning, as it is known in the United States, is practically nonexistent (Pueschel & Fadden, 1975). Not until 1969 were bills introduced in the United States Congress to provide federal assistance to local governments for projects involving the detection and treatment of lead poisoning in childhood. After lengthy public hearings and discussions in various committees, the Lead-Based Paint Poisoning Prevention Act was passed by the legislative branch of government and was signed into law by the president in January 1971. Unfortunately, programs authorized by this act never gained momentum because of the apparent indifference of the Nixon administration to childhood lead poisoning and the limited federal appropriations made available.

In the 1970s, many active citizen groups became involved in the movement to eradicate lead poisoning. Subsequently, many state and local communities initiated lead poisoning prevention programs that dealt not only with identification of children with an increased lead burden but also with ecological factors, since most children with lead poisoning were found in run-down urban neighborhoods where peeling and broken plaster prevailed. In the 1990s, a major concern is low level lead exposure that mandates that all preschool children undergo annual lead screening.

## PREVALENCE OF LEAD POISONING

In the mid-1970s, it was estimated that half a million children in the United States had ingested lead-containing materials (Pueschel & Fadden, 1975). Although the majority of these children did not exhibit overt symptoms of lead intoxication, the increased lead burden constituted an imminent threat to their general health and, in particular, to their intellectual functioning.

Mahaffey, Annest, Roberts, and Murphy (1982) reported on national estimates of blood levels in the United States from 1976 to 1980. These authors found that among children age 6 months to 5 years, the prevalence of elevated blood lead levels was significantly higher (4%) than previously predicted on the basis of fewer data. They noted a higher prevalence of elevated lead levels in black children (12.2%) than in white children (2.0%). A higher mean blood lead level was also found in young children living in central cities (20.0 ug/dl) than in rural areas (13.9 ug/dl), and in children from low-income families (20.0 ug/dl) than in children from families with moderate (16.2 ug/dl) and higher incomes (14.1 ug/dl).

## ABSORPTION OF LEAD

Lead is a heavy metal that has no known useful function in the human body (Lin-Fu, 1972). Lead may enter the human body by different routes. It can be absorbed through the skin following the application of powders and creams containing lead, common in old-fashioned home remedies. Lead can also be absorbed through the respiratory tract. Goldsmith and Hextra (1967) summarized studies reported by the United States Public Health Service Survey of lead in the atmosphere of three urban communities. These authors reported that the average quantity absorbed through the respiratory tract may be of similar magnitude to that absorbed through the alimentary tract. Thus, for many urban residents, respiratory exposure to lead can result in increased storage of lead in the body. In this context, a report by Annest et al. (1983) that analyzed the chronological trend of data from the Second National Health and Nutrition Examination Survey indicated that the average blood lead levels in the United States decreased about 37% from February 1976 through February 1980. The authors feel that this is most likely due to the increased use of lead-free gasoline during this time period, since there is a high correlation of blood lead levels with the lead content in gasoline. Nevertheless, lead originating from automobile exhausts still appears to be an important source of the lead burden in children.

An important route of lead absorption in childhood is via the gastrointestinal tract. It is of note that more than 90% of lead that is ingested by the oral route is excreted in the feces and only less than 10% of ingested lead is absorbed into the bloodstream. In childhood lead poisoning, repeated ingestion of small amounts of lead over weeks or months results in an increased body burden of lead. Most of this lead is stored in the skeletal system. Although generally regarded as inert, stored lead may be mobilized during periods of severe body stress. Whereas the stored lead in the skeletal system does not have any known toxic effects, lead in soft tissues, in particular within the central nervous system, is responsible for the observed toxicity of lead.

## SOURCES OF LEAD

As mentioned, lead can be absorbed through the skin, inhaled through the respiratory tract, and ingested via the oral route. The following discussion focuses primarily on the oral intake of lead-containing materials and the absorption of lead through the gastrointestinal tract.

There have been sporadic reports in the literature of increased lead body burden in young children from chewing on lead pencils, newspapers, magazines, and toothpaste containers, from imported toys with lead-containing paint, and from eating out of inadequately glazed earthenware and pottery. Additional sources of lead poisoning are lead-containing water that is obtained through old lead pipes, burning of old lead battery casings, and lead brought home on clothes by workers employed in lead smelters. Whereas lead poisoning from these sources occurred more frequently in the past, it is rarely observed now.

Most often, lead poisoning in childhood is due to habitual eating of lead from peeling paint and broken plaster that is found in run-down urban neighborhoods. The majority of children with lead poisoning are 1–6 years of age and are living in areas where old buildings still have lead-containing paint. Lead poisoning is also associated with pica (i.e., the eating of nonfood substances by children beyond the physiologic oral stage of early childhood). These children often lack adequate supervision and their parents are rarely aware of the harmful effects of ingesting lead-containing materials. Although lead poisoning has traditionally been felt to be a disease of poverty, primarily occurring in inner-city slums, there are also reports of increased lead burden in children living in rural and suburban areas.

An increasingly recognized danger is that of inappropriate removal of lead-based paint from interior walls and exterior siding of older houses. Torches and sanding machines are particularly dangerous because they can produce a lead fume. In addition, sanding does not only distribute lead as fine dust throughout the house but also creates small particles that are more readily absorbed than paint chips. Also, sandblasting causes large amounts of lead laden dust and debris that, if improperly disposed, may increase the hazard of lead poisoning.

Other sources of low intermediate dose lead poisoning include dust and soil in children's play areas. Dust and soil are primarily contaminated by automobile exhaust and by the deterioration of lead paint from the exterior of old houses. Additionally, soil near lead smelters has been found to contain high concentrations of lead.

One study, carried out in Denmark with focus on traffic as a source of lead exposure in childhood, evaluated the association of individual traffic exposure with individual lead absorption, (Lyngbye, Hansen, Grandjean, Trillingsgaard, & Beese, 1988). The authors found an association between high lead levels and high traffic density in children between the age of 6 months and 2 years. This relationship was of a dose responsive nature. The association was not accounted for by other possible major sources of lead.

## DEFINITIONS OF LEAD TOXICITY

The Centers for Disease Control (1983) determined that lead poisoning exists whenever a child has any one or more of the following:

1. Two successive blood lead levels ≥ 70 ug/dl, with or without symptoms
2. An erythrocyte protoporphyrin level ≥ 250 ug/dl of whole blood and a confirmed elevated blood level ≥ 50 ug/dl, with or without symptoms
3. Erythrocyte protoporphyrin level ≥ 109 ug/dl associated with a confirmed elevated blood lead level (≥ 30 ug/dl) with compatible symptoms
4. Confirmed blood lead levels ≥ 49 ug/dl with compatible symptoms
5. Confirmed blood lead levels ≥ 49 ug/dl with compatible symptoms and evidence of toxicity (e.g., abnormal erythrocyte protoporphyrin levels, edathamil calcium disodium mobilization test, urinary aminolevulinic acid excretion or urinary coproporphyrin excretion)

Although blood lead levels as high as 30 ug/dl were once considered acceptable, new research indicates that there may be no clearly safe level of lead (Marshall, 1984). Neuropsychological dysfunction and biochemical abnormalities have been found in children with blood lead levels below 30 ug/dl. Even at blood lead levels below 10 ug/dl inhibition of delta-aminolevulinic acid dehydrase occurs. Also, ferrochelatase is inhibited in children at blood lead concentration of about 15 ug/dl. Therefore, an expert advisory committee to the Centers for Disease Control has determined that blood lead levels of ≥ 25 ug/dl indicate excessive lead absorption in children and should necessitate intervention.

Shucard, Shucard, Patterson, and Guthrie (1988) reported that the Centers for Disease Control set a blood level of 25 ug/dl as the highest acceptable level for children. The authors also mentioned that research findings have provided evidence that detrimental effects on development can occur when lead levels are below this acceptable value. In addition, it has been found that there is a relationship between prenatal exposure to lead and delayed cognitive development. Because the developing fetus is vulnerable to central nervous system insults, it is of critical importance to further investigate the developmental effects of prenatal exposure to lead.

Careful epidemiologic studies that have controlled for important confounders have set the effect level at 10–15 ug/dl (Needleman, 1988). Animal studies have confirmed these findings. Moreover, biochemical and functional changes have been demonstrated in the heme biosynthetic pathway and in the renal, cardiovascular, endocrine, immune, and central nervous systems.

## INCREASED BODY BURDEN OF LEAD

Controversy exists over the long-term effects of lead at levels considered to be compatible with an increased body burden of lead. During the 1970s and 1980s, many studies were undertaken to address this issue.

Pueschel, Kopito, and Schwachman (1972) reported on a house to house survey of an impoverished section of Boston. They examined preschool children in regard to lead poisoning employing a simple and inexpensive screening procedure based on the analysis of lead in hair. Ninety-eight of 705 children were found to have an increased lead burden. Chelation therapy was administered and elimination of the source of lead poisoning in the environment was initiated. Fifty-eight children with an increased lead burden underwent comprehensive studies, and 1 1/2 years later this population was reexamined. The authors found minor neurologic dysfunction and various forms of motor impairment in 22% in the initial examination and in 27% of the children during the follow-up study. Initial psychological assessment revealed low-average mental abilities in the majority of children, while a significant increase in certain areas of intellectual function was noted in the follow-up study (Pueschel, 1974; Pueschel et al., 1972).

In 1972, Kotok studied children with elevated blood lead levels and a control group of children matched for age, sex, race, environment, neonatal condition, and presence of pica. Deficiencies were found in fine motor, adaptive, and language functions, but these differences were thought to be related to environmental conditions and not solely to lead toxicity (Kotok, 1972).

At about the same time, de la Burde and Choate (1972) evaluated 70 children who had been exposed to lead but who had remained asymptomatic. These children were compared to 72 matched control children with no lead exposure. Sixty-five of the control children as compared to 35 of the lead exposed children performed developmentally in the normal range. Deficits in the lead exposed group occurred most frequently in fine motor function and adaptive behavior. Three years later, de la Burde and Choate (1975) retested the children and compared their performance on a series of psychological tests to 70 matched control children. The lead exposed children had deficits in global IQ, in visual and fine motor coordination, as well as adaptive behavior.

Baloh, Sturm, Green, and Gleser (1975) examined 27 asymptomatic children with chronic increased lead absorption and 27 matched controls. The authors observed a significantly higher prevalence of hyperactive behavior in the subjects with increased lead levels but no significant differences in any of the other tests measuring intellectual performance when compared with the control group. The investigators felt that uncontrolled variables, especially lead absorption in infancy and other adverse environmental factors, left unanswered questions concerning the relationship between chronic lead exposure and behavior and intelligence.

Lansdown et al. (1974) studied 275 school children in England and correlated blood lead levels with their intellectual functioning, reading attainment, and behavior. There was no difference between children with high and those with low blood lead levels in various areas of functioning.

Landrigan et al. (1975) identified 46 children with moderately elevated blood lead levels of 40–80 ug/dl in Texas. A control group of 78 children without elevated blood lead levels was matched for age, sex, socioeconomic status, language spoken at home, and length of time residing in the geographic area. Age-adjusted intellectual functioning on the Wechsler performance test and the results of the fingertapping test proved to be significantly decreased in the group of children with high blood lead levels. Yet, Wechsler Full Scale and Verbal IQs and activity ratings were similar between the two groups.

Needleman et al. (1979) published findings of detailed testing of children with increased dentine lead. Children in specified school districts submitted their shed primary teeth to the investigators; 58 children with high dentine lead levels and 100 children with low dentine lead levels were found. The children with high dentine lead levels scored significantly lower on the Wechsler Intelligence Scale for Children—Revised (WISC—R) than those with low dentine lead levels. There were significant differences on verbal subtests, measures of auditory and speech processing, and measures of attention. An analysis of variance revealed that none of the differences could be explained by any of the other 39 variables studied. Data obtained from the teachers questionnaire indicated that the frequency of nonadaptive classroom behavior increased in a dose-related fashion with higher dentine lead levels. The investigators concluded that lead exposure at doses too low to cause clinical symptoms appear to be associated with neuropsychological deficits and to interfere with school performance.

Ernhart, Landa, and Schell (1981) reported their findings of follow-up testing of children studied 5 years previously. Blood lead levels were determined in 34 of 53 preschool children, and in addition, dentine lead levels were obtained. Using the McCarthy Scales of Children's Abilities (McCarthy, 1972) to assess intellectual functioning, the authors found impairment of those subjects with high lead levels. However, when they controlled for parental IQ, the deficits associated with lead exposure decreased. The authors concluded that the few statistically significant findings remaining could be attributed to methodological difficulties inherent in the research, and if there are behavioral and intellectual sequelae due to the lead burden independent of other variables, these effects are minimal.

In another study, Ernhart, Morrow-Tlucak, and Wolf (1988) reported low level lead exposure and intelligence in preschool years. These authors measured blood lead levels at 6 months, 2 years, and 3 years. They administered the Mental Scale of the Bayley Scales of Infant Development at 6 months, 1 year, and 2 years and the Stanford-Binet Intelligence Scale at 3 years. At 6 months the blood level was not related significantly to any of the five assessments with or without control of confounding variables. However, the remaining three analyses were significant in the initial analyses, but the effect was completely attenuated with statistical control of confounding variables. Thus, the authors found that the results suggested that the obtained correlations between lead exposure and preschool intelligence depended on the caregiving requirement.

From a review of the above cited studies, it appears that the long-term effects of increased body burden of lead, too low to cause significant clinical symptoms, are far from clear. Until further well-planned and controlled research is done, one should consider such exposure to be at least potentially damaging.

## LEAD ENCEPHALOPATHY

Early symptoms of lead encephalopathy are most often nonspecific and difficult to interpret. Children may be anorexic and may exhibit irritability, drowsiness, apathy, decreased interest in play activities, and may complain of abdominal pain. If these symptoms are longstanding, developmental delay or regression in development are frequently observed (Lin-Fu, 1972). Symptoms of the advanced stages of lead encephalopathy include vomiting, lethargy, somnolence, seizures, and coma (Pond, 1982).

Once a child develops lead encephalopathy, the mortality range is 4.5% to 30% (Lin-Fu, 1970). At least 25% of survivors display serious brain damage. The central nervous system insult in lead poisoning in its most severe form does not differ significantly from that which follows any diffuse cerebral injury sustained during early childhood (Chisolm & Kaplan, 1968). Five or more years after lead intoxication, children with lead encephalopathy were found to have an average IQ of 80 with a range of 58 to 104 (Smith, 1964). Other sequelae include seizure disorders, cerebral palsy, optic atrophy, and behavioral disturbances. Children who survive the acute episode of lead encephalopathy but who continue to ingest lead-containing materials will usually have permanent neurological damage (Lin-Fu, 1972).

## LABORATORY TESTS

Most of the early symptoms of lead poisoning are vague and nonspecific. The diagnosis will be made early only if there is a high index of suspicion. In the majority of situations, children will be identified as having lead poisoning or undue lead absorption using specific screening methods.

Although hypochromic microcytic anemia and basophilic stippling are often observed in children with lead poisoning, more specific laboratory methods are employed now. The rationale for using such specific tests is explained with the help of Figure 20.1.

Lead is an important inhibitor of several enzymes in heme synthesis. Lead inhibits the enzymes used to incorporate iron into heme causing anemia in the child with lead poisoning. In addition, there is a build-up of protoporphyrin in erythrocytes that is the basis for the most widely used screening method, the free erythrocyte protoporphyrin test. The latter compound is elevated in children with either iron deficiency or lead poisoning. Orfanos, Murphey, and Guthrie (1977) have developed a simple cost effective fluorometric assay of protoporphyrin in erythrocytes as a screening test for lead poisoning that utilizes filter paper blood specimen. If free erythrocyte protoporphyrin is elevated, a blood lead level should be obtained. It is important to use lead-free containers and proper collecting equipment for such determinations (Pond, 1982).

Quantitative urine coproporphyrin and 24-hour urine collections for lead are other tests that may be used in the diagnosis of chronic lead poisoning. If one is uncertain as to the interpretation of the above tests, the lead content of a 24-hour urine collection may be determined after a single edathamil calcium disodium challenge.

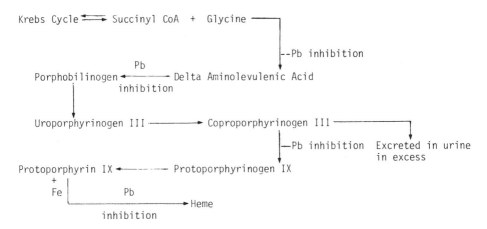

**Figure 20.1.** Steps in heme biosynthesis. (Adapted from Chisolm, 1964.)

Finally, radiologic studies may be useful. A radiograph of the abdomen may show radio opaque flakes of lead in the intestinal lumen in children who recently ingested lead-containing materials. Moreover, so-called "lead lines" at the metaphyses of long bones are often indicators of chronic lead poisoning (Chisolm, 1978; Pond, 1982).

Rosen et al. (1989) reported the L-line X-ray fluorescence of cortical bone lead and compared it with the CaNa2EDTA test in children with lead poisoning. The authors measured the cortical bone lead content by their L-line X-ray fluorescence technique that provides the opportunity to quantify bone lead content. The results of their study indicate that the L-line X-ray fluorescence technique may be capable of replacing the CaNa2EDTA test.

## TREATMENT

All symptomatic children should be regarded as potential cases of acute lead encephalopathy and treated accordingly: 10–20 ug/kg of 10% dextrose in water is administered intravenously over 1 to 2 hours. If urination has not occurred, Mannitol is given in order to induce diureses. Once urine flow is established, fluids are restricted to basic requirements. Seizures are initially controlled with Valium, followed by maintenance therapy with paraldehyde, whenever twitching and increase in muscle tone are observed. Chelation therapy is carried out using 2,3-dimercaptopropanol and edathamil calcium disodium according to a detailed schedule (Chisolm, 1978). Mannitol in repeated doses is used as needed for control of cerebral edema.

The main toxic effects of 2,3-dimercaptopropanol are nausea and vomiting. Therefore, oral intake of food and fluids may be withheld during this form of treatment. Iron should not be given concomitantly since a toxic complex will be formed during therapy for the associated anemia. Edathamil calcium disodium is excreted renally and thus cannot be given to anuric patients. Occasionally, proteinuria and microscopic hematuria are observed. Also, hypercalcemia and fever may be noted. If these symptoms occur, edathamil calcium disodium administration must be discontinued.

D-penicillamine may be used during convalescent periods for long-term chelation by the oral route. As children recover from acute lead encephalopathy, they may exhibit severe behavior abnormalities for 3 to 6 months.

The efficacy and toxicity of D-penicillamine in low level lead poisoning was investigated by Shannon, Graef, and Lovejoy (1988). The authors observed that the use of D-penicillamine was associated with an adverse reaction in 28 cases (33%), transient leukopenia occurred in 8, a skin rash in 7, transient low platelet count in 7, enuresis in 3, and abdominal pain in 2 patients. They conclude that D-penicillamine, although an effective therapy for selected children with low level lead poisoning, has many adverse effects that can complicate or prevent its use in some patients.

Another group of investigators (Graziano, Lolacono, & Meyer, 1988) studied the dose response of oral 2,3-Dimercaptosuccinic acid in children with elevated blood lead concentrations. The authors found that a dose of 1050 mg/m$^2$/day of 2,3-Dimercaptosuccinic acid was significantly more effective than lower doses of this compound or intravenously administered CaNa2EDTA in reducing blood levels and restoring erythrocyte delta-aminolevulinic acid dehydratase activity. Since 2,3-Dimercaptosuccinic acid administration was well tolerated, the authors feel that this is a promising drug that will simplify the management of childhood lead poisoning.

## PREVENTION OF LEAD POISONING

The problem of childhood lead poisoning is so clearly defined that it would seem prevention should be rather straightforward. Yet, this is not the case since the problem of lead poisoning is associated with social, educational, economic, medical, technical, and political factors.

An effective attack on the total problem of childhood lead poisoning is an exercise in environmental management. It requires the marshaling of all community resources, including the medical profession, the communications media, those who manage the housing stock, municipal officials, community leaders, and residents themselves. All must work together as an integrated force to obtain maximum results.

The immediate approach to the control of childhood lead poisoning is threefold:

1.  Members of the professional community as well as lay people need to be educated about the dangers of lead poisoning and its prevention.
2.  The children at risk must be located, screened for lead poisoning, and treated if necessary.
3.  The environments in which children ingest lead-based paint must be located and eliminated. If other sources of lead poisoning are found, they too should be elminated.

Public education through all communication media should emphasize the dangers of lead poisoning in childhood and should acquaint the public with the epidemiology and symptoms of this disease. Parents should be urged to seek professional help if they suspect lead poisoning in their child even in the absence of symptoms. In addition, education of physicians, nurses, social workers, and other public health professionals is needed.

Mass screening programs in high-risk areas using the free erythrocyte protoporphyrin test and/or blood lead determinations should be carried out. Moreover, screening for lead poisoning should take place in well-child conferences, well-baby clinics, hospital outpatient departments, private physicians' offices, and during public health nurses' visits.

Recommendations from the Centers for Disease Control indicate that children in high-risk settings with significant predisposing factors should be screened annually or semiannually. It is important that not only children from run-down neighborhoods be screened but also that all children 6 months to 6 years of age undergo annual screening for lead poisoning. Children who are found to have elevated free erythrocyte protoporphyrin or blood lead levels should be referred to medical centers for further diagnostic studies and prompt treatment if needed.

The American Academy of Pediatrics recommends that, ideally, all pre-school children should be screened for lead absorption using the erythrocyte protoporphyrin test. The following priority guidelines for screening have been developed by the Academy:

1. Children, 12 to 36 months of age, who live in or are frequent visitors in older, dilapidated housing
2. Children, 9 months to 6 years of age, who are siblings, housemates, visitors, and/or playmates of children with known lead toxicity
3. Children of any age living in older housing where renovation is occurring
4. Children, 9 months to 6 years of age, living in older dilapidated housing
5. Children, 9 months to 6 years of age, who live near lead smelters and processing plants or whose parents or other household members partici-pate in a lead-related occupation or hobby

The population with developmental disabilities and mental retardation who live in community residences or who attend school or work in older buildings need to be screened annually. Some of these individuals have pica behaviors and therefore are at high risk for developing lead poisoning. Most important are:

1. Preventing re-exposure of a treated child to lead in the home
2. Close follow-up
3. Retesting of the child who continues to be exposed

Public health workers should routinely inquire about pica and paint in-gestion in all children 6 months to 6 years of age, particularly those from high-risk neighborhoods.

In 1982, a study was undertaken to determine the cost-effectiveness of lead screening programs (Berwick & Komaroff, 1982). It was estimated that at a prevalence of lead poisoning of 7% or more, the use of free erythrocyte protoprophrin screening avoids morbidity and results in a net monetary sav-ings. The authors indicate that for prevalence rates below 7% the net positive cost from screening and early treatment must be weighed against the econom-ic benefits of improved quality of life. Yet, this should not be interpreted to mean that lead poisoning screening programs with a prevalence rate below 7%

should be abandoned. Any screening program that prevents lead poisoning in humans is a worthwhile endeavor.

Parents should be made aware that they can do much to keep children from eating paint chips and chewing on painted surfaces. They can keep paint chips off floors and out of reach of infants. They can complete some remodeling and inexpensive home improvements themselves.

Environmental improvement, including deleading of housing units with lead paint, is a most critical element in the prevention program. Most often landlords are required to remove or effectively cover sources of lead poisoning. Peeling paint and old plaster should be scraped from walls and ceilings and swept from floors. If children have access to lead-containing materials in neighbors' homes, again it is the responsibility of parents, neighbors, and landlords to ensure that children are not exposed to these poisonous materials. Although removal of lead from the environment is often expensive and time consuming, it is imperative that it be done expeditiously in order to avoid further exposure of children to lead. Environmental professionals should strictly enforce housing codes and ordinances.

After deleading, apartments and houses should be thoroughly cleaned and reinspected to ensure compliance with safety regulations. High phosphate detergents are particularly useful in removing lead dust. Children should not return to dwellings until cleaning and removal of lead containing materials are completed.

Moreover, it is paramount that federal as well as state and local legislators become concerned with childhood lead poisoning. Financial assistance should be provided through federal legislation. State laws on lead poisoning should require the establishment of a statewide program for the prevention, screening, diagnosis, and treatment of lead poisoning. Such legislation should also focus on the detection of sources of lead poisoning. When dangerous levels of lead are found, they should be reported to the owner, tenants, and public health agencies. The law should also require the establishment of a reliable laboratory that can accurately analyze large numbers of blood samples. It is important that legislation make landlords responsible for removing existing lead-based paint without delay and that failure to do so be treated as a violation. This means, in legal terms, that the code enforcement agency can initiate criminal prosecution. Violations should be treated as emergencies and given preference by enforcing agencies and speedy hearings by district and superior courts. In short, state and local legislation concerning childhood lead poisoning should be most comprehensive to prevent this man-made disease. It should include an effective screening program with appropriate treatment and laboratory facilities, and prompt environmental remediation as essential components.

Other government regulations should also be enforced, including determining the allowable amount of lead in paint, the Clean Air Act, the Occupational Safety and Health Act, regulations on the use of lead in glazed ceramics and dinnerware, and the control of lead in gasoline. By effecting childhood lead poisoning indirectly, such legislation will contribute to long-term goals for the eradication of lead poisoning in general.

## CONCLUSION

Lead poisoning is a man-made disease. As such, it is one of the truly preventable causes of developmental disabilities. It is imperative that the public, physicians, legislators, and health care workers recognize the seriousness of the problem and that aggressive screening, treatment, and environmental control programs be utilized.

It is essential that all children be screened for lead at regular intervals, especially those with anemia, growth failure, and developmental or behavioral problems (Needleman, 1988). Appropriate treatment, controlling the environment, strengthening the family's supports, enhancing nutrition, and offering remedial education are essential to a successful therapeutic outcome.

## REFERENCES

Annest, J. L., Pirkle, J. L., Makuc, D., Neese, J. W., Bayse, D. D., & Kovar, J. J. (1983). Chronological trends in blood lead levels between 1976 and 1980. *New England Journal of Medicine, 308*, 1373–1377.

Baloh, R., Sturm, R., Green, B., & Gleser, C. (1975). Neuropsychological effects of chronic asymptomatic increased lead absorption. *Archives of Neurology, 32*, 326–330.

Berwick, D. M., & Komaroff, A. L. (1982). Cost effectiveness of lead screening. *New England Journal of Medicine, 306*, 1392–1398.

Centers for Disease Control. (1983). Preventing lead poisoning in young children: A statement by the Centers for Disease Control. *Journal of Pediatrics, 93*, 709–720.

Chisolm, J. J. (1964). Disturbances in the biosynthesis of heme in lead intoxication. *Journal of Pediatrics, 64*, 174–186.

Chisolm, J. J. (1978). Treatment of lead poisoning. *Modern Treatment, 8*, 22–40.

Chisolm, J. J., & Kaplan, E. (1968). Lead poisoning in childhood: Comprehensive management and prevention. *Journal of Pediatrics, 73*, 942–950.

de la Burde, B., & Choate, M. S. (1972). Does asymptomatic lead exposure in children have latent sequelae? *Journal of Pediatrics, 81*, 1088–1091.

de la Burde, B., & Choate, M. S. (1975). Early asymptomatic lead exposure and development at school age. *Journal of Pediatrics, 87*, 638–642.

Ernhart, C. B., Landa, B., & Schell, N. G. (1981). Subclinical levels of lead and developmental deficits: A multivariate follow-up reassessment. *Pediatrics, 67*, 911–919.

Ernhart, C. B., Morrow-Tlucak, M., & Wolf, A. W. (1988). Low level lead exposure and intelligence in the preschool years. *Science of the Total Environment, 71*(3), 453–459.

Felton, J. S. (1965). Man, medicine and work in America: Vol. II. An historical series. Lead, liquor and legislation. *Journal of Occupational Medicine, 7*, 572–579.

Goldsmith, J. R., & Hextra, A. C. (1967). Respiratory exposure to lead: Epidemiological and experimental dose-response relationships. *Science*, *158*, 132–134.

Graziano, J. H., Lolacono, N. J., & Meyer, P. (1988). Dose-response study of oral 2,3-dimercaptosuccinic acid in children with elevated blood lead concentrations. *Journal of Pediatrics*, *113*(4), 751–757.

Kotok, D. (1972). Development of children with elevated blood lead levels: A controlled study. *Journal of Pediatrics*, *80*, 57–61.

Landrigan, P. J., Baloh, R. W., Barthel, W. F., Whitworth, R. H., Staehling, N. W., & Rosenblum, B. F. (1975). Neuropsychological dysfunction in children with chronic low-level lead absorption. *Lancet*, *ii*, 708–712.

Lansdown, R. G., Clayton, B. E., Graham, P. J., Sheperd, J., Delves, H. T., & Turner, W. C. (1974). Blood lead levels, behaviour, and intelligence: A population study. *Lancet*, *i*, 538–541.

Lin-Fu, J. S. (1970). *Lead poisoning in children* (Public Health Service Publication No. 2108). Washington, DC: U.S. Government Printing Office.

Lin-Fu, J. S. (1972). Undue absorption of lead among children: A new look at an old problem. *New England Journal of Medicine*, *286*, 702–710.

Lyngbye, T., Hansen, O., Grandjean, P., Trillingsgaard, A., & Beese, I. (1988). Traffic a source of lead exposure in childhood. *Science of the Total Environment*, *71*, 461–467.

Mahaffey, K. R., Annest, J. L., Roberts, J., & Murphy, R. S. (1982). National estimates of blood lead levels, United States, 1976–1980: Association with selected demographic and socioeconomic factors. *New England Journal of Medicine*, *307*, 573–579.

Marshall, E. (1984). Legal threat halts CDC meeting on lead. *Science*, *223*, 672.

McCarthy, D. (1972). *Manual for the McCarthy scales of children's abilities*. New York: Psychological Corporation.

Needleman, H. L. (1988). The persistent threat of lead: Medical and sociological issues. *Current Problems in Pediatrics*, *18*, 697–744.

Needleman, H. L., Gunnoe, C., Leviton, A., Reed, R., Peresta, H., Mabar, C., & Barrett, P. (1979). Defects in psychology and classroom performance of children with elevated dentine lead levels. *New England Journal of Medicine*, *300*, 689–695.

Orfanos, A. P., Murphey, W. H., & Guthrie, R. (1977). A simple fluorometric assay of protoporphyrin in erythrocytes (EPP) as a screening test for lead poisoning. *Journal of Laboratory and Clinical Medicine*, *89*, 659–665.

Pond, S. M. (1982). Lead poisoning. *Audiovisual Digest*, *28*.

Pueschel, S. M. (1974). Neurological and psychomotor functions in children with an increased lead burden. *Environmental Health Perspectives*, *4*, 13–16.

Pueschel, S. M., & Fadden, M. E. (1975). Childhood lead poisoning and legislative action. *Journal of Legal Medicine*, *3*, 16–20.

Pueschel, S. M., Kopito, L., & Schwachman, H. (1972). Children with an increased lead burden: A screening and follow-up study. *Journal of the American Medical Association*, *222*, 462–466.

Rosen, J. F., Markowitz, M. E., Bijur, P. E., Jenks, S. T., Wielopolski, L., Kalef-Ezra, J. A., & Slatkin, D. N. (1989). L-line X-ray fluorescence of cortical bone lead compared with the CaNa2EDTA test in lead-toxic children: Public health implications. *Proceedings of the National Academy of Sciences of the United States of America*, *86*, 685–689.

Shannon, M., Graef, J., & Lovejoy, F. H., Jr. (1988). Efficacy and toxicity of D-penicillamine in low-level lead poisoning. *Journal of Pediatrics, 112*, 799–804.

Shucard, J. L., Shucard, D. W., Patterson, R., & Guthrie, R. (1988). Prenatal lead exposure and its potential significance for developmental disabilities: A preliminary study of umbilical cord blood lead levels. *Neurotoxicology, 9*, 317–326.

Smith, H. D. (1964). Pediatric lead poisoning. *Archives of Environmental Health, 8*, 256–261.

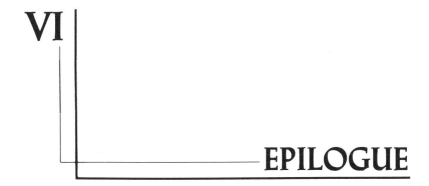

VI

EPILOGUE

# 21 | Allen C. Crocker

# SOCIETAL COMMITMENT TOWARD PREVENTION OF DEVELOPMENTAL DISABILITIES

The word *prevention* has a magic sound and a joyful meaning. It is born of compassion and hope. It implies avoidance of disability and handicap, and it signifies an outreach for the achievement of the maximum potential for all humans. This excitement is the same primal one expressed in the old Jewish exhortation: "Be fruitful and multiply and replenish the earth" (Genesis 1:28). It is also the same aspiration that led the Youth National Association for Retarded Citizens to use the slogan: "To Our Children's Children," for their conference on prevention of mental retardation in 1972. The specific route by which various workers in the field come to focus their activities on prevention may vary, but the theme remains one of a desire for improvement of the human condition.

There are two psychological complications in the circumstances of prevention activities that must be acknowledged, but these can also be accommodated. The first is the risk that there will be some already-present implicit assumption of diminished value regarding the individuals with disabilities

Support is acknowledged by Project 928 from the Office of Maternal and Child Health and Grant #03DD0135 from the Administration on Developmental Disabilities, D.H.H.S.

(inasmuch as the intent exists to prevent the further occurrence of such disabilities). This could take place, for example, if a young person with myelodysplasia or Down syndrome were to perceive that his or her birth was viewed as a systems failure regarding prevention. There is room in prevention activities for designing assistance first, and then future prevention. Furthermore, the commitment of the consumer world to the prevention movement speaks convincingly of the compatibility of these dual pursuits. The second confounding issue is that prophylactic programs may be undertaken primarily for economic rather than humanistic goals, often with exaggerated claims. This becomes a point of contention when testimony about avoidance of expense is emphasized in congressional hearings. The devoted prevention worker may, on occasion, be pressed to follow a double course for pragmatic reasons.

## DERIVATION OF NATIONAL POLICY

Examination of national policy provides a mirror of sorts regarding societal commitment. Richmond and Kotelchuck (1983) pointed out that public policy, as represented by governmental investment, depends on the interaction of an appropriate knowledge base, determination of political will, and the existence of a social strategy or plan. The knowledge base for prevention of mental retardation and other disabilities has been significantly improved since the early 1970s (Crocker, 1986). Enhancement of the political will requires the development of a constituency that will have an impact on the legislative process.

Richmond (1982) described three phases of national public interest on behalf of children and families in the United States. The first phase occurred in the early years of this century, with the first White House Conference on Children and Youth (1909), the establishment of the Children's Bureau (1912), the first infant health programs, the beginning of social work as a profession, and the founding of the first child guidance clinics and children's courts. The second phase took place in the 1930s, culminating in the passage of the Title V Amendments to the Social Security Act, with a new Federal responsibility for the health of mothers and children and provision of services to children with disabilities. The third phase began in 1965 with the "War on Poverty." Involved in this phase were Medicaid, Supplemental Security Income (SSI), neighborhood day-care centers, improved immunization and fluoridation, Head Start, Title XX Day Care, Women-Infants-Children Special Supplemental Food program (WIC) and other nutrition programs, community mental health centers, and many mental retardation programs.

Prevention effects from these efforts have been extensive. There are now vastly improved supports for pregnant women; entirely new systems for assistance to newborn infants, particularly those born prematurely; and a major reduction in hunger and malnutrition. Infant mortality dropped from 24.7 per 1,000 live births in 1965 to 10.4 in 1985. Early intervention programs have done much to change the outlook for those infants who are born with disabilities or who are at risk. Newborn screening for phenylketonuria, galactosemia, and congenital hypothyroidism has allowed effective secondary prevention of the implied mental retardation. Prenatal diagnosis has provided surveillance for many malformation or genetic conditions. Kernicterus and congenital rubella have been virtually eliminated, and measles is no longer an endemic disease.

In spite of these notable achievements, which have drawn heavily on federal support, prevention activities have generally not been focused on a visible or coordinated thrust. Boggs (1980) analyzed the main obstacles that have interfered with the formation of a specific national policy on prevention of developmental disabilities:

1. The real constituency is not aware of the issues. The principal nonprofessional proponents of prevention are those who have suffered but will not benefit, and this altruistic support is necessarily more tenuous than a direct interest.
2. The national service system is largely discontinuous. The sequelae in adult life of childhood disability are not acknowledged in the child oriented health and education movements, so that there is less consciousness of the full impact of handicaps. Many different federal agencies are involved with portions of the concern.
3. National collaborations do not extend to the states. Working relationships established between voluntary and professional organizations on a Washington base may not reach practical applications at a local level.
4. Documentation of successful outcome is often obscure. The ultimate demonstration of disability prevention may be partial, indirect, and difficult.
5. Ethical dilemmas are prevalent in prevention programs. The primary subjects cannot consent to interventions on their own behalf, and genetic counseling and pregnancy interruption can be divisive issues.
6. Competition exists with other public concerns. In current times, there are many demands for national attention.

There is a growing knowledge base but an absence of a national social strategy for the prevention of developmental disabilities. The fragility of the political will justifies real concern. Current events suggest that the reinforcement of commitment to prevention is being handicapped by political realities, including bottom-line reductions in programs for maternal and child health and for children with special health care needs, cuts in nutrition programs, and restriction in support of activities in special education. Vigilance is required to ensure that immunization and newborn screening are not seriously diminished. The policies for regulation of environmental teratogens are still being developed (Ashford, 1980; Halbert, 1980).

## PREVENTION ACTIVITIES IN THE STATES

It is at the state level that the implementation of prevention programs is most visible in this country. Within departments of health, mental retardation, or developmental disabilities, one may find a wide integrated commitment to prevention. Strong efforts in this regard are seen, for example, in New Jersey, Virginia, California, and New York, with public prevention agencies often established as a result of leadership from voluntary organizations.

A particularly eloquent set of resolutions were established in 1981 by the state of Tennessee, as a result of the "Governor's Task Force on Mental Retardation Prevention" (Crocker, 1982). Emphasis is being placed on family life education, family planning, prenatal care, genetic services, newborn screening, nutrition programs, immunization, stimulation programs, and early education. Of special note are the elements of access, standards, evaluation, and coordination that give promise of there being more substantial value. It is reassuring that broad supports have been designed for the pregnant woman and the young child, for it is in their particular circumstances that many of the "unknown" factors of the genesis of developmental disabilities must reside. And, the direct involvement of the governor's office speaks well for the commitment of Tennessee.

Guthrie (1982) provided a draft of the elements that should be included in a "Model State Plan for Prevention." He advised: 1) establishing a state commission for prevention, 2) gathering epidemiological data, 3) estimating costs and developing funding mechanisms, 4) integrating prevention into the service delivery system, 5) coordinating prevention efforts at a high level of government, 6) coordinating private and public sector prevention activities, and 7) involving consumers in all phases of prevention planning and implementation. He also recommended a strong advisory group, program evaluation of each component, and applied research on effectiveness.

## ROLE OF VOLUNTARY GROUPS

Since the 1970s, voluntary associations have provided the critical driving force for most of the reform legislation regarding services for persons with disabilities. In prevention, the story is much the same. It has been the impatience of consumer groups that has moved professionals to be articulate and legislators to respond. Not uncommonly, in each step of progress, a few people with immense energy and motivation have mobilized the needed forces to break through inertia and bureaucracy. Conferences on prevention often have local agency involvement, but one can frequently find the spark of voluntary groups and individuals behind the genesis of a conference and the strength of its agenda. The fragmented aspects of diverse government agencies are seldom coordinated until voluntary organizations provide the stimulus (Crocker, 1987).

The transmission of knowledge to the general public about the potential for prevention has also involved leadership by voluntary groups. In the sensitive area of education for young child bearing couples, there is a large number of informational brochures available (Crocker, 1986). These strive for the prevention of disabilities and are generally sponsored or stimulated by local Associations for Retarded Citizens (ARC) or similar groups. Some such brochures available include: *Take Care of Yourself for Your Baby's Sake* (Indiana); *Take Care of Yourself* (Alabama); *Take Good Care of Both of You* (Illinois); *What Can You Do to Help You and Your Unborn Baby* (Pennsylvania); *The Baby in Your Life* (Virginia); *If There Are Children in Your Future, Know These Facts* (Massachusetts); and *If They Don't Know that Mental Retardation Can Be Prevented, It Won't Be* (Minnesota). It is clear that in the field of prevention of developmental disabilities the commitment of activists in the voluntary associations is a precious resource.

## FEELINGS OF INDIVIDUALS

In the final analysis, programs for prevention will succeed or fail on the basis of the perceptions of individual citizens. As indicated in the introduction, there is an outreach in this direction, influenced by personal experience, education, and cultural factors. It seems apparent that compliance with recommendations regarding prevention is greater when the objects are one's children, rather than when it is one's self. Adjustment of health habits is easier to achieve for the pregnant woman than for the nonpregnant woman (e.g., indiscriminate use of medication, drinking, and smoking). Legislation enforcing restraints in automobiles has proved more acceptable by the public for infants and young children than for adults.

The voluntary utilization of well-publicized opportunities for obtaining relevant diagnostic information regarding risk has a real ceiling, however, in today's society. Genetic screening programs, such as carrier identification for Tay-Sachs disease among young Ashkenazi Jewish couples, are viewed as highly successful when about 25% of the eligible persons come for testing in local projects. At the time of actual pregnancy, this percentage rises dramatically because of modern standards in obstetric practice.

Use of amniocentesis in women 35 years of age or older to detect chromosome abnormalities in the fetus represents a blend of medical advice and personal feelings. Amniocentesis rates in this population have been increasing steadily. In Rhode Island, the figure was 8% in 1978, 20% in 1979, 36% in 1980, and 42% in 1981 (D. Abuelo, personal communication, 1987).

In 1987, the utilization rate in Rhode Island by older women was just over 50% of all pregnancies, and some surmise that this may be about the level expected for some time.

Since the mid-1970s, screening of maternal serum for alpha-fetoprotein levels has been encouraged as an indicator of the possible presence of neural tube defects in the fetus. In Maine, efforts have been made to educate obstetricians about this prevention potential through the Foundation for Blood Research in Scarborough. In 1979-1980, 18% of all pregnancies in Maine were so screened, and the rate in 1986 reached more than 50% (J. Haddow, personal communication, 1987), probably the highest in the United States. In the British Isles, this program has been implemented vigorously because of the relatively greater incidence of neural tube defects there. In parts of Scotland the employment of testing is over 75%. Since 1985, it has been possible to obtain additional data from the maternal serum alpha-fetoprotein level, with screening information now available as well about the fetal risk for certain chromosome abnormalities, including Down syndrome. The double value from the assay will unquestionably lead to greater interest in testing by young couples.

Prevention programs have occasionally moved from the voluntary to the compulsory sphere when the stakes are high and when public health methods are very effective. Examples are the testing of newborn infants for phenylketonuria and congenital hypothyroidism (the latter testing reaching all 50 states in 1981). Immunization for rubella has also become compulsory as a basis for admission to public schools. Legislation proved vastly more effective than consumer education in the states that developed programs for infant restraint in automobiles. Since 1986, in California, there has been mandatory provision of information and access to testing of serum alpha-fetoprotein levels for all pregnant women.

## CONCLUSION

The prevention of developmental disabilities has the characteristics of a "movement," drawing its strength from many sources. A basic hope for full potential for young people is the central factor. Leadership in the implementation of prevention efforts has come particularly from voluntary associations and certain highly motivated individuals. At the state level, these forces have often achieved productive alliances with key agencies. The national commitment has had sectors of immense accomplishment, but lacks a needed coordination. Many elements of the knowledge base are incomplete.

It is reasonable to state that society will act optimally to prevent disabilities when beliefs have been clarified about the value of all humans and human experiences. The prevention story will be completed when the commitment to service is made and when the needed research in etiology is sponsored.

George Tarjan tells the story of having been asked by the president of a developing country what he as a consultant would recommend as a single strategic project that country might undertake to prevent mental retardation, if they could only do one thing. He replied that the president should establish a program that would lead to the postponement of pregnancy from the early teen years until the mid-twenties (Tarjan, 1982). In that inspired suggestion he captured the paramount importance for all humans to be born under circumstances where there is deliberate readiness and high value assigned to them.

## REFERENCES

Ashford, N. A. (1980). Regulatory policy for mutagens and teratogens. In A. Milunsky & G. J. Annas (Eds.), *Genetics and the law: Vol. II* (pp. 413–419). New York: Plenum.

Boggs, E. M. (1980). Toward a national policy for prevention of developmental disabilities. In M. D. McCormack (Ed.), *Prevention of mental retardation and other developmental disabilities* (pp. 641–654). New York: Marcel Dekker.

Crocker, A. C. (1982). Current strategies in prevention of mental retardation. *Pediatric Annals, 11*, 450–457.

Crocker, A. C. (1986). Prevention of mental retardation: 1985. *Annals of the New York Academy of Sciences, 477*, 329–338.

Crocker, A. C. (1987). A comprehensive strategy for the prevention of mental retardation and related developmental disorders. In President's Committee on Mental Retardation, *Proceedings of the National Conference on State Planning for the Prevention of Mental Retardation and Related Developmental Disabilities*. Washington, DC: Department of Health and Human Services.

Guthrie, R. (1982, September). *Model state and community planning for prevention.* Symposium conducted at the National Prevention Showcase and Forum, Atlanta.

Halbert, G. T. (1980). Developing a government policy for the regulation of environmental mutagens and teratogens. In A. Milunsky & G. J. Annas (Eds.), *Genetics and the law: Vol. II* (pp. 421–436). New York: Plenum.

Richmond, J. B. (1982, October). *Current issues in perinatal care.* Paper presented at the Missouri Perinatal Association Clinical Conference, Columbia, MO.

Richmond, J. B., & Kotelchuck, M. (1983). The effect of the political process on the delivery of health services. In C. McQuire, R. Foley, D. Gorr, & R. Richards (Eds.), *The handbook of health professions education*. San Francisco: Jossey-Bass.

Tarjan, C. (1982, September). *Remarks made at the P.C.M.R.* Symposium conducted at the National Prevention Showcase and Forum, Atlanta.

# INDEX